Besant's History of London

The Stuarts

Titles available from The Village Press are:-

The London Library:

Hardback
Village London Volume I
Village London Volume II
London Recollected Volume I
London Recollected Volume II
London Recollected Volume III
London Recollected Volume IV
London Recollected Volume V
London Recollected Volume VI
Village London Atlas
Besant's History of London - The Tudors
Besant's History of London - The Stuarts

Paperback
Village London Pt. 1 West and North
Village London Pt. 2 North and East
Village London Pt. 3 South-East
Village London Pt. 4 South-West
Village London Atlas
Old Fleet Street
Cheapside and St. Paul's
The Tower and East End
Shoreditch to Smithfield
Charterhouse to Holborn
Strand to Soho
Covent Garden and the Thames to Whitehall
Westminster to St, James's
Haymarket to Mayfair
Hyde Park to Bloomsbury
Belgravia, Chelsea and Kensington
Paddington Green to Seven Sisters
Highgate & Hampstead to the Lea
(The above thirteen titles are extracts from the hardback edition of London Recollected.)

Other titles published are:

The Village Atlas - Birmingham and The West Midlands
The Village Atlas - Manchester, Lancashire & North Cheshire

CHARLES I (1600-1649)
From the painting by van Dyck in the National Gallery, London.

Besant's History of London

The Stuarts

The Village Press

First published in 1903 by Adam & Charles Black
under the title *London in the Time of the Stuarts.*

This edition published March 1990
by The Village Press Limited,
7d, Keats Parade, Church Street, London N9 9DP.

British Library Cataloguing in Publication Data
Besant, Walter, *1836-1901*
  Besant's history of London, the Stuarts.
  I. Title   II. Besant, Walter, *1836-1901* : Survey of London

  ISBN 1-85540-002-2

Printed and bound in Great Britain by
Redwood Press Limited, Melksham, Wiltshire

PREFACE

Abundant as is the mass of material for the study of history and manners in the sixteenth century, there is even a greater abundance for the history, political and social, of the century of the Stuarts. There are, however, two difficulties to be faced in such an inquiry. The first is that the history of London is far more closely connected with the history of the nation during the seventeenth than during the sixteenth century. It may, indeed, be advanced that at no time, not even when London deposed Richard II. and set up Henry IV., was the City so closely involved in all the events of the time as in the seventeenth century. The City at that time reached the highest point of its political importance, an importance which vanished in the century that followed.

Therefore the historian of London has before him the broad fact that for sixty years, viz. from the accession of Charles I. to the expulsion of James II., he should be pursuing the history of the country. In this place, however, there is not space for such a history; it has already been well told by many historians; and I have neither the time nor the competence to write the history of this most eventful period. I have therefore found it necessary to assume a certain knowledge of events and to speak of their sequence with reference especially to the attitude of the City; the forces which acted on the people; their ideas; their resolution and tenacity under Charles I.; their servility and obedience under Charles II.; and their final rejection of the doctrines of passive resistance, Divine right, and obedience which made the departure of James possible, and opened the door for constitutional government and the liberties of the people.

The second difficulty is, that while the century contains an immense mass of material in the shape of plays, poems, fiction, pamphlets, sermons, travels, sketches, biographies, trials, reports, proclamations, ordinances, speeches, and every other conceivable document for the restoration of the century, the period was sharply divided into two by the Civil Wars and the Protectorate, the latter being at best a stop-gap, while events were following each other and the mind of the nation was developing. It was, in fact, a revolutionary change which took place. The change was deepened by the Great Fire of 1666, after which a new London arose, not so picturesque, perhaps, as the former London, but reflecting the ideas of the time in its churches, which, from Mass houses became preaching rooms; and in its houses, which offered substantial comfort, more light, loftier rooms, standing in wider and better ordered streets, agreeing with the increase of wealth and the improvement in the general conditions of life. The first half of the century is, in fact, a continuation of the Elizabethan period with decay in literature and development in religion; the second half belongs to the eighteenth century, where we find a development of the last forty years of the seventeenth.

I have endeavoured to meet this difficulty by making such a selection from the things belonging to the daily life as have not been dwelt upon in the study of the sixteenth century with those points which, while they were developed or dropped in the eighteenth, have not been in that volume considered at length.

The events of the greatest importance to the City, apart from those which belong to the whole nation, were the repeated visitations of Plague, and the Great Fire. The former came and went; it destroyed the people, chiefly the common people, by thousands; its immediate effect was a dearth of craftsmen and servants, a rise in wages, and an improvement in the standard of life in the lower levels. The lessons which it taught and continually enforced were learned most imperfectly. They were simple—the admission into the courts and lanes of the crowded City of light and air; the invention of some system of sanitation which would replace the old cesspool and the public latrine; and the introduction of a plentiful supply of water for the washing of the people, as well as for their drink and for the flooding of the streets. Somewhere or other—it must be between Dowgate and Mincing Lane — there is still existing under ground the great Roman Cloaca; it is an additional proof of the desertion and desolation of the City after the Romans went away that the Cloaca was forgotten, choked up, and its mouth covered over; the creation of the foreshore covered it up. Had it been found, say, in the thirteenth or fourteenth century, the whole modern sanitary system might have been invented and developed by its means, and so the Plague would have been stayed. I have attempted to present an adequate account of the Plague from contemporary evidence. As regards the Fire I have essayed a restoration of the City before and after that event.

Turning to events political, I have already stated the difficulties which confront the historian of London in this century. The reader will not look here for a detailed history of the Civil War or the Protectorate. I hope, however, that he will find some indication of the way in which the people of London regarded the events which were working out their redemption for them, in ways which were unexpected, by trials which were hard to bear, and after a time when all seemed lost.

Considering London alone, the Restoration seems to me to have been a natural, a wholesome, and a most fortunate reaction against the successive rule of Presbyterian, Independent, and Captain or Colonel. It must have become quite clear even to men like Milton, who was one of the last to lift his voice against the return of a king, that a Commonwealth was too far in advance of the people, and that a military despotism was intolerable.

In the same way the Revolution was a swing back of the pendulum; it was quite as natural and as salutary as the rebellion against Charles and the Restoration of his son. I read this lesson clearly in the history of London, and I assume it for the history of the country.

Meantime let it be remembered that the seventeenth century secured the country for two hundred years, *i.e.* to the present day at least, and, so far as can be prophesied, for an indefinite period yet to come, from the personal interference of the sovereign. That is an enormous gain to the country. We are no longer called upon to discuss the Prerogative. The attempted encroachments of George III. appear as mere trifles compared with the monstrous claims of Charles the First and the almost incredible acts of tyranny recorded of his son and successor. And in the achievement of this great result London in the seventeenth century played a noble part and earned the deepest gratitude of all those who came, or shall come, after.

WALTER BESANT.

CONTENTS

STUART SOVEREIGNS

RELIGION, GOVERNMENT, AND TRADE

THE GREAT PLAGUE AND FIRE

ix

MANNERS AND CUSTOMS

APPENDICES

ILLUSTRATIONS

SOVEREIGNS

CHAPTER I

JAMES found the City, after a hundred years of Tudor rule, reduced to an admirable condition of submission and loyalty. He was proclaimed in the City and by the City, the citizens of London claiming once more a voice in electing an accessor

JAMES I. (1566–1625)
After the portrait by Paul von Somer.

to the crown. The King returned thanks to the Mayor and Aldermen in a letter which lacks, one perceives at once, the royal style of Elizabeth.

Trustie and Wel-beloved, wee greet you hartily well: being informed of your great forwardnesse in that just and honourable action of proclaiming us your sovereigne Lord and King, immediately after the decease of our late dearest Sister, the Queen; wherein you have given a singular good proofe of your ancient fidelitie (a reputation hereditary to that our Citie of London), being the chamber of our imperial crowne, and ever free from all shadowes of tumultes, and unlawful courses; we could not omit, with all the speed possible we might, to give you hereby a taste of our thankful Mind for the same: and with all assurance, that you cannot crave anything of us fit for the Maintenance of you all in general, and every one of you in particular, but it shall be most willingly performed by us, whose speciall care shall

TRIUMPHAL ARCH ERECTED AT THE TIME OF THE CORONATION OF JAMES I.
From a contemporary print. E. Gardner's collection.

ever be to provide for the continuance and increase of your present happines, desiring you in the mean time to go constantly forward in all doing, in and whatsoever things you shall find necessary and expedient for the good Government of our sayde city, in execution of justice, as you have been used to doe in our sayde deceased Sister's tyme, till our pleasure be known to you in the contrary. Thus not doubting but you will doe, as you may be fully assured of our gratious favours towards you, in the first degree, we bid you hartily farewell. Haly Roodhouse, the 28th of March, 1603.

James left Edinburgh on the 5th of April, arriving at Theobalds, where he rested for four days, on May the 7th; it had taken more than a month to ride from Edinburgh, *i.e.* he had ridden about twelve miles a day. At Waltham he was met by one of the sheriffs with sixty servants; at Stamford Hill by the Mayor and Aldermen in velvet and gold chains and 500 citizens richly apparelled. At that moment the Plague broke out; the Coronation was shorn of its splendour; the pageants and shows were laid aside; only the Mayor, Aldermen, and twelve citizens were present in Westminster Abbey; and James had to postpone his public entry into the City for a twelvemonth.

With the accession of James revived the hopes of the Catholics; they built upon the inexperience and the ignorance of the King; perhaps upon his fears; they magnified their own strength and numbers; and they quite misunderstood the feeling of the country, which grew more and more in distrust and hatred of the Catholics. They began, moreover, just as they had done in the reign of Elizabeth, by plots and conspiracies. The first of these plots was that called the "Main," in which Raleigh, unfortunately for himself and his own reputation, was concerned. With him was Lord Cobham. As to Raleigh's guilt, this is not the place to inquire. As is well known, after twelve years he was suffered to come out of the Tower, and was allowed to command a fleet bound for the coast of South America in quest of gold-mines. The story of his voyage, of his ill success, of his son's death, of his return, of his arrest, may be read in the history of England. But the tragedy of October 29, 1618, when at eight o'clock in the morning Sir Walter Raleigh was led out to die, moved to the depths every English heart, and should not be passed over in any history of London. It was remembered by all that he was the lifelong enemy of Spain, nor could the attacking of a friendly power in time of peace appear as any other than a laudable act to the English mind. That the traitor who arrested and betrayed him, his kinsman who became a paid spy, who also took money from the very man he was watching, that this man, Sir Lewis Stukeley, afterwards fell into misery and madness appeared to everybody an open and visible punishment inflicted by God Himself.

Let us consider the meaning of the fines which play so large a part in the history of these times. If a man is a Roman Catholic he is on no account allowed to attend a church or assembly where any kind of service other than the Catholic is performed. That rule is never, I believe, relaxed under any circumstances. It is a rule, therefore, which can be easily used for the discovery of Catholics. Thus (23 Elizabeth) it was enacted that every person over sixteen years of age who should refrain from attending at church, chapel, or some usual place of common prayer, against the tenor of a certain statute of the first year of her Majesty's reign, for uniformity of common prayer, and should be lawfully convicted thereof, should forfeit, for each month in which he or she should so refrain, the sum of twenty pounds of lawful money. The convictions under this statute illustrate to some extent the proportion of Roman Catholics to Protestants then existing in the country. Thus in the Middlesex Session Rolls (Middlesex County Record Society) may be found a long list of persons brought before the Middlesex magistrates charged with this offence. During the last twenty-four years of Queen Elizabeth's reign there were 408 convictions of this offence in Middlesex alone. They were gentlemen and gentlewomen, clerks, yeomen, tradesmen, wives, widows, and spinsters. They came from many parts of Middlesex, but especially from Westminster, Clerkenwell, Tottenham, Stepney, and Holborn. A fine of twenty pounds a month—about £100 of our money—would be far beyond the means of most of the persons convicted. For instance, on one page of the Rolls there are the names of twenty-six persons all convicted of not going to church for two or three months. Of these, twelve are gentlemen, three are wives of gentlemen, five are yeomen, one is a spinster, four are clerks, and one is a cook. What happened when the fine could not be paid? The number of convictions proves, first, that there were some, but not, in proportion to the whole, many Roman Catholics left in London and the parts around; next, that they were easily detected by their absence from church; thirdly, that there was a hot search after them; and fourthly, that though we find, here and there, a person following a trade or a craft, the Catholics were for the most part gentlefolk.

The secret professors of the ancient faith knew of places where a priest was concealed, and where Mass was sung or whispered with closed doors. There were five or six of these priests tried and condemned before the Middlesex magistrates. Thus John Welden in March 1587, William Hartley in 1588, Robert Walkinson in 1598 were tried and found guilty simply for being priests, i.e. because, "being subjects of the Queen, they were ordained by authority derived from the See of Rome, in contempt of the Crown and Dignity of the said Queen." They were executed as traitors with the cruelties of detail which we know. Other persons were charged with receiving, comforting, and maintaining priests. Thus George Glover and Mary Baylie his wife maintained and comforted Thomas Tycheburne, clerk and priest, and they received the pardon of the Queen; Catharine Bellamy, wife of Richard Bellamy, gentleman, moved and seduced by instigation of the devil, received and entertained Robert Southwell—it does not appear whether she was punished for the offence; and Dorothea White, either sister or wife of Humphrey White of Westminster, gentleman, thus received and entertained William Tedder, priest. Dorothea was hanged—one supposes—because she did not make submission.

If we inquire into the comparative importance of the recusants, it seems that it must have been too small to constitute a real danger. The number, 408, convicted in a quarter of a century over the whole of Middlesex—London not included—that is, no more than an average of sixteen in a year, at a time when the search after them was keen and untiring—hardly warrants the fears which were entertained by the Queen's Council as to the power and numbers of the secret Catholics, or the hopes of support from the south which were entertained during the rising of the north; or the expectations at Rome and at the Court of Spain of a widespread insurrection all over England and a return to the ancient faith.

THE GUNPOWDER CONSPIRATORS

From title-page of *Warhafftige Beschreibung der Verrätherei, etc.* (De Bry), Frankfurt, 1606.

At the same time it is reasonable to believe that there were many thousands who, while they adhered outwardly, went to church and heard the sermon, would have welcomed the return of the Mass and the Romish form.

Action in the case of the recusants was followed by the famous Gunpowder Plot. There can be no doubt that the Catholics were maddened by disappointment, by persecution, by the failure to obtain toleration, and by the fines to which they were subjected. The conspirators proposed, as is well known, to blow up the King, the Lords, and the Commons when the Parliament should assemble. This plot, like that of Raleigh, belongs to the history of the country.

When the Common Council established a Court of Conscience in the City, it was with the design of saving poor debtors from the costs of being sued in the superior courts. But this Court was confined to debtors who were Citizens and

Gun Powder Treafon.

From a contemporary print. E. Gardner's collection.

Freemen of London and the Liberties. Some persons, intending to subvert the good and charitable intent of the Court, took hold of certain ambiguous words and endeavoured by means of these to render the intentions of the Court useless. A new and amending Act was passed which cleared up these difficulties and put the Court of Conscience on a sounder footing. The Act was well meant, but for more than two hundred years after it the miserable annals of the Debtors' Prisons are filled with stories of the exorbitant and extortionate costs charged by attornies, and with the sufferings of the debtors in consequence.

The honour in which the City was held was illustrated when the King joined the Clothworkers' Company, and when the Merchant Taylors, in jealousy, showed him their roll of members containing seven kings, one queen, seventeen princes and dukes, two duchesses, one archbishop, thirty earls, five countesses, one viscount, fourteen bishops, sixty-six barons, two ladies, seven abbots, seven priors, and an immense number of knights and esquires. The King gave them his son Henry as a member.

The New River was completed after eight years of work. The length of the canal was 60 miles; it was crossed by 800 bridges, and five years were spent in the construction; the people were slow in taking their water from the new supply, probably because they detested changing their ways. The City was at first supplied with water from the Walbrook and the Fleet; there were also wells and springs on the rising ground of the Strand; in Moorfields, at Shoreditch, and elsewhere there were wells sunk within the City walls; and there were "bosses" or taps of fresh water brought in from Tyburn. All this, however, was not enough; the principal sources of supply, the Fleet and Walbrook, had long since ceased to be of any use. Powers therefore were sought to bring more water into the City, and were granted to bring water from Hampstead and from the river Lea; these powers were not, however, used. Improved works were set up at Tyburn; water mills were placed in the Thames, by which water was forced up and conveyed as far as Leadenhall. Finally, after a great deal of hesitation the City made use of these powers to construct a canal from springs at Chadwell and Amwell in Herts, and accepted the office of Hugh Middleton, a goldsmith, to execute the work. Middleton would have failed, however, but for the help of James, who agreed to pay half the cost of the work if Middleton gave him half the property. This was done in an assignment of thirty-six "King's shares." Charles parted with them for an annuity of £500. A few years ago an undivided share sold for £94,900. Yet Middleton died in reduced circumstances, unable to pay a loan which the City had advanced him on the progress of his work.

The flight of the Earls of Tyrone and Tyrconnel in 1607 left without an owner a large tract of land in the north of Ireland which was confiscated to the Crown. It was proposed to colonise the district, and a scheme was drawn up for the "Plantation of Ulster." The King proposed that the City should take part in this work; the citizens were assured that their own City was dangerously overcrowded with workmen and traders of all kinds, that the plantation would be an outlet much wanted, that the country was well watered and fertile, good for breeding cattle, well stocked with game and with fisheries; they were even told to consider how great a work had been done by the people of Bristol in settling Dublin. A fuller account of the Irish Estates will be found later on (p. 206).

The conduct of a State Banquet at the Court of King James is minutely related in the following account of the Banquet presented to the Spanish Ambassador by the King.

"The Audience Chamber was elegantly furnished, having a buffet of several stages, filled with various pieces of ancient and modern gilt plate of exquisite workmanship. A railing was placed on each side the room in order to prevent the crowd from approaching too near the table. At the right hand upon entering was another buffet, containing rich vessels of gold, agate, and other precious stones. The table might be about five yards in length, and more than one yard broad. The dishes were brought in by gentlemen and servants of the King, who were accompanied by the Lord Chamberlain, and before placing them on the table they made four or five obeisances. The Earls of Pembroke and Southampton officiated as gentlemen-ushers. Their Majesties, with the Prince Henry, entered after the Constable and the others, and placed themselves at their throne, and all stood in a line to hear the grace said; the

KING JAMES I. ENTERTAINING THE SPANISH AMBASSADOR AT WHITEHALL, 1623
From a contemporary print. E. Gardner's Collection.

Constable being at the King's side, and the Count de Villamediana on the Queen's. Their Majesties washed their hands in the same basin, the Lord Treasurer handing the towel to the King, and the High Admiral to the Queen. The Prince washed in another basin, in which water was also taken to the Constable, who was waited upon by the same gentlemen. They took their seats in the following manner: their Majesties sat at the head of the table, at a distance from each other, under the canopy of state, the Queen being on the right hand, on chairs of brocade with cushions; and at her side, a little apart, sat the Constable, on a tabouret of brocade with a high cushion of the same, and on the side of the King the Prince was seated in like manner. On the opposite side of the table and on the right sat Count Villamediana, and next to him the Senator Rovida opposite the Constable; and on the same side with the senator, nearly fronting the Prince, were seated the President Richardot and the Audiencier, a space in front being left vacant owing to the absence of the Count d'Arembergue, who was prevented by the gout from attending. The principal noblemen of the kingdom were likewise at the table, in particular the Duke of Lennox; the Earl of Arundel; the Earl of Suffolke, Lord Chamberlain; the Earl of Dorset, Lord Treasurer; the Earl of Nottingham, High Admiral; the Earls of Devonshire, of Southampton, and of Pembroke; the Earl of Northumberland; the Earl of Worcester, Master of the Horse; the Earls of Shrewsbury, of Sussex, of Derby, and of Essex, and the Lord Chancellor—all being Knights of the

Garter; also Barons Cecil and Wotton and the Lord Kinross, a privy councillor; Sir Thomas Erskine, Captain of the Guard; Sir John Ramsay and James Lindsay, Scotchmen; and other barons and gentlemen of quality. There was plenty of instrumental music and the banquet was sumptuous and profuse. The first thing the King did was to send the Constable a melon and half-a-dozen oranges on a very green branch, telling him that they were the fruit of Spain transplanted into England; to which the latter, kissing his hand, replied that he valued the gift more as coming from his Majesty than as being the fruit of his

Walker & Cockerell.

HENRY, PRINCE OF WALES (1594–1612)
From the painting by Paul von Somer.

own country; he then divided the melon with their Majesties, and Don Blasco de Aragon handed the plate to the Queen, who politely and graciously acknowledged the attention. Soon afterwards the King stood up, and with his head uncovered drank to the Constable the health of their Spanish Majesties, and may the peace be happy and perpetual. The Constable pledged him in like manner, and replied that he entertained the same hope and that from the peace the greatest advantages might result to both crowns and to Christendom. The toast was then drunk by the Count Villamediana and the others present, to the delight and applause of their Majesties. Immediately afterwards, the Constable, seeing that another opportunity might not be afforded him, rose and drank to the King the health of the Queen from the lid of a cup of agate of extraordinary beauty and richness, set with diamonds and rubies, praying his Majesty would condescend to drink the toast from the cup, which he did accordingly, and ordered it to be passed round to the Prince and the others; and the Constable directed that the cup should remain in his Majesty's buffet. At this period the people shouted out, 'Peace, peace, peace! God save the King! God save the King! God save the King!' and a king at arms presented himself before the table, and after the drums, trumpets, and other instruments had sounded, with a loud voice said in English: 'That the kingdom returned many thanks to his Majesty for having concluded with the King of Spain so advantageous a peace, and he prayed to God that it might endure for many ages, and his subjects hoped that his Majesty would endeavour with all his might to maintain it so that they might enjoy from it tranquillity and repose, and that security and advantage might result to all his people; and therefore they prayed him to allow the same to be published in the kingdoms and dominions of his Majesty.' At length, after other healths and messages from the King and Queen, it was brought to a conclusion, having lasted about three hours. The cloth having been removed, every one immediately rose up; the table was placed upon the ground, and their Majesties standing upon it, proceeded to wash their hands, which is stated to be an ancient ceremony. The Constable invited Count Villamediana to wash in his basin, and the other Commissioners washed in others. Their Majesties then withdrew to their apartment, and the Constable and Count were conducted to a handsome gallery, adorned with various paintings, where they remained more than an hour. In the meantime dancing had begun in the said Audience Chamber, and the Constable and Count were informed in the name of their Majesties that they were then waiting for them to go and see it.

After a little while the Prince Henry was commanded by his parents to dance a galliard, and they pointed out to him the lady who was to be his partner; and this he did with much sprightliness and modesty, cutting several capers in the course of the dance. . . . The ball ended, and then all took their places at the windows of the room, which looked out upon a square where a platform was raised, and a vast crowd had assembled to see the King's bears fight with greyhounds. This afforded great amusement. Presently a bull, tied to the end of a rope, was fiercely baited by dogs. After this certain tumblers came, who danced upon a rope and performed curious feats of agility and skill on horseback. With this ended the entertainment and the day, and their Majesties now retired, being accompanied by the Constable and the other noblemen to their apartment, before entering which, many compliments passed on both sides, and their Majesties and the Prince shook hands with the Constable and the Count; and the other Spanish cavaliers kissed hands and took their departure. The Constable and the others, upon quitting the ball-room, were accompanied by the Lord Chamberlain to the farthest room, and by the Earl of Devonshire and other gentlemen to their coaches, more than fifty halberdiers lighting them with torches until they reached home, where as many others were waiting their arrival. Being fatigued, the Constable and the Count supped that night in private, and the others at the ordinary table."

The mind of the City in 1607 was greatly exercised with a question of precedence. The question, which was submitted to the King, and by him submitted to the Court Marshal, was as follows :—

"Whether a Commoner dignified with knighthood, without any other advantage of honour by employment or otherwise, and using trade and keeping shop in the City, should take place of an Alderman Knight within the same City, contrary to this beautified order, of ancient time settled and confirmed, with such charters and grants from his Majesty; or whether any other Bachelor Knight shall take place of any Alderman within this City?"

The question was decided in favour of the precedency of the Aldermen.

In the year 1606 one is surprised to find an order for the cleansing of the town ditch—the last of such orders. In 1598 Stow wrote that it was stopped up and choked :—

" Now of late neglected and forced either to a very narrow, and the same a filthy channel, or altogether stopped up for gardens planted, and houses built thereon ; even to the very wall, and in many places upon both ditch and wall houses to be built ; to what danger of the City, I leave to wiser consideration, and can but wish that reformation might be had."

It had been cleansed in 1519, 1540, 1569, and 1595, but apparently only in part. Thus in 1519 between Aldgate and the Tower postern, the same part in 1540, the same part again in 1569, and the part between Bishopsgate and the postern of Moorgate in 1595. I do not understand the reason of these repeated cleansings of parts.

In 1614 Smithfield, which had now become the cattle-market of the City, and was therefore a place of very great resort, continued to be without pavement of any kind, so that during or after rainy weather it was absolutely impassable for mud and mire. King James called the attention of the Mayor to this scandal, and ordered that the place should be paved. This was done. The paving was the old-fashioned cobble ; it took six months to lay down, and cost £1600.

At the same time the laying down of broad freestones instead of the old cobbles was commenced. Those of the inhabitants who chose laid down the stones before their own doors. We must understand, therefore, that all the important streets at this time were paved with cobbles ; that in a few of the principal thoroughfares there was a pavement of flat stones, but not uniform ; and that there were many courts and alleys where there was no kind of pavement at all. We may further understand that this was the London of Hogarth as well as of James I.

On July 8, 1614, the Lord Mayor sent a communication to the Lord Chamberlain detailing the steps he had taken in reforming disorderly practices (*Remembrancia*, p. 358) :—

Firstly.—He had freed the streets of a swarm of loose and idle vagrants, providing for the relief of such as were not able to get their living, and keeping them at work in Bridewell, not punishing any for begging, but setting them on work, which was worse than death to them.

Secondly.—He had informed himself, by means of spies, of many lewd houses, and had gone himself disguised to divers of them, and finding these nurseries of villany, had punished them according to their deserts, some by carting and whipping, and many by banishment.

Thirdly.—Finding the gaol pestered with prisoners, and their bane to take root and beginning at ale-houses, and much mischief to be there plotted, with great waste of corn in brewing heady strong beer, many consuming all their time and sucking that sweet poison, he had taken an exact survey of all victualling-houses and ale-houses, which were above a thousand, and above 300 barrels of strong beer in some houses, the whole quantity of beer in victualling-houses amounting to above 40,000 barrels ; he had thought it high time to abridge their number and limit them by bonds as to the quantity of beer they should use, and as to what orders they should observe, whereby the price of corn and malt had greatly fallen.

Fourthly.—The Bakers and Brewers had been drawn within bounds, so that, if the course continued, men might have what they paid for, viz. weight and measure.

He had also endeavoured to keep the Sabbath day holy, for which he had been much maligned.

Fifthly.—If what he had done were well taken, he would proceed further, viz. to deal with thieving brokers or broggers, who were the receivers of all stolen goods.

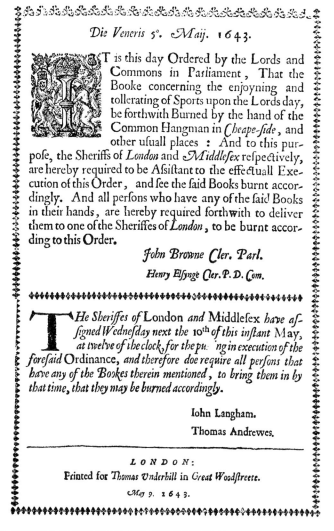

Die Veneris 5°. Maij. 1643.

IT is this day Ordered by the Lords and Commons in Parliament, That the Booke concerning the enjoyning and tollerating of Sports upon the Lords day, be forthwith Burned by the hand of the Common Hangman in *Cheape-side*, and other usuall places : And to this purpose, the Sheriffs of *London* and *Middlesex* respectively, are hereby required to be Assistant to the effectuall Execution of this Order, and see the said Books burnt accordingly. And all persons who have any of the said Books in their hands, are hereby required forthwith to deliver them to one of the Sheriffes of *London*, to be burnt according to this Order.

John Browne Cler. Parl.

Henry Elsynge Cler. P. D. Com.

THe Sheriffes of London *and* Middlesex *have assigned Wednesday next the* 10th *of this instant* May, *at twelve of the clock, for the putting in execution of the foresaid* Ordinance, *and therefore doe require all persons that have any of the Bookes therein mentioned, to bring them in by that time, that they may be burned accordingly.*

Iohn Langham.

Thomas Andrewes.

LONDON:
Printed for *Thomas Underhill in Great Woodstreete.*
May 9. 1643.

A FACSIMILE OF THE ORDER FOR THE BURNING OF THE BOOK OF SPORTS
E. Gardner's Collection.

And lastly, the inmates of infected houses would require before summer to be discharged of all superfluities for avoiding infection, etc.

Returning from Scotland in 1618 James observed that certain persons of Lancashire, whom he called Puritans, and precise people, had interfered by prohibiting such "lawful recreations and honest exercises upon Sundays and other holidays after the afternoon sermon or service " as the peasantry had been accustomed to indulge in ; he therefore issued a declaration setting forth that this prohibition " barreth the common and meaner sort of people from using such exercises as may make their bodies more able for war, when we or our successors shall have occasion to use them ; and in place thereof sets up filthy tiplings and drunkenness, and breeds a number of idle and discontented speeches in their ale-houses : for when shall the common people have leave to exercise, if not upon the Sundays and holidays, seeing they must apply their labour, and win their living, in all working days ? "

The King therefore commanded that no recreations should be denied to his subjects which did not militate against the laws and the canons of the Church. " And as for our good people's lawful recreation, our pleasure likewise is that after the end of divine services our good people may not be disturbed, letted, or discouraged from any lawful recreation, such as dancing, either men or women, archery for men, leaping, vaulting, or any other such harmless recreation : nor from having of May games, Whitsun ales, and Morris dances, and the setting up of May-poles, and other sports therewith used, as the same be had in due and convenient time without impediment or neglect of divine service ; and that women shall have leave to carry rushes to the church for the decorating of it, according to their old custom. But withall, we do here account still as prohibited all unlawful games to be used upon Sunday only, as bear and bull-baiting, interludes, and, at all times in the meaner sort of people by law prohibited, bowling."

The famous Book of Sports, which laid down rules as to games and sports lawful to be played on the Sunday, was ordered to be read in every parish church throughout the country. The reception of the proclamation, especially in the City, seems to have surprised the King's advisers. Neither James nor his son could ever understand the extent or the depth of the new ideas in religion. Sunday, in the eyes of most people who thought about religion at all—that is, in the eyes of all responsible persons in London, which was a hot-bed of religious controversy—had become the Jewish Sabbath. Most of the City clergy refused absolutely to read the Book of Sports in their churches, choosing to be fined or suspended and imprisoned rather than obey. These punishments they endured. But the feeling in the City ran very high, insomuch that the Lord Mayor refused permission for the King's carriages to be drawn through the City on Sunday during Divine Service. There was, naturally, great indignation at Court. The King made the customary observation about two Kings in the country. However, he sent his carriages back with a warrant to let them pass. This the Mayor obeyed, saying that he had done his duty, but that what one in higher authority commanded, he must obey. So no more was said, and the City, in the matter of the Book of Sports, had peace.

The story of the settlement of Virginia is a pleasing episode of this reign. It shows the City at its best, wise, patriotic, generous, and far-seeing. Taking this history with that of the plantation of Ulster, we have a proof that the City was at this time overcrowded and congested. When the latter scheme was first set afoot the citizens were reminded that the City was so crowded that one tradesman was

THE DESTRUCTION OF CHEAPSIDE CROSS AND THE BURNING OF THE BOOK OF SPORTS, MAY 1643

hardly able to live by another, and when the Virginian colony was mooted it was proposed to relieve the streets by sending out all the idle children.

The Company for colonising Virginia was founded in 1609. The promoters assured the Mayor, then Sir Humphry Wild, that if the surplus population of London could be transferred to Virginia there would be far less danger of pestilence and famine. By way of attracting people willing to emigrate, meat, drink, and clothing, with a house, orchard, and garden, and an allotment of land, were offered.

Any alderman subscribing £50 would be reckoned an original member of the Council. "Bills of Association" were given to all who subscribed, entitling them to a *pro rata* share in the profits. Fifty-six of the Companies agreed to take ventures in the plantations. On May 23, 1609, the Company received a second charter, and in the same month the first fleet of seven ships was dispatched. The ships took three months to get across; yellow fever broke out among their crews and passengers, the number of whom were sadly reduced when they landed.

In two years' time the Company had got through all their money, though they had raised £18,000 since their first fleet went out. They obtained, however, a third charter, with the addition of the Bermudas, and they held a public lottery. It is remarkable to find the City Companies and the City churches, or vestries, taking shares in this lottery.

Two years later a second lottery was set on foot. In 1618 it was decided to take up vagrant boys and girls in the streets and to transport them to Virginia. This was done. A beginning was made with 100, who were shipped across so successfully that the Corporation sent over another hundred. The children cost £5 each, including their voyage and their clothing. The Common Council paid for both shiploads by a rate levied on the City.

Next, the King complained that whole companies of lazy rogues and masterless men followed the Court. The Virginia Company laid hands on all, put them into Bridewell, and as soon as possible packed them off for the Plantation. But the infant colony suffered in 1622 from a treacherous attack made upon the people by the Indians, in which 350 of the settlers perished. The Court of Common Council voted another £500 for another shipload of boys and girls. The question of beggars, vagrants, and disorderly persons was constantly before the authorities. The difficulty has always been the same. If they are suppressed one day, they gather again the next.

In the year 1614 the City began a very mean and unworthy practice; that, namely, of electing to the office of Sheriff those who would rather pay the fine than serve. In this year nearly a dozen were elected, all of whom declined to serve.

In the same year the Mayor and Corporation received a reminder that the City was expected to keep a force of militia always equipped and drilled. They therefore resolved on raising a force of 6000 men; the Aldermen were provided with precepts stating the number of men wanted from each ward, with the kind of arms and armour which they were to bring with them. A list of prices at which the arms could be procured was appended to the precept :—

"Jerome Heydon, described as 'iremonger at the lower end of Cheapeside,' was ready to sell corslets, comprising 'brest, backe, gorgett, taces and headpiece,' at 15s.; pikes with steel heads at 2s. 6d.; swords, being Turkey blades, at 7s.; 'bastard' muskets at 14s.; great muskets with rests, at 16s.; a headpiece, lined and stringed, at 2s. 6d., and a bandaleer for 1s. 6d. Henry White and Don Sany Southwell were

2

prepared to do corslets 6d. cheaper, and the same with swords, but their swords are described as only 'Irish hilts and belts to them.' Their bastard muskets, 'with mouldes,' could be had for 13s., or 1s. cheaper than those of Jerome Heydon. The Armourers' Company were ready to supply corslets at 15s., but for the same 'with pouldrons' they asked 4s. more. The Cutlers' Company would furnish 'a very good turky blade and good open hilts' for 6s., thus underselling the private firms."

The interference of James with the Merchant Adventurers in 1615 is difficult to understand. He suppressed the Company, withdrew all licences for the exportation of undyed and undressed cloth, and formed a new company. The Dutch threatened to set up looms for themselves and to destroy the English trade in cloth, but the new company proved a failure, and the old company was restored.

The charter granted by James in the sixth year of his reign confirmed all the ancient rights, liberties, and immunities of the citizens, and added to the bounds of the City and its jurisdiction, the precincts of Duke's Place, St. Bartholomew's the Great and Less, Black and White Friars, and Cold Harbour.

Yet the same anxiety which possessed the Government in the reign of Elizabeth as to the increase of London was shown by that of James in his very first year, when he issued a proclamation putting a stop to the building of new houses in the suburbs. It was ordered that no one should build on new foundations, and that all houses so built should be pulled down. The frequency of these proclamations shows that the Government was in earnest on the subject. No doubt the ordinance was evaded because the suburbs were actually increasing, and that rapidly, but a great many persons would be deterred by fear of breaking the law, and would either remain in the City, which was greatly overcrowded, or go across the river and occupy Southwark, which began to fill up fast, along the causeway and embankment, and to grow also by putting out new streets on either side of the former and along the road to Bermondsey. The year after a third proclamation was issued to the same effect; no one was to build on new foundations within two miles of the City. The people paid no attention to this proclamation, and building went on without molestation for some years, when the builders were called upon either to buy their own houses at an extravagant price or to pull them down. This mode of enforcing the law would not be approved at the present day; in 1617 it put money into James's pocket.

Six years later another proclamation was published to the same effect, acknowledging the futility of the former law.

On a certain Sunday afternoon, the 26th of October 1623, occurred a disaster, called the Fatal Vespers, which was long remembered as a signal proof of Heaven's wrath against those who followed Popish worship. The French Ambassador at that time had a house in Blackfriars, adjoining which there was a large upper chamber, sometimes used as the Ambassador's chapel, about 60 feet long and 20 feet broad. Roman Catholics in London frequented the chapels at the various embassies. But this was not the French Ambassador's chapel, which was within his house. Perhaps the occasion demanded a larger room.

On this afternoon about 300 persons were assembled to celebrate evensong and to hear a sermon from a Jesuit named Father Drury, a person held in great repute for his learning, his blameless life, and laudable conversation. The congregation consisted of English, Scotch, Irish, and Welsh. The sermon began between three and four in the afternoon. The text was the parable of the king and the servant whom he forgave.

In the midst of the sermon the beams and side timbers of the floor suddenly gave way and fell with all the people upon the floor of the room below. This in its turn being broken through, all fell upon the lowest floor, where they lay piled together with the beams and broken planks. The only persons who did not fall were some thirty sitting or standing in a corner where the beams held fast. These people with their knives cut a hole in the wall, and so got safely into the Ambassador's house.

Meanwhile people came running with spades and pickaxes to extricate the sufferers from the ruins.

It took the whole of that day and night to bring out all the people. Out of the 300 who were assembled in the evening some thirty we have said did not fall with the rest. Ninety-five were found to be dead, including the preacher, Father Drury, and a great many were maimed and bruised.

The story of a tumult by the City 'prentices suggests the fourteenth century. It began with one of them crying out when Gondomar, the Spanish Ambassador, was being carried down Fleet Street in his chair, "There goes the devil in a dung-cart." Upon which one of the suite retorted sharply. Then the apprentice knocked down the Spaniard. For this offence he with his companions was ordered to be whipped through the City. Thereupon the apprentices rose, 300 strong, and released their companions. However, it could not be endured that an Ambassador should be insulted, and the sentence was carried out. One of the apprentices died, presumably from the severity of his punishment; the others were released, and when it was known, later on, that the Spanish match had fallen through, the Londoners expressed the liveliest joy, bonfires were lit, bells rung, tables were spread in the streets, casks were broached, and all because the Prince was coming home—without the Infanta.

All that precedes concerning the reign of James I. touches the surface of things. These events might have been observed by any casual by-stander, and understood by him as possessing no significance as to the mind of the people and the City.

We have now to consider the influence of James, not on the country at large, where opinion was slow in coming to a head, so much as in the City, where, with 100,000 gathered closely together, and that within hearing of Whitehall, suspicion and jealousy, once awakened, became rapidly opinion, and opinion became conviction, and the settled conviction of the City, once known and formulated, proved the most important weapon of all those forged by the pedantry and obstinacy of James, and the equal obstinacy and wrongheadedness of Charles. In other words, it is necessary in this place to show, if possible, that in a closer sense than is usual the years 1603-1625 were a preparation for the appeal to arms, by which the liberties of the country were secured. I prepare, therefore, to pass in very brief review some of the leading political events of the time, in order to show how the City was affected by them.

To begin with, the City was fiercely Protestant. The Catholic reaction, which had stayed the spread of Continental Protestantism, only made England more doggedly Protestant. That a new life had been imparted to the Catholic Church by the Jesuits and the new orders made the Englishman only the more hostile to a church which threatened his nationality, his liberties, everything that he held most sacred. Again, to the Protestant spirit belonged the right of free thought and free doctrine as against authority. Scholars and divines were satisfied with the purely personal relations between God and man, which they had substituted for the priest and the sacerdotal authority. What the Protestant clergy wanted, what they asked of James in the Millenary Petition was a reform in the ecclesiastical courts, the removal of certain superstitious usages from the Prayer Book, the more rigorous observance of Sunday, and the training of preachers. "Why," asked Bacon—he might have asked the same question to-day—"should the civil state be purged and restored by good and wholesome laws made every three years in Parliament assembled, devising remedies as fast as time breedeth mischief, and contrariwise the ecclesiastical state still continue upon the dregs of time, and receive no alteration these forty-five years and more?"

However, James had not the least intention of making any change in the ecclesiastical courts.

Moreover, he had already declared his views as to the rights of the sovereign. "A king, he said, is not bound to frame his actions according to law, but of his own free will, and for giving an example to his people." Convocation was quick to adopt this view and to denounce as a fatal error the doctrine that all power is derived from the people. Later on, the University of Oxford proclaimed the doctrine of passive resistance. It is difficult to speak with moderation of these two opinions, or to estimate how far they are responsible for the bloodshed of the Civil War.

How James carried on his government for seven years without a Parliament belongs to national history. We may, however, picture the wrath and exasperation of the City at the encroachments of the spiritual courts, the subserviency of the lawyers and judges, the extortions, the sale of peerages, and the dismissal of the

Chief Justice. We can also imagine the whispers that went round concerning the Court, its extravagance, the shameless promotion of favourites, the scandals, the attempt to form a Spanish alliance.

We may sum up this ignoble reign, so far as concerns London, by saying that the attitude of the City during the whole of it was one of observation and endurance. We have seen something of what was observed. There were, however, other things of which the City took silent note. To begin with, James, while he proclaimed the Royal prerogative, threw away the Royal dignity. He was extravagant and in foolish ways ; he loved favourites and they were unworthy ; his son was the idol of the people, but James affected no grief for him, nay, it was even whispered that the young Prince was poisoned, and with the guilty knowledge of his father ; he hated Puritans and persecuted Catholics ; he spent most of his time in hunting ; it was commonly reported that he drank heavily ; his servants were left without their wages ; his purveyors refused supplies until they were paid ; he was always preaching the Royal prerogative ; he was anxious to enter upon a marriage with Spain, the arch-enemy of the Protestant religion ; he tried to bully the House of Commons, but got nothing from them ; he granted monopolies, a thing abhorrent to the commercial mind. All these things London observed and marked, and they bore their fruit in the reign of James's son, and those of his two grandsons. But as yet resistance—armed resistance—was not even thought of. Plots and conspiracies there were, but of small account. Of armed resistance on behalf of the liberties of the country as yet there was no idea.

CHAPTER II

CHARLES I

THE history of Charles shows, if we consider nothing more than his dealings with the City of London, a wrongheadedness which is most amazing. It is true that two at least of the Tudor sovereigns had ruled the City with a strong hand, but they

CHARLES I. (1600–1649)

From the replica of the portrait by Van Dyck painted by Sir Peter Lely.

knew how to make themselves loved as well as feared, and they knew, further, how timely concessions in small things may overcome resistance in great things. Moreover, we have seen how James had endeavoured to make himself an absolute

CHEAPSIDE—QUEEN HENRIETTA MARIA'S ENTRY INTO LONDON

From a contemporary print.

monarch, and the results which followed. As the event proved, the side taken by London in this reign was once more the winning side; as it was with Richard the Second and Henry the Sixth, so it was with Charles the First.

I have attempted to indicate something of the effect produced upon the City by the reign of James I. I have now to show the fruits of that reign, followed by another even more obstinately arbitrary; even blinder to the threatening wave that was rising and swelling before the King's feet, so that it was impossible, one would have thought, not to see it and to understand it. The unbroken contumacy of the House of Commons, whenever it had a chance of speaking, was not that a sign which might have been read by the King and his Ministers? The sullen attitude of the City—was not that a sign? Charles, however, saw nothing, or, if he saw, then he thought the opposition feeble compared with the forces at his own disposal. Nothing, however, seems to have been further from his thoughts than armed resistance. Let us remember, however, that at the outset Charles had to face an angry and discontented City; angry on account of the ecclesiastical courts and the impossibility of redress; discontented on account of the late King's deliberate trampling upon all its liberties.

On the 28th of April, Charles was proclaimed King at Ludgate Hill, himself being present. On the 1st of May he was married by proxy in Paris to Henrietta Maria. The new Queen came over at once, and received a kindly welcome from the citizens. The public entry, which was arranged for June 18, was postponed on account of another outbreak of plague. The number of deaths from this visitation is returned at 35,417, about one-third of the whole population. As in 1603, and later on in 1665, the richer sort hurried out of the town on the first outbreak, leaving behind them the population which cannot leave the place of work, namely, the apprentices, craftsmen, servants, and porters. The rich carried away what they could, but they were refused entrance into the villages, even the barns being closed to them. Many of them died on the highway, their pockets stuffed with money.

In the midst of this terrible time Charles called upon the City to raise and equip 1000 men for the new expedition. This was done, and the men were raised somehow, and marched down to Plymouth, where they awaited the arrival of the Fleet with no pay and no provisions. Finally the Fleet arrived, and they went on board, bound for Cadiz, there to experience failure.

The Parliament of 1626 refused to grant supplies until grievances had been considered. Charles therefore dissolved it. This was like his father. He would get on without the Parliament. He began by calling upon the City to lend him £100,000. The City refused, they had no money, they were just recovering from the Plague; they lent, however, £20,000 on good security. Next came a demand for 4000 men and 20 ships, the first for the defence of Sheppey, and the second in order to carry the war into the enemy's country. To the first the City replied that the order came from some of the lords and not from the King, and that by charter their soldiers were for the defence of the City and must not go farther than the Mayor himself may go. As we have seen in the past, this right was always put forward when the City did not want to obey the King, and always neglected when the City was willing that its troops should go anywhere, as, for instance, in the deposition of Richard the Second, in the siege of Winchester under Stephen, and in the defence of the country against the Spanish Armada.

As for the ships, the Mayor was instructed to reply that the City was in a most impoverished condition, that they could not get the ships ready in the time, and that the merchants would far rather have letters of mark and go out privateering. However, the City gave way. It is an indication of the poverty of the City at this time that the small sum of £18,000 wanted for fitting out the ships could not be raised. Many of the people steadfastly refused to pay their rate ; the constables refused to distrain ; the people helped one another when the constables tried to do their duty. Meantime the streets of the City were thronged with sailors clamouring for their pay ; they mobbed the Duke of Buckingham, who put them off with promises. Charles had no money to give them. He endeavoured to get supplies by the "Forced Loan" of 1626. The City was left for a time, but when in 1627 war broke out between France and England it became necessary to press for the loan. Some persons refused to give any money and were committed to prison ; the judges declared the loan illegal. The City, however, after long discussions, resolved on lending the King another sum of £120,000, provided it was amply secured.

The following is part of the assessment, showing the demands divided among the leading companies :—

Merchant Taylors	£6300
Grocers	£6000
Haberdashers	£4300
Drapers	£4608
Vintners	£3120
Goldsmiths	£4380
Mercers	£3720
Fishmongers	£3390
Clothworkers	£3390

The masters and wardens of the plumbers, saddlers, founders, joiners, and glaziers were sent to prison for neglecting to collect the company's quota.

The unpopularity of Buckingham, upon whom was laid the odium of failure, is shown in the very strange story of the murder of Dr. Lambe. Lambe was an astrologer and a creature of Buckingham's. The account of his death is told in three ways. First, that of Dr. Reginald Sharpe (*London and the Kingdom*, ii.

p. 105). He says that Lambe was set upon by some of the people in the City on his way home after supper, that they did him nearly to death, and that no one would receive the wounded man, who was taken to the compter, and died the next day. The other accounts are more elaborate and more unreal. They are as follows :—

1. He was insulted by a few boys, who were joined by the rabble, so that he took refuge in a tavern in the Old Jewry. The vintner, for his own safety,

HENRIETTA MARIA (1609–1669)
From an engraving by Voerts, after Van Dyck.

turned him out, whereupon the mob beat him to death before the Mayor's guard could reach the spot.

2. He was in Cheapside, where he was insulted by the boys, who were joined by the mob; he ran into a house of Wood Street, where the people broke all the windows. He was forced to leave his refuge, and was then seized by the mob, who dragged him along, striking and kicking him. The account goes on to say that the news of the tumult reaching the King, he rode, accompanied by a small guard, into the City, and found in St. Paul's Churchyard the mob, still beating and kicking the man; that he addressed the mob and bade them desist; that they replied that they had already judged him; and in fact they had so dislocated his limbs that he was dead. Charles, having so small a guard, was obliged to retire.

The second of these two accounts is clearly false, because Wood Street is only a few minutes' walk from St. Paul's Churchyard; the noise of a City disturbance would not reach Whitehall; when the news of it did reach Whitehall, the thing must have been over, unless the kicking and striking lasted for an hour; it would take quite an hour for the riot to be reported to the King, and for him to get ready his escort and to ride to St. Paul's.

In any case there is no doubt that the man Lambe was murdered by the London mob; also that the King was greatly incensed at the matter, for he wrote an angry letter to the Mayor calling for the punishment of the murderers. The Mayor replied that he could not find any; the City was therefore fined £6000, which, on their arresting a few men, was reduced to 1500 marks or £1000. It has been suggested that the money was all that Charles wanted. If so, why did he reduce the fine? It is much more probable that he was personally concerned at the murder.

There are many indications that the people were getting beyond the control of the Mayor and Aldermen. The murder of Lambe was only one of the many riotous affairs which occurred during this reign. In 1630 the Sheriff's officers having arrested a man in Fleet Street, the populace rose and attempted a rescue. The Sheriff's officers were supported by watchmen, constables, and some of the citizens who joined them; a fight ensued, in which many were killed and wounded. The Mayor, with a company of the trained bands, arrived upon the scene and stopped the battle. Several ringleaders were arrested, and one, Henry Stamford by name, was executed.

Again, in 1640, the City being greatly enraged against the Archbishop of Canterbury, a body of five hundred 'prentices gathered together by night and ran to Lambeth, intending to sack and destroy the Palace; the Archbishop, however, had got wind of their design, and was strong enough to beat them off. The 'prentices also broke up the sittings of the High Commissioner of St. Paul's.

Another pestilence visited the City in 1629, remaining till 1631. It was followed, as usual, by distress and scarcity of provisions. Doggerel rhymes (*Sharpe*, ii. 109) appeared showing the temper of the people :—

> " The corne is so dear,
> I doubt many will starve this year;
> If you see not to this
> Some of you will speed amiss.
> Our souls they are dear,
> For our bodies have some care.
> Before we arise
> Less will suffice."

One of the advantages of keeping all the shops of one trade in the same quarter is illustrated by the story of the Queen's loss by robbery. It was in the year 1631 that a part of her plate and jewels was stolen. The purchasers of the stolen property must have been the goldsmiths, and unless the stolen plate had been sent abroad, it might be recovered by finding to what goldsmith it had been offered on purchase. Until the beginning of the seventeenth century all the goldsmiths lived together in Cheapside. As early as 1623 it was observed that many of them were leaving their old quarters and setting up shops elsewhere. They were ordered to go back to their old quarters, but, as generally happened with such orders, there were no means of enforcing them, and the goldsmiths continued to scatter themselves about the town. Then came the Queen's loss, and it was found that the order had been entirely neglected. The Lords in Council, therefore, renewed the order on the ground that by leaving Cheapside and setting up their shops in other places, they offered facilities for "passing away of stolen plate." This order of Council was issued in 1635. As very little attention was paid to the order, which was certainly vexatious, it was renewed on May 24, 1637, and was followed by an order of the Court of Star Chamber that if any other tradesmen besides goldsmiths should keep shop in Cheapside or Lombard Street, the Alderman should be imprisoned for permitting it. As little attention was paid to this order, a fourth, to the same effect, was issued in January 1638. In the last the names of some offenders were given; there were two stationers, a milliner, a bandseller, a drugster, a cook, and a girdler. This interference with the conduct of trade was part of a general and systematic attempt to make the King master in everything. He could not possibly have made a greater mistake than to interfere with the trading interests or to meddle with the way in which a money-making community conducted its affairs. The goldsmiths who had left Cheapside had done so in their own interests; by scattering, each shop formed its own circle; to give up that circle would be to give up the shopkeeper's livelihood; they had found out by this time that in a great city of 150,000 people, trade is more successful when the shops of the same kind are scattered. Imagine the wrath of Cheapside at the present day if all the shops except those of one trade were ordered to depart!

The business of the ship money is by some historians considered the greatest of all the King's mistakes; but that of the Cheapside tradesmen touched a lower level, and therefore a wider area. To bleed the rich merchants was one thing, to deprive an honest tradesman of his shop was more serious, because of tradesmen there were more than of merchants. A charter confirming the City liberties produced no change in the King's policy. It was signed while the disputes concerning ship money, Irish Estates, and interference with trade were at their height, and it cost the City £12,000.

When we read of ships being fitted out by London, of the fleet equipped by Sir John Philpott, of the solid support given to the fleet which engaged the Spanish Armada, and of other occasions, it is difficult to understand the objections of London to raise the ship money, save on the supposition that they now perceived that the King meant to go as far as he could in the way of despotic power, and that it behoved them to make a stand and to fight every inch of ground. This they prepared to do. First they set their law officers to hunt up charters and Acts of Parliament. The case complete, they presented a petition to the King, stating that by certain Acts recited the City was exempt from such obligations. However, the City got nothing by its petition except a peremptory order to raise the £30,000 wanted, and to raise it at once. The City gave way and proceeded to obey and to fit out seven ships.

The impost of ship money, which ultimately caused Charles I. so much trouble, was suggested to him in 1631 by Sir William Noye, Attorney-General, who had found among the records in the Tower, not only writs compelling the ports on certain occasions to provide ships for the use of the King, but others obliging their neighbours of the maritime counties to contribute to the expense. Writs were issued to London and the different ports, October 20, 1634, ordering them to supply a certain number of ships of a specified tonnage, sufficiently armed and manned, to rendezvous at Portsmouth on the 1st of March 1635. The writ is set out in Howell's *State Trials*, vol. iii. pp. 830-832, and also the proceedings of the Common Council, and their petition to the King against it. By this contrivance the King obtained a supply of £218,500, which he devoted to providing a fleet. Twelve of the judges decided that the King had the right to make the levy. In the speech of Lord Keeper Coventry to the judges assembled in the Star Chamber on the 14th of February 1636 he stated that, " In the first year, when the writs were directed to the ports and the maritime places, they received little or no opposition; but in the second year, when they went generally throughout the kingdom, although by some well obeyed, have been refused by some, not only in some inland counties, but in some of the maritime places."

Charles then called upon the whole nation to provide ship money. London was ordered to equip two more ships of 800 tons apiece. One, Robert Chambers by name, brought the question of the King's right into the Court of the King's Bench. Mr. Justice Berkeley, with amazing servility, refused to allow the case to be argued, because, he said, " there is a rule of law, and another of government," thus actually separating the law and government. It was by this time fully evident that the King and Council were resolved upon the humbling of the City. If there was any doubt left in men's minds, that doubt was surely dispelled by the action of the Star Chamber concerning the Irish Estates. The Star Chamber, after hearing a suit against the City charging them with mal-administration of their Irish property, condemned the City to forfeiture of all their lands in Ireland—lands which, as we have seen, the City had been forced to take up by James the First, and on which they had spent very large sums of money. In addition to losing their estates the citizens were fined £70,000.   As for the fine, it was easier to inflict it than to levy it.   The City let the Irish Estates go for the present, and paid the sum of £12,000 in full discharge of the fine.   But the thing remained in their minds, and one of the first acts of Parliament, when it was called, was to reconsider the whole question (see p. 209).

Walker & Cockerell.

GEORGE VILLIERS, FIRST DUKE (SECOND CREATION) OF BUCKINGHAM (1592–1628)
From the portrait by Gerard Honthorst.

I purpose in this place to interrupt the direct course of events in order to show, by reference to certain political events of the time, the mind of London.

In 1626 occurred the famous impeachment of the Duke of Buckingham by Sir John Eliot, when the Commons pronounced their first refusal to grant subsidies till grievances had been redressed.   Eliot was arrested and confined to the Tower; after ten days he was released, but the Parliament was dissolved.   The King appealed to the country to grant as a free gift what the Commons had refused.

The answer to this appeal should have left no doubt in the minds of the King's friends that the words of Sir John Eliot stated the mind of the whole country.   As regards London and Westminster they replied to those who would collect the subsidy with cries of " A Parliament ! A Parliament !"

Charles then tried the expedient of a forced loan with equal want of success. It was found impossible to collect it.

In 1628 a new Parliament was called. In this House the Petition of Right was drawn up, in which, among other things, it was claimed that no man should be compelled to pay any kind of tax without the consent of Parliament.

Charles gave way, secretly, after his manner, reserving certain rights of his own, as that of imprisonment without appeal. The City knew nothing of this duplicity ; bells were rung ; bonfires lighted ; it was assumed that the King had honestly given way, and the House granted a subsidy. Then came the news of Buckingham's murder.

There were two of Charles's friends, and only two, for whom the City afterwards entertained a hatred equal to that they felt for Buckingham. But at that moment there was no one whose death was so ardently desired. When the news was brought to London, grave citizens drank the health of Felton. When the murderer was brought to London, the crowd followed praying that the Lord would comfort him. Such was the mind of the City towards the man whom Eliot had impeached ; they received the news of his murder with savage exultation. Then Charles made Laud Bishop of London—the third of the three men whose death a few years later the City welcomed with shouts of joy. It was not enough to trample on the liberties of the people, he must now proceed to deprive them of their religion. The memorable sitting in the House when the Speaker was held in his chair while the Commons passed resolution after resolution against innovations in religion and the illegal levy of taxes, belongs to national history. It was with passionate excitement, hardly restrained from tumult, that the news of this sitting and these resolutions was received in the City. There were as yet no newspapers to furnish day by day a report of the proceedings in the House, but the tidings of each protest of the Commons and each arbitrary measure of the King flew through the streets of the City as quickly as if by means of the daily paper, so that every house was filled with the angry murmurs of the citizens, and men in the streets and on 'Change looked at each other and asked what would happen next.

Yet no word of armed resistance. The old time when one King could be put down and another set up in his place was forgotten. Rebellion was not yet even thought of. The Parliament was dissolved.

Laud, free to do what he pleased, proceeded whither his pleasure led him. What he did is national history. The people of London, of whom nine-tenths were Puritans (see p. 137), or, at least, strong Protestants, saw with rage the severance of the ties connecting the Church of England with the foreign Protestant churches ; they saw the forcible introduction of rites and ceremonies offensive to Puritan feeling; the expulsion of Puritan clergy; the suppression of Puritan lectures; the prohibition of the Geneva Bible, loved by all the people; the desecration, as they thought, of their so-called Sabbath; the restoration of ritualism; the return, as they believed, to Rome.

There seemed no hope of redress. The High Church party were in power; the return to Rome seemed certain.

It was at this time (1629-1640) that the first great emigration to America took place. It was an emigration of men and women of every station and every trade; there were men of family and property among them; there were also husbandmen and humble craftsmen; 1700 emigrants went out in one year, 1630; in eleven years (1629-1640) 20,000 went away. It seems as if the magnitude of the emigration should have caused uneasiness, but probably the exodus of 2000 people a year, many of whom went abroad to better themselves without regard to religion, was considered to be useful to the plantations, and, so far as they departed for the sake of religion, in no way prejudicial to the State.

The lists published in *The Original Emigrants to America* show that from the Port of London—the only port we need mention here—in the year 1635 there were embarked and were transported—not in a criminal sense—no fewer than 4890 emigrants, a fourth part of the whole number mentioned above. There must have been some special reason for the departure of so many in one year. We may find it, perhaps, in the tyrannical and oppressive proceedings of Laud. He had deprived the French and Flemish refugees of their right to worship after their own manner, and thousands emigrated in consequence; he had assumed a censorship of the Press which forbade such books as Foxe's *Book of Martyrs;* he restored the "wakes" or dedication feasts, the church ales, the Sunday sports, the surplice, kneeling at the Communion; he insisted on uniformity of worship; these are sufficient causes for the great emigration of 1635. The book in which I find the names of the emigrants gives them in separate lists according to the ships in which they sailed; in most cases it gives their ages, in a few cases their occupation and station—unfortunately in very few cases. Again, in some cases the list gives the name of the parish where the statutory declaration was made, viz. the oaths of allegiance, that of conformity to the Church of England, and the assurance that the emigrant was not a "subsidy man"—that is to say, a person owing money to the State on account of subsidy due. One need not attach much importance to this declaration, as yet no one had begun to dispute the duty of allegiance; the Church of England included the Puritans, and as regards the subsidy, those who were of humble rank owed nothing; those of the better sort may very well have protested that they owed nothing—as by a strictly legal view they did not.

It is a great pity that the names of the places from which the emigrants came are not always indicated. We cannot, for instance, learn how far this movement affected London. Certain City parishes are given in which the emigrants made the statutory declaration, but in the majority of cases the parishes are not indicated. I have compiled a table, manifestly very incomplete, of those parishes which are mentioned. It is quite evident that many of the lists belong to London, though the fact is not stated. Thus there seems no reason why St. Katherine's—is it St. Katherine Cree or St. Katherine Coleman, or St. Katherine's by the Tower?— should have sent out 157 emigrants; St. Mildred's, Bread Street, 27; and other London parishes two or three only.

St. Andrew, 1	Tower Precinct, 2
St. Alphege, 4	St. Saviour, Southwark, 3
All Hallows, Staining, 6	St. Olave, Southwark, 5
St. Botolph, Billingsgate, 1	"Westminster," 3
St. Mildred, Bread Street, 27	"Wapping," 6
St. Katherine's, 157	"Lombard Street," 8
St. Giles, Cripplegate, 6	"Cheapside," 3
Minories. 4	"Fenchurch," 1
Stepney, 33	

The greatest contributor, however, to the 5000 was Gravesend, from which place 1875 persons took the oaths and were sent on to the Port of London to be shipped.

The sight of these crowds flocking to the Port of London to embark on the ships bound for America; the provisioning of the ships for the voyage; the talk about the places whither these persons were to be carried; the reasons why they went; the escape for some from the Laudian persecution; the hope, for others, of a new country where the divine right of Kings would not be a subject of discussion; the grave and serious divines who went on board these ships; the gentlemen who joined them; the humble craftsmen who went with them, the Geneva Bible in hand; can we doubt that these sights sank deep into the hearts of the people? Can we doubt that the example, the prayers, the touching farewells of these emigrants were sowing seeds which should produce fruit eventful and terrible? "Our hearts," said Winthrop, "shall be fountains of tears for your everlasting welfare when we shall be in our poor cottages in the wilderness."

Doubt not that the people of London knew very well what a wilderness this New England was; how hard and barren was its coast; how cruel was its winter; how deadly and implacable were the Indians; they had heard of seasons when the shell-fish of the sea-shore were the food of the emigrants, when in the evening they knew not where they would find their food in the morning, and when they assembled to worship under escort and with armed sentinels.

We must not be led away to believe that after the first rush, when divines, scholars, country gentlemen, and lawyers joined the list of emigrants, the same class was continued. The lists before us point rather in the other direction, as if in 1635, five years after the first movement began, by far the larger number were craftsmen and rustics. The age of the emigrants points to this conclusion. I have taken a few consecutive pages at random. I find that out of 409 names there were 106 under twenty; of these many were children and boys, but the majority were eighteen and nineteen years old; 259 were men and women—the men far out-numbering the women—in the full vigour of early manhood, namely, over twenty and under thirty. There were only thirty-four over forty and under fifty, and ten only of fifty and upwards. In other words, I conclude from these lists that while religion may have had a good deal to do with the emigration of this year, a very large part of the attraction was the thought of adventure, change, and better meat, which has always made the Englishman restless and enterprising.

Where did the emigrants go? There were six places open to the emigrant of the seventeenth century. And he went to them in the following proportion during the year 1635 :—

New England .	.	69 ships	St. Christopher's	.	6 ships
Virginia	.	21 „	Providence	.	2 „
Barbadoes	.	10 „	Bermudas	.	2 „

Let us return to the constitutional part of the history.

Charles called no Parliament for eleven years. During that time, as he could get no subsidies, he was compelled to practise every kind of extortion; he enforced the old obligation to take the honour of knighthood; he imposed fines for encroach-ments, for defective title deeds, for recusancy.

Where he touched the City was, first, in reviving the old laws against building in the suburbs, and in fining those living in houses built twenty years before in assurance that the law was a dead letter; next, in the levy of illegal and extortionate customs duties, which were resisted by the City merchants, but at their peril. One of them said that it was better to be a merchant in Turkey than in London; for this he was sent to the Tower and fined £2000: thirdly, by the system of monopolies, against which the City had protested under Elizabeth. Everything became the subject of a monopoly. As was said afterwards in the Long Parliament, " They sup in our cup; they dip in our dish; they sit by our fire; we find them in the dye-fat, the wash bowls, and the powdering tub. They have marked and sealed us from head to foot."

All these grievances continued to roll up like a snowball, as silently and as rapidly; yet it was an invisible snowball. Outwardly the King and his friends were deceived by the general tranquillity; there was offered very little resistance; there were manifested few open signs of discontent; a general prosperity prevailed; trade was better than it had been for many years; the English flag was flying over new seas and in ports hitherto unknown; agriculture was advancing; the country gentry were growing more easy in their means; every one seemed quiet. In fact it was felt by the better class that there was no hurry. Sooner or later there must be a Parliament; sooner or later the makeshifts of the King would come to an end; there was no hurry. And the bill kept rolling up. But the King, and Laud, and the Court party were deceived. They mistook the quiet of the people, and especially of the City, for submission and subjection; they thought that the spirit of resistance was quelled.

Perhaps enough has been said to show the temper of the City. One or two notes more.

We find a London clergyman calling on all Christians to "resist the Bishops as robbers of souls, limbs of the Beast, and fathers of Antichrist." One pays very little heed to ecclesiastical censure, which is generally cursing, at any time, but the vehemence of this language seems worthy of remark.

When Prynne was carried from Palace Yard after the sentence which deprived him of his ears, he was escorted by a hundred thousand Londoners with prayers and cries of encouragement and of comfort.

In 1638 Hampden's judges laid down the principle that "no statute prohibiting arbitrary taxation could be pleaded against the King's will." To this monstrous doctrine the City said nothing, the people said nothing; they waited; sooner or later there must be a Parliament.

Next year began the Scotch troubles, the beginning of the end for Charles.

In 1640 the King found himself compelled to call a Parliament; he must have money.

This was the Short Parliament. I am quite sure that the news of the summons was received on 'Change and wherever the merchants and citizens of London met together with the quiet laughter of those who saw that the day of redemption was drawing nigh. At last after eleven years the Parliament was called together. Would the members prove staunch? No fear of that. The City knew—no other institution or place knew so well—the feeling of the country. The City always knew the feeling of the country; there were a thousand correspondents between the City and the country; the merchants had no doubt that the country was sound. Laud's clergy marked the change in the defiant air of the City, in the exulting looks of the people; there were changes close at hand.

The House did prove staunch. Once more the Commons refused a subsidy till grievances were redressed, and until security was obtained for religion, for property, and for the liberties of the country. The House was dissolved. Then the City laughed again and its people rubbed their hands. For the King must have money, and without a Parliament he could not get money. The Scotch business went on, and the snowball of discontent and of grievances was now visible even to Charles the Blind.

Then began an interesting and an exciting time.   The King tried to persuade the City to lend him £100,000.   The City steadfastly refused.   The Mayor and Aldermen were summoned to Whitehall; the King addressed them; they were ordered to make out lists of the wealthier citizens; they were dismissed, but were

KING CHARLES I. THROWN OVERBOARD
From a satirical print in the British Museum.

summoned again, and told that if they did not pay £100,000 they would have to pay £200,000; and that if they still refused that they would have to pay £300,000. They were again dismissed, and told to prepare the list of rich citizens by the following Sunday.

By this time the temper of London was roused.   The Mayor and Aldermen came on the following Sunday, but without that list. Instead they brought a petition asking for redress. Some of them refused absolutely to make out such a list, and were committed to prison, viz. Sir Nicholas Rainton to the Marshalsea, Alderman Somers to the Fleet, Alderman Atkins to the King's Bench, and Alderman Gayre to the Gatehouse. It was on Sunday, the 10th of May, that the Aldermen went to prison. The reply of the City was a tumult, in which the Archbishop's Palace at Lambeth was attacked and the Archbishop's life was threatened. A royal warrant was issued commanding the Lord Mayor to raise as many men as might be needed for the suppression of riots. At the same time it was thought best to let the Aldermen go.

In June the Mayor was again summoned to show cause why the ship money was not collected. He replied, plainly, that no one would pay it. Here we see the secret of the City's strength; the people only had to sit down; they could not be forced to pay, either by the King, who had no force at his disposal, or by the Aldermen, who had no police. The people sat down and refused to pay. There were threats of debasing the coinage unless the City yielded; the answer was that the Common Council had no power to dispose of the citizens' money. Charles then endeavoured to raise £120,000 from the livery companies; they replied—it was impossible to let go so fine an opportunity—that their "stocks" had all been consumed in the Irish Estates—confiscated by the King.

On the 3rd of November 1640 Charles, evidently suffering under great depression of spirits, opened the Long Parliament.

Between the dissolution of the Short Parliament and the assembling of the Long the City petitioned the King to call a Parliament for the redress of grievances. Laud and the Privy Council tried to frighten the City against signing it, but in vain. It was signed by 10,000 citizens. Maitland gives it in full:—

"MOST GRACIOUS SOVEREIGN—

Being moved with the Duty and Obedience, which by the Laws your Petitioners owe unto your sacred Majesty, they humbly present unto your princely and pious Wisdom the several pressing Grievances following, viz.—

1. The pressing and unusual Impositions upon Merchandize, importing and exporting, and the urging and levying of Ship-Money, notwithstanding both which, Merchants' Ships and Goods have been taken and destroyed both by Turkish and other Pirates.

2. The Multitude of Monopolies, Patents, and Warrants, whereby Trade in the City, and other Parts of the Kingdom is much decayed.

3. The sundry Innovations in Matters of Religion.

4. The Oath and Canons lately enjoined by the late Convocation, whereby your Petitioners are in Danger to be deprived of their Ministers.

5. The Great Concourse of Papists, and their Inhabitations in London, and the Suburbs, whereby they have more Means and Opportunity of plotting and executing their designs against the Religion established.

6. The seldom Calling, and sudden Dissolutions of Parliaments, without the redress of your Subjects' Grievances.

7. The Imprisonment of divers Citizens for Non-payment of Ship-Money, and Impositions ; and the prosecution of many others in the Star-Chamber, for not conforming themselves to Committees in Patents of Monopolies, whereby Trade is restrained.

8. The great Danger your sacred Person is exposed unto in the present War, and the various fears that seized upon your Petitioners and their Families by reason thereof ; which Grievances and Fears have occasioned so great a stop and distraction in Trade, that your Petitioners can neither buy, sell, receive, or pay as formerly, and tends to the utter Ruin of the Inhabitants of this City, the Decay of Navigation, and Clothing, and the Manufactures of this Kingdom.

Your humble Petitioners conceiving that the said Grievances are contrary to the Laws of this

From a contemporary print in the British Museum.

Kingdom, and finding by Experience that they are not redressed by the ordinary Course of Justice, do therefore most humbly beseech your most sacred Majesty to cause a Parliament to be summoned with all convenient Speed, whereby they may be relieved in the Premises.

And your Petitioners and loyal Subjects shall ever pray, etc."

The fanatical temper of the people as regards the Catholics was shown in their attack upon the Spanish Ambassador's house in Bishopsgate Street :—

"Upon the twenty-ninth of April the first tumultuous disorder (of these Times) happened in London, when a great number of Apprentices and others beset the Spanish Ambassador's house in Bishopsgate Street, threatening to pull it down, and to kill the Ambassador, for permitting English papists to frequent his Chapel. For the appeasing of this Commotion, the Lord-Mayor immediately repaired to the Ambas-

THE TRUE MANER OF THE EXECUTION OF THOMAS EARLE OF STRAFFORD. LORD
Lieutenant of Ireland. vpon Tower hill, the 12ᵗʰ of May, 1641.

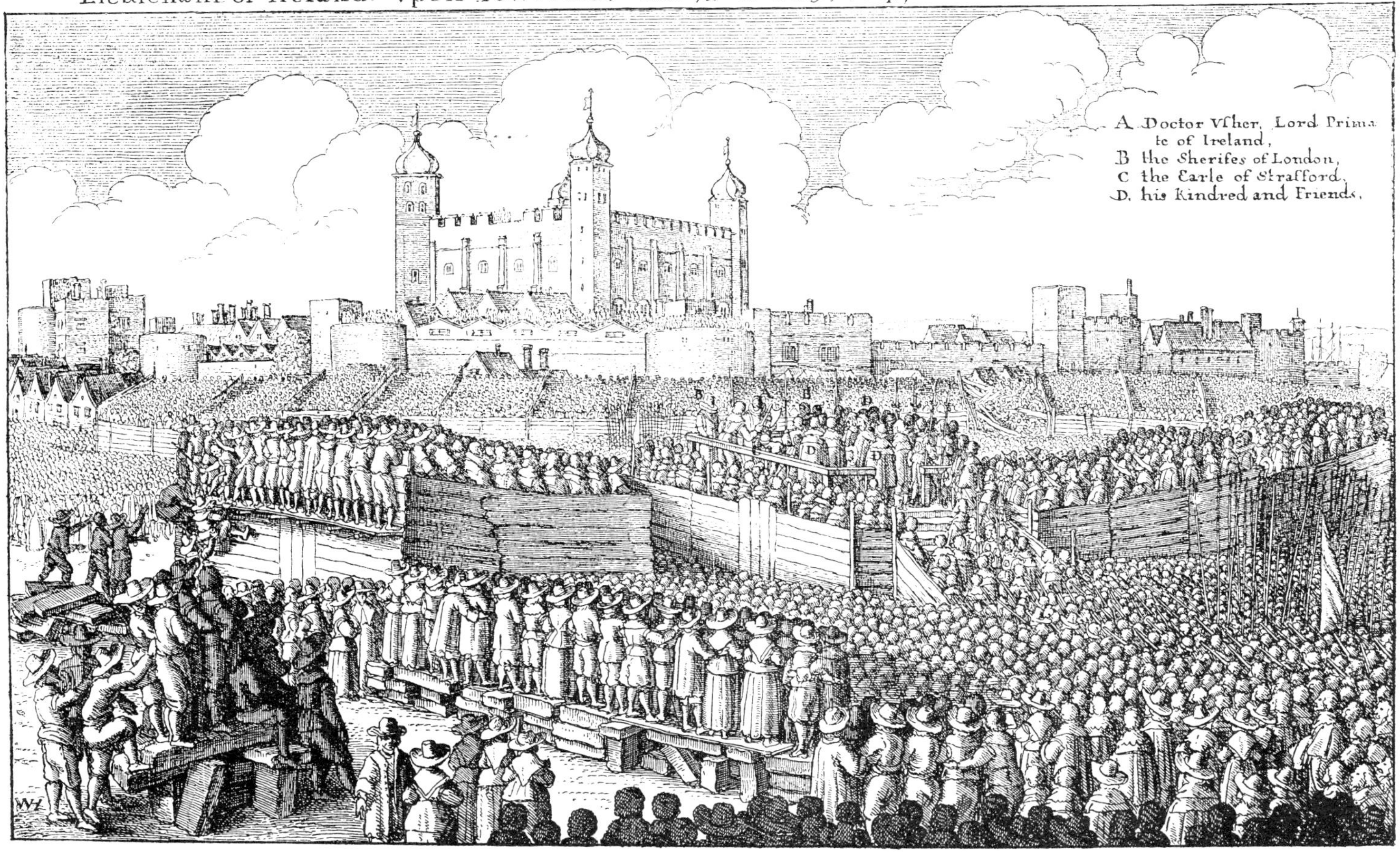

A Doctor Vsher, Lord Prima-
te of Ireland,
B the sherifes of London,
C the Earle of Strafford,
D his kindred and friends.

From a contemporary Dutch print. E. Gardner's Collection.

sador's, where with much difficulty he prevailed upon the Populace to disperse and return home.   His
Lordship had no sooner allayed the fury of the Multitude, than he entered the Ambassador's House, and,
being met by that Minister, was desired to drop the point of the City Sword that was carried before him,
acquainting him, That he was then in a Place where the King of Spain, his Master, had Jurisdiction ; which
the Mayor complying with, the Ambassador told him that he had never seen so barbarous an attempt ;
and desired to know whether this could justly be called a civilized Nation, where the Laws of Nations and
Hospitality were so horribly violated ?   The Mayor replied, That the Rioters were the very Refuse of the
People, therefore entreated his Excellency not to impute the Sedition to the City : to which the Ambas-

THOMAS WENTWORTH, FIRST EARL OF STRAFFORD (1593–1641)
From the portrait by Sir Anthony Van Dyck.

sador smartly answered, That he hardly knew how to call that a City, or even a Society of Rational
Creatures, which was seemingly divested both of Humanity and Government.

The Mayor, to extenuate the Crime as much as possible, told the Ambassador, That the People were
enraged because Mass was publicly said in his Chapel.   To which he replied, That the English Minister
at Madrid enjoyed the free Exercise of his Religion without the least Disturbance ; and that he would rather
choose to lose his Life than the Privileges due to him by Contract and the Law of Nations : the Mayor
returned, That the People were the more incensed against him because the Citizens of the Popish Communion were permitted to frequent his House at Mass, contrary to Law : The Ambassador answered,
That if the Mayor would prevent their coming, he would not fend for them ; but, if they came, he could
neither in Conscience to his Religion, nor his Master's Honour, deny them Access to their Devotions, or
Protection to their Persons, while they were with him.   Wherefore a Guard was placed at his House, which
not only protected him from further Insults, but likewise the Popish Citizens from frequenting Mass.

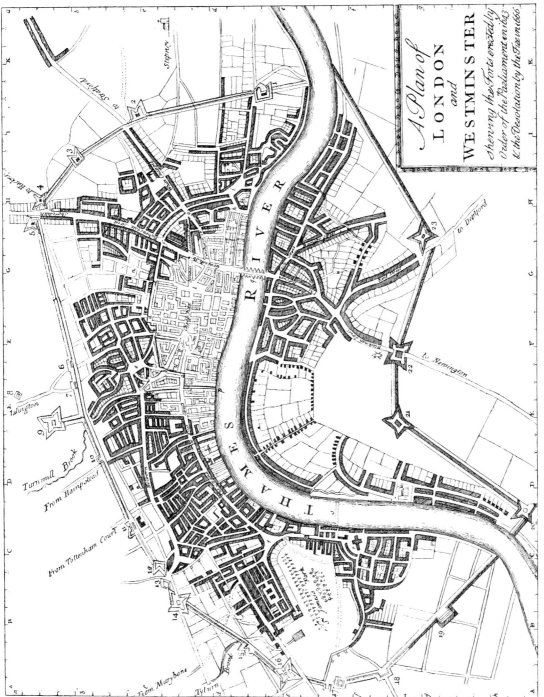

A Plan of
LONDON and
WESTMINSTER

shewing the Forts erected by
Order of the Parliament in 1643
& the Desolation by the Fire in 1666

This Storm was no sooner over than another far more impetuous began ; for a Discovery being made of some desperate Designs both at home and abroad, of bringing up the Army to London to surprise the Tower, and favour the Earl of Strafford's escape, divers Ministers from their Pulpits, on the Sunday following, shewed to their several Auditories the Necessity of having Justice speedily executed upon some great Delinquents ; which so greatly irritated and inflamed the Citizens, that the Day after they, to the Number of Six Thousand, armed with Swords, Staves, and Cudgels, ran to Westminster ; and posting themselves in the Avenues leading to the House of Lords, stopped all Coaches, and incessantly cried out for Justice against Strafford."

We now come to events which belong to the national history. We may therefore pass them over except where they specially touch upon London.

The discovery of the " Army Plot " made Strafford's fate certain, and his death was the cause of savage exultation in the City ; a countless multitude assembled to see him die ; the people ran and rode from the scene waving their hats and crying " His head is off."

The Grand Remonstrance laid before the House called forth the opposition of a small Royalist party, which only strengthened the cause. London was zealous for the cause ; associations were formed in every county. I pass over the events which followed.

Civil War began in July 1642. Marston Moor in 1644 and Naseby in 1645 practically finished it.

The importance of the City in making the war possible can hardly be overestimated. They began with a force of 8000 trained bands, well drilled and well handled. When the breach between King and Commons could no longer be averted, the City raised £100,000 with alacrity at the request of the latter. An immense quantity of plate was brought in, and a levy of £50,000 was laid upon all strangers and aliens residing in the City. That was in June 1642. When in the autumn it was reported that Prince Rupert was marching on London, the City became a huge camp ; nothing went on but arming, training, practising, marching. The whole City was Roundhead ; those few who remained loyal—the " malignants " —were arrested and clapped into prison as soon as they could be caught. This unanimity did not continue. The Royalists presently plucked up heart and, appearing with their badges, found out how strong they were. A reaction set in when it was discovered that the war would not be finished in a single campaign and that it entailed heavy sacrifices, including the shutting of shops and the temporary ruin of trade. A stormy gathering was held in the Guildhall, at which there were loud cries for peace. The Common Council therefore drew up two petitions, one for the King and one for the Parliament, advocating peace, or at least a truce for deliberation.

They even sent a deputation to the King, who received the members graciously and promised a reply, which quickly followed. It is a very long document, in which the King pointed out the wickedness of fighting against him ; and he ordered his loyal subjects to begin the cause of peace by arresting the Mayor.

On the 21st of November 1642, about a month after the battle of Edgehill, a suspicious-looking boat was discovered by the pinnace guarding the Thames for the City and Parliament. She was a Gravesend boat and should have put in at Billingsgate. Instead of this, the tide being favourable, she continued her course and shot the bridge. The pinnace gave chase, and presently caught up with her and seized her. The only passenger on board was a gentleman, who was carrying from Colonel Goring a letter—it is not stated to whom—containing lists of the supplies of men expected by the King from Holland and Denmark. Nothing could have been more opportune than such a capture; the City was still lukewarm in the cause; to afford them clear proof that the King intended to fight them with Danes and Dutchmen would fire their blood as nothing else would do, not even defeat and disaster. Pennington, who was Mayor and a Parliamentarian heart and soul, joyfully received the letter, ordered copies to be made and to be read in every church on Sunday, the very next day, and a subscription to be opened at once for carrying on the war. In the church of St. Bartholomew by the Exchange, twenty-seven persons subscribed various sums, amounting in all to £290. In St. Margaret's, Lothbury, about £350 were subscribed. Mr. Edwin Freshfield, who relates this story (*Archæologia*, xlv.), is of opinion that the whole business was invented by the Mayor. He wanted money, he wanted to rouse the citizens, he wanted them to be committed openly. In this he succeeded perfectly; he raised £30,000, he fired their passions, he made them commit themselves in writing. From this moment there was no looking back for the City of London.

In February 1643, as the attack upon London by the Royalist army seemed threatening, the Common Council passed an Act for the defence of the City by a line of redoubts and fortifications, which were taken in hand and executed without delay. It has been assumed that this work consisted of a wall with redoubts and bastions at intervals. A plan of the wall shows an enormous work, eleven miles long, running all round London. This view has been adopted by later writers. No one seems to have remarked on the impossibility of so colossal a fortification being constructed in the brief space of three or four weeks even if the whole population worked day and night; and no one seems to have discovered that it was absurd to construct such a wall where the enemy could not possibly attack it, or that it should have been thought desirable to construct a wall which it would have required at least 200,000 men to defend. The historian also might have thought it still more remarkable that such enormous earth-works, with stone bastions, entailing such enormous labour, should have been undertaken with so much zeal and unanimity; and, finally, he might have asked himself how it came to pass that not a vestige of the work should have remained, even though the greater part of the ground covered was free from buildings down to the beginning of this century.

Sharpe, however (*London and the Kingdom*, iii. 431), gives the actual " Resolution of the Common Council for putting the City and Suburbs into a posture of defence, 23rd February 1643 : "—

"*Journal* 40, fo. 52.

That a small fort conteyning one bulwark and halfe and a battery in the reare of the flanck be made at Gravell lane end.   A horne worke with two flanckers be placed at Whitechapell windmills.   One redoubt with two flanckers betwixt Whitechapel Church and Shoreditch.   Two redoubts with flanckers neere Shoreditch church with a battery.   At the windmill in Islington way, a battery and brestwork round about.   A small redoubt neere Islington pound.   A battery and brestwork on the hill neere Clarkenwell towards Hampstead way.   Two batteries and a brestworke at Southampton House.   One redoubt with two flanckers by St. Giles in the Fields, another small worke neere the turning.   A quadrant forte with fower halfe bulwarks crosse Tyborne highway at the second turning that goeth towards Westminster.   At Hide parke corner a large forte with flanckers on all sides.   At the corner of the lord Gorings brick wall next the fields a redoubt and a battery where the Court of Guard now is at the lower end of the lord Gorings wall, the brestwork to be made forwarder.   In Tuttle fields a battery brestworke, and the ditches to be scowred.   That at the end of every street which is left open to enter into the suburbs of this citty, defenceable brestworks be made or there already erected, repayred with turnepikes muskett proof, and that all the passages into the suburbs on the north side the river except five, viz. : the way from St. James towards Charing Crosse, the upper end of Saint Giles in Holborne, the further end of St. John Street towards Islington, Shoreditch church, and Whitechapell be stopped up.   That the courtes of guard and the rayles or barrs at the utmost partes of the freedome be made defensible, and turnpikes placed there in lieu of the chaynes all muskett proof. And that all the shedds and buildings that joyne to the outside of the wall be taken downe.   And that all the bulwarkes be fitted at the gates and walls soe that the flanckes of the wall and streets before the gates may be cleared and that the gates and bulwarkes be furnished with ordnance."

It will be seen that there is not one word about a new wall round London. The so-called fortifications were simply small redoubts and bastions at certain fixed points.

How the London trained bands went out to fight, how well they stood their ground, in what actions they took their part, will be found in the many histories of that war which still claims its fierce adherents and still awakens the passions of a partisan, whoever relates it.   The constancy of the City was rewarded by the stoppage of trade and the ruin of many merchants, while the soldiers in the trained bands were shopkeepers and skilled craftsmen, to whom long continuance in the field was ruin.   In 1644 the disaffection of the men amounted almost to mutiny.

On the temper and discipline of the City trained bands Sharpe thus speaks :—

"That the city trained bands had done good service in their day no one will deny, but the time was fast approaching when it would be necessary to raise an army of men willing to devote themselves to the military life as a profession.   For permanent service in the field the London trained bands were not to be relied on. 'In these two days' march,' wrote Waller (2 July) to the Committee of Both Kingdoms, 'I was extremely plagued with the mutinies of the City Brigade, who are grown to that height of disorder that I have no hope to retain them, being come to their old song of "Home! Home!"'   There was, he said, only one remedy for this, and that was a standing army, however small :—'My lords, I write these particulars to let you know that an army compounded of these men will never go through with your service, and till you have an army merely your own, that you may command, it is in a manner impossible to do anything of importance.' The junction of his forces with those under Browne, who had been despatched (23 June) to protect the country between London and the royalist army, served only to increase the general discontent. 'My London regiments,' he wrote (8 July), 'immediately looked on his [*i.e.* Browne's] forces as sent to relieve them, and without expectation of further orders, are most of them gone away; yesterday no less than 400 out of one regiment quitted their colours. On the other side, Major-General Browne's men, being most of them trained band men of Essex and Hertfordshire, are so mutinous and uncommand-able that there is no hope of their stay. They are likewise upon their march home again. Yesterday they

A SOLDIER OF THE TIME OF KING JAMES THE FIRST ARMED WITH A CALIVER
From a contemporary print.

were like to have killed their Major-General, and they have hurt him in the face. . . . I am confident that above 2000 Londoners ran away from their colours.' The same spirit of insubordination manifested itself again when Waller threw himself (20 July) into Abingdon. Most of his troops were only too anxious to leave him, whilst the Londoners especially refused to stir 'one foot further, except it be home.'"

The City, however, despite these rules, remained staunch to the Parliamentary cause; in spite of hard times, London raised the money to carry on the war; and, as in former cases, the winning side proved to be that which London had espoused.

Early in 1645 the army was remodelled on a more permanent footing, in which the men were to receive regular pay and the officers to be appointed for efficiency alone. Parliament resolved on borrowing £80,000 of the City; the Committee of Militia raised a sufficient number of men to guard the new redoubts and forts, and the City regiments were brought up to their full strength.

In June 1645 the Common Council presented a petition to Parliament calling attention to what they considered the causes of their ill success, and asking, among other things, that Fairfax might have a free hand and not be hampered by orders from Westminster. This view was favourably received. Fairfax chose his own tactics; he marched in pursuit of the Royal army, which he met—and fought—at Naseby on June 14.

After Naseby the City entertained both Houses of Parliament with a Thanksgiving sermon in Christ Church, Newgate. This was the old Grey Friars Church, a splendid building then still standing, though its monuments and fine carved work were gone. After the sermon there was a banquet in Grocers' Hall; the Hall was not large enough for everybody, therefore the Common Council dined at another Company's hall. The day after the dinner the Council had to consider what was to be done with the 3000 Royalist prisoners. They confined them in the south cloister and the Convocation House of St. Paul's. How long they were kept there; how they were fed; what became of them ultimately, one knows not. Perhaps they were treated as Cromwell afterwards treated the Scotch prisoners taken at Worcester (see p. 68).

The City also raised £31,000 for the pay of the Scots who were marching south. In July of the same year they raised 1000 light horse and 500 dragoons, and in September 500 light horse and the same number of dragoons.

The events which followed Naseby until the trial and execution of the King would not concern us but for the part played by the City. They constitute a chapter in which the completion of the Civil War is mixed up with the dissension of the Presbyterians and the Independents, two sects equally intolerant and equally determined to obtain the supremacy. I have abridged the business so far as the City is concerned in the paragraph which follows. The whole story, when one reads it in detail, makes one almost inclined to condone the crimes of the King against the civil liberties of the people, since his enemies were themselves so determined against their religious liberties.

The Parliament desired to force a Presbyterian form of worship on the City, and to lay down laws for the election of elders. This was not at all the view of the City, which desired freedom from Parliamentary control in matters of religion. The ministers of the City parish churches drew up their own list of reforms; the citizens themselves sent a petition to Parliament giving their views. The House of Commons returned an answer of an ungracious character. They knew their own duties and would carry them through.

TRIAL OF KING CHARLES I., JANUARY 1648

From an engraving of the painting by William Fisk.

The City at the same time came to a quarrel with Parliament on the governing of the militia raised within the weekly bills of mortality. Parliament was ready to allow them the command over the militia within the Liberties, but the City wished to include within the area of command all the parishes and parts covered by the weekly bills of mortality.

The three years preceding the execution of Charles were a troubled and an uneasy time for the City.

On September the 7th, 1646, the City was asked by Parliament to consider ways and means for raising £200,000, being half of the sum claimed by the Scots for their expenses. On the 9th they reported a scheme for raising money by the excise and by the sale of the Bishop's lands.

On December 19th the City sent a petition to Parliament for the redress of grievances. They demanded the disbandment of the army, the suppression of heresy, the union of the two kingdoms, the free election of members of Parliament, and the command of their own militia. The "disbandment of the army" is a point that must be especially noted because it marks the growing terror of the army.

It was necessary, before the army could be disbanded, to settle the arrears of pay. The men were invited to volunteer for service in Ireland. They asked for their pay. Parliament proposed to raise £200,000, not for the arrears, but for service in England and Ireland.

At the same time application was made to the City for ways and means to raise this large sum. And the City was put into good temper by an ordinance for a new Militia Committee.

But the disbanded army had to look on while they themselves could get no pay, and the City militia received their pay regularly. Riots took place; companies of the disbanded besieged the House of Commons demanding their arrears. These riots took place early in June 1647.

On the 11th of June the City was informed that Fairfax, with the army, was on his way to London. The Mayor replied that they had no quarrel with the army; that they had themselves presented a humble address to Parliament in favour of the just demands of the army; and that if Fairfax would kindly keep at a distance of thirty miles, the City would be much obliged.

Fairfax declared that the last demand was impossible so long as enlistments were continued in the trained bands and auxiliaries, and that the movements of the army depended very much on the reception that might be given to certain papers just laid before the House of Lords. The "papers," in fact, asserted the right of the army to speak in the name of the people, and demanded the expulsion from the House of eleven members who had misrepresented the army and raised forces for a new war. Among them was Glyn, the City Recorder.

The Mayor, Sir John Gayre, on finding that the army was really marching south, called out the newly-enlisted trained bands. It appeared that they only existed on paper; in many companies not ten men appeared; in many others none but officers. It became evident that a different tone must be adopted. Fairfax was assured that the new enlistments had been stopped. Even then that general was not satisfied. He now said that he could not stop his army until the Parliament had returned a satisfactory answer to the "papers" already mentioned. The

SIR THOMAS FAIRFAX (1612–1671) AND HIS WIFE
From the painting by William Dobson in the National Portrait Gallery, London.

sending of these letters backwards and forwards produced little effect for a time— except tumults of apprentices and disturbances by *reformadoes*, or disbanded soldiers.

On July 9th the Parliament agreed to the demands of Fairfax, and ordered all disbanded soldiers to quit the City. On July 11th the Army Council recommended the Parliament to take into their own hands again the command of the City militia. This was done, but the City had their say in the matter. Petitions to the House were drawn up; they were carried to Westminster by the sheriffs and members of the Common Council, followed by an enormous crowd of angry and excited apprentices and citizens. There was a long debate; the Commons refused to give way; the crowd grew more threatening; at last, at eight o'clock in the evening, the Commons yielded.

It was now time for the City to consider measures of defence. The trained bands were sent to man the works, and all the citizens who could carry arms were ordered to attend at a general muster. It became obvious, however, that armed resistance to the army was out of the question, and the City made haste to submit and to hope for favourable terms. The City forts were surrendered. Fairfax entered the lines of fortification and marched upon Westminster. On the following

TRIAL OF KING CHARLES I. JANUARY 20-27, 1648
" It was remarkt yᵗ the Gold Head dropt of yᵉ King's Cane yᵗ day wᵗʰout any visible cause.'
From a contemporary print. E. Gardner's Collection.

day the army marched through the City doing no kind of harm to any one. Fairfax and his officers were invited to a grand banquet at Grocers' Hall, and so the business ended amicably, as it seemed.

The banquet did not interfere, however, with the projects of Fairfax and the army. The City was called upon for £50,000 towards the arrears of pay; the Lord Mayor, Sir John Gayre, Thomas Cullons, one of the Sheriffs, and three Aldermen were impeached for threatening the Commons and for inciting to fresh war. They were all sent to the Tower. When they were brought for trial before the Lords, they refused to kneel, took exception to the jurisdiction of the Houses, and were all fined and committed again to the Tower, where they lay for two months more, when they were liberated.

In 1648 the City carried one point and gained the command of their own militia. A deputation of Lords and Commons attended the Court of Common Council, and assured them that not only did they cheerfully commit to them the command of the militia, but that they had resolved on making no change in the constitution of the country with King, Lords, and Commons. The City at this juncture resolved to stand by the Parliament; they asked for the return of the Recorder, the Aldermen, and the other citizens who were imprisoned in the Tower.

The miserable condition of trade naturally brought about discontent, which turned to disaffection. The Royalist party made an excuse of a rising in Kent to petition the Parliament for a personal treaty with the King; the same people also called upon the Court of Common Council to summon a Common Hall—that is, a meeting of the whole body of freemen. The Court took time to consider the matter: in other words, to see their way to refusing it, which they did at last, on the ground of the distraction of the times. The longing for peace was shown by petition after petition from the City, all in the same strain, that the King should be approached personally; the City offered to assure his safety if he were placed in their hands.

In addition to the other troubles, the mob was now growing more Royalist. They insulted the Speaker; they rescued war prisoners; they secretly enlisted and sent out horses for the Royalist enemy. The Council asked the House that a death penalty should be inflicted on any person who caused a tumult or riot, and that no man who had ever fought against the Parliament should be allowed to reside within thirty miles of London. These two requests reveal a time of great uneasiness and general suspicion.

The end of this state of things was now rapidly approaching. The Parliament sent fifteen commissioners to open the Treaty of Newport in September. At the end of November the army declared that the Parliament must be dissolved. Fairfax marched into London (November 30, 1648) and demanded a sum of £40,000 to be paid the next day. The Council sent him £10,000 and promised the rest; Fairfax took up his quarters at Whitehall, and sent into the City for 3800 beds. A week later, neither money nor beds having been provided, Fairfax arrested Major-General Browne, one of the sheriffs, with certain others, on a charge of having joined in calling upon the Scots to invade England. He also seized on the sum of £27,000 lying in Goldsmiths' and Weavers' Halls. This money, he told the City, he intended to keep until they sent him the £40,000. He refused meantime to withdraw his troops who were quartered on the City. The money was found. In the municipal elections the new Mayor, Abraham Reynardson, was a Royalist,

ENGLANDS ROYAL PATTERN or the Execution of KING CHARLES y.ᵉ 1.ˢᵗ Jan.ʸ 30.

EXECUTION OF CHARLES I., JANUARY 30, 1648

From a contemporary print.   E. Gardner's Collection.

and well known to be such. It was feared by the Commons, now the Rump, that the elections of December to the Common Council would also be Royalist. Accordingly the House passed an ordinance excluding " malignants." In this way no citizen was admitted who had subscribed to any petition for a personal treaty with the King. When the new Council assembled, the Mayor ordered them to take the oath of allegiance, which had not yet been abolished. This they refused. The Commons ordered the Mayor to suspend the oath altogether. Under these conditions the Council met, and although the Mayor refused to acknowledge their authority, they proceeded to consider a petition asking the House " to execute justice impartially and vigorously ' upon all the grand and capital authors, contrivers of and actors in the late wars against Parliament and kingdom, from the highest to the lowest,' and to take steps, as the supreme power of the nation, for the preservation of peace and the recovery of trade and credit."

The Royalist Lord Mayor with his Aldermen—only two being present—rose and left the Court rather than sanction such a petition by their presence. It must be remembered that the date of this meeting was the 18th of January 1648, and that the Court for the trial of Charles had been already determined. When the Mayor and Aldermen had left there was no Court. But those present proceeded with their petition. Among the judges of King Charles were nominated five Aldermen, viz. Isaac Pennington, Thomas Andrews, Thomas Atkins, Rowland Wilson, and John Fowke. Only the two first took part in the trial, and Wilson refused to serve. Bradshaw, the President, had been judge of the Sheriffs' Court in the Wood Street Compter. Two citizens, Tichborne and Row, were on the Commission. The trial of Charles—the most momentous in its consequences of any event since the Conquest or the granting of the Great Charter—belongs to the national history. It began on the 20th of January; it concluded on the 27th; and on the 30th the King was beheaded.

they drew out a paper, which they read,—whether a pretense of authority or what else I cannot easily conjecture. And thereupon they rushed into the house, rifled him of all that was in the house, breaking and battering many of the goods, and, having brought them out, sold them to such persons as would buy them at any rates, and this at noone day, and in the sight of one thousand people : one feather-bed I saw sold for four shillings, and one flock-bed for one shilling ; and many other things at I know not what prises, leaving him nothing but naked walls and one stoole, which the old man sate upon, he being lame and decrepit with old age. The head-borough of the place endeavoured to rescue some of the goods, which were afterwards violently taken againe out of his house. After the riot was thus ended, they marched away with a drum ; and then I made bold to goe into this distressed man's house, where I found him sitting upon his only stoole, and with the teares falling downe his hoary beard, from whence, having administered the best comfort that I could, I departed."

Before long it became manifest that the war was pressing very severely upon the City. The complaints of all classes were deep and loud ; there arose the inevitable reaction. It seemed at one time as if history was about to repeat itself and that the desertion of London by the Britons in the fifth century, owing to the stoppage of supplies, was about to be repeated in the seventeenth. There was no foreign trade ; the Royalist ships commanded the German Ocean ; the west of England sent up no wool ; the east sent up no provisions ; the north sent up no coal ; there was no money ; the shops stood open, but the master was away with the trained bands ; the craftsman's children wanted bread, but the breadwinner was away with Fairfax. The industries ceased, for the markets were closed ; after every battle, soldiers, either disbanded or deserters, swarmed into London as a place of refuge ; the Royalist minority was a constant source of danger ; there were religious differences innumerable, each as intolerant as the Church of Rome ; the citizens were, for the most part, Presbyterian ; but they desired not to have a national, but a free, Church ; they wanted the Church to be governed by herself, and not by Parliament ; they petitioned Parliament in this sense ; they also petitioned the House for intolerance pure and simple ; they would have no freedom of thought, or speech, or doctrine in religion.

To take instances of hardship. In 1642 the people in the Strand, who chiefly lived by letting lodgings, were in despair, having to pawn their furniture in order to pay the rent, their lodgings being all empty. The lawyers at the Guildhall were busy, but it was over the affairs of an incredible number of bankrupts ; at the Royal Exchange there was no business transacted, nor any discourse all day long except about the news of the day. In the shops the keepers had nothing to do but to visit and to condole with each other. London, as it always had been, was a receiving house and a distributing house for the whole country, and in this time of civil war there was nothing to distribute and nothing to receive. As a finishing stroke, it is added that the ladies who formed the greater part of the population of Covent Garden, Drury Lane, and Long Acre were reduced to a condition which is described in a tract of the time as a "lump of amazement." For this quarter and these ladies existed not by the citizens, though the morals of the City were by no means without reproach, but by the visitors who in quiet times flocked to London.

Amid a confused babble of petitions and letters, and imprisonments and fines, one episode stands out clear and strong. It is the petition of the women, calling themselves "many civilly disposed women," to the Parliament, praying for a peace. The petition was cleverly drawn up—one suspects a masculine hand :—

"That your Petitioners (tho' of the weaker Sex) do too sensibly perceive the ensuing Desolation of this Kingdom, unless by some timely Means your Honours provide for the Speedy Recovery thereof. Your Honours are the Physicians that can, by God's special and miraculous Blessing (which we humbly implore), restore this languishing Nation, and our bleeding Sister the kingdom of Ireland, which hath now almost breathed her last Gasp.

We need not dictate to your Eagle-eyed Judgements the Way; Our only Desire is, that God's Glory, in the true Reformed Protestant Religion, may be preserved, the just Prerogatives and Privileges of King and Parliament maintained, the true Liberties and Properties of the Subject, according to the known Laws of the Land, restored, and all honourable Ways and Means for a speedy Peace endeavoured.

May it therefore please your Honours, that some speedy Course may be taken for the Settlement of the true Reformed Protestant Religion, for the Glory of God, and the Renovation of Trade, for the Benefit of the Subject, they being the Soul and Body of the Kingdom.

And your Petitioners, with many Millions of afflicted Souls, groaning under the Burden of these Times of Distress, shall (as bound) pray, etc."

It was taken to Westminster by two or three thousand women with white ribbons in their hats. The Commons received and heard the petition; they even gave them an answer. They had no doubt of speedily arriving at a peace; meantime the petitioners were enjoined to return to their own homes. By this time their numbers were swollen to five thousand and more, among them being men dressed as women. They flocked round the door of the House of Commons, crying "Peace! Peace!" and presently, "Give us those Traitors that are against Peace, that we may tear them to pieces! Give us that dog Pym!" The trained bands were sent for, but were received by these Amazons with brick-bats, whereupon the soldiers fired upon the women, killed some, and dispersed the rest.

The violence and insolence of the mob during this unhappy time shows the want of executive strength in the City. Measures are passed; no one heeds them; a riot is suppressed and it breaks out again; disbanded soldiers swarm in the streets and rob and plunder as they please. We have seen how the mob murdered Dr. Lamb. On another occasion the mob had forced its way into the Court of High Commission. They had assembled at Westminster, crying "No Bishops!" They had been driven down King Street by officers with drawn swords. After the war broke out the mob was divided between the two factions, each having its own badge. When the war brought the usual troubles, with want of money and of trade, both sides joined and riotously clamoured for peace.   As early as 1643, with six years of war before it, the mob besieged the House of Commons, clamouring for peace.   The most remarkable effort of the mob was that of the "Solemn Engagement" in 1647 related by Sharpe :—

"A week later (21 July) a mob of apprentices, reformadoes, watermen and other disaffected persons met at Skinner's Hall, and one and all signed a solemn Engagement pledging themselves to maintain the Covenant and to procure the king's restoration to power on the terms offered by him on the 12th May last, viz. the abandonment of the episcopacy for three years and the militia for ten.   An endeavour was made to enlist the support of the municipal authorities to this engagement, but a letter from Fairfax (23 July) soon gave them to understand that the army looked on the matter as one 'set on foot by the malice of some desperate-minded men, this being their last engine for the putting all into confusion when they could not accomplish their wicked ends by other means.'   On the 24th both Houses joined in denouncing the Solemn Engagement of the City, their declaration against it being ordered to be published by beat of drum and sound of trumpet through London and Westminster, and within the lines of communication.   Any one found subscribing his name to the engagement after such publication would be adjudged guilty of high treason."

Another serious outbreak took place later, on Sunday, April 10, 1648.   A multitude was assembled in Moorfields to drink and play.   A company of trained bands endeavoured to suppress the profanation of the day, and were themselves set upon and dispersed.   The mob, gathering greater strength, went off to Whitehall, where they were driven back by the troops.   Returning to the City, they broke open houses and magazines, seized the gates and chains, attacked the Lord Mayor's house, and called upon everybody to join them for God and King Charles.   General Fairfax let them alone one night, and in the morning sent out troops, and after some resistance dispersed them.

Every success or partial success made the Royalist party in the City more fearless and undisguised ; sometimes they mounted cockades ; sometimes they burned bonfires ; sometimes they openly cried for the King ; the 'prentices, who had been so ready to petition against the Bishops, turned round.   Though the actual weight of numbers and of opinions was in favour of the Parliament, there was a very strong party who were always looking for an opportunity to demonstrate, if not to rise, for the King.   One has only to consult the pages of Evelyn in order to understand the strength of the Royalist party even in times of the deepest adversity.

I have already quoted from Howell.   Let him speak again concerning the condition of the City at this time :—

"Touching the condition of Things here, you shall understand that our Miseries lengthen with our Days ; for tho' the Sun and the Spring advance nearer us, yet our Times are not grown a whit the more comfortable.   I am afraid this City has fooled herself into a Slavery ; the Army, tho' forbidden to come within ten Miles of her by order of Parliament, quarters now in the Bowels of her ; they threaten to break her Percullies, Posts, and Chains, to make her previous upon all occasions ; they have secured also the Tower, with Addition of Strength for themselves ; besides a famine doth insensibly creep upon us, and the Mint is starved for want of Bullion ; Trade, which was ever the Sinew of this Island, doth visibly decay, and the insurance of ships is risen from two to ten in the hundred ; our Gold is engrossed in private hands, or gone beyond Sea to travel without License ; and much I believe of it is returned to the Earth (whence it first came) to be buried where our descendants may chance to find it a thousand years hence, if the world lasts so long ; so that the exchanging of white earth into red (I mean Silver into Gold) is now above six in the hundred ; and all these, with many more, are the dismal effects and concomitants of a Civil War.   'Tis true, we have had many such black days in England in former Ages ; but those paralleled to the present are as a Shadow of a Mountain compared to the Eclipse of the Moon."

The weaker side always takes refuge in epigrams.   I have before me a little book called *Two Centuries of Paul's Churchyard*, which contains (1) a list of imaginary books, (2) questions for tender consciences.   The following extracts will show the temper of the Royalists in London during the Civil War :—

"Σεληναρχία.   A discourse proving the World in the Moon is not governed by States because her Monthly Contributions do still decrease as much as increase, but Ours increase and never decrease."

"Ecclesiasticus.   A plain demonstration that Col. Pride (alias Bride) was Founder of St. Bride's Church, and not found in the Porch, because the Porch was built before the Church, that is, not behind it."

"Severall Readings on the Statute of Magna Charta by John Lylburn ; with a Treatise of the best way of boiling Soap."

"Domesday Book.   A clear manifesto that more Roundheads go to heaven than Cavaliers, because Roundheads on their death-beds do repent of their former cause and opinions, but not Cavaliers."

"An Act for expunging the word King, and inserting the word ——— in all text of Scripture, beginning at Isa. xxx. 33.   'Tophet is prepared for the ———' "

"An Act concerning the Thames, that whereas at Westminster it ebbs six hours and flows but four, it shall henceforth ebb four hours and flow six."

"An Act for Canonizing those for Saints that die in the State's service ; who, since there are but two Worlds, ought at least to be honoured in one."

"An Act commanding all malignants to use onely their surnames, their proper Names (with all other properties) being forfeit to the State."

"That the Army ought to march but two abreast, since all creatures at Noah's Ark went by Couples."

"A Vindication of the Citizens of London, that as yet they want nothing but wit and honesty."

"Whether that Text (they are all become abominable ; there is none that doeth good, no not one) doth concern Committee men ? "

"Whether we (as well as Seneca) may call a common woman Respublica ? "

"Whether now more bodies and souls are saved when every man doth either practise Physick or preach."

"Whether the Parliament had not cause to forbid Christmas when they found their printed Acts under so many Christmas Pies ? "

"An Act for admitting Jews into England, with a short proviso for banishing the Cavaliers."

"An Act of oblivion for malignants to forget that ever they had estates."

"The humble petition of the City of London that those Citizens who can raise no Horse may raise a troop of Oxen."

"Sepelire Mortuos.   A List of those Scots who, dying in prison, were denied Christian Burial and (left in the Fields) were eaten by Hogs, which now makes Pork so cheap in London."

"Whether it is not a horrible imprecation against the state to wish that every man might have his due."

"Whether there now live more men or women in the Inns of Court ? "

"Whether it is not clearly proved that there are Witches, since England hath been bewitched eleven years together ? "

"Why Lucian makes Hell governed by a Committee ? "

"Whether Major-General Harrison be bound to give no quarter because his Father is a Butcher ? "

" *Vox Populi*, or the joynt opinion of the whole kingdom of England, That the Parliament is hell, because the torments of it are like to everlasting."

" An Act for reforming divers texts of Scripture, as being of dangerous consequence and contrary to the very being of this present State, beginning at Rom. xiii., where it is said, ' Let every soul be subject to the higher Power,' which words are thus to be reformed, ' Let every soul be subject to the Lower House.' "

" Whether when Colonel Pride goes to quarter with old Nick, the Proverb will not be verified, ' Pride feels no cold' ? "

Although the Royalists ventured to proclaim their opinions, though they openly wore ribbons or badges in their hats, they were not so strong as the Parliamentary party; they had to take their part in the fortification of the avenues and approaches to London, and they had to pay their share in the weekly tax of £10,000 imposed upon the City.

In " A True Relation of two Merchants of London who were taken prisoners by the Cavaliers and of the Misery they and the other Puritans endured "—a pamphlet of 1642—I think we have one of those documents, of which Napoleon so well understood the use, which were meant to stimulate enmity and provoke wrath. It is an interesting paper, but one remarks that the only cruelty endured by the two merchants was due to a smoky chimney; that they report various hangings, but they were not themselves hanged; and various slashings of ears, but they brought their own away with them; and, as is common in such documents, they report the evil case of the enemy and their resolution to destroy the City of London when they get in.

I take an extract from it as follows :—

" Warre hath seemed always sweet to those who have been unexperienced with it, who, blinded with its flourish and its glory, observe not the tragicall events that doe attend it. Of all war the civill is most grievous, where all the obligations of friendship and nature lye cancelled in one another's blood, and violated by their hands who should bee most carefull to preserve them. In civill warres there hath been no greater stickler than religion, whose innocent and sacred garment hath been too often traduced to palliate all dissolute and bloody acts, and (as if heaven suffered flatterers as well as Princes) religion and loyalty have been induced to beleeve they are protected most by those men who most dangerously and most closely doe oppose them, and who, while both are trampled on them by them, doe still cry out, For God and the King.

Every day brings in many sad demonstrations concerning this subject; the burning of houses, the pillaging of goods, the violating of all lawes, both divine and humane, have been arguments written in blood by too many swords. What I shall now relate concerning the sufferings of these two Gentlemen, who were taken by the Cavaliers, and what outrages they have performed in the time of their durance, will bee a compendious mixture of all distresses in one story, wherein I shall bee carefull to satisfie the reader with the manner of it, as myselfe with the truth, not doubting but it will find as much beliefe in the reader as it hath done compassion in the writer.

Two Citizens of London, Gentlemen of good repute and quality (who will be ready upon their oaths to give an attestation of what is here reported), travelling not many days towards Hartly Row, concerning some private occasions of their owne, were taken in their way at Hounsloe, at the sign of the Katharine Wheele, by a

PRINCE RUPERT (1619-1682)

party of some fifty Cavaliers, who had then been forraging up and downe the County of Middlesex, to see what good booty and pillage they could bring.

These Gentlemen no sooner alighted, with an intent for an houre or two to refresh themselves, and bait their horses, but the Cavaliers had notice of it, who rudely and violently did breake into the Chamber wherein they were, and tooke them prisoners. From their Chambers they made haste downe into the Stable, and seized upon their horses, and inforced these captive Gentlemen to ride behinde two of them unto Eggham, to be examined there by Prince Robert. They found their journey, though short, extreamly troublesome, beeing never used to ride before without a saddle; and having such desperate companions on either Saddle before them to conduct them. Comming to Eggham they found Prince Robert in bed, his clothes being on; for he had made a vow that he would never undresse nor shifte himselfe till he had resetted King Charles in White Hall. In the examination it was laid to the charrge of one of these Gentlemen, that his wife was a Roundhead, and if they had her there present, they did sweare they would hang her. It was alledged against the other Gentleman, that hee was a Preacher in a Tub, which, being with much scornfull sport and vehemency prosecuted, at length they espied (having seldome seen in a preacher) a great branch of Ribbands in his hat; the Prince took the paines to look them over himselfe, and turned and tossed them up and downe, and not finding what he searched for, he swore there was none of the King's favours there. The Gentleman replying that they were his Mistress's, Prince Robert smiling, without giving any word at all, returned him his favours and his hat againe.

From thence they were committed to the Court of guard, and a Captain had a charge over them, who was a Frenchman; he placed them both together by the fireside, where the winde did drive all the smoke into their eyes. Though they were almost blinded and choaked with the smoake, which still in waving tumults did issue from the Chimney upon them, they durst not stirre, though to discharge the most earnest Offices of Nature, but had a guard set over them, who threatened and swore, God darne them, they would pistoll them.

That night Prince Robert was to march from Hounsloe, and either wanting guides in earnest, or their cruelty making mirth with these honest Gentlemen, they made their conducts, and following them with their pistols, they did sweare, that if they led them but a yard out of the way they immediately would shoot them.

It was a lamentable condition that these two Gentlemen were in; they were not well acquainted with the way, the smoke had almost blinded their eyes, the night was as darke as cold, which were both then in extreames, they saw their lives at the mercy of these mercilesse men; and to make their condition yet worse, there did arise a thick and sudden mist, which tooke from them the little knowledge of the way they had before; they were not suffered to eate or drinke one drop, though they offered to pay freely for it, and were ready to starve for cold and hunger, but were still pursued with reproachfull and contumelious words, as, Lead on, lead on, you Parliament dogges; if you lead us but one yard out of the way, we will hang you, wee will pistoll you both. The Army being come to the Rendezvous, they were driven before it with many other prisoners, being coupled in cords two by two.

That day the Army being to march towards London, with a resolution to take the Citie, they were left in bonds at the Rendezvous.

The King and Prince were then on Hounsloe Heath, and were marching towards Brainford;[1] they made full account (whatsoever is suggested to the contrary) to have surprized the Citie of London. Prince Robert put off his scarlet coat, which

---

[1] Brentford.

was very riche, and gave it to his man, and buckled on his armour, and put a gray coat over it, that he might not bee discovered; he talked long with the King, and often in his communication with his Majesty he scratched his head, and tore his haire, as if hee had been in some great discontent.

There was that day apprehended a Gentleman cloathed in Scarlet, and hanged in a with upon a tree, as it is conceived for speaking in honour of the Parliament, and no man suffered to cut him downe or cover his face, untill he had been made a publicke spectacle to the whole Army which was then marching by. This was done in the way betwixt Eggham and Staines.

Dr. Soame, vicar of Staines, having four or five daughters, in great jollity did ride up and downe the Army, and was very familiar with the Commanders, and it was thought some of those Commanders were as familiar with his daughters; for they did ride behinde some Captaines, who took them up on horsebacke, and being more mindfull of them than of their souldiers, shewed them the whole Army, as they marched by.

The Army being prevented, and their hopes frustrated for the surprizing of the Citie of London, they were driven back to their Rendezvous, where these two honest Gentlemen, after many solicitations for their release, procured at length some men to passe their words for their ransome; and after eight dayes imprisonment, finding a convenient opportunity for their escape, they stole away to Brainford, making so much haste, that when they came thither they had not one dry threed about them. The misery these two Gentlemen indured hath beene almost inexpressible; they were cudgelled by the Cavaliers, and drove with the other prisoners, like beasts before the Army; their eyes were tormented to see the slaughter and execution of their friends, their eares furred to heare the blasphemies of their enemies, their bellies were pinched with hunger, their whole bodies with cold, their understandings with the apprehension of some infamous death; for not an houre hardly passed away, wherein they were not threatened to be hanged. Whatsoever calamity the insolency of men could inflict, they indured, and doe believe the bondage under the Turk to be humanity and mercy compared to their slavery, who being now in the armes of safety, have drawne my sad pen from the relation of their sorrowes to touch a little on the tyranny of the Cavaliers, and on the extremities of those men who were fellow captives with them.

The poore people that were not able to pay ransomes, they did put into a pond stark naked, up to the knees in durt, in a cold night, and drove them the next morning before the Camp, the basest of the Army inveighing against them with most opprobrious language, calling them Round-headed Citizens, Parliament Rogues, and Parliament Dogges.

They took one in Thistleworth, an honest and religious man, who, because he said he was for the King and Parliament, they most inhumanely did cut off his

eares and gave him besides 30 wounds in his body, and not content with this
butchery, they threw him afterwards on the Dunghill with this most unchristian
scoffe, ' Let the dogs lick him.'

They took another in the same towne, who, flying from their fury, got into a
house, and, having barred fast the gate, not long after he was inforced to open it to
let in his wife, when the Cavaliers came violently rushing in after her, and, fastning
a cord unto his feet, they dragged him about the streets ; and weary of their cruelty,
they said, ' Why do we trouble ourselves any longer with this Dogge,' and so dis-
charging their pistols on him, they discharged him of his torments, and his life
together.

They are very poore in cloathes, especially the foot, but are very full of money ;
wheresoever they come, they pay for nothing, yet make pillage of whatsoever they
come at ; and what they get in one towne at very easie rates, they doe sell in
another, and doe inforce the inhabitants to buy their commodities and stolne goods
of them, whether they will or no. There was a Captaine who offered to lend three
hundred pound to any man upon good security, and that being lent forth, hee made
no question, he said, but in a few days to be able to lend as much more.

The Cavaliers and all are driven unto such necessity, as they are constrained
sometimes either to fast or to feed on carrion ; they have killed Ewes great with
lambe, and one Ewe that was great with two lambes. Whatsoever they cannot eat
at any time, bee their diet never so good, they throw away ; and whatsoever is left
of their hay and provender (their horses many times feeding on good wheat, which
they take from the owner), they fling away at their departure, alledging they will
leave nothing behind them for the Parliament Roundheads.

They drinke and sweare extreamly, and although they lately were prevented in
their designe upon the Citie of London, wherein they verily expected a great and
strong party to assist them, they say, that ere it be long, they will returne to it
againe, and are so confident either by stratagem or by strength to win it, that when
anything comes crosse them, they will say, ' No matter, ere it be long, London shall
make amends for all.' "

CHAPTER IV

AFTER the execution of the King, the Commons, by an Act, abolished Monarchy and erected a Commonwealth in its place. Orders were sent to the Mayor and Sheriffs requiring them to make proclamation accordingly. The Mayor, however, Reynardson, who had always shown Royalist leanings, refused to obey on the ground that he had already, in entering upon the various offices which he had held, taken so many oaths of loyalty that he could not, in conscience, obey. He was therefore committed to the Tower for two months, deprived of his Mayoralty, and fined £2000 for contempt. And the City was ordered to elect a new Mayor with all convenient speed.

The City obeyed; Alderman Atkins was chosen Mayor, and on the 30th of May the proclamation was duly made, but not without hooting and groaning from the crowd. Two Aldermen, Soames and Chambers, were not present. On being questioned at the Bar of the House, Soames said boldly that the proclamation was against his judgment and conscience; Chambers that his heart was not in the business. They were therefore degraded from their position and declared incapable of filling any City office for the future.

A day of public thanksgiving was then appointed, when the City invited the House of Commons to hear a sermon at Christ Church, Newgate, and afterwards to a noble entertainment at the Grocers' Hall. The day after, the City presented Fairfax with a basin and ewer of gold, and Cromwell with a hundred pounds' worth of plate and a purse of £200 in gold.

The exchange of presents and courtesies ended, for the time, with the presentation to the City, by the House of Commons, of Richmond Park.

On the 19th of September 1650 another day of thanksgiving was held for the victory of Dunbar, and another after the victory of Worcester.

Cromwell was received on his return to London by the Mayor, Aldermen, and Sheriffs, who invited him to a Banquet.

On the forcible dissolution of the old Parliament, petitions were presented to Cromwell by the City for and against the reinstatement of the Parliament. Cromwell met them both by constituting a certain number of persons the " Supreme

CROMWELL DISSOLVING PARLIAMENT

From a Dutch satirical print in the British Museum.

5

Authority." The City, recognising this body, presented a petition in which they prayed :—

" 1. That the precious Truths of the Gospel may be preserved in Purity ; and the Dispensers thereof, being approved to be learned, godly, and void of Offence, may be sent forth to preach the Gospel.   2. That their settled Maintenance by Law might be confirmed, and their just Properties preserved.   3. That the Universities may be zealously countenanced and encouraged." (*Maitland*, vol. i. p. 421.)

The "Supreme Authority" surrendering its power, Cromwell was made Protector, a step which the City hastened to recognise by inviting him to dine at the Guildhall, and receiving him with all the honours of a sovereign.

HACKNEY COACHMAN
From a contemporary print published by
John Overton.

On the discovery of a conspiracy against his person, Cromwell sent for the Mayor and Aldermen, and, after acquainting them with the nature of the plot, recommended to them the safety and peace of the City, giving them at the same time, in order to strengthen their hands, the entire control of the City Militia.   He also sanctioned the revival of the Honourable Artillery Company.

As regards affairs municipal, Cromwell limited the number of hackney coachmen to two hundred, under the license of the Mayor and Corporation ; and for the sake of the poor he allowed the entrance into the port, free of duty, of 4000 chaldrons of coals every year.

Cromwell also renewed the attempts of Elizabeth, James, and Charles to stop the erection of new buildings ; all those persons who had built houses—except on four acres of ground— since 1620 were fined one year's rent, and all those who should build after 1656 were to be fined £100.   These successive Acts caused great vexation at the time, but as they were never enforced save at irregular intervals, the chief effect was to drive across the river into the Borough those of the craftsmen for whom there was no room in the City.

The Common Council proceeded to consider the allowances for the expenses of the Mayor and the Sheriffs ; these were now fixed at £208 : 6s. a month for the former, and £150 a month for each of the latter.

A Committee was appointed " to manage and to let to farm a number of offices, including those of garbling, package, and scavage, metage of grain, coal, salt and fruit, as well as all fines, issues, amerciaments and estreated recognizances under the greenwax."

The condition of the poor was taken in hand at this time very seriously. A project was started to raise money by establishing a post in Scotland and other parts of the country; but the House of Commons resolved that the office of postmaster in every part of the country is in the power and the disposal of the Parliament; the project, therefore, fell through; meantime the poor remained. It was decided to raise £4600 in order to find work for them; a storehouse was set apart for them in

Walker & Cockerell.

OLIVER CROMWELL (1599–1658)
From a painting in the National Portrait Gallery, London.

the Minories and the King's Wardrobe, part of the Palace so-called, one court of which remained until recently—to be used as a workroom.

The weariness of civil war felt by the Londoners was further displayed in the autumn of 1650 when a contingent of recruits was marched from London to the North to join the army in Scotland. Half of them deserted by the way. In the following year the City remonstrated on the heavy taxation from which they suffered, stating that the City was assessed at a fifteenth part of the whole kingdom; that the foreign trade had suffered grievously from Prince Rupert's piracies; that the wealthier citizens were withdrawing from London to the suburbs, and so evading taxation. The last clause is remarkable. The time had not yet come when the wealthier merchants desired to leave the City and to live outside; the practice shows simply that in this way they avoided taxation.

The battle of Worcester, September 3, 1651, put an end to the Civil War. A few days later the unhappy Scottish prisoners were marched through the City, ragged, barefoot, bareheaded, starving—a terrible spectacle. Meal was collected for them from house to house; they were taken to Tothill Fields in Westminster, where they lay in the open under rain and suffering from the cold winds of autumn. Twelve hundred of them died. The rest were sent away to the Gold Coast, whence none ever came back.

War with Holland broke out in 1652 and a subscription of £1071 : 9 : 5 for the wounded sailors and soldiers was raised in the City.

On December 16, 1653, the Lord Mayor carried the City Sword at the installation of Cromwell as Lord Protector. Two months later he dined with the Mayor and Corporation at Grocers' Hall. This interchange of courtesies continued during the rest of Cromwell's rule.

The connection of the City with the Protector offers very little of importance. When the proclamation was made, six weeks after the execution of the King, abolishing monarchy, the City made no protest either by its Common Council or by any popular movement. When a Commonwealth was proclaimed in May there were many refusals among the clergy and others to promise fidelity to the new order, but no remonstrance came from the City. When Cromwell dissolved the Rump " not a dog barked " either in the City or outside.

The Fifth Monarchy men, a small minority, gave some trouble in the City. They were fanatics of the deepest dye. They would have no King but Jesus Christ, and no Parliament but a Sanhedrin of Saints—meaning themselves.

Among all the sects which drove men mad perhaps the most mischievous was that of the " Fifth Monarchy " men. It was a sect whose adherents were principally found in London. At one time they were numerous enough to be important. They supported Cromwell's Government at first in the faith that it would become the " Fifth Monarchy," in succession, that is, to the Assyrian, the Persian, the Grecian, and the Roman. During the Fifth Monarchy, they thought, Christ would reign, with the saints, for a thousand years. Their leader was one Venner, a wine cooper, but among them were certain officers, as Major-General Harrison, Colonel Rich, and others. When the proposal that Cromwell should assume the title of King was first brought forward, the Fifth Monarchy men, being disappointed in their hopes and acknowledging no King but Christ, prepared for a rising; they were to meet at Mile End Green, where they expected to be joined by thousands from the country as well as from the City. They were arrested with arms in their hands and sent to the Tower, but none were executed. The man Venner gave more trouble afterwards. There were, however, signs of Royalist disaffection, rumours of proposed risings and the suppression of actual risings, both before and after Cromwell's death, in which the apprentices of London were more or less implicated.

What followed Cromwell's death belongs to the general history of the country. Lambert treated the Parliament with the greatest insolence and arrogance. Monk marched south, pretending to vindicate the rights of Parliament; the apprentices rose and rushed about the streets clamouring for a free Parliament; Colonel Heron

GENERAL MONK, FIRST DUKE OF ALBEMARLE (1608–1670)
After an engraving by David Loggan, 1661

with a company of soldiers fired upon them. The Aldermen exchanged explanations on the subject with the Committee of Safety. The Common Council petitioned Fleetwood for a Parliament as in 1642; the petition was returned. The City Remembrancer was sent to expostulate with Fleetwood, who finally promised a free Parliament. It is difficult to understand what else he could do; there was no second Cromwell; the City called out six regiments of its own militia, commanded by its officers nominated by the Common Council.

If we inquire why a city which before the death of the King seemed Republican and Presbyterian through and through, should in ten years become in the same thorough manner Royalist and Episcopal; or, to put it more exactly, why the

Republican majority became so unmistakably a Royalist majority, we shall find that many forces were at work in this direction.

First of all, though the governing body was both Republican and Presbyterian, there were numbers of citizens who had preserved their loyalty to the Crown, and many more who, for divers reasons, hated the Puritan rule. We have seen the petition of the women and that of the apprentices; we have seen the rioting and discontent at the prohibition of the old sports and the closing of the play-houses. There were also other causes; the Londoners were ready to go forth and fight a

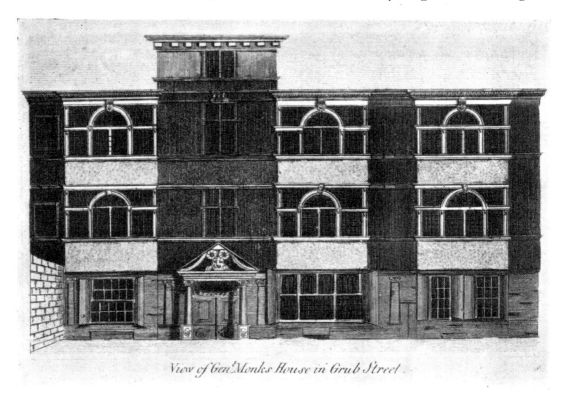

View of Gen¹ Monks House in Grub Street.

battle, but not to carry on a long war; further, they distrusted the standing army which had taken the place of the trained bands. Again, trade was depressed; many ships were taken by Prince Rupert off the Nore and in the narrow seas, and the whole City was kept in perpetual controversies and quarrels over points of doctrine. With a decaying trade, a city divided against itself, religious quarrels without religious peace, the young folk longing for the restoration of the old sports, every tavern full of discontented men, every church a brawling place, what wonder if, after ten years and more, the City suddenly turned round and cried for the King and the Church to come back again.

Yet the events which followed Cromwell's death and preceded the Restoration were very closely connected with the City of London. The domination of the City

A LETTER

Of His Excellencie

The Lord General Monck,

To the Speaker of the Parl. From *Guild-Hall, London.*

Right Honourable,

IN obedience to the Commands received from the Council laſt night, I marched with your Forces into the City this morning, and have ſecured all the perſons except two, ordered to be ſecured, which two were not to be found: The Poſts and Chaines I have given order to be taken away, but have hitherto forborn the taking down of the Gates and Portcullifes, becauſe it will in all likelihood exaſperate the City : and I have good ground of hopes from them, that they will Levy the Aſſeſs; They deſiring onely firſt to meet in Common-Council, which they intend to do to morrow morning. It ſeems probable to me, that they will yeild obedience to your Commands, and be brought to a friendly Complyance with you; for which reaſon I have ſuſpended the execution of your Commands touching the Gates and Portcullifes, till I know your further pleaſure therein, which I deſire I may by this Bearer ; I ſhall onely deſire, that (ſo your Commands may be anſwered with due obedience) ſuch tenderneſs may be uſed towards them, as may gain their affections ; They deſired the Reſtauration of thoſe Members of their Common-Council that are ſecured, which deſires of theirs I ſhall onely commend to your grave Conſideration, to do therein as you ſhall think moſt expedient, and, in attendance upon your further Commands, Remain

Guildhall Feb 9. 1659.

Your moſt Humble and Obedient Servant

George Monck.

To the Right Honourable William Lenthal, *Speaker to the Parliament of the Common-Wealth of* England *at* Weſtminſter.

POSTSCRIPT

I ſhall become an humble ſuiter to you, That You will be pleaſed to haſten your Qualifications, that the Writs may be ſent out; I can aſſure you it will tend much to the Peace of the Country, and ſatisfie many honeſt Men.

Thurſday Afternoon, January 9. 1659.

THis Letter from General *George Monck* from *Guild-Hall, London,* of the 9th of *February,* 1659, was read.

Reſolved, Upon the Queſtion by the Parliament, That the Anſwer to this Letter be, to ſend General *Monck* the Reſolve of the Parliament, That the Gates of the City of *London,* and the Portcullifes thereof be forthwith deſtroyed , And that he be ordered to put the ſaid Vote in Execution accordingly, and that M. *Scot* and M. *Pury* do go to General *Monck* and acquaint him with theſe Votes.

Tho. St. Nicholas, *Clerk to the Parliament.*

Thurſday, February 9. 1659.

REſolved upon the Queſtion by the Parliament, That the Gates of the City of *London,* and the Portcullifes thereof be forthwith deſtroyed, and that the Commiſſioners for the Army do take Order that the ſame be done accordingly

Tho. St.Nicholas, *Clerk to the Parliament.*

LONDON, Printed by *John Macock* in the Year 1659.

by the army deeply moved the people. The clamour for a Parliament prevailed; on the 29th of December 1659 the old Rump was recalled. It was not a full and a free Parliament. But such as it was, the House viewed with jealousy the repair of the City gates and the restoration of the chains, with the calling out of the City militia. The City, however, which had but one representative in the House, refused absolutely to pay or to levy any tax until there was full representation. Meantime Monk was advancing from the north. He entered London on the 3rd of February 1660, and was quartered at Whitehall. For the moment he either dissembled his real intentions or he was simply waiting.

The Rump hastened its own fall. In consequence of the attitude of the Common Council it declared that body dissolved; it also ordered the gates and chains of the City to be removed, and troops to be quartered there in order to reduce the City to obedience.

Monk, in order to carry out these instructions, removed into the City, where he conferred with the Aldermen. They would do nothing; the Common Council being dissolved, there was no body which had the power of speaking for the City.

Monk met them again on the following day. He read them a letter which he had sent to the House. He demanded that writs for every seat should be ready for issue within a week.

Great was the joy of the City; bonfires were lighted; bells were set ringing, and the soldiers were feasted by the people.

The next day, being Sunday, Monk attended service at St. Paul's.

On the 13th, Monday, he conferred with the Mayor and Aldermen in Drapers' Hall.

On the 15th he informed the Mayor that he was about to return to Whitehall, but that he should take care of the safety of the City. However, he did not go back; he remained in the City.

Meantime his order about the writs had been obeyed; many of the old members were taking their places, including those ejected for various reasons. The order dissolving the Common Council was rescinded and the gates were allowed to be repaired. It does not appear that much damage had been done to them. The House also allowed the City to place its militia in the hands of Commissioners of its own choice. On March 16 the Parliament—the old Long Parliament which had done so much, suffered so much, and gone through so many vicissitudes—dissolved. Writs were issued for a new Parliament to meet on April 25. Meantime the Government was in the hands of the Council of State.

And now people began to talk openly and freely of the Restoration. One man boldly set a ladder against the wall of the Royal Exchange and brushed out the inscription, " Exit Tyrannus Regum Ultimus," which had been set up in August 1650. The Skinners' Company set up the Royal Arms once more in their Hall.

The Common Council issued a Declaration in which they set forth their disavowal of many acts committed by themselves during the last twenty years on the ground that they were the work of "men of loose and dangerous" principles who had got into the Council "in the general deluge of disorder introduced into these kingdoms." They also expressed satisfaction at the thought of an end having been put to the destructions of the country and of a return to the old order of King, Lords, and Commons.

This Declaration was scarcely issued before a letter came from Charles II. conveying his assurance that he had no thoughts of revenge, and promising the City the confirmation of its Charters. He also pledged himself to grant liberty of conscience in religion, to leave questions of title to land to Parliament, and he promised the soldiers their arrears of pay.

The new Parliament met on the 25th of April. Charles's Declaration reached the House on the 1st of May. Parliament instantly sent to the City to borrow £100,000, which was cheerfully advanced, and half of it was at once sent over to the King. On the same day the City companies raised the sum of £10,000 for Charles, and £2000 to be divided between the Dukes of York and Gloucester. Sixteen commissioners were appointed to wait on Charles at the Hague in order to take over this Royal gift.

Charles was proclaimed on May the 18th.

CHAPTER V

THE RESTORATION

THE welcome with which Charles was received amounted to frenzy. Bonfires were made all over the City; up went the maypoles again; the church bells rang; the mob paraded rumps of beef, which they afterwards roasted and devoured; they made

MOB AT TEMPLE BAR
From the Crace Collection in British Museum

everybody drink the health of the King upon their knees; they broke the windows of leading Puritans; they made Monk's soldiers drunk. It was not only the King who had come to his own again; it was the return of merriment, feasting, dancing, singing, mumming, sports, music, laughing, the pride of the eye, the delight of the ear, the joy of the world, the careless, reckless, headlong happiness of youth in the things that belong to youth. The kingdom of God upon the earth had been attempted. Perhaps the Puritans mistook the nature of that kingdom; perhaps they were only wrong in believing that the time was ripe for the advent of that kingdom.

But let us begin this reign with the words of those who looked on at the Restoration :—

" Mem. that Threadneedle Street was all day long and late at night crammed with multitudes crying out, ' A free Parliament!—A free Parliament!' that the air rang again with their noise. One day, he, coming out on horseback, they were so violent that he was almost afraid of himself, and so, to satisfy them (as they used to do to importunate children), said, ' Pray be quiet, ye shall have a Free Parliament! This was about seven, or rather eight, as I remember, at night ; immediately a loud halloa and shout was given, all the bells in the city ringing ; and the whole city looked as if it had been in a flame by the bonfires, which were prodigiously great and frequent, and ran like a train over the city ; and I saw some balconies that began to be kindled. They made little gibbets, and roasted rumps of mutton ; nay, I saw some very good rumps of beef. Health to K. Charles II. was drunk in the streets, by the bonfires, even on their knees."

And Pepys writes :—

"In Cheapside there were a great many bonfires, and Bow bells and all the bells in all the churches as we went home, were ringing." [Hence he went homeward, it being about ten at night.] "But the common joy that was everywhere to be seen ; the number of bonfires!—there being fourteen between St. Dunstan's and Temple Bar ; and at Strand Bridge I could at one time tell thirty-one fires ; in King Street seven or eight ; and all along burning, and roasting, and drinking for rumps ; there being rumps tied upon sticks, and carried up and down. The butchers at the May-Pole in the Strand rang a peal with their knives, when they were going to sacrifice their rump. On Ludgate Hill there was one turning the spit that had a rump tied upon it, and another basting of it. Indeed, it was past imagination both the greatness and the suddenness of it. At one end of the street you would think there was a whole lane of fire and smoke, so hot that we were fain to keep on the other side. . . . Everybody now drinks the King's health without any fear, whereas before it was very private that a man dare do it. Monk this day is feasted at Mercers' Hall, and is invited, one after another, to all the twelve Halls in London. Many think that he is honest yet, and some or more think him to be a fool that would raise himself by endeavouring it. . . . This morning comes Mr. Edward Pickering ; he tells me that the King will come in, but that Monk did resolve to have the doing of it himself or else to hinder it."

When Parliament met all the members must have understood what was going to happen. On the 3rd of May, Sir John Greville presented to the House a letter from Charles. It was resolved that his promises were satisfactory and that the Government should be once more by King, Lords, and Commons. Six Commissioners representing the House of Lords, twelve for the House of Commons, and twenty for the City of London, were appointed ; they were instructed to take over £50,000 for the King, £10,000 for the Duke of York, and £5000 for the Duke of Gloucester ; the City Commissioners added a gift of £10,000 for the King.

" There was great joy in London," Pepys states, " and at night more bonfires than ever, and ringing of bells, and drinking of the King's health upon their knees in the streets, which methinks is a little too much."

On the 26th of May 1660 the King landed at Dover ; on the 29th he entered

London. The cavalcade which did honour to the occasion was worthy of a mediæval riding.

"First marched a gallant troop of gentlemen in Cloth of Silver, brandishing their Swords, and led by Major-General Brown; then followed another troop of two hundred in velvet coats with footmen and liveries attending them in purple; then another troop, led by Alderman Robinson, in buff coats, with cloth of silver sleeves, and very rich green scarves; and after these a troop of about two hundred, with blue liveries laid with silver, with six trumpeters, and several footmen, in sea-green and silver; then a troop of two hundred and twenty, with thirty footmen in grey and silver liveries and four trumpeters richly habited. Then another troop of an hundred and five, with grey liveries and six trumpets; and another of seventy, with five trumpets. And then three troops more, two of three hundred, and one of one hundred, all gloriously habited and gallantly mounted. After these came two trumpets with his Majesty's arms; the Sheriffs' men in red cloaks, richly laced with silver to the number of fourscore, with half-pikes in their hands; then followed six hundred of the several companies of London on horseback, in black velvet coats with gold chains, each company having footmen in different liveries, with streamers, etc. After these came kettle-drums, and trumpets, with streamers, and after them twelve Ministers at the head of His Majesty's Life Guards of Horse, commanded by the Lord Gerrard; next the City Marshall, with eight footmen in divers colours; with the City Waits and Officers in order; then the two Sheriffs, and all the Aldermen of London in their scarlet coats and rich trappings, with footmen in liveries, red coats laid with silver and cloth of gold; the Heralds and Maces in rich coats; then the Lord Mayor carrying the Sword, bare, with his Excellency (the General) and the Duke of Buckingham, bare also; and then, as the last to all this splendid triumph, rode the King himself between his royal brothers, the Dukes of York and Gloucester; then followed a troop of Horse with white colours; and after them the General's Life-Guard led by Sir Philip Howard, and another Troop of Gentry; and last of all five regiments of the Army Horse, with Back, Breast, and Head-Pieces, which diversified the Shew with delight and terror."

At the Coronation in April of the following year, the City, still in a fever of loyalty, raised four triumphal arches, and organised a procession as magnificent as that of the entry. After the Coronation was the Banquet, at which Pepys was so fortunate as to be a spectator :—

"A little while before the King had done all his ceremonies (in the Abbey) I went round to Westminster Hall all the way within rayles, with the ground covered with blue cloth, and scaffolds all the way. Into the Hall I got, where it was very fine with hangings and scaffolds one upon another, full of brave ladies. The King came in with his crowne on and his sceptre in his hand, under a canopy borne up by six silver staves carried by barons of the Cinque Ports, and little bells at every end. And after a long time he got to the farther end, and all set themselves down at their several tables. . . . I went from table to table to see the bishops and all others at their dinner. And at the lords' table I met with William Howe, and he spoke to my lord for me, and he did give him four rabbits and a pullet, and so Mr. Creed and I got Mr. Minshell to give us some bread, and so we at a stall eat it as every one else did what they could get. I took a great deal of pleasure to go up and down and look upon the ladies, and to hear the musique of all sorts; but, above all, the twenty-four violins. About six at night they had dined. And strange it is to think that these two days have held up fair till now, that all is done, and the King gone out of the Hall, and then it fell a-raining and thundering and lightning as I have not seen it do for some years, which people did take great notice of. I observed little disorder, only the King's footmen had got hold of the canopy and would keep it from the barons of the Cinque Ports, which they endeavoured to force from them again, but could not do it till my lord Duke of Albemarle caused it to be put into Sir R. Pye's hand, till to-morrow, to be decided."

The Fifth Monarchy men who have already been mentioned as rising against

THE CORONATION OF CHARLES II. IN WESTMINSTER ABBEY, APRIL 23, 1661

From a contemporary print.

Cromwell were, on the reappearance of Charles, mad enough, or fanatical enough, to attempt a second rising, the history of which is curiously picturesque, and shows also the strange religious distractions of the time.

Between the King's accession in May and the end of the year these fanatics seem to have done nothing. Many of their leaders, including Colonel Overton, Major Wild, Cornet Day, and others, were arrested on suspicion of dangerous

CHARLES II. (1630-1685)
From an engraving by P. Vanderbanc.

symptoms. The Fifth Monarchy people had a meeting-house in Swan Alley, Coleman Street. Here on the sixth day of January 1661, the Sunday after the arrest of their leaders, they assembled in a state of mind approaching frenzy. What followed was madness pure and simple. Their preacher, Thomas Venner, the wine cooper, had acquired a competent fortune by his trade. He was believed to be a man of sense until his understanding was confused with enthusiasm. He, in common with his sect, looked on Charles as a usurper upon Christ's dominion. On this particular Sunday his madness and the madness of his followers broke out. He assured them that the time of the Fifth Monarchy had arrived; that those who believed in it and expected it should be protected by Divine interference so that no weapon should hurt them, and not a hair should be touched among them all;

but one should chase a thousand and that two should put ten thousand to flight; that the Reign of Jesus was beginning that day upon the earth. Filled with enthusiasm the people drew up a declaration called "A door-of Hope opened," in which they affirmed they would never sheath the sword till Babylon (meaning the Monarchy) became a hissing and a curse; till there would be left neither remnant, son, nor nephew; that when they had led captivity captive in England, they would go forth into France, Spain, and Germany; that they would rather die than take the oaths of supremacy and allegiance; that they would make no league with monarchists, but would rise up against the carnal, to possess the gate of the world; to bind their kings in chains and their nobles in fetters of iron.

When they had adopted this promising declaration they marched out in a body of sixty only, but well armed, down Cheapside to St. Paul's Churchyard, shouting as they went for "King Jesus." In St. Paul's Churchyard they were accosted by a man who cried out for King Charles. Him they slew immediately. By this time the Mayor, Sir Richard Brown, heard of the tumult, and sent a company of the trained bands to suppress it. The number of the company thus sent out is not known, but they were not strong enough. Instead of suppressing the fanatics they were themselves totally routed and put to flight. The Fifth Monarchy men then marched through the City without opposition; they passed out at Bishopsgate; then, evidently not knowing what to do next, they crossed Moorfields, marched along Chiswell Street, and, turning south again, re-entered the City at Cripplegate. It would have been better for them had they dispersed and gone home for the night, satisfied with their triumph and now convinced of their invulnerability. Unfortunately they heard of a troop of horse waiting for them somewhere, and so retreated, killing a headborough on the way, to Beech Lane. Here they encountered some opposition which caused them to march north as far as the heights of Hampstead. They found shelter, such as it was, for the night in Ken Woods, which are still left exactly as they were then. In the morning—they must have been wretched after a winter night in the open and with no food—they were attacked by more troops and dispersed, some of them being taken prisoners and committed to the Gatehouse, Westminster.

Next day they rallied again and returned to London. This was the last day of the Rising. It was a day of sturdy and obstinate fighting. I do not know any other example where such a handful of men held out so long against such odds. Nor can one understand where the men got their ammunition. They fought on Sunday evening, Monday and Tuesday; they are described as firing in good order; where, then, did they procure their ammunition?

When they arrived once more in London they divided into two small parties; one of them marched towards Leadenhall, where they were followed by the trained bands which dispersed them. The other party, under Venner, marched on

INCIDENTS IN THE REBELLION OF THE FIFTH MONARCHY MEN UNDER THOMAS VENNER, AND THE EXECUTION OF THEIR LEADERS

E. Gardner's Collection.

Haberdashers' Hall in Maiden Lane, hoping to catch the Mayor. But he evaded them. They then repaired to Wood Street, presumably intending to go out again by Cripplegate; the Horse Guards now came upon the scene, and a fierce fight ensued, in which Venner was dangerously wounded and two of their preachers killed. They then retreated in good order; outside the gate they stationed ten men in an alehouse with instructions to hold it; seven of the ten were killed, a large number of the trained bands, and twenty of the rebels. Fourteen were taken; eleven were executed with the customary formalities; and here they made an end; probably no further search was attempted after the rest of the rioters. It was wiser not to ascertain how many of these fanatics there were and who they were. We hear, however, very little more of the Fifth Monarchy men. As for the poor fanatics, they affirmed to the last that if they had been deceived, the Lord Himself was their deceiver.

On the 30th day of January 1661, the anniversary of King Charles's execution, in the year following the Restoration, a remarkable procession took place through the streets of London to Tyburn. Horsemen led the way and brought up the rear; there were trumpets and drums; guards marched on either side; in the middle, one behind the other, on their sledges, sat Lord Munson, Sir Henry Mildmay, and Robert Wallop with ropes about their necks. The Act of Indemnity had spared their lives, but it had not spared them other penalties, and they went through the form of being drawn to execution. Arrived at Tyburn they were taken off the sledges and carried back to the Tower, there to pass the remainder of their days.

Three more of the regicides, Okey, Corbet, and Berkstead, who had escaped to Hanau in Germany, were decoyed by Sir George Downey, the King's resident at the Hague. He treacherously assured Okey that he had no directions to look for him; whereupon all three left Hanau and repaired to Delft, where they were arrested and sent home for trial. They were of course convicted and executed. No more honourable and conscientious man than Corbet ever existed. The death of these three was followed by that of Sir Harry Vane. Neither Vane nor Lambert was among the judges of the King. The House of Lords wished, however, to exclude both from the Act of Indemnity; the House of Commons desired to include them. The Chancellor assuring them that their lives were safe, both Houses agreed in a petition to the King :—

"Your Majesty having declared your gracious pleasure to proceed only against the murderers of your royal Father, we, your Majesty's most humble subjects, the Lords and Commons assembled, not finding Sir Henry Vane or Colonel Lambert to be of the number, are humble suitors to your Majesty that, if they shall be attainted, execution of their lives may be remitted."

Charles broke his word and Vane was executed, showing to the last the firmness and courage which only a good conscience could give, this belongs to national history. He suffered on Tower Hill. His friends urged him after his sentence to make submission to the King. He replied :—

" If his Majesty does not think himself more concerned for his honour and word than I am for my life, I am very willing he should take it ; and I declare that I value my life less in a good cause than the King does his promise." (*Clayton*, ii. p. 164.)

Sir Harry Vane was a scholar of Oxford ; he had travelled in France and stayed awhile in Geneva, where he had adopted the religious principles which ruled him through life. So much was he considered when quite young that the King entreated Laud to bring him to a more orthodox way of thinking. To avoid Laud's frequent reproofs Vane went to America, where, at the age of four-and-twenty, he became Governor of Massachusetts Bay.

The Act of Indemnity excluded the late King's judges and certain persons who had been active in procuring the King's execution. The trials of the State prisoners under the exceptions of this Act took place at the Old Bailey. On October 11 they were all sentenced to death as traitors, with the customary barbarities. Major-General Harrison, the Rev. Hugh Peters, Mr. Thomas Scot, Mr. Gregory Clement, and Colonels Scroop (or Scrope), John Jones, Francis Hacker, and Daniel Axtell were sentenced. Most of them were executed at Charing Cross.

The case of Harrison was the most important. There is no doubt that he took an active part in bringing Charles to the block ; yet he subsequently refused to assist Cromwell in his ambitions ; he was imprisoned by Cromwell and deprived of his commission ; on his release he retired to a private life, and refused to fly when the King returned. Brought before the Court, he made no attempt to deny the fact ; on the contrary he gloried in it :—

"The act of which I stand accused was not a deed performed in a corner ; the sound of it has gone forth to most nations ; and, in the singular and marvellous conduct of it, has chiefly appeared the sovereign power of Heaven. . . . I have often, agitated by doubts, offered my addresses, with passionate tears, to the Divine Majesty, and earnestly sought for light and conviction. I still received assurances of a heavenly sanction, and returned from such devout supplications with tranquillity and satisfaction. These frequent illapses of the Divine Spirit I could not suspect to be interested illusions : since I was conscious that for no temporal advantage would I have offered injury to the poorest individual. All the allurements of ambition, all the terrors of imprisonment have not been able, during the usurpation of Cromwell, to shake my steady resolution or bend me to a compliance with that deceitful tyrant : and, when invited by him to sit on the right hand of the throne—when offered riches, splendour, and dominion, I have disdainfully rejected all temptations, and, neglecting the tears of my friends and family, have still, through every danger, held fast my principles and my integrity."

He then refused to say more and submitted to the sentence of the Court. The scene of the execution was Charing Cross ; the day, October the 14th, 1661. Evelyn met the carts carrying away the mangled quarters. "Oh!" he cried, "the miraculous providence of God!"

CHAPTER VI

THE REIGN

THERE is, perhaps, no time in the history of Great Britain of deeper interest and importance than that which witnessed the restoration and, later, the final expulsion of the Stuarts. We find the City at the outset weary of its Commonwealth, and longing for that security and order which are the best recommendations of a settled succession. And then the old business begins again. It seems as if the history of the last twenty years had been in vain, that the struggles and the victories had been forgotten.

I have here to recount only the part played by London between the years 1660 and 1688. Not, that is, the part played in London, otherwise we should have to consider nearly all the important events of the reign, which was passed almost entirely at Whitehall. In many cases it is difficult to decide between what belongs to London alone and what belongs to London and the country.

The execution of Venner and his men did not clear the City of dangerous elements. The Fifth Monarchy people and the Presbyterians exhorted each other to withstand the introduction of the Book of Common Prayer and the idolatry of the Court. Some of them refused to obey the law unless the spirit ordered them. The City was full of disbanded officers and men who were ready and anxious to take up arms again. The King complained that the night watch was unable to cope with these turbulent people, and ordered that only able men should be appointed, and that their watch should continue all night.

The Act of Uniformity of 1662 ordered every minister, if he would continue in his benefice, to assent to everything contained in the Book of Common Prayer. On Sunday, August 17, all the Presbyterians took leave of their congregations amid their tears and lamentations. Then persecution set in. It must be confessed that the language and action of some of the Nonconformists seemed to justify, in a certain measure, the rigours of the Government. For instance, the Baptists are said to have spoken openly of the King as the "Beast"; it was reported that Presbyterians and Baptists together were preparing to resist by force of arms; it must be remembered that these people represented the Roundheads of twenty years before.

The Act of Uniformity, rigorously enforced, filled the prisons, made the Church of England hateful to the people, and drove hundreds away to America and to Holland.

In the same year an Act was passed for raising money for the paving of the streets of London by making every hackney coach—of which there were then four hundred—pay a tax of five pounds a year ; every load of hay, sixpence ; every load of straw, twopence. The Act provided especially for the paving of Hedge Lane (Whitcomb Street), from Petty France to St. James's Palace, St. James's Street, and Pall Mall. The paving was the old-fashioned round cobbles ; before they were laid down the road was simply a trodden way, in the summer throwing up clouds of dust, in the winter knee-deep in mud. The Act further provided for the widening of certain ways and passages in the City. It is idle to ask if they were widened, because the Fire came a few years later and swept all away.

The King in the same year formally restored to the City their Irish estates, which the Parliament had long before restored.

On June 24, 1663, Charles granted the Inspeximus Charter.

Accounts of the Plague of 1665 and the Fire of 1666 will be found in other places (pp. 215, 240).

As soon as things were more settled after the Great Fire, the Corporation considered how best to avoid the recurrence of such a calamity. They divided the City into four divisions, each to be supplied with 800 buckets, 50 ladders, from 12 to 42 feet in length, 2 brazen hand-squirts to each parish, 24 pickaxe sledges, and 40 "shod" shovels. Each of the twelve great companies was to be provided with an engine, 30 buckets, 3 ladders, 6 pickaxe sledges, and 2 hand-squirts. The inferior companies were to have such a number of engines, etc., as should be fixed by the Court of Aldermen. The Aldermen who had passed the Shrievalty were to keep 24 buckets and 1 hand-squirt each in his house. Those who had not yet passed the Shrievalty, half that number of buckets. Fire-plugs were to be placed in the main water-pipes. The companies of carpenters, bricklayers, plasterers, painters, masons, smiths, plumbers, and paviours were to appoint for each company 2 master workmen, 4 journeymen, 8 apprentices, and 16 labourers, to be ready on an alarm to turn out. And lastly, all the workmen belonging to the several water-works, the sea coal meters, Blackwall Hall, Leadenhall, ticket, package, and other porters, were to attend the Lord Mayor and Sheriffs in such services. In other words, a fire brigade was established of several hundreds, with means of putting out fires amounting to about 1500 buckets and 300 hand-squirts. The weak point in this machinery was the difficulty of getting at the men when they were wanted, and the feeble nature of the hand-squirt.

The Fire produced confusion in ecclesiastical property, for the tithes which had been levied from house to house could no longer be collected owing to the changes of site, the substitution of a small house for a great house, or *vice versâ*. It was therefore resolved that each parish should be assessed at so much per annum in lieu of tithe, and that each house should be assessed at its share of this amount. Trouble afterwards arose in the working of this Act in consequence of houses standing empty.

The rebuilding of London was a great time for the passing of ordinances and regulations for the better preservation of order and cleanliness in the City. Thus the foot-passage, or way along the streets, was at this time ordered to be of flat or broad stone. The Fellowship of Carmen was ordered to send round carts for the collection of all waste stuff, which was to be conveyed to the nearest laystall.

The traffic in the streets was regulated. Carts had to stand along, not across, the street; brewers and others were not to use more than one horse, nothing was to be thrown into the streets, every householder had to keep his own part of the street clean, and things offensive were not to be carried about the streets before eleven o'clock at night.

The heavy losses caused first by the Plague, which stopped trade of all kinds and destroyed many thousands of craftsmen and servants, and next by the Fire, had reduced the City to a very low condition. No one will ever be able to estimate the losses of or consider the number of respectable families reduced to poverty, and plunged down into the lowest depths. A Committee, appointed by the Common Council to investigate the financial position of the City, had to recommend the abolition of certain offices and resolute retrenchment in many departments. Among other measures of economy the Committee recommended the abolition of their chronologer (see p. 178).

On June 10, 1667, the City, which was as yet only half-built, presented a most melancholy appearance. It had been devastated by plague, its people lay by thousands in the burial-grounds, it had been destroyed by fire, and now it seemed as if the last and crowning misery was to be inflicted upon it. Men's hearts sank within them. They asked if their afflictions were laid upon them for their persecution of the Quakers and the Baptists, for their imprisonment of the saints, for the idolatries of the Court, and the corruption of the times. For it was known on that day that the Dutch had sailed up the Medway and burned the English men-of-war which were lying there, either without a crew or with half their company discharged. For defence—an ignoble defence—ships were sunk in the bed of the Thames at Barking, Woolwich, and Blackwall. Every able-bodied man in the City was called out. Had the Dutch continued, they must have been able to take the City. Luckily they did not continue, and the Treaty of Breda put an end to hostilities.

The City at this time returned to the mediæval use of passing long and intricate regulations for the better management of the markets. The most noteworthy provisions were two: that the Market Bell should ring at six every morning, at which the market was to open *for housekeepers only* and such as bought for their own use; at ten the bell was to ring again, at which time retailers and those who bought to sell again should be allowed to enter.

Was the Temple within the City and its Liberties or not? The question was answered in a practical manner by the Lord Mayor in March 1669, when, with the Aldermen, he went to dine with the Reader of the Inner Temple. He claimed that it was within his jurisdiction, and ordered his sword-bearer to precede him carrying the sword up. The students, as sticklers for the honour of the Temple, came out and ordered him to lower the sword; they tried to snatch the sword away; they hustled the marshal's men and compelled the Mayor and Aldermen to take refuge in the chambers of the Auditor Phillips while the Recorder and Sheriffs hastened to Whitehall in order to lay the matter before the King. It is not stated what message was sent by the King, but when the Sheriffs came back and the Mayor attempted to get away there was another fight, and the Aldermen were treated with the greatest disrespect. They again retreated to the Chambers and again sent to the King. When the Sheriffs returned, however, the students had gone to dinner and the unfortunate civic procession was enabled to get out in an extremely undignified manner.

In 1670 an Act of Parliament was passed suppressing conventicles. The Act was carried out with great rigour; but the meeting-houses were handed over to the Church of England to be used as churches until the parish churches themselves should be rebuilt.

The attempted robbery of the Tower by Blood in 1671 may be mentioned on account of the extraordinary interest excited everywhere by the audacity of the crime. Otherwise it belongs to the history of the country rather than to that of the City. There was whispering on 'Change, murmurs and rumblings of discontent when it became known that the man had not only received the King's pardon, but also the King's favour and a grant of land. But, in fact, during the whole of this reign, in which the King was encroaching as much as he dared, having learned nothing from his father's fate, and the City was defending her liberties now feebly, now strongly, the air was filled with murmurs of discontent and with whispers of approaching rebellion. It was as if an impending earthquake announced its coming by subterranean rumblings. How much the King heard and understood, how far he was prepared, if necessary, for a new appeal to the sword, it is for the historian of the country to investigate.

As a means of compensating those loyal and necessitous officers who had suffered for their adherence to the Royalist cause, Charles granted them one or more plate lotteries. Thus he presented the officers with certain plate as a gift from the Crown; they were authorised to put it up in lottery by tickets which were sold for the purpose. Thus, if the plate was worth, say £1000, tickets to the value of £3000 were issued, ensuring a large profit to the proprietor if all the tickets were sold.

We have now to consider the treatment of London by the King during the latter part of his reign. One may ask with amazement how the City, which had deposed Richard the Second for acts not nearly so arbitrary as those of Charles the Second, which had driven Charles the First from the throne for attempts far less despotic, could sit down in submission, nay, almost without a protest, under tyrannies and encroachments which indicated the determination to recognise neither liberty nor privilege.

The bankers of the Middle Ages were the great merchants, the merchant adventurers. Whittington held money for the landowners, advanced money on the security of land, and in nearly all respects carried on the business of a private bank. The merchant adventurers, who were mostly mercers, were succeeded by the goldsmiths, who were private bankers, kept the money of their customers—"running cash"—gave them cheques under the name of "goldsmiths' notes," received money on deposit account and gave interest for it; they made their own profits by lending it out at higher interest. The customers were allowed 6 per cent at twenty days' sale and $3\frac{1}{2}$ per cent for money on demand. The bankers took assignments of the public revenue for payment of principal and interest as it came in.

Of these bankers the most important was Edward Blackwell. He was the King's intermediary in many important transactions. The pay of the troops in Dunkirk passed through his hands; he went to France on business for the King; he advanced money to the King, who owed him in 1672 more than a quarter of a million. There were nearly forty goldsmiths and bankers in Lombard Street. The money these bankers had lent to the Exchequer on security of the public revenue amounted to £1,300,000. In the year 1671 Charles wanted money. He was about to enter upon the war with Holland. Parliament was prorogued; he would always get money, if he could, without going to the House for it. In this case he listened to the advice of Clifford and took a step, the nature of which, one would hope, he did not comprehend. He resolved upon closing the Exchequer. The meaning of this step is perhaps not at once intelligible. It means that the repayments due to those who had lent money to the Exchequer were withheld, and it means that the interest due on these loans was refused payment. Imagine, if you can, the consternation and the despair which would be spread around if the interest on Bank of England Stock, or the London County Council Debt, or any other large security were to be suddenly stopped at the present day! Charles laid his hands on the whole amount. He took it. He promised to resume payment within a year, with interest. He took this money. And yet the City did not rise! Blackwell, with all the goldsmiths in Lombard Street, was ruined. Those rich bankers who had placed all their money in the King's hands were utterly ruined; so were the lesser folk, the hundreds of people who had entrusted their money to the bankers of Lombard Street.

Not even Henry the Third, not even Richard the Second, ever inflicted such a blow as this upon the City. In money of our day, and considering the poverty of the City, it represents at least £6,000,000—nay, more, because the interest was then more than double that of the present day, say £8,000,000. Imagine the rage and consternation were such a blow to be delivered at the Bank of England! Imagine the consternation if there were to be no interest on a great part of the National Debt for a whole year! Nay, the blow was far greater, because London two hundred years ago was far, far less wealthy than at present, not only actually, but in proportion to its population. Looking on London only as a trading community it is quite certain that such a blow could never be forgiven. When the opportunity should arise it would be remembered. It was not his religion only that drove James from Whitehall, it was the memory of this act of confiscation and the other acts of oppression which followed.

The absence of resistance is at first sight most remarkable. I can only account for this fact on the theory that the poverty of the City and its weakness were much greater than is generally supposed. The Plague, which swept away many thousands of bread-winners, left behind it many thousands of penniless orphans. The Fire, which spared the lives of the people, destroyed all they owned in the world: house, furniture, stock in trade, tools, everything. The long civil wars had helped to impoverish the City; the Dutch War was calamitous; in other words, the City for many years had been living on its capital, and now this was coming to an end. Again, the religious dissensions of the City contributed to its weakness. It was the influence of the Church of England which brought back the King; it was therefore with an ill grace that they complained of the Royal exactions. The Church of England had joined in persecuting the Nonconformists just as, in the fifties, the Independents and the Presbyterians had joined in persecuting the Anglicans. Moreover, from many a pulpit in the City, day after day, the doctrine—the monstrous suicidal doctrine—of passive obedience was preached. The "Judgment and Decree" of Oxford, issued a few years later, was already on the lips of the High Church preachers. It declared to be "false, seditious, and impious, even heretical and blasphemous," to hold that "authority is derived from the people; that if lawful governors become tyrants, they forfeit their right of governing; that the King hath but a co-ordinate right with the other two estates, the Lords and the Commons, etc.," and that passive obedience is "the badge and character of the Church of England."

The secret of the submission of the City under so many blows was therefore (1) its poverty, (2) its internal dissensions, (3) the doctrine of passive obedience inculcated by so many of the clergy. Perhaps there was still some memory among middle-aged men of the sour austerities enforced during the Commonwealth.

Many of the natural leaders of the City, those of the merchants who were still in good circumstances, had withdrawn from the scene of certain strife and possible disaster; they had taken houses in the suburbs, especially those on the north and the east of the town. One result was that their houses stood unoccupied. At this time we begin to find the suburbs becoming the place of residence for City merchants; at first the favourite quarters were in and about Stepney. Many substantial houses were built in the midst of large gardens at Mile End, Hoxton, Hackney, Ratcliffe, and Norton Folgate.

In February 1674 the general complaints about trade were so loud that an attempt was made to seek redress from the Parliament. A petition, setting forth the miserable condition of the City, was drawn up and presented on February 23. Nothing was done, however, and on the 24th the House was prorogued.

In the year 1675 compliments and presents passed between the King and the City, noticeable only as showing the apparently unabated loyalty of the City, and in 1677 the City offered a magnificent entertainment to the King and Queen, the Duke of York, the Princesses Mary and Anne, and the Prince of Orange, to celebrate the betrothal of the Princess Mary.

After the regulation of the Provision Markets the Common Council turned their attention to the Cloth Market and produced a set of regulations which, one may confidently assume, could never have been mastered by the honest vendors of cloth. They may be found set forth at length in Maitland's *History*.

Then followed one of those dreary disputes which can hardly be read with patience. It was the old question whether the Court of Aldermen had the power to veto the decisions and orders of the Common Council. How was it ended? I quote the words of Sharpe (*London and the Kingdom*, ii. p. 454):—

"One result of the *contretemps* which had occurred in the Court of Common Council of the 12th March was that the Court of Aldermen resolved to retain certain counsel to advise them as occasion should arise on the question of their rights and privileges, and to create a fund by subscription among themselves to meet the necessary expenses.

In April the Town Clerk and the Four Clerks of the outer court (*i.e.* mayor's court) were instructed to search the books and records of the city on the question whether or not it was the province of the lord mayor (1) to direct and put the question in the Common Council, (2) to name committees, and (3) to nominate persons to be put in election to any office. This last point especially affected the right claimed by the Mayor to nominate (if not to elect) one of the sheriffs by virtue of his prerogative—a claim which had already been more than once canvassed, and which was destined shortly to bring the City and the Crown into violent opposition.

On the 7th September 1675 the Court of Aldermen directed that the opinion of counsel should be taken on the power of the mayor and aldermen to put their veto on matters passed by the Common Council. After the lapse of fifteen months the opinions of Sir William Jones, the attorney-general, Sir Francis Winnington, solicitor-general, Sir John Maynard and Sir Francis Pemberton, sergeants-at-law, and of 'Mr. William Steele' (*not* a former Recorder of that name as some have supposed) were presented to the court (5th Dec. 1676); and with the exception of the last mentioned, all the lawyers declared in favour of the mayor and aldermen. There the matter was allowed to rest for a year or more until in February 1678 the opinions of Sir William Dolben, not long since appointed the city's Recorder, and of

FORVM
VTILITATI publicæ per quam necessarium
REGIA CAROLI 2 di annuente MAJESTATÆ.
proprijs Sumptibus erexit perfecitq
D. EDOARDVS HVNGERFORD
Balnei Miles
ANNO MDCLXXXII

HUNGERFORD MARKET, NEAR YORK BUILDINGS, STRAND.

Built by Sir Edward Hungerford, created Knight of the Bath at the Coronation of King Charles the Second.

From a contemporary print.

Jeffreys, the Common Sergeant, who was destined in a few months to succeed Dolben on the latter's promotion to the bench, were taken and found to coincide with the opinions already delivered with the exception of that of William Steele."

On the termination of the French war, Charles asked the City to lend him another £200,000. The City consented amid gloomy forebodings. What did the King want with the money? What was he going to do with it? Would he introduce foreign troops and so destroy the liberties of the people? It is a singular illustration of the affection which the City is said to have always entertained for Charles that these things should have been whispered about. It was not affection, it was fear. This Prince, whom we suppose to have been always under the influence of women, always wallowing in pleasure, had proved himself a strong man and a crafty man; he showed when he seized that money, not only his own strength, but also the weakness of the City. He did what he pleased with them, and he continued to do what he pleased with them as long as he lived. In one point, however, Charles was powerless; he could not abolish the national hatred and suspicion of the Catholics. The Popish Plot, invented by Titus Oates, drove the City into a state of panic meaningless and causeless. Sir Edmondbury Godfrey was found dead on Primrose Hill the day after he had received the deposition of Titus Oates. Murdered by the Papists of course! Why, then, did they not murder Titus Oates himself? No one felt safe. The City gates were closed, the streets were protected by post and chains, the City was in a state of siege, with no enemy in sight or existence.

In the year 1679 the King was attacked by fever, and for some time was believed to be in danger. The City realised, then, at least, that his successor was a Catholic. Therefore when Charles recovered, the joybells and the bonfires represented much more than a common and perfunctory rejoicing. The King recovered, and made haste to show the true nature of his sentiments towards the City. He was very much annoyed by the presentation of a number of petitions from all parts of the country, including London, in favour of calling a Parliament. He went so far as to prohibit (December 1672) "tumultuous petitions," the adjective meaning petitions such as might lead to civil war. Nothwithstanding this prohibition the City of London dared to present another petition urging his Majesty "for the preservation of his royal person and government, and the Protestant religion, he would graciously please to order that parliament, his Great Council, might assemble and sit to take measures against the machinations of Rome."

When, in November 1680, the House did meet, the City sent up another petition. They urged the King to lend an ear to the advice tendered by the House for his own safety and the preservation of the Protestant religion; "they promised to be ready at all times to promote his Majesty's ease and prosperity, and to stand by him against all dangers and hazards whatsoever."

The deputation which presented the petition were bluntly told to go home and mind their own business.

Six months later the City presented another petition expressing surprise at the prorogation of the House, "whereby the prosecution of the public justice of the kingdom has received an interruption," and prayed that the House might resume its sessions on the day to which it had been prorogued as being "the only means

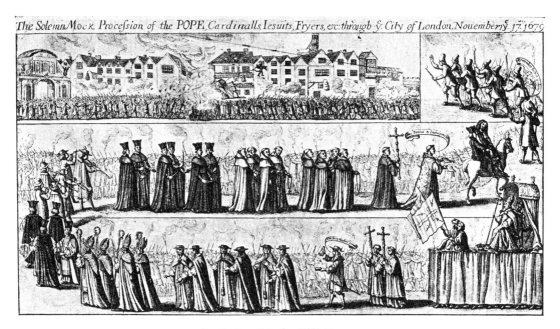

The Solemn Mock Procession of the POPE, Cardinalls, Iesuits, Fryers, &c: through ẙ City of London, Nouember ẙ 17 1679

From the Crace Collection, British Museum.

to quiet the minds and extinguish the fears of your Protestant subjects." The King's answer was the dissolution of Parliament, and the announcement that he would call another for March 1 to sit at Oxford.

All this anxiety meant that the Duke of York was not to succeed if he could be kept out. And Charles, for his part, was not going to take any steps to prevent the succession of his brother.

There were, however, other instruments at work to keep up the anti-Papal feeling. Chief among these was the King's Head Club. The King's Head Tavern stood over against the Inner Temple. The members of the Club were at first Lord Shaftesbury's friends, but others, especially young men of good family, were admitted. In order to be known by each other they wore a green ribbon in their hats. Their principal discourse turned upon the perils of Popery. The true purpose of the founders was to foster the anti-Catholic spirit, and to keep it alive and strong enough to prevent the succession of James. Among other things, for instance, they got up processions, in which the Pope was carried in effigy with two or three devils to decorate his chair. In the end Pope, devils, and all were tumbled into the bonfire.

The Oxford House of Commons lasted a week only. The City presented another address of remonstrance. For a second time they were told to mind their own business.

When a really clever thing is done in the name of the King he always gets the credit of the cleverness. The reduction of the City into a collection of men and women without rights, liberties, or government, other than what the King might grant and allow, was a piece of work which reflects the highest credit on whoever devised it, designed it, or carried it out.

The last years of Charles's reign were occupied in a determined and a successful effort to reduce the Corporation to submission and to make it, so to speak, a pocket borough. In these efforts he completely succeeded. Where the first Charles had failed, the second Charles succeeded.

The petitions of the Corporation were counterbalanced by others from the Borough of Southwark, from the Lieutenancy of London, and from 20,000 'prentices to the opposite effect.

The last of these petitions gave the greatest pleasure to the Court. The loyal 'prentices were rewarded with a splendid banquet given to them in the Merchant Taylors' Hall. The Duke of Grafton, the Earl of Mulgrave, Lord Hyde, and Sir Joseph Williamson acted as stewards, and 1500 tickets were given away among those who had signed the petition. The tickets contained the following invitation : "You are invited, and desired, by the Right Honourable and others of the stewards, elected at a meeting of the loyal young men and addressers, July 28, 1682, to take a dinner (together with other loyal young freemen and apprentices of the City of London) at Merchant Taylors' Hall, on Wednesday the 9th of this instant August, at 12 o'clock." The King himself, to grace the board, sent a brace of "very good bucks." They were carried into the City upright in a cart, stuck with boughs. Three thousand sat down to this entertainment.

Charles, in fact, discovered with joy that there were two parties in the City, and that the loyal party was apparently of strength nearly equal to the "country" party He resolved, therefore, so to manage the conduct of the City as to bring the election of all the officers into the hands of the Royalists—that is to say, into his own hands. The contest began with the election of the Sheriffs.

There had been many attempts made from the commencement of the fourteenth century to take away the election of the Sheriffs from the Commonalty. But in 1347 the Mayor obtained the right, or took the right, of nominating and electing one of the Sheriffs, while the Commonalty elected the other. For 300 years this right was exercised, either without opposition or with faint grumblings.

The Lord Mayor continued to exercise this right for 300 years. In the year

1641, when everything began to be questioned, the Commonalty protested against this custom. The question was referred by the King to the House of Lords, who refused to settle it, ordering that for that year the Mayor's nominee should be chosen by the Commonalty, without prejudice to the Mayor's right in the matter.

Here, then, was established a very pretty ground of quarrel. For the next nine years the Mayor continued to nominate and the Commonalty continued to protest. Then for the following nine years the Mayor abandoned his privilege. But it still remained open for him to claim it and to exercise it. In fact, in 1662 he did both. The Commonalty protested but elected his man. For seven years after this the Mayor continued to exercise his right. In 1674, however, the Common Council appointed a Committee to investigate the case. The Mayor drank, as usual, to the man whom he chose. The Committee recommended an Act of Common Council to settle the question. No such Act was passed.

In 1680 the question proceeded to the acute stage. It was just before the discovery by Charles of the strong Court party in the City.

The Mayor nominated one Hockenhall, who refused to serve, and paid his fine. The Commons therefore elected Slingsby Bethel and Henry Cornish, both men of the Puritan party, and the former a strong republican and an enemy to everything that looked like feasting and joy. The nominees of the Court party who suffered defeat were Box and Nicholson. Cornish refused, for instance, to give the customary dinner to the Aldermen. He was regarded with great aversion by the Court party for his republican tendencies.

In the following year the two Sheriffs, Pilkington and Shute, were of the same party and were elected against the same Court nominees as in the previous year. The King, when the Recorder and the two Sheriffs waited upon him, expressed in the presence of the latter the fact that they were personally unwelcome to him.

One would think that the Common Council had had enough rebuffs over their petitions. But they drew up another, which they presented to the King, with the same result as before.

In September 1681 the Court party got a Mayor of their own, one Sir John Moore. It was their first success. The King expressed his satisfaction at the election of so loyal and worthy a magistrate. And, in order to mark his sense of the late elections of Sheriffs, he issued, in January 1682, a writ calling upon the citizens to show by what warrant they claimed their liberties and franchises :—

"These were (1) the right to be of themselves a body corporate and politic, by the name of mayor, commonalty and citizens of the city of London, (2) the right to have sheriffs of the city and county of London and county of Middlesex, and to name, elect, make and constitute them, and (3) the right of the mayor and aldermen of the city to be justices of the peace and hold Sessions of the Peace" (*Sharpe*, ii. 477).

The City received the writ much as their ancestors had received notice of an

Iter. It was troublesome, but it was lawyers' work. They were not afraid of having exercised any usurpation of rights; let the lawyers deal with it. The lawyers, therefore, took it in hand for a time, and while they prepared the case, matters rested.

LORD MAYOR AND ALDERMEN
From Pennant's *London*, in British Museum.

Meantime the people of the City were ranged definitely into two factions; on the one side were those who stood for rights and liberties; for toleration of religion—it was notorious that they would have no toleration while they were in power—and for Parliamentary government. This party contained the better class of citizens, the merchants, the responsible citizens, and the whole of the Nonconformists. The other party, which remembered the severe times when the theatres were closed and dancing and singing were criminal offences, contained the most of the clergy of the Church of England, all the Catholics, all those who were connected with the old Royalist families, and that powerful body, the 'prentices of London.

The former party was under the leadership of Pilkington ; the latter under that of the Lord Mayor.

The shrievalty of Pilkington was terminated in an extremely disagreeable manner by the Duke of York bringing an action against him for libel. The Sheriff was accused of saying that the Duke had burned down the City and was going to cut the throats of the citizens. The Duke had little cause to be friendly with the City, where his portrait had been cut and hacked, and where such things were openly said about him. At the same time it was a vindictive action, and one which he did not dare to have tried in a City court. He removed it, one knows not by what authority, to the county of Hertford, where it was heard by a packed jury. It is quite uncertain whether Pilkington uttered the words attributed to him. Alderman Sir Henry Tulse and Sir William Hooker swore that he did say these words. Sir Patience Ward swore that if the words were said, it was before Pilkington's arrival on the scene. However, there was no hesitation on the part of the jury. They found for the plaintiff with £100,000 damages.

The name of Pilkington belongs to two or three Protestant champions of a somewhat earlier time. Thomas Pilkington, born about 1620, the son of a country gentleman of good family, like so many London citizens, was probably related to, or descended from, James Pilkington, Bishop of Durham, Leonard Pilkington, Master of St. John's, Cambridge, and Richard Pilkington, Archdeacon of Leicester ; all these were controversialists in their generation. Thomas Pilkington, therefore, had Protestantism in his blood. He was Master of the Skinners' Company, one of the City members, Alderman of Farringdon Without, and, as we have seen, Sheriff in 1681.

He was a marked man at Court ; not only did he never disguise his principles, but entertained at his house Shaftesbury, Essex, and other leaders of the Whig party.

On hearing the result of the libel case he made no effort to escape but quietly surrendered to the bail, was committed to prison, and resigned his aldermanry, to which Sheriff North succeeded. He remained in prison four years, when the King released him. Sir Patience Ward, for giving evidence in his favour, was proceeded against for perjury and found guilty. Like Lord Shaftesbury he took refuge in Holland.

To complete the history of Pilkington. When the opportunity arrived he did his best to send James on his travels and to welcome William ; he was reinstated in his office of Alderman ; he was three times Lord Mayor, and at his first installation banquet he entertained the King and Queen.

Before the trial which condemned him, Pilkington had to take his part in the election of the new Sheriffs, June 24, 1682.

It was not to be thought that the Lord Mayor would neglect his opportunity of securing one of the Sheriffs for his own side. He therefore drank to one Dudley North, and issued a precept to the companies to meet for the purpose of informing his nominee and electing another Sheriff. The following is his letter (*Maitland*, i. p. 474) :—

" BY THE MAYOR.

"These are to require you, That on Midsummer-Day next, being the Day appointed as well for Confirmation of the Person WHO HATH BEEN BY ME CHOSEN, according to the ancient Custom and Constitution of this City, to be one of the Sheriffs of this City and County of Middlesex for the Year ensuing, as for the Election of the other of the said Sheriffs, and other officers, you cause the Livery of your Company to meet together at your common Hall early in the Morning, and from thence to come together decently and orderly in their Gowns to Guildhall, there to make the said Confirmation and Election. Given the Nineteenth of June, 1682. JOHN MOOR."

On Midsummer Day, we read, the Liverymen assembled in the Guildhall in great numbers. When the Mayor and Aldermen were arrived upon the Hustings, the Common Crier made proclamation: "You Gentlemen of the Livery of London, attend your Confirmation;" upon which there arose a tumult of voices crying, "No Confirmation! No Confirmation!" and so continued for half an hour. The Recorder at last procured silence and made a speech upon their privileges. The Lord Mayor and Aldermen then withdrew, and the Common Serjeant offered to speak amid cries of "Election! Election! To the Day's Work!"

The question of confirmation was shelved, and there were put in nomination for Sheriffs, Dudley North and Ralph Box, of the Court side, and Thomas Papillon and John Dubois, of the other side.

On a show of hands the two latter had an enormous majority. But a poll was demanded. It was noticed that a great many persons were present who had no right of entry, not being citizens; they carried swords and insulted the Liverymen and endeavoured to make a disturbance. In this they were unsuccessful. About seven in the evening the Lord Mayor came to the Hall and ordered all to depart till three days later. But the Sheriffs took no notice of this order and continued the Poll, hoping to finish that day. At nine o'clock, there being three or four thousand people in the Guildhall, the Sheriff closed for the day, and adjourned the Poll till the Tuesday following (it was then Saturday).

So the Sheriffs went home, followed by crowds crying out "God bless the Protestant Sheriffs! God bless Papillon and Dubois!" This was construed into a riot, for which the Sheriffs Pilkington and Shute were committed to the Tower, but immediately afterwards admitted to bail. On the 1st of July they met a Common Hall, and refusing to obey the order of the Lord Mayor to adjourn the meeting, declared Papillon and Dubois duly elected Sheriffs.

Had the Sheriffs the right to ignore the Mayor's orders? That remained to be proved. Meantime on the 7th the Mayor repaired to the Guildhall to carry on the Poll, taking no notice of the Sheriffs' proceedings. There was a dispute, naturally, and the Mayor adjourned the Hall until the 11th.

The matter was laid before the King, who decided that a new election should take place. Sharpe gives two versions of what took place at this new election.

According to the official account, Dudley North was duly confirmed and gave his consent to take office. On taking votes for the other three, Papillon had 60 voices, Dubois 60, and Box 1244. Therefore Box was elected.

According to a tract of the time, a separate poll was opened on the same day by the Sheriffs; all four candidates were submitted to the Hall. Only 107 voted for the confirmation of North, and 2414 against it. After the declaration of this result the Mayor caused the reading of the other, which caused so great an uproar that the Mayor and Aldermen left the Hall, and the Sheriffs declared Papillon and Dubois duly elected.

Then petitions were drawn up, praying that as Papillon and Dubois had been duly elected, the Court would call them; also that a *caveat* should be entered against North and Box being admitted. The Mayor returned an evasive answer. The huge majority in favour of Box at the Mayor's poll is explained by a remark of Maitland, that nobody voted for Papillon and Dubois because they had already carried them at the Sheriffs' poll.

Box at this point retired, paying the fine. The Mayor therefore ordered another Common Hall for the election of his successor, and put forward one Peter Rich. There was a great tumult in the Hall. The people shouted for their own men, Papillon and Dubois; the Mayor, going through the ceremony in dumb show, declared Rich duly elected. He then dissolved the Common Hall and went home. Then the Sheriffs proceeded to open the Poll, and found 2082 votes in favour of their former choice, and only 35 for Rich.

The Sheriffs—who were still Pilkington and Shute—proclaimed the result of the Poll, and the election of Papillon and Dubois.

Then the Mayor and some of the Aldermen went to Whitehall and informed the King what had happened. The Sheriffs were summoned before the Council. They were ordered to enter in their own recognizances for £1000.

Two days afterwards Rich and North were sworn in as Sheriffs, the Guildhall being guarded by the trained bands. It was ominous of the feeling in the City that the Mercers' Company, to which North belonged, refused to pay him the common compliment of going with him to the Guildhall on entering upon office.

So far the Court had won. They now had the Lord Mayor and the Sheriffs; the next thing was to secure the successor to the Mayoralty.

This was done, apparently, by making a false return of the votes. Four

Aldermen were put up. The Poll placed first and second on the list Gold and Cornish, both belonging to the popular side. A scrutiny was made by the Court of Aldermen (October 24) that maintained this result, but the Mayor, on the 25th, brought in a result which put Pritchard, a man of the Court party, at the head of the list. It is true that the first difference between Gold and Pritchard was only 56, so that a very little manipulation was required.

In order to obtain a Royalist Common Council, Charles ordered that none should be elected who had not conformed to the Corporation Act.

In February 1683 the hearing of the *Quo Warranto* case came on. The points at issue have already been detailed. The pleadings in the case may be found in Maitland.

The following judgment was pronounced by Mr. Justice Jones on June 12 :—

"That a city might forfeit its Charter; that the Malversations of the Common Council were the Acts of the whole City; and that the two Points set forth in the Pleadings were just grounds for the forfeiting of a Charter. Upon which Premises the proper Conclusion seemed to be, That therefore the City of London had forfeited their Charter."

The Attorney-General moved that the judgment might not be recorded. After this judgment the City was greatly astonished and perplexed. The popular party wanted to enter the judgment and to leave the King to do what he pleased. The Court party were for absolute surrender of their liberties and submission to the King. Maitland gives in full a paper which was circulated at that time, showing what would be lost if the City surrendered its Charter :—

"There being so great a Murmur, and so much discourse, that the Charter of this City of London is to be made forfeit, or else surrendered by a Common Council, 'tis fit for every member of this City to understand, that the Meaning or Intent of such a Forfeiture or Surrender, is to dissolve the Body Corporate or Politic of the City, to spoil it irrecoverably of all its antient Government, Laws, Customs and Rights, which have been its glory throughout Europe near two thousand Years, to bring it into the same State with the Country Villages, only capable to be created a new Body politick by the Grace and Favour of his Majesty, and to obtain such Privileges as the Crown can grant, which are infinitely inferior to the Customs, Franchises, Rights and Government it now holds by the Laws and Statutes of the Kingdom.

If then there be any Danger either of a Forfeiture or Surrender of this City's Charter, every Member of it is concerned, not only in Interest, but in Duty, to contribute what Assistance he can to perserve and secure it.

For that Purpose every Citizen upon taking his Freedom is sworn to maintain the Franchise and customs of the City, and to keep the City harmless, to his Power; and whatsoever Citizen shall openly attempt, or privately contrive, the Destruction of the Corporation, its Customs, or Franchises, betrays the Community, and violates his said oath, from which no Power on Earth can absolve."

The writer then enumerates all the rights, privileges, and possessions which the City would lose, never to regain them again, and concludes :—

"The death of a Corporation reduceth it to nothing; and 'twill then be, as if it had never been, in respect of Debts or Credits; there can be no Successor, Heir, or Executor to demand or answer for the Body that was:

Therefore all the Goods and Chatels of the City must fall to the King, to be given and disposed of, as he pleaseth.

And all its Lands and real Estate in the Exchange, Guildhall, etc., must of right revert unto the Heirs of the Donors, if there be any, or escheat to the Crown, for want of such Heirs.

But the Face of Confusion is so full of Horror, that will appear after the Dissolution of this mighty Body by Forfeiture or Surrender of its Charter, that I tremble to look upon it afar off.

The Lord Cook says, It would require a Volume of itself to treat of the great and notable Franchises, Liberties and Customs of this City. And no less a Volume would be necessary to describe the Disorders, Losses, Distractions, Mischiefs and Confusions that must attend the Destruction and the Death of so great a Body Politick.

And the City of London by this Means, which is now one of the antientest Cities in the whole World, will at the time of such Surrender be the youngest City and Corporation in England" (*Maitland*, i. pp. 481, 482).

However, the City submitted.

They were informed by the Lord Keeper that the King accepted their submission in consideration of the many loyal citizens in London, but with conditions, which were as follows :—

" 1. That no Lord Mayor, Sheriff, Recorder, Common-Serjeant, Town-Clerk, or Coroner of the City of London, or Steward of the Borough of Southwark, shall be capable of, or admitted to, the Exercise of their respective Offices, before his Majesty shall have approved them under his Sign Manual.

2. That, if his Majesty shall disapprove the Choice of any Person to be Lord Mayor, and signify the same under his Sign-Manual to the Lord Mayor, or, in default of a Lord Mayor, to the Recorder, or senior Alderman, the Citizens shall within one Week proceed to a new Choice. And, if his Majesty shall in like Manner disapprove the second Choice, his Majesty may, if he please, nominate a Person to be Lord Mayor for the ensuing Year.

3. If his Majesty shall, in like Manner, disapprove the Persons chosen to be Sheriffs, or either of them, his Majesty may appoint Persons to be Sheriffs for the ensuing Year by his Commission, if so he please.

4. That the Lord Mayor, and Court of Aldermen may also, with the Leave of his Majesty, displace any Alderman, Recorder, etc., *ut supra*.

5. Upon the Election of an Alderman, if the Court of Aldermen shall judge and declare the Person presented to be unfit, the Ward shall chuse again ; and, upon a Disapproval of a second Choice, the Court may appoint another in his Room.

6. The Justices of the Peace are to be by the King's Commission ; and the settling of these matters to be left to his Majesty's Attorney and Solicitor-General, and Council learned in Law."

The City were also informed that if they accepted these conditions all would be well with them. If, on the other hand, they refused, the Attorney-General would enter upon judgment on the following Saturday.

The Court of Common Council was called to consider the propositions. Some of them declared that rather than accept such slavish conditions they would sacrifice everything. But, by a majority of eighteen, the conditions were accepted.

While these things were going on Papillon obtained a writ of Latitat on an action upon this case against the Mayor, Dudley North, and some of the Aldermen. They were all served with this writ by one Brown, an attorney, and a clerk to the Skinners' Company. He not only served them with the writ, but he arrested them all and carried them off to Skinners' Hall, where he kept them as prisoners till one o'clock in the morning. He was then, however, himself arrested for debt and carried off to the Compter, so that the prisoners were able to walk home.

This story to my mind, untrained in legal subtleties, is mysterious. By whose authority could the chief magistrate of the City be arrested within his own jurisdiction? And why did the Lord Mayor, the Sheriff, and the Aldermen go meekly in the custody of an attorney-clerk to a City company?

The conclusion of the story, however, is an action brought by Pritchard when his time of office was expired. It was heard before Judge Jeffreys, and resulted in damages against Papillon of £10,000. He therefore made haste to put the sea between himself and prison.

Then came the question whether the City should voluntarily surrender their liberties. The Recorder was strongly against this step; if they freely surrendered their liberties there would be no redress open to them; if they did not and judgment was entered, they could take proceedings by writ of error. Finally, by 103 to 85 it was resolved not to surrender.

Judgment was therefore entered against the City. The King was now therefore absolutely master of the City. He allowed Pritchard to continue as Mayor and the two Sheriffs to remain; eight Aldermen were dismissed; sixteen were made Justices of the Peace; the Recorder was dismissed and another appointed, and Sir Henry Tulse was nominated Mayor to succeed Pritchard.

Now had Charles the First been clever enough at the outset to secure and use for his own interest the Court party in the City, all his troubles might have been avoided. On the other hand, had Charles the Second begun his reign instead of ending it with the enslaving of the City, he might have died the same death as his father, with the certainty that there would have been none to lament him. The City was not yet, however, made safe; there remained the companies. These also, being served with a *Quo Warranto*, had to surrender their charters and receive new ones with certain trifling conditions.

I have said nothing of the national aspect of this struggle. Let us remind ourselves that the conquest of London was only part of the conquest of the kingdom; that the triumph of despotism in London was accompanied by the triumph of despotism in the country. The country party was broken up. Shaftesbury had fled; with him many of the London merchants; Essex had committed suicide; Lord Russell and Algernon Sidney had been executed; Monmouth had fled. The towns attacked, like London, with *Quo Warranto*, surrendered their charters and received them back, with conditions. Oxford had declared for passive obedience. All but the most thorough loyalists were excluded from the franchise; Charles had the representation of every borough in his own hands. More than this, he had an army of 10,000 men.

The wonderful ability with which this Revolution was effected may be credited to Charles's ministers; one seems, however, to perceive the King's brain devising and the King's hand executing the whole. And the master-stroke of all was that by which he acquired the whole power; he violated no law and executed no overt acts of tyranny. He was using the forms and institutions of liberty for the purpose of crushing liberty. He did not even restore old abuses; the Star Chamber and the Court of High Commission did not reappear. Freedom of the press was granted. The Habeas Corpus Act was passed. And the City of London, stripped of all real power, retained the form of it, and on the strength of the form seemed to preserve the old loyalty and the old personal affection for the King who had taken away its powers and its privileges. And this was even a more wonderful achievement for Charles than his triumph. Yet the loyalty and the affection were but forms and shadows like the ghostly form of its liberties left to the City.

What the King would have done with his absolute authority one knows not, because in the very hour of his success he was stricken down by death. I have refrained from speaking much of Charles's Court, because by this time the Court and the City were entirely separate, and were drifting apart more and more. Yet one cannot avoid asking what the better class of people, what the baser sort, knew of the Court and the life led by King Charles and his courtiers. Something of the King's mistresses they knew; witness the well-known story of Nell Gwynne and the mob; witness also that other story of the riot in 1668 when the 'prentices pulled down and wrecked certain disorderly houses in Moorfields, saying that they did "ill in contenting themselves with pulling down the little brothels and did not go to pull down the big one at Whitehall." Eight of the rioters were hanged for this offence, which did not stop the appearance of the Remonstrance pretending to be a petition from the women whose houses had been destroyed to the King's mistresses at Whitehall. But they could not have known the corruption, the venality, and the profligacy of Whitehall; that could only be learned by the *habitués;* there were no papers to spread the infamy abroad; there was no fierce light of journalism thrown upon the King's private life.

The general belief concerning the Court of Charles II. is that it presented to the world nothing but a long-continued pageant of profligacy, extravagance, luxury, waste, and open contempt of morals. We remember Evelyn's often-quoted account of the last Sunday evening before the fatal seizure; Pepys tell us what he saw and heard; De Grammont's book is well known to all; the name and the fame and the shame of the King's mistresses are notorious; the men seem devoid of honour, and the women match the men. It appears, to one who would restore the palace in the days of the Merry Monarch, that all day long the courts of Whitehall echo with the tinkling guitar; at every window is a light o' love; below one of these the King converses gaily and carelessly; we hear the laughter, loud and coarse, of the titled harlots; with painted faces and languishing eyes they roll by in their coaches; the singing boys practise the latest part song by Tom D'Urfey; the courtiers are loud with ribald jest.   I suppose that these things cannot be denied.   It is, however, a great mistake to suppose that there was no serious side to the Court.   In the first place, it is impossible to conduct the business of the kingdom without an immense amount of ceremony and state.   Charles was not an Edward the Second; there is nothing to show that he did not do what was expected of a king with as much dignity as his father, even though he did not take himself so seriously.   There were

NELL GWYNNE (1650-1687)
From the painting by Sir Peter Lely in the National Portrait Gallery, London,

grave and weighty troubles and difficulties in his reign; domestic troubles such as the Fire of London; foreign troubles such as the war with the Dutch; the King's counsellors were for the most part grave and serious men.   Add to this that every officer in the numerous household and following of the King desired and expected his rank and dignity to be respected.

There were daily duties to be performed.   The King held a levée every morning; he went in state to prayers; he received his ministers and sat at the Council; he dined in public; the Court was open to any one who might venture to claim the rank and consideration of a gentleman; the King was accessible to all.

The quiet, dull Court of the Georges was a new thing altogether in the land. Charles kept open house, like the kings of France. He walked fearlessly and almost unattended in the Park and in his gardens; one cannot, I repeat, deny the gambling, singing, and love-making which the King permitted and encouraged; but I plead for Charles that amount of serious attention to his state and dignity of his position, no small amount, which was necessary for the mere maintenance of kingship. In other things the laxness of his morals did not prevent the assertion of his prerogative, especially in his dealings with the City of London. No king before him, for instance, had dared to inflict upon the City so enormous a fine as that when Charles shut up the Exchequer and robbed the merchants of a million and a half of money. This one action, so bold, so calculated both as to the occasion and the probable impotence of the City to resist it, ought to be alone sufficient to set aside completely the old theory of the jaded voluptuary. It was not, again, the jaded voluptuary who plotted, planned, and carried out the destruction of the City liberties; it was a Stuart, with all the cleverness of his race, with all the tenacity of his father and his brother, and with all the inability to discern the forces that were arrayed against him and to comprehend the certainty of their success. He died in the moment of his success, leaving to his brother the fruits of his despotic measures in ruin and deposition (*see* Appendix I.).

A Perspective of WESTMINSTER-ABBEY from the High-Altar to the West end shewing the manner of His Majesties CROWNING.

THE CORONATION OF JAMES II. IN WESTMINSTER ABBEY

From a contemporary print.   E. Gardner's Collection.

CHAPTER VII

JAMES II

THE short reign of James afforded to the City a time of continual surprises and ceaseless anxiety, with the corresponding emotions of joy, sorrow, disappointment, and despair.

The reign began with an assurance that the established government, that of Church and State, would be respected and maintained. The King, however, showed

TITUS OATES FLOGGED AT THE CART TAIL

what he understood by the proclamation when he continued to receive the customs which had been settled on Charles for life, and which could not be exacted by his successor without the assent of Parliament. James announced his intention of speedily calling a Parliament at the same time as he proclaimed his continuance of taking the customs. In the same illegal way he took over the excise duties.

Meantime the Mayor and Aldermen, in accordance with the successful craft of Charles, were mostly nominees of the King; they were instructed to admit to the liveries of the City Companies none but persons of "unquestionable loyalty"; so that, as Charles had provided, the whole of the governing bodies in the City were mere creatures of the Court.

One can hardly be surprised at the arrest and punishment of Titus Oates when James succeeded. At the same time to flog a man all the way from Aldgate to Newgate, and two days afterwards from Newgate to Tyburn, seems, short of the tortures of a Damiens,[1] the most horrible barbarity ever inflicted on a criminal since the time when a Roman could flog a slave to death. The first day's march at the cart tail was a mile and a quarter in length; the next was over two miles and a half. Titus was flogged the whole way, with an interval of two days. If the cart was driven slowly, as was always the case, say at the rate of three miles an hour, and if the whip descended fifteen times a minute, the wretched man would receive 375 lashes on the first day, and two days after he would receive 750 lashes. Perhaps the

TITUS OATES IN THE PILLORY

executioner was less rapid in his movements; perhaps the cart moved more quickly. Perhaps the executioner was one of the many who still believed in the perjured wretch and sympathised with him. Yet even the closest friend would have to make a show of laying it on with a will. The man survived, showing how much agony a man may suffer before it kills him.

Short as was the reign of James, it provided for the Londoners many other scenes and dramatic situations.

On July 15 the populace gathered together in immense crowds to witness the execution of the unfortunate Duke of Monmouth. They brought him out of the Tower surrounded by a strong guard, while commanding officers had orders to shoot the prisoner should any attempt be made at a rescue. This was more than probable, seeing that in the vast concourse of people who were collected on Tower Hill, nine out of ten wished in their hearts that the Protestant champion had won the day at Sedgemoor, while some of them had even been with him on that fatal night, though they were by no means anxious that their friends should know the fact. The prisoner, still young, still the loveliest man to look upon in the three kingdoms, mounted the scaffold; he showed a firm countenance at the end. Did any of the spectators ask each other whether this handsome face had in it the slightest sign of kinship with the black and dour face of Charles? He knelt down; the headsman, trembling, delivered three strokes, then threw down the axe and swore he would not go on; but, taking up the axe again, in two more strokes severed the head from the body. Then the people, sick and sorry, returned to their homes.

The fall of Monmouth offered an opening, which James was not likely to forego, for the enjoyment of private revenge, and for giving a lesson to zealous Protestants.

[1] Damiens in 1757 made an attempt on the life of Louis XV., for which he was first tortured, and then torn to pieces by wild horses. Brewer's *Dictionary*.

Henry Cornish, late Sheriff, had shown activity against Catholics on the occasion of the Rye House Plot.   Let him, therefore, be legally murdered.

Henry Cornish was by trade a "factor"; was Alderman of the Ward of Bassishaw, and a resident in Cateaton Street.   As we have seen, he was made Sheriff in 1680 with Slingsby Bethel.   The events connected with his election were not calculated to make him a *persona grata* with the Court.   He was not only a Whig but a Presbyterian.   He was one of the five Aldermen chosen for the defence

DUKE OF MONMOUTH (1649-1685)
From an engraving after Sir Peter Lely.

of the civic liberties against the *Quo Warranto*.   In February 1683 Cornish, with Pilkington, Shute, Bethel, Sir Thomas Player, the City Chamberlain, and Lord Grey of Wark, were brought to trial for the disturbances in June of the preceding year.   They were all found guilty and all were fined; Cornish, for his part, had to pay a fine of 1000 marks.   He had already been tricked out of his election to the office of Mayor by wholesale tampering with the votes.   At the time of the Rye House Conspiracy, one John Rumsay, arrested on suspicion, offered to give evidence implicating Cornish.   At the time his offer was not accepted.

Then James succeeded.   Evidently he regarded Cornish as one of his most dangerous enemies.   He waited until the Monmouth rebellion gave him an excuse. There had been an actual rebellion ; if it could be proved that Cornish had any hand in it, there would be a way of getting rid of him.

Monmouth was executed on July 15.   Three months passed, during which nothing was done to Cornish.   This interval was employed, it is now certain, in getting up a case against him ; we cannot suppose that James was ignorant of this plot—it was nothing less—to take the life of the sturdy Whig.   The man Rumsey found another man, a private enemy to Cornish, named Goodenough, to join him in bearing witness which should implicate Cornish in the Rye House Plot and show

THE EXECUTION OF MONMOUTH, JULY 15, 1685
From a contemporary Dutch print.   E. Gardner's Collection.

him to be a friend of Monmouth.   On Tuesday, the 13th of October, Cornish was arrested and taken to Newgate.   On the Saturday he learned for the first time that he was in prison on a charge of high treason, and that he would be tried on the Monday.   The trial took place accordingly.   It was marked by the customary brow-beating and bullying.   The man must have known that he was doomed ; the fact that two days only were allowed him to prepare his case and bring forward his witnesses might have warned him what to expect.

[1] " His attitude before the judges was calm and dignified.   Before pleading not guilty to the charge of having consented to aid and abet the late Duke of Monmouth and others in their attempt on the life of the late King (the Rye House Plot), he entered a protest against the indecent haste with which he had been called upon to

[1] Sharpe, ii. p. 512.

plead, and the short time allowed him to prepare his case. He asked for further time, but this the judges refused.

One of the chief witnesses for the Crown was Goodenough, who had a personal spite against Cornish for his having objected to him (Goodenough) serving as under-sheriff in 1680-81, the year when Bethel and Cornish were sheriffs. Goodenough had risked his neck in Monmouth's late rebellion, but he had succeeded in obtaining a pardon by promises of valuable information against others. With the King's pardon in his pocket he unblushingly declared before the judges that he, as well as Cornish and some others, had determined upon a general rising in the city at the time of the Rye House Plot. 'We designed,' said he, 'to divide it (*i.e.* the city) into twenty parts, and out of each part to raise five hundred men, if it might be done, to make an insurrection.' The Tower was to be seized and the guard expelled.

Cornish had been afforded no opportunity for instructing counsel in his defence. He was therefore obliged to act as his own counsel, with the result usual in such cases. He rested his main defence upon the improbability of his having acted as the prosecution endeavoured to make out. This he so persistently urged that the judges lost patience. Improbability was not enough, they declared; let him call his witnesses. When, however, Cornish desired an adjournment, in order that he might bring a witness up from Lancashire, his request was refused. His chief witness he omitted to call until after the Lord Chief Justice had summed up. This man was a vintner of the city, named Shephard, at whose house Cornish was charged with having met and held consultation with Monmouth and the rest of the conspirators. The Bench after some demur assented to the prisoner's earnest prayer that Shephard's evidence might be taken. He showed that he had been in the habit of having commercial transactions with Cornish and was at that moment in his debt; that on the occasion in question Cornish had come to his house, but whether he came to speak with the Duke of Monmouth or not the witness could not say for certain; that he only remained a few minutes, and that no paper or declaration (on which so much stress had been laid) in connection with the conspiracy was read in Cornish's presence; that in fact Cornish was not considered at the time as being in the plot. Such evidence, if not conclusive, ought to have gone far towards obtaining a verdict of acquittal for the prisoner. This was not the case, however. The jury, after a brief consultation, brought in a verdict of guilty, and Cornish had to submit to the indignity of being tied—like a dangerous criminal—whilst sentence of death was passed upon him and three others who had been tried at the same time.

The prisoner was allowed but three clear days before he was hanged at the corner of King Street and Cheapside, within sight of the Guildhall, which he had so often frequented as an Alderman of the City, and on which his head was afterwards placed. He met his end with courage and with many pious expressions, but to the last maintained his innocence with such vehemence that his enemies gave out that he had died in a fit of fury."

It is pleasing to add that four years later an Act of Parliament was passed reversing the attainder of Cornish. It is also pleasing to think that the blood of this innocent man, like the blood of the martyrs, was remembered by his fellow-citizens, that it strengthened the side of freedom and accelerated the fall of James.

On the same day the people of London had a choice between two spectacles: that of Henry Cornish's hanging, which was calculated to make every citizen thoughtful; or that of the burning of Elizabeth Gaunt at Tyburn—an act of brutal wickedness which ought to have made every citizen mad with indignation. Elizabeth Gaunt was a woman of great piety and charity; she visited the prisoners in the gaols; she relieved the sick; she fed the poor; she helped all who were afflicted, or in want, or in danger. Among others she helped a man named Burton, who was an outlaw, to escape. For this she was actually burned alive! The wretched man, Burton, turned King's evidence and informed against his benefactress. One feels that it would be a moral lesson if we could ascertain the after-lives of Messrs. Rumsey, Goodenough, and Burton. The unfortunate gentlewoman behaved with fortitude, arranging with her own hands the straw around her so that she might the more quickly die. To us it seems incredible that judges should pass such sentences or should have such cases as those of Henry Cornish and Elizabeth Gaunt brought before them. As for the effect produced by these executions, they might, and no doubt did, terrify for a short time, but it was a terror which led to exasperation.

We must remember that the temper of the City during the whole of the seventeenth century was profoundly hostile to the Catholics. The Gunpowder Plot; the Romish leanings of Laud; the Fire of London; the so-called Romanist plots; the Protestant literature of the period; the terrible stories of the Spanish Inquisition; everything conspired to keep alive the hatred and suspicion of the Catholic Church. And an event which happened in October 1685 taught the people, who were ripe for such a lesson, what was to be expected of a Roman Catholic Government.

From time to time London has been enriched by the arrival of foreigners—Danes, Normans, Flemings, Italians, Palatines—who have brought with them new industries, and have settled down among the people, becoming English in the next generation. The most important of these immigrations was that of 1685, which came over here from France in consequence of the Revocation of the Edict of Nantes, under which the Protestants of France had enjoyed the freedom of worshipping according to their own religion. A great many of them—probably about 60,000—came to this country, bringing with them what money they had, amounting, as was estimated, to £3,000,000. Among them were artificers of various kinds, especially silk-weavers, gold and silversmiths, watchmakers and carvers.

These refugees came over just before the death of Charles the Second; they were received with warm welcome; collections were made for them. There can be no doubt that the presence of these victims to Catholic bigotry largely stimulated the feeling against Catholicism which two or three years later ended in the expulsion of James. They were always in evidence. "See," they said, "we are Protestants like yourselves; we have been driven from our own country for no other crime but our religion. What will happen to you when your King has had his own way and turned this country again to the Roman Catholic faith?" This was a question which was

JAMES II. (1633-1701)

asked by everybody, and answered by every man and woman, however mean and illiterate, by one word.

With all these facts before him, in the face of feeling so strong that it seems impossible that he could fail to understand it, James persisted in his purpose. Perhaps he relied on assurances of support from the Catholic gentry; perhaps he thought of using Irish troops; perhaps he even looked forward to assistance from Louis; perhaps he counted on Roman Catholic officers carrying with them the army. However this may be, James resolved that there should be no mistake about his intentions. The laws against the Catholics were disregarded. Roman Catholic chapels were openly built and the Romish services were openly performed in them; there were tumults in the City; the mob would have no wooden gods and tore down the crucifix; they put up a cross and mocked it; they set upon the priests and ill-treated them; they would not believe that the Mayor really wished them to disperse. The trained bands actually refused to disperse the crowd while they were engaged on such pious work. Then James took a step which at first sight appears clever; it was really most unwise. He issued the famous Declaration of Indulgence which suspended all laws against Catholics and Dissenters alike. The Church of England, as he was going to find, was stronger than Roman Catholics and Dissenters put together. Indeed, many of the Dissenters very clearly understood that the Declaration was simply a measure of relief for the Catholics.

James next took up his late brother's plan, which was to gain over the Corporations in the country; six Commissioners were sent round to turn out all those persons who were in favour of the Test Act and the penal laws. The companies of London were treated in this way, with the result that some 900 persons were turned out of the Courts of Assistants. As for the City itself, which, it must be understood, was still deprived of its charter, Jeffreys was instructed to inform the Aldermen that in future their Court should recommend to the Crown persons fit to be Aldermen. Many of the Aldermen resigned rather than vote an address to the King for this liberty, which was in reality another link in the chain which kept the City in servitude. Recommending to the King is not exactly the same thing as free election. However, they did recommend and nominate persons to serve, but it was found extremely difficult to get any one to accept office. No less than £8500 were paid in fines by those who refused.

In a very short time the City offices were nearly all held by Dissenters. A Dissenter was Lord Mayor, one Sir John Shorter, said to be an Anabaptist. The installation of Sir John was accompanied by a great dinner, to which every Alderman contributed £50; the King was present, with the Queen and the Papal Nuncio. The City Companies had turned out most of their Church of England members, and the Lord Mayor, Sir John Shorter, "a very odd, ignorant person, a mechanic, I think, and an Anabaptist" (Evelyn), openly attended a conventicle every Sunday.

Among those who accepted office was William Kiffin. He was a leading Nonconformist in the City. Two of his grandsons, Benjamin and William Hewling, had been executed by Jeffreys for their share in the Monmouth rebellion. He was just seventy years of age, and had retired from active business when the King sent for him and made him accept office by telling him that if he refused he might be fined £20,000 or £30,000, or anything that the judges pleased. So the old man accepted. His account of the work entrusted to the Court of Aldermen is amazing. The King used to send them lists of liverymen who were to be turned out of their companies, with other lists of those to be put in. There were seven hundred so discharged without any charge or accusation, and all Protestants of the Church of England.

The winter of 1687-88 passed quietly; but there were messengers secretly passing between London and Holland and the end was rapidly approaching. The King received addresses from all quarters thanking him for his Declaration of Indulgence; not only from Nonconformists about the country, but from the newly reformed City Companies, of whom, however, not all were found to join in the cry of gratitude. It would seem, however, as if the absence of any rebellion, coupled with the fact of their dutiful addresses, made James believe that he had a clear majority in support of his Declaration of Indulgence. He seems never to have understood the strength and the magnitude of the Established Church, just as he

THE SEVEN BISHOPS ON THE WAY TO THE TOWER
From a contemporary print. E. Gardner's Collection.

certainly never understood the strength and the extent of the popular hatred of his own Church. To the latter form of ignorance we may ascribe James's acts and their consequences. He could not understand how the Catholic Church could be so deeply hated. Himself the son of a Catholic; his second wife a Catholic; his brother's wife a Catholic; surrounded by Catholics in his own house, he was in no way able to comprehend why the country hated and feared his religion. In the same way the mediæval Jew could not understand that he was loathed and hated. Why should he be? He was a man, like the Christian, of similar body, parts, and passions. He could never understand it. Now that loathing has become a thing of the past, he cannot yet understand it. So with James; he could not understand it.

In the spring, therefore, of 1688 James, still unable to understand, issued a

Second Declaration of Indulgence. Another interesting and dramatic spectacle was, in consequence of this mistake, provided by James for his loving subjects of London. This was the carriage of the Seven Bishops by water to the Tower. Their arrest was the King's reply to their petition praying that the clergy might not be compelled to read the Second Declaration of Indulgence from the pulpit in the midst of public service. Only a few of the London clergy obeyed the order; one of them told the people that though he was ordered to read it, they were not ordered to hear it, and so waited till the Church was empty before he read it. In some churches the

1. The King.
2. The Prince of Denmark.
3, 4. The Archbishops of Canterbury and York.
5. The Speaker.

6. The Chancellor with the Great Seal.
7. The Bishops, twenty-five in number.
8. The Dukes and Peers.
9. The Members sitting on Woolsacks.

10. The Barons and Lords of the Kingdom.
11, 12. The Lawyers.
13. The Herald.
14. The Spectators.

PARLIAMENT IN THE REIGN OF JAMES II.
E. Gardner's Collection.

congregation, with one accord, rose and left the church as soon as the clergyman began to read the Declaration.

The objections of the Bishops are stated by Evelyn :—

"Not that they were averse to the publishing of it for want of due tendernesse towards Dissenters, in relation to whom they should be willing to come to such a temper as should be thought fit, when that matter might be consider'd and settl'd in Parliament and Convocation; but that, the Declaration being founded on such a dispensing power as might at pleasure set aside all Laws Ecclesiastical and Civil, it appear'd to them illegal, as it had done to the Parliament in 1661 and 1672, and that it was a point of such consequence that they could not so far make themselves parties to it, as the reading of it in Church in time of divine service amounted to."

The Bishops were sent to the Tower for refusing to give bail, "as it would have prejudiced their Peerage. The concern of the people," says Evelyn, "was wonderful, infinite crowds on their knees begging their blessing and praying for them as they passed out of the barge along the Tower wharf."

That was on the 8th of June. On the 13th Evelyn visited four of the Bishops in the Tower. On the 15th they were brought to Westminster, where their indictment was read and they were called in to plead. They were called upon to give bail, but they refused ; in the end they were dismissed on their own recognizances to appear that day fortnight.

JUDGE JEFFREYS (1648-1689)
From a print in the British Museum.

On the 29th they appeared and the trial took place. It lasted from nine in the morning until six in the evening. At that hour the jury, who had been drawn from Middlesex, not from London, retired to consider their verdict. They could not at first agree, and were locked up all night. All were for acquittal except one. At last he, too, agreed with the others.

"When this was heard," says Evelyn, "there was great rejoicing : and there was a lane of people from the King's Bench to the waterside on their knees, as the Bishops passed and repassed, to beg their blessing. Bonfires were made that night and bells rung, which was taken very ill at Court."

It is pleasing to note that the Bishops not only refused to give bail, but refused to pay any fees to the Lieutenant of the Tower.

It was during their short imprisonment that the Prince of Wales, the Elder Pretender, was born, " which will cause disputes," says Evelyn.

8

Well assured of the spirit in which he would be received, the Prince of Orange made haste to prepare for his descent on England. In September the news came that a fleet of sixty sail was in readiness. Then James began to make concessions. The City should have its charter returned. This was done. But the City was no more inclined to Catholicism than before.

The rest we know; William landed on the 5th of November.

James sent for the Mayor and Aldermen, entrusted the care of the City to them, and instructed them, should he fall in battle, to proclaim the infant Prince of Wales successor to the Crown. He then set out for the west, to meet the invader. His army deserted him, and he returned to London, where there had been some riots and plundering of Roman Catholic chapels. A fortnight later, the Queen and her child having been got safely out of the country, James himself attempted to escape. As soon as this fact was known, many of the Lords, spiritual and temporal, met at the Guildhall and there drew up a declaration that they would stand by the Prince of Orange in maintaining the religion, the rights, and the liberties of the country. The declaration was communicated to the Court of Aldermen, who called a Court of Common Council, at which another address to the same effect was drawn up. James, as we know, failed in his first attempt to escape, being stopped by certain fisher folk at Feversham. Lord Winchilsea, for whom he sent, persuaded him to return to London. He was received, we are told, with the liveliest indications of joy, as if he had been the best Prince in the world. Perhaps the historian mistook rejoicings over the capture of a prisoner for those over the return of a well-beloved sovereign. A London mob may be fickle, but there was absolutely no reason for such a change of front as would justify a demonstration of joy. Rather must we believe that every shout which went up meant that the King was in the hands of his faithful subjects, and that the faithful subjects would be able to give him the same trial, with the same termination of it, which they gave to his father.

Another of those dramatic scenes which enlivened the City during this reign was provided by the flight and capture of Judge Jeffreys.

The Judge, who had presided over the butcheries in the west of England, who became the willing creature and tool of James in every illegal act, was regarded all over the country with a hatred exceeding that which any Englishman has achieved for a thousand years and more. No one knew this better than himself. When, therefore, the power of his master crumbled away he sought safety in flight.

Why he did not escape to France; whether his nerve failed him; whether there was no time; whether there was no one he could trust, one knows not. It is, however, certain that he was suffering from a cruel disease, which caused him the greatest agonies and was partly the cause of that roaring voice, those bullying tones, which made him the terror of the Court and aggravated the agonies of punishment. I think it not impossible that a severe attack of this disease prevented him from moving till it was too late; he then assumed the disguise of a sailor and took refuge in a humble tavern at Wapping. Here, however, he was recognised as he looked out of a window, and was dragged out and committed to prison, having been so roughly handled by the mob that he died of the injuries he received. According to another account, however, he drank to excess, and so killed himself. As for the

THE ARREST OF JEFFREYS
From a satirical print in the British Museum.

King, he was permitted to escape, the Prince of Orange doubtless feeling that though he did not hesitate about taking his father-in-law's place, he did not desire his head.

And so James vanished from the scene and a new king reigned. But neither in the reign of William nor in that of any following sovereign were there so many splendid sights and anxious moments as in that of the unfortunate king whom we have learned to despise more profoundly than any other sovereign who ever sat upon the sacred Coronation chair.

The events connecting London with the reign of James II. belong for the most part to the history of the country. I have not thought it necessary, therefore, to dwell at length upon them.

The following, on the condition of London after the abdication, is an extract from the *English Courant and London Mercury*. It is quoted by Malcolm (*Manners and Customs*, 1811) :—

"No sooner was the King's withdrawing known, but the mobile consulted to wreak their vengence on papists and popery : and last night began with pulling down and burning the new-built Mass-house near the arch, in Lincolns Inn Fields : thence they went to Wild-house, the residence of the Spanish Ambassador, where they ransackt, destroy'd and burnt all the ornamental and inside part of the chappel, some cartloads of choice books, manuscript, etc. And not content here, some villanous thieves and common rogues, no doubt, that took this opportunity to mix with the youth, and they plunder'd the Ambassador's house of plate, jewels, mony, rich goods, etc. : and also many other who had sent in there for shelter their money, plate, etc. : among which, one gentlewoman lost a trunk, in which was £800 in mony, and a great quantity of plate. Thence they went to the Mass-house, at St. James's, near Smithfield, demolisht it quite ; from thence to Blackfryers near the Ditchside, where they destroy'd Mr. Henry Hill's printing-house, spoil'd his forms, letters, etc., and burnt 2 or 300 reams of paper, printed and unprinted : thence to the Mass-house in Bucklersbury and Lime-street, and there demolisht and burnt as before : and this night they went to the Nuncio's, and other places at that end of the town ; but finding the birds flown, and the bills on the door, they drew off : thence they went into the City, threatening to pull down all papists' houses, particularly one in Ivy Lane, and the market house upon Newgate Market, for no other reason but that one Burdet, a papist, was one of the farmers of the market ; but by the prudence of the citizens and some of their trained bands, they were got off without mischief doing anywhere.

Tuesday night last, and all Wednesday, the apprentices were busy in pulling down the chappels, and spoiling the houses of papists : they crying out the fire should not go out till the Prince of Orange came to town. There were thousands of them on Wednesday at the Spanish Ambassador's, they not leaving any wainscot withinside the house or chappel, taking away great quantities of plate, with much money, household goods and writings, verifying the old proverb 'All fish that came to the net.' The spoil of the house was very great, divers papists having sent their goods in thither, as judging that the securest place.

Then they went to the Lord Powis's great house in Lincoln's Inn Fields, wherein was a guard, and a bill upon the door, 'This house is appointed for the Lord Delameer's quarters :' and some of the company crying, 'Let it alone, the Lord Powis was against the Bishops going to the Tower,' they offered no violence to it.

Afterwards they marched down the Strand with oranges upon their sticks, crying for the Prince of Orange, and went to the Pope's Nuncio's, but finding a bill upon the door, 'This house is to be let,' they desisted. Lastly, they did some damage to the house of the resident of the Duke of Tuscany, in the Haymarket, carrying away some of his goods, when one Captain Douglas, coming thither with a company of trained bands to suppress them, a soldier, unadvisedly firing at the boys with ball, shot the Captain through the back, of which he lyes languishing. They also went to the houses of the French and other Ambassadors, but finding them deserted and the landlords giving them money, they marched off.

On Thursday, an order of the Lords coming forth, warning all persons to desist from pulling down any house, especially those of the Ambassadors, upon penalty of the utmost severity of the law to be inflicted on them : since which they have been very quiet."

ENTRY OF THE PRINCE OF ORANGE INTO LONDON

E. Gardner's Collection.

CHAPTER VIII

WILLIAM THE THIRD

AT the Coronation Banquet the Lord Mayor, the Aldermen, and the members of the twelve principal companies attended as butler and assistants. The City plate was also lent for the occasion. This was on the 11th of April 1689. Since the Prince of Orange had entered London on December 18, 1688, when James fled, the country had been left without King or Government. The "Convocation," as it was called, met on January 22. On the 28th the Commons declared the throne to be vacant, and on the 6th of February the House of Lords passed a similar resolution. A Declaration of Rights was next drawn up condemning the unconstitutional acts of James and offering the throne to William and Mary. After their proclamation their Majesties made haste to convert the Convocation into Parliament.

The reign of William presents few surprises or dramatic scenes so far as the City of London is concerned. On the other hand, there was a great deal done towards the strengthening and definition of the City rights and liberties. The Stuart kings, who could learn nothing and forget nothing, were gone, never to return; in future it would be quite as impossible for the sovereign to rob London of her liberties as to reign without a Parliament. Out of the arbitrary acts of the two Charleses, the elder and the younger, out of the civil wars, out of the expulsion of James, came to London the secure possession, henceforth unquestioned, of her charters, just as to the three kingdoms came constitutional government and a sovereign bound by the will of the people. These were great gains; one who could realise the state of the country even under the well-beloved despot Elizabeth, and compare it with its condition under the Georges, might well acknowledge that the gain was worth all the fighting and struggle, all the trials and executions which had to be endured in achieving it.

Of the loyalty of the City throughout this reign there can be no question. The address drawn up by the Lord Mayor and Sheriffs soon after it began on the occasion of a discovery of a plot against the King strikes a note which was maintained throughout :—

"And we most humbly beg leave to assure your Majesty that we will, as far as our Power extends, oppose ourselves to, and suppress all designs of that Nature; and will search after, disarm, seize, secure, and bring to Justice all Persons concerned therein, or contributing thereto: And we are unanimously, firmly, and unalterably resolved and determined to stand by, defend, and maintain your Majesty, and your Government, with the uttermost Hazard and Expence of our Lives and Estates, against all Persons whatsoever, that shall conspire or attempt any Thing against the same" (*Maitland*, i. p. 491).

The pageant on Lord Mayor's Day was attended by the King and Queen, who sat in the usual place reserved for them in Cheapside—the balcony of St. Mary le Bow. After the pageant they dined with the Lord Mayor at Guildhall. The pageant itself may be found briefly described in Fairholt's *Book of Pageants*. It will be seen by those who look up the passage that we are indeed far from the pageants of Edward the Third or Henry the Fifth.

It was natural that the first desire of the City should be to obtain an Act of Parliament declaring the forfeiture of their charter to be illegal. On March 8, 1689, the Grand Committee of Grievances reported that the rights of the City of London in the election of Sheriffs were invaded in the year 1682, and that the judgment given upon the *Quo Warranto* was illegal. The Act of Parliament by which the charters of the City were formally declared is a lengthy document of very great importance. An abridgment of this Act follows:—

"Whereas a Judgment was given in the Court of King's-Bench, in or about *Trinity-Term*, in the thirty-fifth Year of the Reign of the late King Charles the Second, upon an Information, in the Nature of a *Quo Warranto*, exhibited in the said Court against the Mayor and Commonalty and Citizens of the City of London, That the liberty, Privilege, and Franchise of the said Mayor, and Commonalty, and Citizens, being a Body Politick and Corporate, should be seized into the King's hands as forfeited; And forasmuch as the said Judgment, and the proceedings thereupon, is and were illegal and arbitrary; and for that the restoring of the said Mayor and Commonalty and Citizens to their antient Liberties, of which they had been deprived, tends very much to the Peace and good Settlement of this Kingdom.

2. Be it declared and enacted, . . . That the said Judgment given in the said Court of King's Bench in the said Trinity Term, in the thirty-fifth year of the reign of the said King Charles the Second, or in any other Term; and all or every other Judgment for the seizing into the late King's Hands the Liberty, Privilege, or Franchise of the Mayor, and Commonalty, and Citizens of the City of London, is, shall be, and are hereby reversed, annulled, and made void, to all Intents and Purposes whatsoever; and that Vacates be entered upon the Rolls of the said Judgment, for the Vacating and Reversal of the same accordingly.

3. And be it further declared and enacted, by the Authority aforesaid, That the Mayor and Commonalty, and Citizens of the City of London, shall and may for ever hereafter remain, continue, and be, and prescribe to be a Body Corporate and Politick, in *re, facto and nomine*, by the Name of Mayor and Commonalty, and Citizens of the City of London, and by that Name, and all and every other Name and Names of Incorporation, by which they at any Time before the said Judgment were incorporated, to sue, plead, and be impleaded, and to answer and be answered, etc."

At the same time the City proceeded to lay down and define the rights of the inhabitants in voting for Aldermen and Common Council men. The following is the Act of Common Council :—

"It is hereby declared, That it is, and antiently hath been the Right and Privilege of the Freemen of the said City only, being Householders, paying Scot and bearing Lot, and of none other whatsoever, in their several and respective Wards, from Time to Time, as often as there was or should be occasion, to nominate Aldermen, and elect Common Council men for the same respective Wards. That all and every the Beadle and Beadles of the respective Wards shall do, prepare, return, and deliver to the Aldermen at their several and respective Courts of Wardmote, or to their Deputies authorized to hold the same,

WILLIAM III. (1650-1702)
After an engraving of the painting by Sir Godfrey Kneller.

one List of all and every the Freeman Householders aforesaid, dwelling and residing within the respective Wards, to which they are Beadles, and of no others, apart and by themselves : And also one list of all and every other Householders within the said respective Wards only, apart and by themselves : To the intent that such Freemen Householders, may nominate Aldermen, and elect their Common Council-men : And they, together with the other Householders, may chuse their Constables, Scavengers, Inquest and Beadles."

So that those who were not Freemen of the City had no right to vote at all. This limitation of the vote was confirmed in 1711, 1712, in 1714, and by an Act of Parliament of 11 George I.

There were scares in the City, first after the defeat of the Dutch fleet on

June 30, 1691, by the French, when the latter were expected to attempt a landing up the Thames; and next when a report was raised that King James was at the head of a powerful French army. On both occasions the City put on a bold front, called out and equipped 10,000 men, and invited the Queen to appoint officers. It will be remembered that on the scare of the Spanish Armada, doubts were cast on the efficiency of the London contingent because the men would only obey their own officers, who were notoriously incompetent. Here we see a change.

MARY II. (1662-1694)
After an engraving of the painting by Sir Godfrey Kneller.

The City now recognises the fact that an officer cannot be made out of a merchant in a single day.

The City next had to go before Parliament in the humiliating position of a trustee who has lost trust money. The case was this. It had long been the custom of the City to take care of orphans, being children of Freemen, their fortunes or portions being received by the Chamber and administered for them. The Mayor now declared that this money had so grievously diminished that they simply could not pay the orphans on coming of age their own estates. Several reasons were alleged for this loss: the stoppage of the Exchequer, Charles's act of robbery; a large part of the fund had been lent to the Exchequer; other sums had been lost in various ways, and the City now found itself in debt to orphans for £500,000, and £247,500 in other ways, the whole being far more than it could pay. A committee was appointed to investigate the case, and on their report an Act was passed, of which the following are the heads :—

"That towards settling a perpetual Fund for paying the yearly Interest of four Pounds, for every hundred Pound due by the City to their Creditors, all the Manors, Messuages, Lands, Markets, Fairs, and other Hereditaments, Revenues and Income whatsoever, belonging to the Mayor, Commonalty, and Citizens, in Possession or Reversion, and all Improvements that shall be made thereof (excepting the Estates and Possessions belonging to Christ's, St. Bartholomew's, St. Thomas's, Bridewell, Bethlehem, or any other of the City Hospitals, and the Estates appropriated for the repair of London Bridge), are for ever charged, from the twenty-fourth of June in the present Year, for raising annually the sum of eight thousand Pounds, clear of all Deductions.

2. That all the Profits arising from the several Aqueducts belonging to the City be applied towards the Payment of the said Interest.

3. Towards the Support of the said Fund, the Lord Mayor and Common Council are impowered annually to raise the Sum of two Thousand Pounds, by an equal Assessment upon the personal Estates of the Citizens.

4. Towards the Support of the said Fund, be paid the annual Sum of six hundred Pounds, being the Fine or Rent paid by certain Persons for the Privilege of illuminating the Streets of the City with Convex Lamps. This tended very much to the Dishonour of the City, to make a pecuniary advantage of a publick Benefit; but the same being removed, to the no small honour of the Gentlemen in the present Direction of the City Affairs, I shall say no more on that Head.

5. That every Apprentice, at the Time of his being bound, shall pay towards the said Fund two shillings and six Pence.

6. That every Person, upon his being admitted a Freeman of the City, shall pay towards the Support of the said Fund five Shillings.

7. That every Ton of Wine imported into the Port of London, shall pay towards the support of the said Fund five Shillings.

8. That, towards the increase of the said Fund, all Coals imported into the Port of London shall pay four Pence the Chaldron Metage above what was formerly paid.

9. And, as a further Increase to the said Fund, all Coals imported into the Port of London after the twenty-ninth of September, Anno 1770, the Measurable to pay six Pence the Chaldron, and the Weighable six Pence the Ton, for the term of Fifty Years. And to the Intent that the said Fund may be perpetual, it is enacted, That, after the Expiration of the said Term of fifty Years, when the said six Pence per Cauldron and Ton upon Coals shall cease, then all the Manors, Messuages, Lands, Tenements, Markets, Fairs, and the Duties thereof, and other Hereditaments, Revenues and Income whatsoever, belonging to the City either in Possession or Reversion, shall stand charged with the yearly Sum of six thousand Pounds, over and above the already named Sum of eight Thousand Pounds per Ann."

Dissensions over elections and the mode of elections, scares about plots and the rumours of plots, rejoicings over victory, make up the history of London during the next few years. The losses of the Turkey merchants when, for want of a sufficient convoy, their ships were taken or burned by the French, were a national disaster. The merchant fleet was valued at many millions; the convoy forwarded the merchantmen safely as far as the Land's End, when it left them to a smaller convoy of seventeen ships under Rooke. They found their way barred by the French fleet; in the fight that followed some of the merchantmen escaped, but the greater number were lost. " Never within the memory of man,"

Macaulay says, "had there been in the City a day of more gloom and agitation than that on which the news of the encounter arrived. Money-lenders, an eye-witness said, went away from the Exchange as pale as if they had received sentence of death." The Queen expressed her sorrow and sympathy and promised an inquiry. The probable cause of the desertion of the merchant-men by the main convoy was that it was not safe to leave the Channel unguarded so long.

Everybody who studies London possesses among his collection pictures of the street cries. These drawings generally belong to the later years of the eighteenth century or the beginning of the nineteenth. They establish the fact that the streets were filled with a never-ending procession of men and women with baskets, carts, wheel-barrows, trays, boxes, all bawling their wares at the top of the voice. You may look into the shop now called an "Oilman's"; nearly all the things he sells were formerly vended in the street. The conversion of the wheel-barrow and the tray into the shop would prove a chapter in the history of London trade.

It is therefore interesting to learn that these hawkers and pedlars had already, at the end of the seventeenth century, increased so greatly as to become a nuisance to the Citizens. The Common Council proceeded against them with an Act providing that

"No Person should presume to sell any Goods, or Merchandize, in any Street, Lane, Passage, Tavern, Inn, Ale-house, or other Publick Place within the City or Liberties thereof, other than in open Markets and Fairs, upon the Penalty of forty Shillings for every such Offence. And, for the more effectual Prevent-ing such Practices, all Citizens buying Goods of such Persons to forfeit the like Sum of forty Shillings for every such Offence. And, as farther Discouragement to all Hawkers and Pedlars, every Citizen that should permit or suffer such Persons to expose to Sale any Goods or Merchandize in his, her, or their Houses, should for every such Offence likewise forfeit the Sum of forty Shillings" (*Maitland*, i. p. 479).

At the same time an Act of Parliament imposed a tax upon them. The hawker or pedlar played an important part in the country life from an early period. He it was who circulated among the villages, and from farm to farm, the things for which in the country there existed no shops. Autolycus belongs to all ages, and in all ages he is a jovial, sharp, ready-witted rascal who will pass off his damaged goods for new, will buy cheap and sell dear. The hawkers escaped legislation in mediæval England, and are first noticed in a statute of Edward VI., in which "they are treated in a very contemptuous manner, being described as more 'hurtful than necessary to the commonwealth.' But the case of pedlars was not seriously taken in hand before the reign of William III., who put a tax upon them and, ominously enough, bound them to certify commissioners for transportation how they travelled and traded."

We have seen how the Franciscans became pedlars,

"Thai dele with purses, pynnes and knyves,
With girdles, gloves for wenches, and wyves."

The hawker of London was not exactly the same as the hawker of the country. In the first place, it is evident that the City disliked his setting up a stall outside the markets or the streets where special things were sold; the companies still exercised the power of regulating trade; there was still the old jealousy which would not allow one trader to sell things belonging to another company. But the object of hawkers was to sell everything wanted for the daily life; like the Franciscan, he would not only sell mercery but also cutlery. This kind of hawker was effectually

LONDON STREET CRIES
From contemporary prints in British Museum.

banished from the City, even though shopkeepers had now begun to mix up various companies and crafts in the same counter. The London hawker was reduced to selling one thing, and one thing only. In all the pictures of the street cries we find the hawker engaged in crying one thing for sale; he offered to catch rats, or sold sand, small coal, boot laces, door-mats, baskets, sausages, and so on, whatever was wanted for everyday use and could not be found in the shops.

The hawkers of 1695, since they could not set up stalls or sell in the streets, tried to force an entrance into the markets. Upon which the Council laid down the law that the markets were not to be used as a place of sale for goods sold in the shops or warehouses of Freemen of the City. This important Act, which continued in force until the nineteenth century, should be quoted :—

" Whereas by the Laws, Customs, and antient Usages of the City of London, confirmed by Parliament, every shop and warehouse within the said City, and Liberties of the same, having open shew into any Streets and Lanes thereof, have, Time-out-of-Mind, been known and accustomed to be, and in very deed is an open and Publick Market Place for Persons free of the said City, for every Day of the Week, except Sundays, for Shew and Sale of Wares and Merchandizes, within the said City and Liberties thereof :

And whereas all other publick Markets within this City, and the Liberties of the same, that is to say, Leadenhall-Market, the Green-Yard or Herb-Market, Stocks-Market, Honey-Lane-Market, Newgate-Market, and all other such like Markets, were and are appointed and ordained, by the Laws and Constitutions of this City, to be held and used upon particular and certain Days only in the Week, and on certain Hours of such Days, as open Markets for all Foreigners and Freemen and Women to use and resort unto for Sale of Flesh, Fish, Butter, Cheese, Eggs, Fruit, Herbs, Roots, and such like Victuals and Food, for the Support and Sustenance of the Citizens and other Inhabitants of the said City and Liberties of the same ; and were not appointed for any other Use or Purpose whatsoever, save for the Sale of Raw Hides, Tanned Leather, Tallow and Wool, as appears by the Laws and Orders of the Court of Aldermen and Common Council, for regulating the same :

But nevertheless, for Want of due Encouragement, in the Execution thereof, several Hawkers, Pedlars, and Petty Chapmen and others, contrary to the said Constitution and proper Use and Intention of the said Markets, do now come to the said Markets, and there sell and expose to Sale Mercery Wares, Lace, Linen, Grocery Wares, Confectionery Wares, Drapery Wares, Millinery Wares, Glass and Earthen Wares, Ironmongers' Wares, Braziers' Wares, Turners' Wares, Hosiers' Wares, Cutlers' Wares, Tin Wares, Toys, and other Wares and Merchandizes, and such like Commodities, which, by the Usage and Customs of this City ought only to be sold in the Shops and Warehouses of the Freemen of this City, and Liberties of the same ; by Reason whereof the publick Markets and Market-places appointed only for the sale of Victuals, Food, Herbs, Roots, Raw Hides, Tanned Leather, Tallow and Wool, as before-mentioned, are become incumbered and made inconvenient for the exposing the same to sale, and the Prices of Victuals much enhanced thereby, and the Trades used to be exercised in the Shops and Warehouses in the said City and Liberties thereof are much hindered and decayed, to the great Prejudice and Damage of the Citizens of the City :

Now, for the effectual preventing and suppressing the said Mischiefs for the Time to come, be it enacted and ordained, by the Right Honourable the Lord-Mayor, Aldermen, and Common Council assembled, and it is hereby enacted by the said Court, and by the Authority of the same, That from and after the twenty-fifth Day of December, now next ensuing, no Person or Persons whatsoever, whether free or not free of this City, shall sell or expose to Sale in the said publick Markets called Leadenhall-Market, the Green-Yard or Herb-Market, Stocks-Market, Honey-Lane-Market, Newgate-Market, or in any other such like Market or Market-Grounds thereunto belonging, within this City and Liberties of the same, any Mercery Wares, Lace and Linen, Grocery or Confectionery Wares, Ironmongers' Wares, Braziers' Wares, Hosiers' Wares, Cutlers' Wares, Tin Wares, Drapery Wares, Millinery Wares, Glass or Earthen Wares, Toys, or any such like Commodities or Merchandizes, which are sold in the open Shops or Warehouses of the Freemen of this City, and Liberties thereof, upon Pain to forfeit and pay for every such Offence (by him, her, or them committed or done to the contrary), the Sum of three Pounds of lawful Money of England, to be sued for and recovered, with reasonable Costs of Suit, by Action or Actions of Debt, to be brought and prosecuted within fourteen Days after such Offence or Offences shall be committed, in the name of the Chamberlain of this City for the Time being, in the open Court holden before the Lord-Mayor and Aldermen of the said City.

Which said Sum or Sums of Money, so forfeited and recovered from Time to Time (the necessary Charges for the Recovery thereof being first deducted), shall be to the Uses, and disposed of as followeth : That is to say, one Moiety thereof to be paid and delivered to the Treasurer of St. Thomas's Hospital, to be employed towards the Relief of the Poor, Sick and Maimed, provided for and maintained in the said Hospital : And the other Moiety to him or them that shall and doth prosecute and sue for the same (in Manner as aforesaid) from Time to Time : Any Law, Custom or Usage contrary thereof notwithstanding."

In 1695 we hear of the first indications that the Jacobite party was still strong in the City as elsewhere. It was on the 10th of June, the birthday of the Prince of Wales, that a number of Jacobites assembled in a tavern of Drury Lane, where they proceeded to drink the health of the Prince. Thence they went out into the streets with drums and flags and insisted upon everybody's drinking the same toast. It was a time when the people could not wait for the interference of the police, because there were none; they were obliged to act for themselves, and often acted in a more efficient manner than any police. On this occasion they poured out into the streets, armed, and with one consent set upon the Jacobites, put them to flight, took one prisoner, and sacked the tavern. In the same year we read of another Jacobite ebullition when, the King being abroad carrying on the war with France, a man rode through the streets crying aloud that King William was dead: an adventure which might have done great mischief. The King, who was not dead after all, returned in October. Then occurred the assassination plot. He was to be murdered after hunting in Richmond Park. Fortunately the plot was discovered and the ring-leaders arrested. The trained bands were called out and an address of loyalty was drawn up by the Corporation.

In 1697 the King returned to London on the Treaty of Ryswick. He consented to make a public entry. It was made the occasion of a procession of great magnificence, though falling very far short of the old pageants.

The following notes from the letters of Richard Lapthorme to Richard Coffin cover the greater part of King William's reign :—

1688. Sir C. Pym, dining at a tavern in Old Fish Street, quarrelled with a stranger—went out into the street, drew—Sir C. died.

1688. July 21st. Fireworks on Thames cost £20,000. Present 100,000 people.

„ Judge Rotherham, Oxford Circuit, took with him Burgess N. Comminuta; asked him to pass a short tract for instructions and admonitions of criminals condemned.

„ Captain tossed the Mayor of Scarboro' in blanket. Came up to complain to King.

„ Nov. Two rich aldermen died, one Alderman Jefferys, Tobacconist, £300,000, no children. Alderman Lacy very rich, 1 daughter.

„ 11 Dec. "Mobile" pulling down mass-houses.

1688. 29th Dec. Lord Jefferies confined in chamber of one Bulle, a warder. Pen, ink, and paper. Town church very full in hopes of seeing him. Did not come.

1689. 20th Dec. Anniversary of King's arrival in London. Representation in effigies. Procession 1000 torches to Temple Bar. All King James's ministers: all hung on gallows—bonfire—gallows fall in with pillory. Whipping posts and everything.

1690. 20th Sep. People shut shops for monthly fast, but clergy will not open church. . . . preached everywhere.

1690. 22nd Nov. Two ladies of fortune abducted.

„ 18th Dec. 22 condemned to be hanged, including the Golden Farmer, a highwayman, and Sir John Jepson for abducting Mrs. Coherton.

„ 28th Feb. In Duke Street, Covent Garden, a gentlewoman bewitched. A voice speaks within her blasphemously—tho' lips and teeth are shut; sometimes she is visibly lifted up, chair and all, no one touching the chair.

1691. 11th Apr. Fire at Whitehall.
,, 31st May. New Diving bell.
,, 4th July. Fray between Alsateans and gentlemen of the Temple. A fight; one of the sheriff's posse killed; several wounded. 70 Alsateans sent to the various prisons.
,, 25th July. Murder by one Bird.
,, 15th Aug. ,, ,, a young gentleman.
,, 22nd ,, 2 grenadiers shot in Hyde Park for mutiny. Murders nearly every day.
Dr. Clench sent for to a patient—strangled in coach.
1692. 18th Aug. Packet from Holland blew up—60 perished. 40 picked up.
The Lord of Banbury fought with his brother-in-law, Capt. Laurie, and killed him. Young, clerk, fought Graham, clerk, and killed him. Lord Mohun killed Montfort the player. Reprieves used to be sent after the prisoners on their way to Tyburn. They were brought back on Sheriff's horse, yet after all executed.
Miracle of the lame F. Girl.

A long succession of cold and rainy seasons caused many bad harvests, in so much that for some years there was a great dearth of corn, wheat being sold at as high as three pounds eight shillings a quarter. Considering the value of money then —it was almost twice as much as at present—we may understand the cost of wheat bread. But the working classes did never eat wheat bread except as a luxury. They lived on oaten bread.

In the year 1699 occurred another scare about the wicked Papists. The Mayor and Aldermen were summoned before the Privy Council, when the King informed them that he had heard of a great increase of Papists in the City; that they openly attended Mass-houses in spite of the law; that he had commanded all Jesuits and Popish priests to leave the country; that he had recalled all those English students who were educated abroad, and that he looked to the Lord Mayor for vigilance in searching out Papists, especially those who had arms concealed, destroying Papistical books, shutting up Mass-houses and Catholic schools, and administering the oaths to suspected Papists.

Almost the last act of the City of London in this reign was to send a loyal address to the King when James the Second died and Louis XIV. acknowledged as his successor the young Prince of Wales.

On the 8th of March 1702 William III. died.

CHAPTER IX

QUEEN ANNE

THERE is nothing picturesque and very little that is important in the history of London during the reign of Queen Anne. An address to the new Queen, a public reception of Her Majesty by the City, several days of Thanksgiving for successes

ANNE (1665-1714)
After the portrait by J. Closterman.

over the enemy, quarrels about elections, High Church riots, mainly exhaust the annals of this reign.

On Friday, November 26, 1703, the greatest hurricane of wind and rain ever known in this country "o'er pale Britannia passed." This really belongs chronologically to the eighteenth century, and has been described in that volume, but some reference to it here is also necessary. It began about seven o'clock in the evening, and raged all night long. It overturned houses, uprooted trees, blew down stacks of chimneys, rolled up the lead on the roofs of churches, overthrew walls, and tore off tiles, which it blew about like snowflakes. The streets were covered with brick-bats, broken signs, tiles, bulks, and pent-houses; the houses in the City at daybreak looked like skeletons, being stripped of their roofs, with their windows blown in or out; the people destroyed were said, and believed, to number thousands; all business was suspended while the houses were made once more weather-proof; the price of tiles rose from a guinea to six pounds a thousand; at sea twelve men-of-war were destroyed with 1800 men on board, and the whole of the shipping in the Pool except four vessels were driven from their moorings to beat against each other and to founder off Limehouse.

The Common Council in 1704 considered the condition of the night watch. They ordered that 583 men, strong and able-bodied, should watch all night, divided among the respective wards. When we read that for the small precinct of Black-friars alone six men were ordered to patrol the streets all night, that for Monkwell Street alone two men were to walk up and down all night, one wonders at the stories of midnight violence, burglary, and robbery belonging to the eighteenth century. What were those able-bodied men doing? It is another illustration of the difference between a strong law and a strong executive.

The Union of England and Scotland being at last happily accomplished, the Queen was carried to St. Paul's in a solemn procession for a Thanksgiving service.

In 1709 arrived in London a body of helpless and destitute people from the Palatinate, which had been devastated by the French; there were nearly 12,000 of them. At first they were maintained by charity, over £22,000 being subscribed for their immediate necessities. They were then settled in various places; about 3000 were sent to Ireland, to each of the provinces of North and South Carolina about 600, and to the Province of New York about 3500. This settlement was made by a Committee appointed by the Queen. It consisted of the Great Officers of State, many of the nobility, the Lord Mayor and Aldermen of the City and other persons of distinction, in number 121. These Trustees, as they were called, met every after-noon in the week at four o'clock, either at Whitehall or at the Guildhall Council Chamber. There were not wanting malcontents who thought that the country had paupers enough of its own without importing others. The example of the Huguenots, whose reception in this country brought new industries and increased wealth, might have taught a lesson, but it did not. Perhaps the double example of the welcome given to the Huguenots first and the Palatines next may serve for another lesson at the present moment when the immigration of Polish and Russian Jews by the thousand terrifies some of us.

THANKSGIVING SERVICE IN ST. PAUL'S

From Pennant's *London*, in the British Museum.

9

During the whole of this reign, and in that of its successor, party feeling ran high with High Churchmen and Moderates, including Dissenters.

In the autumn of the year 1709 two sermons were preached, by one Henry Sacheverell, D.D., which produced consequences not often due to the pulpit. The preacher himself has been represented by those of the opposite side as an obscure divine, of bad moral character, of no learning, of no eloquence, and of boundless impudence. This description of the famous Doctor must be taken with a very large deduction for the personal equation. Henry Sacheverell was the son of a clergyman, Rector of Marlborough, Wilts, and the grandson of a strong Presbyterian. He was entered at Magdalen College, Oxford, where he had Addison for his fellow-student and his friend. Certain Latin verses of his are inserted in the *Musæ Anglicanæ*, and certain English verses of his may be found in Nichol's Collection. He was born in 1672, was Master of Arts in 1696, and Doctor of Divinity in 1708. He lectured or took pupils at Oxford for a few years, and then became successively vicar of a country parish and Chaplain of St. Saviour's, Southwark. In August 1709 he delivered a sermon at the Derby Assizes, in which he maintained the doctrine, which many Oxford men then held, of passive obedience. To us the doctrine appears too ridiculous to need refutation; to the Tories and High Churchmen of that time it was a very serious position indeed, and one which was maintained by the support of Scripture. On November the 5th of the same year he was invited to preach before the Mayor and Corporation at St. Paul's Cathedral. His sermon on this day was to the same effect. He took for his text the words " Perils from false brethren." He asserted in the strongest terms the doctrines of passive obedience and non-resistance; he spoke of the Revolution as a crime never to be forgiven, and he called the Bishops perfidious prelates and false sons of the Church because they approved of toleration. It was customary for the Mayor to command the printing of any sermon preached before the Corporation. But in this case the Mayor did not make the usual order, the reason being that many of the Aldermen and Common Council were alarmed at the extreme views advanced.

Let us understand that if this man had been the impudent, arrogant, self-seeking quack which some histories represent him, it is quite unlikely that the Mayor would have invited him to preach. Vain, carried away by his sudden popularity, he may have been, but he was eloquent, he was scholarly, and he undoubtedly possessed the power of moving his audience. Other divines on the High Church side had raged against the Revolution but to no purpose; there is talk of a certain Higgins who is said to have made loud outcries against the condition of the Church and the general wickedness. Yet no one heeded Higgins. But Sacheverell they did heed.

His sermons, both that of Derby and that of St. Paul's, were published. The Tories ran after them eagerly, cried them up, ordered everybody to buy them, with the result that 40,000 copies were sold throughout the kingdom. The number, to us who are accustomed to see popular papers sold by millions, does not seem large, but think what it really meant at that time; it meant about two copies for every parish in the kingdom. In the town parishes the pamphlet was handed about from one to the other. Forty thousand copies of a sermon represent ten times that number of readers; it means the whole nation moved and agitated. All who could read did read these sermons; all who could not listened to the discussions on them.

They were considered by the Council. All were of the opinion that the preacher ought to be prosecuted; there were differences as to the method and as to the court by which he should be tried. It was finally resolved that he should be impeached before the two Houses of Parliament.

There were delays before the impeachment could be carried out. Meantime the High Church party and the clergy in general were actively engaged in proclaiming that the Church was in danger, and in inflaming the minds of the people against the Dissenters. And then occurred one of those strange tumults in which the lowest classes in London have risen up, from time to time, in favour of religion and morality, as if they understood in the least what these words mean. The 'prentices waging war against disorderly houses, the craftsmen destroying the Savoy in defence of their Bishop, the mob tearing down Mass-houses, the mob throwing up their hats for Sacheverell, the mob following Lord George Gordon—all these are risings of the same kind. Other reasons are assigned in each case; the one and only reason, apart from the general love of a fight, which lies always in the heart of the Londoner, was a blind desire for truth and justice. Who were the Dissenters? They were Puritans; they were the people, who, when they had the power, forbade the old sports, and persecuted those who would still play them; they were the masters who commanded the way of their people in matters of religion as in matters of politics; they had turned merry London into morose London. It is generally believed that the common people did not go to church, and therefore had no love for the church. This is most untrue. The City was still full of the craftsmen; all those who lived in the City went to church. How many of those who lived outside the walls, what proportion of those who were settled beyond the walls, went to church one has no means of ascertaining. But within the walls all the people went to church. So that when we hear that 'prentices, butchers, chimney-sweepers, scavengers, fellowship porters, and the like made up the mob which bawled in the streets the cry of "The Church in danger," we need only remark that respectable people never join a mob and never bawl in the streets for any cause whatsoever. In a word, there is every reason to believe the mob to have been filled with an honest conviction that this cause was that of religion, pure and undefiled.

On the 27th day of February, Dr. Sacheverell was brought to the bar before the Lords and Commons in Westminster Hall. Immense importance was attached to the case; the Queen was present, but privately. Seats were arranged for the

Commons and for the noble ladies who were here in crowds; galleries were set up at the end of the hall for the people, and a raised platform for the managers of the impeachment and for the defendant. We need not follow the course of the trial. On the 23rd day of March, more than three weeks after it began, the case ended. The Doctor was ordered to abstain from preaching for three years. Meantime the mob had been showing the sincerity of its conviction not only by cheering the defendant every day as he went to the Hall or returned, but by wrecking the Dissenting chapels. They broke into the Gate Street Chapel, took out everything

HENRY SACHEVERELL, D.D. (1674?-1724)

—pulpit, pews, Bibles, cushions, sconces—and carried the whole into Lincoln's Inn Fields, where they made a bonfire of the things, shouting "High Church and Sacheverell!" In Blackfriars, Clerkenwell, Long Acre, Shoe Lane, and Leather Lane they also wrecked the chapels. The rioters were dispersed by a detachment of Guards without any bloodshed.

The sentence passed upon the Doctor was considered as an acquittal. Bonfires illuminated the City in the evening; drink flowed; every one was made to drink the health of the Doctor. The subsequent career of Sacheverell was tame. He made a kind of triumphal progress through the country, though some of the towns refused to admit him. Oxford received him as if he was a martyr, or a confessor at least.

Finally, he settled down at St. Andrew's, Holborn, where he died at the age of fifty. Such a man must needs make many enemies. Among them was the Duchess of Marlborough. She calls him "a lewd, drunken, pampered man," and says that "he had not learning enough to speak or write true English, but a heap of bombast, ill-connected words at command." He had a "haughty and insolent air" which helped him with the public. She acknowledges, however, that he had "a good assurance, clean gloves, white handkerchief, well managed, with other suitable accomplishments, which moved the hearts of many at his appearance." She says that his speech in defence was written for him; that many of the "weaker" ladies were more like mad or bewitched than like persons in their senses. It might seem to us, who live so very far from passive obedience and non-resistance, as if the occasion were enormously exaggerated. That, however, was certainly not the case. The clergy were only too ready, one and all, to join in the prosecution of the Nonconformists, in the suppression of free thought, and in the corresponding doctrines of non-resistance. It was most certainly desirable, above all things, if the Protestant succession were to be secured, that these doctrines should be placed before the people in their true light; whatever the mob might bawl, whatever ecclesiastics might preach, the men of sense and understanding must not only go on their way, but must show the world the reason of their action. By the impeachment of a greatly overrated preacher before both Houses of Parliament the Government committed both Houses to the maintenance of religious toleration, to the Protestant succession, and to the liberties of the country. Considered from that point of view the case of this person must be regarded as the most important State trial. The Doctor is reproached with having his head turned by the honours bestowed upon him. We may forgive him. Who would not have his head turned, first, by the enormous success of a sermon; next, by being thought worthy of a State trial in Westminster Hall; lastly, by receiving every evidence of popular approval that a shouting, bawling mob can give, to say nothing of the gifts, the letters, the assurances of great ladies and noble lords? Of course his head was turned.

When the Sacheverell tumults were finished and over, the Lord Mayor issued an order for the suppression of such assemblies of rude and disorderly persons by the constables. We have already noted the appearance of these documents and proclamations and their futile character, because without sufficient force of police in reserve such general orders are powerless.

The Statute for the erection of fifty new churches in the suburbs of London indicates the growth of the City outside the walls. Fifty churches would provide accommodation for fifty thousand people; or, allowing for the infants, the aged, the infirm, and those who attended service only once a day, probably a hundred thousand. At the present day the parishes of Greater London frequently include eight thousand to twenty thousand souls.

The last years of Queen Anne were distracted, as readers of history know, by secret conferences, correspondence, and conspiracies to secure the succession of the elder Pretender, James Francis. The reports and whispers of these things kept London in a state of continual alarm and ferment; rumours were constantly spreading around; it was said that a large number of disaffected persons calling themselves Mohocks and Hawkabites came out at night and scoured the streets, assaulting and wounding harmless persons; it was also said that they flattened the noses of those they seized, or slit them; that they cut off their ears; that they stretched their mouths or gagged them; that they cruelly pricked and stabbed them; that they set women on their heads, with other terrible things. The citizens were afraid to go into the streets at night for fear of being "mohocked." A proclamation was issued offering a reward of one hundred pounds for the conviction of every such offender. But no one was apprehended, nor could any one be found who had suffered from the cruelties of the so-called Mohocks and Hawkabites. In fact it was a scare, baseless except for the occasional acts of violence which took place in the streets. Another scare was started about the same time. It was bruited abroad that the suburbs and fields around London were haunted by a wretch called Whipping Tom, whose practice it was to seize on all the women he met with and flog them. No one asked how this could be done if the woman resisted or ran away, because one would want both hands for the purpose, and the fields— meaning Moor Fields—and suburbs were not so lonely that a woman's cries could not be heard. However, the women of London were put into a state of great terror in consequence of this report, and for a long time none would venture abroad without an escort.

At this time there were complaints that many shopkeepers employed assistants who were not Freemen of the City. The Mayor and Common Council passed a strict order that this practice was to cease, and that the persons employed in the City in any capacity should be Freemen of the City.

Queen Anne died on August 1, 1714.

RELIGION, GOVERNMENT, AND TRADE

CHAPTER I

LET us consider the religious side of London in the first half of the seventeenth century. It was not so much the abolition of the Mass and all that went with it, not so much the Smithfield fires and all that they meant, that changed the mind of London, but the acquisition of the Bible and the continual delight which the people found in reading it, in hearing it read, in hearing it expounded, and in making out for themselves the meaning of passages and the foundations of doctrine. The Bible gave them histories more entrancing than any that had ever been presented to them. They read of Abraham and of Jacob, of Joshua, of the Strong Man, of the rash King's vow, of Saul and David, of Hezekiah, of Elijah and the prophets of Baal. They read the words of the Prophets and applied them to the events and the kings and statesmen of their own time; if they longed to praise their God, the Psalms of David gave them words; if they were sad they found consolation in those poems; for the conduct of life there was the Book of Proverbs; for example, under every possible circumstance was a gallery of portraits, the like of which could nowhere else be found. In the Gospel they read of a Christ whose image rose always higher than they could reach; and in the Epistles they gathered materials for the doctrines of a hundred sects. With this book in their hands, containing history, poetry, morals, example, admonition, the way of eternal life and, scattered about, the materials for the Creed or Articles of Faith, without which it seemed impossible to live, the old authority was gone, never to return so long as that book remained in the hands and sank into the minds of the people.

For forty years and more before the Stuarts came, the book had been read and read again and again by every one; children had read it at school; they had been catechised in it; they had been taught that it contained in itself the whole of religion, so that what had been added since was superfluous or superstitious.

The attitude of the people towards Catholicism at the beginning of the seventeenth century was that of hatred far beyond the hatred of fifty years before, because it was intensified by the terror of the Papacy, which seemed recovering its old ground and quickly seizing on one country after another. It seemed to those that could look beyond the sea that in a short time there would be another, and a far more dangerous attempt than that of the Spanish Armada, upon the religion and the liberties of the country. The horrors of Catholic victory were impressed upon them

ST. PAUL'S CROSS

"An accurate delineation, the only Correct Vestige that remains of this Ancient and Curious Object, as it appeared on Sunday the 26th of March 1620; at which time, it was visited by King James the I., His Queen, and Charles, Prince of Wales; attended by the Archbishop of Canterbury, Bishops, Officers of State, Nobility, Ladies, etc. etc.; Who were received with great magnificence by Sir William Cockaine, Lord Mayor of London; assisted by the Court of Aldermen, Recorder, etc.; When a most excellent Sermon was preach'd from a text purposely selected by his Majesty (Psalm cii. Verses 13, 14), by Dr. John King, Bishop of London; recommending the speedy reparation of the Venerable Cathedral of St. Paul; which, with its unsteepled Tower, and incumbrances of Houses, etc. appear on the back and side grounds."

From a print engraved from an original picture in the possession of the Society of Antiquaries, and published by Richard Wilkinson, London, 4th June 1811.

by the spectacle of the Huguenot fugitives and the unfortunate Palatines, by stories of the Spanish Inquisition and its ruthless tortures. The preachers—those "lecturers"—who were added to the parish churches, fed this feeling of hatred and of terror. What, then, was the indignation, what was the dismay, when the citizens of London found the ecclesiastical authorities separating themselves more and more from the reformed churches of Germany and Switzerland, and, as they thought, advancing with no uncertain steps towards a reconciliation with Rome!

The early years of the seventeenth century saw the Puritan at his best. That he should prefer and hold a narrow creed was inevitable; there was no creed or sect possible which was not narrow. In this respect the Puritan was in no way below the Catholic, the Episcopalian, the Presbyterian, or the Brownist, or the Fifth Monarchy man, or any other sectarian. He was not, however, necessarily a gloomy and austere person. He might be a man of many accomplishments; Colonel Hutchinson fenced, danced, and played the viol. But the Puritan was, above all, conscious of his own individual responsibility. Between himself and his God he wanted no priest; he would not acknowledge that there was for any man the need of a priest, or for any priest the possession of supernatural power; he wanted no ceremonies; he remembered that symbolism, as all history proclaims aloud, leads infallibly to the worship of the symbol. He would not allow so simple a thing as the sign of the cross in baptism or the ring in marriage. The key-note of Puritanism, the thing which made it strong and glorified it in the persons of the best and noblest spirits, as Milton and Hutchinson, was that the man was master of himself. Consider, therefore, the wrath and the dismay when such a man saw himself, or thought himself deprived of his liberty of thought, compelled to conformity with what he held to be superstitions, dragged unwillingly and in chains along the road to Rome.

Among the lower ranks, the shopkeepers and the craftsmen of London, the same spirit prevailed; but it led to extravagances. The Bible was kept open on every counter; men discussed texts in every tavern; the barbers quoted Paul while they shaved their customers. A certain description of a citizen's wife suggests the thought and discourse of a London household of this time. "She was very loving and obedient to her parents, kind to her husband, tender-hearted to her children, loving all who were godly, much misliking the wicked and profane; . . . very ripe and perfect in all stories of the Bible; *likewise in all stories of Martyrs.*" The martyrs were the Marian martyrs; this good woman knew them all; there would be more martyrs, she knew full well, if the Catholics came back. And she knew, and delighted in, all the stories of the Bible; she was ripe in them and perfect in them. If the Catholics came back, her Bible would be taken from her. Consider the dismay of this poor woman when she was told that Laud was doing all he could to bring them back!

Green points out, very forcibly and truly, how the claims of despotic authority, of crown and church, jarred with all that was noblest in the temper of the time. "These were everywhere reaching forward to the conception of law. Bacon sought the law in material nature; Hooper asserted the rule of law over the spiritual world. The temper of the Puritan was eminently a temper of law. The diligence with which he searched the Scriptures sprang from his earnestness to discover a Divine

Will, which, in all things, great or small, he might implicitly obey.   But this implicit obedience was reserved for the Divine Will alone: for human ordinances derived their strength only from their correspondence with the revealed law by God." Against such a temper, with such a stubborn people, fully persuaded that their

WILLIAM LAUD (1573-1645)
Archbishop of Canterbury.

eternal welfare depended upon their adherence to their own convictions, Charles and Laud were bound to fail.

It must be admitted that the better type of Puritan was apt to degenerate and to give way to a narrower and a stricter school.   There appeared the Puritan who pulled down and cut in pieces the Maypoles —those of St. Andrew Undershaft, and of Basing Lane, for example.   Also there appeared the Puritan who put down games and sports :—

> "I've heard our fine refined clergy teach,
> Of the commandments, that it is a breach
> To play at any game for gain or coin ;
> 'Tis theft, they say—men's goods you do purloin ;

For beasts or birds in combat for to fight,
Oh, 'tis not lawful, but a cruel sight.
One silly beast another to pursue
'Gainst nature is, and fearful to the view ;
And man with man their activeness to try
Forbidden is—much harm doth come thereby ;
Had we their faith to credit what they say
We must believe all sports are ta'en away ;
Whereby, I see, instead of active things,
What harm the same unto our nation brings ;
The pipe and pot are made the only prize
Which all our spriteful youth do exercise.' "

There appeared also the Puritan who objected to the study of Latin and Greek as encouraging idolatry and pagan superstition. And the Puritan who would have no Christmas festivities, who put down the custom of plum porridge, and changed the name of Christmas pie to mince-pie, which it is still called. The gloomy face of the Puritan belongs to later developments, as do the texts worn on the sleeve, the lank hair, and the hat without a band.

With such a temper in the people, against such leaders, Charles and Laud began their campaign for the overthrow of civil and religious liberty. It is easy to exclaim against a short-sighted policy, and against the blindness of those who could not observe the signs of the times. In the absence of newspapers and public meetings, how was a statesman to understand the signs of the times ? The King, like his father, had not been brought up in the knowledge of English liberties and their history. To this ignorance a great deal of the blundering, both of James and of Charles, may be attributed. Laud, for his part, was an ecclesiastic through and through. It was not for him to seek out the opinions of the unlearned or of the dissentient. It was his business to enforce the ecclesiastical law as he found it, and as he designed to make it.

The number of London clergy afterwards ejected sufficiently proves the support which he obtained from that class. It is, indeed, always safe to expect support from the clergy whenever steps are taken to magnify the ecclesiastical office or to advance the sacerdotal pretensions. As it is in our time, so it was in the days of Laud.

The Archbishop ordered conformity with the ceremonies of the Prayer Book. The surplice was enforced ; the sign of the Cross in Baptism was continued ; the ring in marriage remained in use ; kneeling, and not sitting, at the administration of the Holy Communion became obligatory. The Geneva Bible, the old favourite of the people, with its short and pithy notes, was prohibited ; those ministers who refused to conform were ejected ; the lectures, which in London had been mostly on the Puritan side, were suppressed.

It became evident fifteen years later that the intolerance of Laud was not so much a subject of complaint as the enforcement of ritual and teaching abhorrent to the mind of Puritan, Presbyterian, and Independent. In 1644 it was proved that intolerance belonged equally to all sects. The possibility of allowing people differing in creeds to live in peace was not as yet admitted; nor would it be admitted until all alike, Anglican, Presbyterian, Independent, Quaker, Anabaptist, Socinian, Roman Catholic, had each and all in turn felt and realised that religion

A TRIMMER

From a contemporary print in the British Museum.

would mean continuous persecution, ejection, rebellion, and suffering, unless a *modus vivendi* were arrived at.

Meantime those who would be intolerant in their turn, but as yet could not, found the situation gloomy. They looked across the Atlantic and began to emigrate by thousands; not, as is too often asserted, to find across the ocean that freedom which they could not find here, but to find the power of living under the creed that they accepted, and of imposing it upon all who would live among them.

"The Land," says Clarendon, "was full of pride and mutiny." It seemed, at one time, as if the best blood of the country was going across the ocean. Hundreds of the clergy gave up their houses and went into poverty because they would not turn a table into an altar, and because they refused to take the least step which pointed in the direction of Rome.

And persecution and public punishment of men like Leighton and Prynne

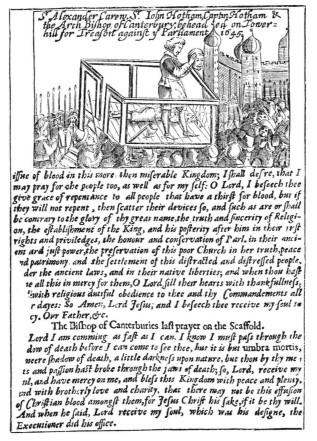

EXECUTION OF WILLIAM LAUD, ARCHBISHOP OF CANTERBURY (1645)

only had the effect of bringing the discontent of the people to the point of exasperation.

In the year 1633 appeared Prynne's *Histrio Mastix*, a violent attack on play-acting, dancing, and masques. In all these things the Queen took great delight. Therefore the work was supposed to be directed against her. A brutal sentence was inflicted upon Prynne, and was duly carried out, and after pillory, branding on the forehead, having his nose slit and his ears cut off, the wretched man was condemned to be disbarred, to be deprived of his University degree, and to be imprisoned for life.

The freedom of the press was of course attacked. Laud assumed a censorship over all new books and over the sale or circulation of old books. Among other books prohibited were Foxe's *Book of Martyrs* and Bishop Jewel's *Works*. Prynne, and with him Dr. Bastwick, a physician, and Henry Burton, a divine, all three being prisoners in the Tower, were prosecuted in the Star Chamber for writing libellous and schismatical books. They were sentenced to pay £5000 each; to stand in pillory; to lose their ears, or, in Prynne's case, to lose what was left of his ears; to be branded and to be imprisoned in Launceston, Lancaster, and Carnarvon. An immense multitude gathered to see the sentence carried out; they "cried and howled terribly"; they followed the prisoners with shouts of good wishes and groans for their persecutors; they threw money into the coach in which Burton's wife was sitting. Laud complained afterwards that the prisoners were suffered to speak to the people, and that notes were taken of their speeches and circulated in the City. At Chester, on his way to Carnarvon, Prynne was entertained by the Sheriff and a number of gentlemen, who refreshed him with a good dinner, and gave him tapestry and carpets for his cell.

Let us turn to the other side of religious opinion. If the Bible, and especially the Old Testament, furnished the popular side with arguments in support of every doctrine they professed, the same authority was called in for the maintenance and defence of the High Church and Loyalist party. Laud and his friends were by no means without Scriptural defence. For instance, the most rigid rule of conduct advanced by the divines of Charles the Second's reign was that of passive obedience, together with the corollary that resistance to the King's authority was a mortal sin. This doctrine seems to us absurd, we who inherit the training of two hundred years in the belief that all power is conferred by the people and may be withdrawn by the people. But, in fact, the doctrine was perfectly logical if one admitted that the English monarchy was an Oriental despotism such as that of Solomon or any other Eastern king. I have before me a sermon preached on February 6, 1668, in Ripon Cathedral, by the Dean, in which the doctrine is boldly advanced and upheld. The text is from 1 Kings viii. 66, and relates how, after the great and solemn function of the dedication with the blood of 22,000 oxen and 120,000 sheep—surely there is here a superfluity of ciphers—and after a great feast, the people went away blessing the King. One would think this a weak text for the support of such a doctrine, but the learned Dean bolsters it up with an abundance of instances and texts. Thus "St. Paul says that Kings are, not by God's sufferance but by his ordinance, and therefore, even supposing them never so bad, they are not to be resisted. You may take up the Buckles of Patience; but you must not take up Arms against them; for Rebellion is such rank Poison to the Soul, that the least Scruple of it is Damnable, the very intention of it in the Heart is Mortal."

In our passive obedience we may, if times are bad, console ourselves with the imitation of " Jeremiah in Prison ; Daniel in the Lion's Den ; Amos struck through the Temples ; Zachariah murdered between the Porch and the Altar ; our Blessed Saviour living under Herod and Tiberius and crucified under Pontius Pilate ; His Disciples under Caligula, Claudius, Nero, and Domitian ; Christian Bishops, under Heathen Persecutors ; none of whom ever reviled their Princes or resisted them." One might object that in these cases resistance would have been useless. But he goes on, " Who questioned Saul for slaying the Priests and revolting to Idolatry ? Who questioned Joram a Parricide and murderer of his nobles ? Or Joash for his Idolatry and slaying the High Priest ? Did the Sanhedrim do it ? Who questioned Theodosius for murdering six Thousand innocent Persons ? Who questioned Constance, or Valeros, or Julian the Apostate ? " Again, one objects the people had not the power to question. Again, " Mephibosheth said of David, ' My Lord the King is an Angel of God. Do therefore what is good in thine eyes.' "

" Did not God ordain Adam to rule over his wife without giving her or her children any commission to limit his power ? What was given to him in his Person was also given to his Posterity ; and the Paternal Government continued Monarchical from him to the Flood, and after that to the Confusion of Babel when Kingdoms were first erected and planted over the face of the Earth ? And so what right or Title, the People can have . . . to restrain the supremacy which was as untouched in Adam as any act of his will (it being due to the Supreme Father-hood) or from what time it commenced, the Scripture nowhere tells us. Where is the People's charter extant in Nature or in Scripture, for invading the Rights of the Crown ? Or what authority can they have from either to introduce their Devices of presiding over him whom God and Nature hath set over them ? "

This was the kind of preaching which was heard from a hundred pulpits in the City of London as well as in country churches and cathedrals during the whole reign of Charles II. and the beginning of his successor's short period of power. There can be no doubt that it persuaded many, that the preachers themselves were in earnest, and that there were few indeed among the congregation who were able to point to the weakness of a doctrine which rested on an absurdity so great as the parallel between the King of a free people whose liberties had slowly developed from prehistoric customs and an Oriental despotism.

Let us note one or two points of custom and popular belief and practice which should be taken into account when we consider the religious spirit of the time.

Fasting, for instance, was still practised and enjoined by the Church, as it is to this day. The Puritans, while they rebelled against the observance of days, maintained the duty of occasional fast days. The High Church party insisted vehemently on the duty of fasting, and the Restoration brought back the usage of fasting as part of the Church discipline. By this time, however, the poorer classes

10

had lost the habit of eating fish only on Fridays and in Lent, and it was impossible to enforce the practice.

Other customs and beliefs, survivals of the old faith, remained. Sanctuary, for example, although the ancient privileges had been abolished, although a criminal could no longer take refuge in a church, still continued under another form (see p. 170). That is to say, certain places remained where Sheriffs' officers could not venture, where a writ could not be served, and where a rogue could not be arrested. Among these places were the streets on the site of Whitefriars: Ram Alley, Salisbury Court, Mitre Court, the Precinct of the Savoy, Fulwood's Rents in Holborn, and on the other side of the river, Deadman's Place, the Mint, and Montagu Close. These pretended privileges were not abolished by law until the year 1697. Some of the places, in spite of this abolition, preserved their immunity for a time by the terror of their lawlessness and violence. The "humours" of Alsatia have been immortalised by Scott, but it must be remembered that there were many other places besides Whitefriars at that time equally entitled to the privileges of sanctuary.

The abolition of Episcopacy was followed by a persecution of those of the clergy who were known to sympathise with the Anglican forms. They were accused of immorality or malignancy; they were haled before the House, which deprived them of their livings and gave them to persons of better principles. Of the sufferings of the London clergy, Walker's well-known work gives a full account. He sums up as follows :—

"Thus were about One Hundred and Ten of the London Clergy turned out of their Livings (nor do I know whether the List be yet compleat), above Forty of which were Doctors of Divinity, and most of them Plunder'd of their Goods, and their Wives and Children turned out of Doors. About twenty were imprisoned in London, and in the Ships, and in the several Jayls and Castles in the Country; upward of that Number fled to prevent the like Imprisonment. About Twenty Two died soon after in remote Parts, in Prisons, and with Grief; and about Forty Churches lay void, having no constant Minister in them.

They were most, if not all, of them turned out in the Years 1642 and 1643. Some few more immediately by the House of Commons; but most of them by the Committee of Religion, and that of Plunder'd Ministers, and chiefly, as I conceive, by the latter: The Resolutions of which Committee were in the beginning, if I mistake not, mostly reported to the House: But when that Godly Work increas'd upon their hands, a Power was lodg'd in the Committee, as I take it, which made their Resolutions Final. I must here add that a Learned and Eminent Person who liv'd through, and suffer'd under those Times, gives this Character of the then London Clergy in general: 'That for a more Pious, Learn'd, and Laborious Ministry, no People ever Enjoy'd it, even their enemies themselves being Judges'" (John Walker, *Account of the Sufferings of the Clergy*, 1714, p. 180).

For a list of the London clergy ejected see Appendix II.

In June 1643 a council or company of one hundred and twenty divines, called " Pious, godly, and judicious," was summoned to meet at Westminster to consider the new form of national church. With them were joined thirty laymen, namely, ten Lords and twenty Commoners. The Houses laid down rules for the form of the meetings and the subject of the debates. Among the hundred and twenty was a certain proportion of Episcopalians, who, however, refused to attend; the majority were Presbyterians, anxious to establish the discipline and doctrine of the foreign reformed churches; but there was also among them a small body of Independents. The difference between the two parties was very important. The former desired a church resembling that of the old Established Church in a gradation of spiritual authorities in presbyteries, classes, synods, and assemblies, giving to these bodies the power of censure, punishment, deprivation, and excommunication. The latter held that every congregation stood by itself, that there should be no central authority, and that churches should be left free to differ in doctrine.

The Council were unanimous in minor points; they removed organs; they prohibited the surplice and the cope; they destroyed monuments of idolatry, but they could not agree as to church government. Finally, they agreed in the production of a Directory of public worship, which introduced order into the service and regulated the administration of the sacraments, the ceremony of marriage, the visitation of the sick, and the burial of the dead.

On Friday, January 3, 1645, the Ordinance for the abolition of the Book of Common Prayer, and for the establishment in its place of a new Directory for the public worship of God, was passed:—

"In the Preamble it is set forth that the 'Lords and Commons assembled in Parliament, taking into serious consideration the manifold inconveniences that have arisen by the Book of Common-Prayer in this Kingdome, and resolving according to their Covenant to reforme Religion according to the Word of God and the example of the best Reformed Churches, have consulted with the Reverend, Pious and Learned Divines, called together to that purpose; And doe Judge it necessary that the said Book of Common-Prayer be abolished, and the Directory for the Publike Worship of GOD herein after mentioned, bee established and observed in all the Churches within this Kingdome."

"And that the Directory for publike Worship herein set forth shall bee henceforth used, perused, and observed according to the true intent and meaning of this Ordinance, in all Exercises of the Publike Worship of God, in every Congregation, Church, Chappell, and place of Publike Worship within this Kingdome of England, and Dominion of Wales; Which Directory for the Publike Worship of God, with the Preface thereof followeth " (*The Directory*, p. 4).

The same preamble ordered that in every church there should be kept a register for the names of all who were baptized, married, or buried in the churchyard.

The Directory may be condensed as follows:—

1. Orderly behaviour in Church without salutations, greetings, or whispering.
2. Commencement with Prayer.

"In all reverence and Humility acknowledging the incomprehensible Greatnesse and Majesty of the Lord (in whose presence they doe then in a speciall manner appeare) and their owne vilenesse to approach so neare him; with their utter inability of themselves, to so great a work: And humbly beseeching him for pardon, Assistance, and Acceptance in the whole service then to be performed; and for a Blessing on that particular portion of his Word then to be read: and all, in the Name and Mediation of the Lord Jesus Christ."

3. After prayer reading of the scriptures; the length and the portion chosen to be left to the Minister, with a recommendation to read one chapter of the Old and one of the New at every meeting.

4. Expounding of the Scripture read to be performed after the reading.

5. After the Reading, Public Prayer, the general heads of which are set forth at length.

6. The Sermon.
   Here follow instructions for the preacher.

7. After the sermon, another prayer.

8. The Prayer ended, let a Psalm be sung, if with conveniency it may be done.

The rite of baptism is ordered; one notes that the sign of the Cross is omitted.

The celebration of the Lord's Supper is to take place after the sermon and psalm. The communicants are to sit round a table covered with a white cloth. Prayer is to be offered, in which it is to be specially noted that the bread and wine remain bread and wine, but that by faith the body and blood of Christ are taken by the communicant.

The "Sanctification of the Lord's Day" assumes that it is the Sabbath, and orders that no unnecessary work be carried on, and that the same not spent in church is to be devoted to reading, meditation, and catechising.

The marriage service is very short. There is to be a prayer with a declaration of Scripture on the subject, after which the man and the woman are to take hands and take each other for wife and husband :—

"Concerning the Burial of the Dead," the *Directory* says, "and because the customes of kneeling down, and praying by, or towards the dead Corps, and other such usages, in the place where it lies, before it be carried to Buriall, are Superstitious : and for that, praying, reading, and singing both in going to, and at the Grave, have been grosly abused, are no way beneficiall to the dead, and have proved many ways hurtfull to the living ; therefore let all such things be laid aside."

On days of fasting there is to be total abstinence from all kinds of food and from all kinds of work.

As for singing of Psalms :—

"The voice is to be tunably and gravely ordered : but the chief care must be, to sing with understanding, and with Grace in the heart, making melody unto the Lord."

"That the whole Congregation may joyne herein, every one that can read is to have a Psalme book, and all others not disabled by age, or otherwise, are to be exhorted to learn to read. But for the present, where many in the Congregation cannot read, it is convenient that the Minister, or some other fit person appointed by him and the other Ruling Officers, doe read the Psalme, line by line, before the singing thereof" (*Directory*, p. 43).

On the 23rd of August following, another ordinance was passed for the taking away of the Book of Common Prayer from all churches and chapels in the kingdom. It was also ordered that the knights and burgesses of the counties should send copies of the Directory, bound in leather, to the constables and other officers of every parish in the kingdom, and that within one week after receiving the books, the constables should hand the books to the minister of the parish.

Pains and penalties for disobedience to these orders conclude the Ordinance.

There are abundant materials for showing the violence of the passions excited in London by the religious controversy of the time. We see the soldiers on guard at Lambeth breaking into the church in time of service, tearing the Prayer Book to pieces, stripping the clergyman of his surplice, and desecrating the altar, until the Thames watermen come to the assistance of the people and there is a fight in the body of the church. We see a party of horse riding through the streets, four of them attired in surplices, tearing the Book of Common Prayer in pieces, leaf by leaf, with gestures unseemly. We find the clergy accused of the most infamous crimes—"common drunkenness, looseness of life, adultery," and worse. We find some of the people in church sitting with their hats on, and some with their hats off, and riots in consequence. We hear of fanatics preaching the wildest doctrines and forming the most wonderful sects. There is neither tolerance, nor charity, nor patience. There is no authority; there is no respect for learning; every one, in every station, interprets Scripture in blind confidence that he is fully equal to the task of framing a bran-new constitution for a bran-new sect. And with it all, a power almost pathetic, of sitting out the longest sermons. On one occasion two ministers, one after the other, engaged the attention of the House of Commons for seven long hours. The people presently grew weary of the incessant wranglings over doctrine; sane persons began to understand that the task of making ignorant men and women agree in matters of creed was hopeless; it became understood that divergence of opinion would be no more tolerated by Independents than it was by Presbyterians; at this point of weariness it was extremely fortunate for the country that the reaction restored them to the Church of England instead of the Church of Rome. It was wonderful how the great mass of the people sank back contentedly into their old form of faith, relieved to find at last that they might leave the dogmas of religion to divines and scholars and be free themselves to illustrate in their private lives the virtues of religion by the exercise of faith, hope, and charity, which, for twenty years and more, seemed to have deserted the City of London.

A single example of the religious dissensions of the time will doubtless stand for many more. I have before me a pamphlet written by the Rev. J. Dodd, which originally appeared in the *English Historical Review* (Spottiswoode, 1895), on the troubles of St. Botolph, Aldgate, during this period. To quote Mr. Dodd's own words, " it is a fairly complete picture of the state of discord, and probably had many a parallel throughout England."

In 1642 the then Vicar, a follower of Laud, one Thomas Swadlin, was deprived of his living and sent to Newgate. After his departure the living was held by a succession of obscure preachers, probably of Puritanic views, till 1654, when Laurence Wise, the last of them, either died or resigned. In August of that year, by popular election, one John Mackarness, a clergyman in Anglican orders, was appointed.

Cromwell, however, intervened, and a Presbyterian, Zachary Crofton, was appointed in his place. Crofton was an Irishman who had been in arms against the King; he was then pastor, first of Newcastle-under-Lyne, next of Winbury, in Cheshire. He refused to take the oath to the Government of 1649 "without King or House of Lords," and lost his living. In London he obtained the church of St. James's, Garlickhithe. Here he made himself known as a hot-headed controversialist, and by no means a friend of Cromwell, who, however, nominated him to St. Botolph's.

Crofton went, therefore, to St. Botolph's, and found a congenial field for a fighting man. He was himself a Presbyterian; the afternoon lecturer was one John Simpson, who had also, like Crofton, been in the Army, and was now an Independent and an Anabaptist. Crofton alienated some of the former sect by attempting to revive "disception" in his church—that is to say, he forbade unworthy persons from approaching the Lord's Table. He enraged the Anabaptists by the importance which he attached to the baptism of infants. He also desired to catechise the children, and printed a short catechism for them. Simpson held that you might as well buy rattles or hobby horses for children as catechisms. Crofton began by refusing to recognise Simpson as afternoon lecturer; the parishioners petitioned Cromwell to allow him one lecture in the church on the Lord's Day and one in the week. This was granted, and Crofton had to give way.

Then occurred a charge which Crofton always denied, but which was brought up against him continually. A certain maid-servant accused him of chastising her with a rod in an improper manner. Afterwards she swore that she had been bribed to bring the accusation.

In 1657 Crofton sent a letter to John Simpson; he was going to take possession of his own pulpit, and Simpson might commence an action as soon as he pleased. Simpson, however, complained to the Council of State, and an order was granted him to preach in the afternoon. Accordingly on Sunday, Crofton being in the pulpit and surrounded by his friends, John Simpson and his party entered the church and presented the order. It was addressed to Grafton, not Crofton. "This order is not for me," said the Vicar; whereupon the Simpson party retired, beaten for once. The Council of State again interfered and Crofton had to submit. He took revenge by charging Simpson's three principal friends with brawling in church. They were acquitted; he made a public protest in the church. John Simpson then began to preach against infant baptism; Crofton charged him with heresy and demanded of him a defence of his position. Simpson preserved silence. But he took other steps. He charged Crofton with being a declared enemy to the Government and with preaching sedition and insurrection. Crofton refused to acknowledge the jurisdiction of the Court. He published a pamphlet, however, in which he defended himself and told a pretty story of parish dissensions and persecutions. After this came the whirlwind. Cromwell died. Crofton went into the country just before the Cheshire rising, and was charged with preaching to the rebels; from this he cleared himself. He then threw himself into the politics of the time, strongly advocating a free Parliament; he preached at St. Peter's, Cornhill, for the restoration of Charles the Second; meantime John Simpson had vanished and the magnanimous Crofton preached a sermon on peace. He lost his church at the Restoration; he was consigned to the Tower for a twelvemonth; he went down into Cheshire and turned cheese-factor; he was again arrested for sowing sedition; he went back to London and started a grocer's shop; under the pressure of the Five Mile Act he left London and took a farm at Little Barford in Bedfordshire; after the Plague he returned to London and set up a school in Aldgate; it was here that he preached a course of sermons in St. James's, Duke's Place, which he afterwards published under the title of "The Saints' Care for Church Communion." He died just before Christmas 1672, and his body lies buried in the churchyard of his old parish.

This story illustrates the feverish unrest of the time: the parish divided into furious parties; one clergyman preaching infant baptism; the other preaching that it was as idle to give the child a catechism as a rattle; calumniations and recriminations of the vilest kind; the Restoration; ejections; an attempt to earn a living by making cheese, by farming, by keeping a shop, by keeping a school. A strange story of a strange time!

As a part of the religious aspect of the City one must not omit the desecration of St. Paul's, which, during the twenty years 1640-1660, was carried out in a manner so resolute and thorough as to show the deliberate intention of giving the citizens, who still gloried in their venerable Cathedral, a lesson in the revolution of religious thought.

The Cathedral, as Dean Milman says, was, under the Puritans, a vast useless pile, the lair of old superstition and idolatry. It would have been pulled down but for the trouble and the expense. The Parliament, however, did what they could to procure its destruction; there was a sum of £17,000 lying in the chambers of the City which remained out of the subscriptions for repairing the church. This was seized. There had also been erected round the tower a scaffolding of wood which was taken down and sold for £174, the whole being given to Colonel Jefferson's regiment for arrears of pay. When the scaffolding was taken away, part of the roof of the south transept fell in. Whereupon the Mayor and Aldermen represented the necessity of getting more water into the City, and begged the lead that covered the roof towards the pipes for carrying the water.

In 1642 the removal of crucifixes and other superstitious objects was ordered. In the same year all the copes belonging to the Cathedral were burned. In 1645 the silver plate of St. Paul's was sold, and the money spent in providing artillery.

The Cathedral, according to the story, was offered by Cromwell to the Jews, who refused to buy it. The east end was walled off for the congregation of the lecturer, Cornelius Burgess. Inigo's portico was let out in small shops to sempstresses and hucksters, with chambers above and stairs leading to them. The body of the church became a cavalry barrack and stable. Paul's Cross was pulled down.

The intolerance of the time may be illustrated by a hundred stories. Take, for instance, the punishment of the unfortunate James Naylor.

On the 18th day of December 1656 a man stood in pillory for two hours at the Old Palace Yard, Westminster. The case attracted some attention because the man was a crack-brained enthusiast, originally in the Society of Friends, who had been parading on horseback accompanied by three women and one or two men singing, " Holy, Holy, Holy is the Lord God of Hosts." These people also called him the Everlasting Son of Righteousness, the Prince of Peace, the Fairest of Ten Thousand. The whole company were arrested and sent to London, where Parliament considered the case of the man, whose name was James Naylor.

In accordance with their sentence, he was first placed in pillory at Westminster for two hours; he was then taken down, tied to the cart's tail, and whipped by the hangman all the way to the Old Exchange in the City. He received three hundred and ten strokes, and should have received one more, " there being three hundred and eleven kennels "—I know not what this means. By this time he was in a most pitiful condition, as may be imagined. According to the sentence, he should have stood in pillory for two hours more, and then have had his tongue bored with a red-hot iron, but he could no longer stand. Therefore he was respited for a week. At the end of that time, although many people petitioned for his pardon, the other part of the sentence was most cruelly inflicted. This was not all. As soon as he recovered he was sent on to Bristol, where he was flogged through the town and laid in prison.

The case of James Naylor happened in the Commonwealth. But religious toleration was no more understood under a King than under a Protector. The sufferings of the Quakers in the reign of Charles the Second prove this fact. In 1662 there were 4200 of this Society imprisoned in various parts of England either for frequenting meetings or refusing to take oaths or for keeping away from Church. Some of them were crowded into prisons so close that there was not room for all to sit down at once; they were tradesmen, shopkeepers, and husbandmen; their property was confiscated; they were refused straw to lie upon; they were often denied food. Here is an extract from Sewel :—

"At London, and in the suburbs, where about this time no less than five hundred of those called Quakers, imprisoned, and some in such narrow holes, that every person scarcely had convenience to lie down; and the felons were suffered to rob them of their clothes and money. Many that were not imprisoned, nevertheless suffered hardships in their religious meetings, especially that in London, known by the name of Bull and Mouth. Here the trained bands came frequently, armed generally with muskets, pikes, and halbards, and conducted by a military officer, by order of the city magistracy ; and rushing in, in a very furious manner, fell to beating them, whereby many were grievously wounded, some fell down in a swoon, and some were beaten so violently, that they lived not long after it. Among these was one John Trowel, who was so bruised and crushed, that a few days after he died. His friends therefore thought it expedient to carry the corpse into the aforesaid meeting place, that it might lie there exposed for some hours, to be seen of every one. This being done, raised commiseration and pity among many of the inhabitants ; for the corpse, beaten like a jelly, looked black, and was swoln in a direful manner. This gave occasion to send for the coroner, and he being come, empannelled a jury of the neighbours, and gave them in charge according to his office, to make true enquiry upon their oaths, and to present what they found to be the cause of his death. They, viewing the corpse, had a surgeon or two with them, to know their judgment concerning it ; and then going together in private, at length they withdrew without giving in their verdict, only desiring the friends to bury the corpse, which was done accordingly that evening. And though the coroner and jury met divers times together upon that occasion, and had many consultations, yet they never would give in a verdict ; but it appeared sufficiently, that the man was killed by violent beating. The reasons some gave for the suspense of a verdict were, that though it was testified that the same person, now dead, was seen beaten, and knocked down ; yet it being done in such a confused crowd, no particular man could be fixed upon, so that any could say, that man did the deed. And if a verdict was given that the deceased person was killed, and yet no particular person charged with it, then the City was liable to a great fine, at the pleasure of the king, for conniving at such a murder in the city in the day-time, not committed in a corner, but in a publick place, and not apprehending the murderer, but suffering him to escape. In the meanwhile the friends of the deceased were not wanting to give public notice of the fact, and sent also a letter to the lord mayor, which afterwards they gave out in print, together with a relation of this bloody business. In this letter it was said, ' It may be supposed thou hast heard of this thing, for it was done not in the night, but at the mid-time of the day ; not suddenly, at unawares, or by mishap, but intendedly, and a long space of time a doing ; and not in a corner, but in the streets of the city of London ; all which circumstances do highly aggravate this murder, to the very shame and infamy of this famous city and its government ' " (William Sewel, *History of the Quakers*, 1722, p. 346).

CHAPTER II

THE CHURCH AND DISSENT

AFTER the Restoration the religious condition of the City was greatly modified. First the Church of England was enormously stronger than it had been in any part of Charles the First's reign. Then the persecution of Roman Catholics and Non-

John Bunyan's Meeting-house, Zoar-street, Gravel-lane, Southwark.

conformists affected London more than the country, first because many of the former had taken refuge in London, and next because the City contained thousands of the latter, some of whom obstinately refused any show of conformity. In 1666 the King banished all Roman Catholic priests; in the following year he forbade his subjects to hear Mass at the Queen's or any Ambassador's chapel. At the same time he called upon the civil officers to enforce the statutes provided. In 1671, when as yet few City churches were rebuilt, he ordered that certain places hitherto used as conventicles should be used as churches, served by orthodox ministers appointed by the Bishop of London :—

" In Fisher's-folly, in Bishopsgate Street—a convenient place, with two galleries, pews, and seats.

In Hand-alley, in Bishopsgate Street—a large room, purposely built for a meeting-house, with three galleries, thirty large pews, and many benches and forms, known by the name of Vincent's congregation.

In St. Michael's Lane—a large room, with two galleries and thirty-nine forms.

In Mugwell Street—Mr. Doolittle's meeting-house, built of brick, with three galleries, full of large pews ; and thirty-eight large pews below, with locks and keys to them, besides benches and forms.

The Cockpit in Jewin Street—a meeting-house of one Grimes, many pews, forms, and benches.

In Blackfriars—Mr. Wood's meeting-house ; four rooms, opening into one another, with lattice partitions, each room conveniently fitted with benches and forms.

In Salisbury Court—four rooms, opening into one another, in the possession of John Foule, a schoolmaster.

In New Street, within Shoe Lane—four rooms, opening into one another, with seventeen pews, and divers benches, in the possession of Mrs. Turner."

During the Commonwealth we find certain games forbidden, as the " Whimsey Board," which used to be played in Lincoln's Inn Fields. Persons guilty of playing the virginals in taverns were punished for " living loosely." Search was continually made for Catholics. There were dissensions in certain City churches about altar rails and other things. The word saint was omitted. Weddings were celebrated by the Alderman of the ward, and banns were published in Leadenhall Market. The hospitals, with revenues greatly diminished, were used for the wounded soldiers. In the same year it was thought necessary to repeat the order for the banishment of priests, and in 1673 Catholic recusants were forbidden to enter the Palace or Park of St. James's or the precincts of Whitehall. The Catholics, however, continued to flock to the Ambassadors' chapels. It was therefore ordered that messengers of the Chamber or other officers should be stationed at the approaches to these chapels in order to arrest those proposing to attend service there.

In 1679 all Roman Catholics in London were ordered to leave the City and to withdraw at least ten miles from it.

The constant repetition of these ordinances proves that they were never enforced save by occasional fits of zeal ; the Catholics went away ; a week later they returned ; no doubt the officers were bribed to shut their eyes. Yet the system was most exasperating; for a Catholic to be compelled to attend a Protestant service was almost as bad as for a Mohammedan to be compelled to eat pig; the Catholic rule about attending heretical services is never relaxed; while a zealous church-warden, armed with blank warrants, which he could fill up as he pleased in order to arrest and to fine, might make life intolerable. A good many young Catholics went abroad for education, and presently found it expedient to stay there. The Non-conformists, for their part, had no intention of submitting meekly. There were riots and tumults in the City. In 1681 the Middlesex magistrates endeavoured to put in execution the Act of Charles II. :—

"Which enacts, that all those who preached in conventicles or meetings, contrary to the statutes of the realm, shall not come within five miles of a corporation; that no person shall teach in any school under the penalty of £40, unless he attend the established church. And that of the 20th year of the same reign, which ordains, that if any person above sixteen years of age attended a religious assembly in a house where more than five others, exclusive of the household, were present, except the rites were according to the established church, any person preaching there should forfeit a certain sum."

It was presently reported, to the blind terror and indignation of the zealous, that in certain houses lately erected Catholics had opened schools, and had attracted many pupils and numbers of people, their parents and relations. It was therefore enacted that those persons who, having licences for keeping houses of entertainment, did not attend church and, instead, attended any kind of conventicle, should lose their licence, and—a very serious blow against Catholics and Nonconformists—money should not be given to the poor unless they attended church. The Privy Council, having a list of Catholic tradesmen in St. Martin's-in-the-Fields, St. Giles's, and St. Paul's, Covent Garden, set an example to the City by ordering the Justices of the Peace to proceed against them according to law.

The history of Nonconformity in London has been treated in the book of the Eighteenth Century. The following, however, is a list of conventicles and preachers in the year 1680 :—

"Holborn, Short's Gardens, Case, Presbyterian Minister.
Chequer Yard, Dowgate Hill, Watson, Presbyterian, 300.
Cutler's Hall, Cole, Presbyterian, 400.
Hand Alley, Bishopsgate Street, Vincent the Elder, 800.
Glovers' Hall, Beech Lane, Cripplegate, Fifth Monarchy Meeting.
Devonshire House, Bishopsgate, Harcostell, Anabaptist.
New Street, Fetter Lane, Cross.
Gracechurch Street, Gibson.
Devonshire House, Haward, drysalter.
Barking, Benj. Antrobus.
The Golden Harrow, Bishopsgate Without, linen-draper.
Plaistow, Clement Plumstead, ironmonger.
Three Cranes, Thames Street, R. Haward, coal merchant.
Barking, T. Bagley, Lothbury, clockmaker.

Little Eastcheap, R. Whitepace, butcher.
Cornhill, W. Mead, draper.
Leadenhall Street, S. Loveday, Anabaptist.
Star Alley, East Smithfield, Isaac Lamb, shoemaker."

The example of religious discussion and the examination of doctrine penetrated, as has been set forth, to the lower classes. A case in point is that of Oliver
Cromwell's porter. This man, whose Christian name was Daniel, learned in
Cromwell's service much of the cant that prevailed at that time. He was a great
plodder in books of divinity, especially in those of the mystical kind, which are
supposed to have turned his brain. He was many years in Bedlam, where his
library was, after some time, allowed him, as there was not the least probability of
his cure. The most conspicuous of his books was a large Bible given him by Nell
Gwynne. He frequently preached and sometimes prophesied, and was said to have
foretold several remarkable events, particularly the Fire of London. One would
think that Butler had this frantic enthusiast in view when he says :—

> " Had lights where better eyes were blind,
>   As pigs are said to see the wind ;
>   Fill'd Bedlam with predestination."
>   (*Hudibras*).

Mr. Charles Leslie, who has placed him in the same class with Fox and Muggleton,
tells us that people often went to hear him preach, and " would sit many hours
under his window with great signs of devotion." That gentleman had the curiosity
to ask a grave matron who was among his auditors, " What she could profit by
hearing that madman ? " She, with a composed countenance, as pitying his ignorance,
replied, that " Festus thought Paul was mad."

In the year 1692 one Robert Midgley was moved to speak out on behalf of the
churches and their services. His pamphlet is useful in showing the conduct of the
religious services in the City of London at that time. He imitated the methods of
the theatres in issuing a printed paper of services and hours. I omit a portion of
his preamble :—

"And now considering the ways and methods which Satan and his Emissaries have taken to fill *his*
Chirches, the Theatres, with Votaries, have been (not by Bells, which make a great noise near hand and are
not heard afar off, but) by silently dispersing their Bills, and setting them up at the corners of the streets,
whereby they do draw People from all Parts to their contagious Assemblies, I was easily convinced of the
Success of the like Undertaking for the Service of Almighty God, and therefore could no longer excuse
myself for the Omission thereof. These are, therefore, Dearly beloved in Christ Jesus, to acquaint you
where ye may daily, with the congregations of the Faithful, assemble together at the House of Prayer ; where
you may, in Imitation of the Apostles of our Lord, every Lord's Day partake of the blessed Sacrament of
the Lord's Supper ; and lastly, where there are any extraordinary regular Lectures to be heard ; in all which,
for your good, I have spared no pains for the certainty of my own information nor Charges in the Dispersing
hereof for yours. And now know that the wilful Neglect of these means will one day have a sad after-
reckoning, and that this Paper will then rise up in judgment against you.

If this Paper[1] have its desired effect, I trust Almighty God will open the hearts of his faithful Labourers, to set up Daily Prayer and weekly Communion in many of their own churches, where at present it is not.

For the sake of such as, during the whole time this is dispersing, may happen, either by sickness, Absence, or otherwise, not to come in the way of it, there shall be of them to be bought, *Price one Half-penny*, which is also *Corban*, and therefore put into the hands but of one person to sell; whoever else, therefore, does sell them, does also Print them, and consequently does not only rob this Bookseller of his Copy (which cost the Author so much labour to form) but all the Poor also of their just due herein, which it is hoped every Christian Buyer will remember and consider.   ROB. MIDGLEY."

From his list it appears that there were four daily services in one church, three in seven churches, two in forty-one, and one in thirty-six. That the Holy Communion was administered every Sunday in eight churches, three times a month in two, twice at two churches, viz. the chapels of Gray's Inn and Lincoln's Inn, and on the first Sunday of the month at all the other churches. As regards the hour, at two churches there were two celebrations at 7 A.M. and noon, in two at 6 A.M., in one at 8 A.M.; in all the rest at noon.

There were lectures in three churches at 6 A.M. every Sunday, in one church at 7 A.M., in one at 10 A.M., in two at 4 P.M., in ten at 5 P.M., and in one at 6 P.M. On week days there were four churches where a lecture was given once a week at 6 A.M., one at 9 A.M., twelve at 10 A.M., one at 11 A.M., one at 2 P.M., three at 3 P.M., four at 4 P.M., one at 5 P.M., and one at 6 P.M. Of evening service, as we understand it, there was none. It is, however, without doubt that all the churches were open practically every day for service, and that all the week round a pious person might hear a sermon in the morning and another in the evening; or he might run round from church to church and hear sermons all day long.

Charity has always been closely coupled with church-going in theory at least. In Appendix III. will be found a list of the almshouses of London of this period.

This list, containing forty-one almshouses in which hospitals are not included and seventeen schools, appears to speak well for the charity, well directed and deliberate, of the seventeenth century. Out of the whole number of almshouses in existence in the year 1756, when this list was compiled, the seventeenth century founded nearly the half, and of the whole number of endowed schools existing in 1753, the seventeenth century contributed exactly one half.

Of the greatest of all the "almshouses" founded in the Stuart period, viz. Chelsea Hospital, I do not speak in this place, as a full account of it is given elsewhere in the Survey.[2]

---

[1] The *Second Impression, Corrected and Enlarged,* Price one Halfpenny. Sold by Samuel Keble at the Turk's Head in Fleet Street, 1692.

[2] See *Chelsea* in the "Fascination of London Series." A. and C. Black.

CHAPTER III

SUPERSTITIONS

FOREMOST among the superstitious beliefs of the century was that of witchcraft. It became, indeed, more actively mischievous and more real in the minds of the people on account of the universal habit, considered as a Christian duty, of referring everything to the Bible, as much to the Old as to the New Testament. Theologians of all sects believed in witchcraft and in the active interference of the Devil. Erasmus and Luther, for instance, were believers in witchcraft, while King James wrote on witches. The persecution of miserable old women, accused of being witches because they were old and poor, was carried on throughout the seventeenth century; it is a frightful record of cruelty and superstition, especially in the eastern counties, which were mainly Puritan, and therefore even more inclined than the rest of England to accept the literal application of the Old Testament to their own time. " Thou shalt not suffer a witch to live," said the Book of Exodus. " There shall not be found among you," said the Book of Deuteronomy, "one that useth divinations, or an observer of times, or an enchanter, or a witch, or a charmer, or a consulter with familiar spirits, or a wizard, or a necromancer." Could anything be plainer? Again, " Regard not them that have familiar spirits, neither seek after wizards to be defiled with them. I am the Lord your God."

The belief in witchcraft was universal, but the persecution was not; in London, though there is no reason to doubt the belief, there are few cases on record of the actual persecution of witches. One case is that of Sarah Mordyke, who was apprehended at Paul's Wharf, charged with bewitching one Richard Hetheway, near the Falcon Stairs in Southwark. She was taken before certain learned Justices in Bow Lane. The victim swore that he had lost his appetite, voided pins, etc., but recovered when he had scratched and brought blood from Sarah Mordyke, the witch.

Another case is that of Sarah Griffith. She lived in Rosemary Lane. She had long been considered a bad woman, but nothing could be proved against her, though it was suspicious that her neighbours' children were affected with strange distempers, and were affrighted with apparitions of cats. One day, however, she was buying soap in a shop when the apprentice laughed at the scales not being right, and said they must be bewitched. Whereupon the old woman thought he was laughing at her and vowed vengeance. Sure enough, in the night everything in the shop was turned topsy-turvy.

Two or three days after, the apprentice, with two or three friends, was walking towards New River Head when they met Sarah Griffith. It was a favourable opportunity to try her, so they tossed her into the canal. Instead of drowning she swam like a cork—a sure sign of her guilt. When they let her come out she smote the young man on the arm, making a mark as black as a coal, and told him he should pay dear for what he had done. So he went home in a great fright and died. After this his master took a constable and brought her before the Justices, charging her with compassing the death of his apprentice by witchcraft. She was accordingly committed to the Clerkenwell Bridewell, and I know not what became of her afterwards.

I have before me a short pamphlet on the tragic history of a young gentleman of Stepney who sold himself to the Devil.

When one remembers Defoe's mystification about Mrs. Veal one suspects that this story is also an invention, devised for the purpose of inspiring godly fear, and based upon popular superstition rather than a narrative put together on hearsay, exaggerated as it passed from lip to lip. The story is quite in Defoe's circumstantial manner. A young gentleman named Watts, son of Mr. William Watts of Stepney and of Anne, daughter of Squire Wilson of Brentwood, was the only survivor of four children. He was therefore treated with the greatest indulgence and tenderness. After five years at St. John's College, Oxford, he returned home and began to keep evil company, being already ripe in wickedness. His parents remonstrated with him, but in vain. Finally, his father refused to give him any more money for the support of his extravagances. The son, in a great rage, swore that he would be revenged upon his parents even to the hazard of his soul. He took a lodging at some distance from his father's house, and fell to devising how he might get the estate into his own hands.

Now, as he was thus meditating, Satan himself came into the room and asked the reason of his sadness. After a little conversation the young man consented to sign away his soul with his own blood in return for as much money as he could spend in twelve years.

When the time approached he went home, struck with terror and remorse, and confessed to his father all that he had done.

His father sent for certain divines who are duly mentioned, viz. Dr. Russel of Wapping, Dr. Sannods, Dr. Smithies, and Dr. Paul. These clergymen gathered round the poor wretch, now weeping and wringing his hands, and entreated him to pray ; but he could not, so they prayed for him, but in vain ; for in the middle of the night there arose a dreadful storm of thunder, lightning, rain, and hail, and in the midst of the storm the Devil came into the room " in dreadful shapes," snatched the young man from their midst, dashed out his brains against the wall, tore him limb from limb, and scattered the fragments on the dunghill behind the house.

The pamphlet concludes with a sermon preached upon this doleful occasion. The story is, as I said before, either an exaggerated account of some local rumour, or it is a deliberate invention, which is, of course, the more probable. In either case it proves the continued existence of the old traditions about selling one's self to the Devil, of which we find abundant examples among the mediæval chronicles. The superstition must be added to those already recorded of the seventeenth century.

It is needless to add that the bagful of superstitions was swallowed whole by people of every rank and class. In the *Spectator* we read how the girls vied with each other in telling ghost stories. They watched for omens, and made themselves miserable when these were unlucky; they remembered their dreams carefully and consulted the *Dictionary of Dreams* or the nearest wise woman; they learned what was coming by the tingling of the ears, irritation of the nose, specks on the nails, and other signs; the meeting of birds and creatures filled them with terror; they read warnings in the candle and in the fire; the dogs howled in sign of approaching death. Most of these superstitions are still with us, more or less. It must, however, be observed that London, with its crowded, busy, active life, was far less troubled with superstitions than the country; people had no time to worry over signs and omens in the midst of their full and busy lives.

Lucky and unlucky days played a very important part in the conduct of life. Cromwell's lucky day was the 3rd of September. Thursday was an unlucky day for Henry VIII. and his children. Every change of moon brought an unlucky day; there were also certain unlucky days in every month. Lord Burghley, who despised these observances as a rule, kept three days in the year as especially unlucky. The reasons why he considered them unlucky mark a great gulf between his time and ours. The first Monday in April was one, because on that day Cain was born and Abel was killed. The second Monday in August was another, because then Sodom and Gomorrah were destroyed. The remaining day was the last Monday in December, because at that time Judas Iscariot was born. How these days were discovered, and why they should be unlucky for all time to follow, are questions which it is impossible to answer.

Almanacks containing lists of lucky and unlucky days were in great request, and continued until quite recently. They were consulted by everybody before entering upon any kind of work.

The autobiography of William Lilly is valuable for its unconscious exposure of fraud, impudence, credulity, and superstition. He lived throughout the greater part of the seventeenth century. It was an age in which the so-called science of astrology flourished exceedingly. The astrologer not only cast nativities and foretold in general terms the future of a man, but also condescended to answer questions concerning doubtful points, as in matters of love ; found lucky days for the commencement of any business or enterprise ; discovered thefts and thieves ; practised physic without preliminary training, and compelled, by means of the crystal ball or some other magic, spirits and angels to perform their bidding. In all these pretensions and powers Lilly firmly believed ; yet he was unable to prove them by making the spirits, his servants, obey him in great things—such as the rescue of King Charles and the triumph of his cause. Moreover, in his simple chat about his brethren of the fraternity he is quite unable to see how he gives away the whole of his own pretensions by exposing their weakness and their failures. Thus one of them " sets a figure " about himself. He learns from this figure that he is to be a Lord or great man within two years. Alas ! in two years he was in Newgate Prison. Another time he set his figure, and learned that he was to be a great man within a year. But in that year he advanced not one whit. And being consulted by a friend about to undertake a voyage, he learned by astrology that it would be a fortunate adventure. Unhappily it proved the reverse, for the adventurer was taken prisoner by pirates and lost his all. He set down four or five other judgments, in every one of which he was wrong. Lilly, however, sees in these failures no reflection on the " science " at all. Another of them, Evans, a clergyman who had to give up his benefice on account of some scandal, lived by giving judgment on things lost ; he was " much addicted to debauchery," very abusive and quarrelsome ; he made and sold antimonial cups, and he was in correspondence with an angel named Salmon, whom he ordered to fetch and carry for him. His portrait, if it is genuine, represents a face like a dog's—the most ill-favoured, ill-conditioned, repulsive face imaginable. Another, Alexander Hart, used his wonderful powers for finding lucky days for young gentlemen about to gamble. Lilly does not seem to have grasped the elementary fact that any one actually possessing magical powers would certainly use them for his own enrichment. And there was Captain Bubb, who " resolved horary questions astrologically." He, however, was found out and put into pillory. There was one Jeffrey Neve, who brought Lilly two hundred " verified questions," desiring him to correct them for publication, but of the first forty, thirty were untrue. There was Dr. Ardee, who declared that an angel had offered him a lease of life for one thousand years ; yet the poor man died at fourscore.

The crystal ball was not an astrological instrument, but many of the astrologers practised by means of it. This instrument of pretence and imposture has been revived in our own times. The ball was held in the hand by those who had " the sight." Then things and persons were seen. Thus there was one Sarah Skelhorn who had a perfect " sight." She could see in the ball what any persons were doing at any time or in any place, but seems to have used this remarkable gift for objects quite paltry, as when she observed her mother, who was many miles away, taking a red waistcoat out of a trunk—a really terrible waste of good power. How useful would Sarah be in time of war in order to tell exactly where the enemy was and what the enemy was doing! She was also familiar with angels, who were so fond of her that they followed her about until she was really tired of them.

There was Ellen Evans, daughter of the scandalous *défroqué* above mentioned. She could call up the Queen of the Pigmies whenever she pleased merely by saying, "O Micol! O tu Micol, Regina Pygmeorum, veni!" There was also Sir Robert Holborn, Knight, who "formerly had sight and conference with Uriel and Raphael, but lost them both by carelessness." And so on. The volume is redeemed from intolerable silliness by the firm belief of the author in the science. It shows, however, that the whole of the country was filled with credulity and childish superstition.

The following lines are the commencement of a Latin epitaph composed for Lilly by one George Smalridge, student of Christ Church, Oxford :—

> "Occidit, atque suis annalibus addidit atram
>   Astrologus, qua non tristior ulla, diem.
> Pone triumphales, lugubris Luna, quadrigas ;
>   Sol, maestum picea nube reconde caput.
> Illum, qui Phoebi scripsit, Phoebesque labores,
>   Eclipsen docuit Stella maligna pati.
> Invidia Astrorum cecidit, qui sidera rexit ;
>   Tanta erat in notas scandere cura domos
> Quod vidit, risum cupiit, potiturque, cupito
> Coelo, et sidereo fulget in orbe decus."

Two official superstitions must be recorded, if only because they were practised and no doubt fully believed in London. They were touching for the King's Evil and the blessing of the Cramp Ring. The ceremonies for both these observances are here described.

First, the touching for the King's Evil—

" *The King, kneeling, shall say,*
     In the Name of the Father, and of the Son, and of the Holy Ghost. Amen.
And so soon as He hath said that, He shall say,
     Give the blessing.
The Chaplain, kneeling before the King, and having a Stole about his Neck, shall answer and say,
     The Lord be in your heart and in your lips, to confess all your sins. In the name of the
Father, and of the Son, and of the Holy Ghost. Amen.
Or else he shall say,
     Christ hear us. In the name of the Father, and of the Son, and of the Holy Ghost. Amen.
Then by and by the King shall say,
     I confess to God, to the blessed Virgin Mary, to all Saints, and to you, that I have sinned in
thought, word, and deed through my fault ; I pray Holy *Mary*, and all the saints of God and
you, to pray for me.
The Chaplain shall answer and say,
     Almighty God have mercy upon you, and pardon you all your sins, deliver you from all evil,
and confirm you in good, and bring you to everlasting life. Amen.

The Almighty and Merciful Lord grant you absolution and remission of all your sins, time for true repentance and amendment of life, with the grace and comfort of his Holy Spirit.　Amen.

This done the Chaplain shall say,

The Lord be with you.

The King shall answer,

And with thy spirit.

The Chaplain,

Part of the Gospel according to St. Mark.

The King shall answer,

Glory to thee, O Lord.

The Chaplain reads the Gospel:

Last he appeared to those Eleven as they sat at the Table : and he exprobated their Incredulity and hardness of Heart, because they did not believe them that had seen him risen again.　And he said to them : Going into the whole World, Preach the Gospel to all Creatures.　He that believeth and is Baptised, shall be saved : But he that believeth not, shall be condemned. And them that believe, these Signs shall follow : In my name shall they cast out Devils, they shall speak with new tongues.　Serpents shall they take up, and if they drink any deadly thing it shall not hurt them ; they shall impose hands upon the sick, and they shall be whole.

Which last clause (They shall impose, etc.) *the Chaplain repeats as long as the King is handling the sick person.　And in the time of repeating the aforesaid words* (They shall impose, etc.) *the Clerk of the Closet shall Kneel before the King, having the sick person upon the right hand ; and the sick person shall likewise kneel before the King : and then the King shall lay his hand upon the sore of the sick Person.　This done, the Chaplain shall make an end of the Gospel :*

And so our Lord Jesus after he spake unto them was assumpted into Heaven, and sate on the right hand of God.　But they going forth preached everywhere ; our Lord working withal, and confirming the Word with signs which followed.

Whilst this is reading, the Chirurgion shall lead away the sick person from the King.　And after the Gospel the Chaplain shall say,

The Lord be with you.

The King shall answer,

And with thy spirit.

The Chaplain,

The beginning of the Gospel according to St. *John.*

The King,

Glory to thee, O Lord.

The Chaplain then shall say this Gospel following :

In the beginning was the word, and the word was with God, and God was the word.　This was in the beginning with God.　All things were made by him, and without him was made nothing that which was made.　In him was life, and the life was the light of men.　And the light shineth in darkness, and the darkness did not comprehend it.　There was a man sent from God, whose name was *John.*　This man came for testimony : to give testimony of the light, that all might believe through him.　He was not the light, but to give testimony of the light.　It was the true light which lightneth every man that cometh into this world.

Which last Clause (It was the true light, etc.) *shall still be repeated so long as the King shall be crossing the sore of the sick Person, with an Angel of Gold Noble, and the sick Person to have the same Angel hang'd about his neck, and to wear it until he be full whole.　This done, the Chirurgion shall lead away the sick Person as he did before ; and then the Chaplain shall make an end of the Gospel :*

He was in the world, and the world was made by him, and the world knew him not.　He came into his own, and his own received him not.　But as many as received him, he gave them power to be made the Sons of God, to those that believe in his name.　Who not of blood, nor

London Printed for Dorman Newman at the Kings Armes in the Poultry &c:

F. H. van Houe Sculp:

TOUCHING FOR KING'S EVIL.

of will of the flesh, nor of the will of man, but of God are born. And the word was made flesh and dwelt in us, and we saw the glory of him, glory as it were of the only begotten of the Father, full of grace and verity.

Then the Chaplain shall say,

The Lord's name be praised.

The King shall answer,

Now and for ever.

Then shall the Chaplain say this Collect following, praying for the Sick Person or Persons,

O Lord, hear my prayer.

The King shall answer,

And let my cry come unto thee.

The Chaplain,

Let us pray :

Almighty and everlasting God, the eternal health of them that believe ; graciously hear us for thy servants for whom we implore the aid of thy mercy, that their health being restored to them, they may give thee thanks in thy church, thro' CHRIST our Lord. Amen.

This Prayer following is to be said secretly, after the Sick Persons be departed from the King, at his Pleasure :

Almighty God, Ruler and Lord, by whose goodness the blind see, the deaf hear, the dumb speak, the lame walk, the lepers are cleansed, and all sick persons are healed of their infirmities : By whom also alone the gift of healing is given to mankind, and so great a grace, thro' thine unspeakable goodness toward this Realm, is granted unto the Kings thereof, that by the sole imposition of their hands a most grievous and filthy disease should be cured : Mercifully grant that we may give thee thanks therefore, and for this thy singular benefit conferr'd on us, not to ourselves, but to thy name let us daily give glory ; and let us always so exercise ourselves in piety, that we may labour not only diligently to conserve, but every day more and more to encrease thy grace bestowed upon us : And grant that on whose bodies soever we have imposed hands in thy name, thro' this thy Vertue working in them, and thro' our Ministry, may be restored to their former health, and being confirmed therein, may perpetually with us give thanks unto thee, the Chief Physician and Healer of all diseases ; and that henceforwards they may so lead their lives, as not their bodies only from sickness, but their souls also from sin may be perfectly purged and cured : Thro' our Lord JESUS CHRIST thy Son, who liveth and reigneth with thee in the Unity of the Holy Ghost, God World without end. Amen."

Next, the blessing of the Cramp Ring by the King on Good Friday according to the form prescribed. It was as follows :—

" First, the singing of the Psalm *Deus Misereatur Noster.*

Then the King reades this prayer :

Almighty eternal God, who by the most copious gifts of thy grace, flowing from the unexhausted fountain of thy bounty, hast been graciously pleased for the comfort of mankind, continually to grant us many and various meanes to relieve us in our miseries ; and art willing to make those the instruments and channels of thy gifts, and to grace those persons with more excellent favours, whom thou hast raised to the Royal dignity ; to the end that as by Thee they reign and govern others : so by Thee they may prove beneficial to them ; and bestow thy favours on the people : graciously heare our prayers, and favourably receive those vows we powre forth with humility, that Thou mayst grant to us, who beg with the same confidence the favour, which our Ancestours by their hopes in thy mercy have obtained : through Christ our Lord. Amen.

The Rings lying in one bason or more, this prayer is to be said over them:

O God, the maker of heavenly and earthly creatures, and the most gracious restorer of mankind, the dispenser of spiritual grace, and the origin of all blessings; send downe from heaven thy holy Spirit the Comforter upon these Rings, artificially fram'd by the workman, and by thy greate power purify them so, that all the malice of the fowle and venomous Serpent be driven out; and so the metal, which by Thee was created, may remaine pure, and free from all dregs of the enemy. Through Christ our Lord. Amen.

The Blessing of the Rings:

O God of Abraham, God of Isaac, God of Jacob, heare mercifully our prayers. Spare those who feare thee. Be propitious to thy suppliants, and graciously be pleased to send downe from Heaven thy holy Angel: that he may sanctify ✠ and blesse ✠ these Rings: to the end they may prove a healthy remedy to such as implore thy name with humility, and accuse themselves of the sins, which ly upon their conscience: who deplore their crimes in the sight of thy divine clemency, and beseech with earnestness and humility thy most serene piety. May they in fine by the invocation of thy holy name become profitable to all such as weare them, for the health of their soule and body, through Christ our Lord. Amen.

A Blessing.

O God, who has manifested the greatest wonders of thy power by the cure of diseases, and who were pleased that Rings should be a pledge of fidelity in the patriark Judah, a priestly ornament in Aaron, the mark of a faithful guardian in Darius, and in this Kingdom a remedy for divers diseases: graciously be pleased to blesse and sanctify these rings, to the end that all such who weare them may be free from all snares of the Devil, may be defended by the power of celestial armour; and that no contraction of the nerves, or any danger of the falling sickness may infest them, but that in all sort of diseases by thy help they may find relief. In the name of the Father, ✠ and of the Son, ✠ and of the Holy Ghost. ✠ Amen."

After another psalm the following prayer was read :—

"Wee humbly implore, O merciful God, thy infinit clemency; that as we come to thee with a confident soule, and sincere faith, and a pious assurance of mind: with the like devotion thy beleevers may follow on these tokens of thy grace. May all superstition be banished hence, far be all suspicion of any diabolical fraud, and to the glory of thy name let all things succeede: to the end thy beleevers may understand thee to be the dispenser of all good; and may be sensible and publish, that whatsoever is profitable to soule or body is derived from thee: through Christ our Lord. Amen.

These prayers being said, the Kings highnes rubbeth the Rings between his hands, saying:

Sanctify, O Lord, these Rings, and graciously bedew them with the dew of thy benediction, and consecrate them by the rubbing of our hands, which thou hast been pleased according to our ministry to sanctify by an external effusion of holy oyle upon them: to the end, that what the nature of the mettal is not able to performe, may be wrought by the greatnes of thy grace: through Christ our Lord. Amen."

Then with another prayer holy water was thrown on the rings and the ceremony was complete.

CHAPTER IV

SANCTUARY

THERE is a somewhat dreary allegory of a voyage called "The Floating Island, or a New Discovery relating the Strange Adventure on a late Voyage from Lambethana to Villa Franca, *alias* Ramallia, to the eastward of Terra del Templo."

It was published in the year 1673, and it contains an account of certain parts of London which give it some interest. The humour of the piece is that places described are mentioned as new discoveries lying at the distance of many days' voyage from one to the other. Thus, to take a single example, the following is the description of the Savoy. The sanctuary of this quarter is, of course, Alsatia :—

"The Palace is a very stately Fabrick, and hath been formerly employed for charitable uses, and still serves as an excellent Refuge and Sanctuary for such who are either forced by banishment, or voluntary Exile, to desert their native or long lov'd habitations, where they may live obscurely, and yet take their pleasure abroad in the Countries round about, by the means of those several convenient Avenues belonging thereunto, viz. for sporting on a brave River, the Stairs; for the Land, the Great Gate butting Norwards and separated but by a very small channel from Excestria. To the eastward there is an outlet which leadeth two ways, the one on the left into the Dutchy, the other turning a little on the right, into Somersetania; by the first you have a conveyance into the Country called Maypolia, and so have the whole Country before you to make choice of; by the last a safe passage by water, or a conduct short and commodious through the Provinces of White-Hart into Hortensia (vulgarly called Covent Garden), from whence you may travail through the whole kingdom.

The Slavonian women supplied us with Fish and fruits of all sort, which they bring down in abundance from the Upland Countries; insomuch that we could not fear want of Provision so long as we had Money; nor question our security, whilst we did put ourselves under the Protection of this place or of the Dutchy Liberty."

The sanctuary was for debtors, but not for felons or traitors, and bailiffs occasionally effected an entrance by pretending to have a warrant for the arrest of the latter. But on the cry of "Arrest, Arrest," the whole of the residents flew to arms and drove out the offenders, perhaps with the loss of their ears. There were punishments inflicted on those who invaded the rights of sanctuary.

Not far from the Savoy the adventurous voyagers discover a floating island, called the Summer Island, or Scoti Moria, viz. "There were two Ports or landing Places, one guarded by 'Knights of the Blue Aprons,'" *i.e.* waiters, who wore aprons of that colour; and the other by a woman with a white apron. They landed; they found, to leave the allegory, a company assembled playing skittles on the deck and down below drinking bad wine in worse company. The whole of the vessel was filled with bottles; and for commodities for sale or exchange there were none except "what were wrapped in silken Petticoats, and like a Pig in a Poke you must buy, or not at all." There was also a billiard table on the ship, and tobacco was their only "breath and breathing while." The next land they touch is the Island of Ursina, or the Bearbaiting, on which it appears that the charge of five shillings covered a ticket for drink as well as entrance. The description of the sport, which follows, affords nothing new. Sailing from Ursina, they arrive at the *Ne plus ultra*, where they are deafened by the "great fall and hideous noise of the waters"—in other words, at London Bridge. Not far from this place they discovered mermaids, both male and female; but the latter only swam at night, being shy. I do not understand this allusion.

The author is pleased to represent Terra del Templo, or the Temple, as a place occupied chiefly by a people constantly engaged in defending themselves against an enemy.

"In the Description of this Ramallia, I must look into Terra del Templo, but shall not pry into its Court, nor any of the standing houses, the Housekeeper's lodging, nor into the menial precincts of the Inns of Court, farther, than they stand for Refuge and Relief of the neighbouring Privileges about them. And indeed (since the general purgation by fire) the first, and chiefest of all, which for advantage of ground, for fortifications, for Water Works, Posterns, Passages, Supplies, and provisions by land, or otherwise, is that so far famed and so fitly named Ramallia; in it are several Garrisons of old Soldiers, every one of the which is able to lead a whole Army of Younger Debtors.

They call their Muster rôle in the Round Church, which might more properly be called their Corps du Guard; then they draw them out into the Cloysters, and either exercise them there, or in the Garden, which is an excellent Military Spot for that purpose; but under the Blowers in the Rum Stampers (called the King's Bench walk) they pitch their set Battles, where every evening that ground (which was lifted in and level'd for their use) is fil'd with men of desperate and undaunted resolution.

The first work in Ramallia is rais'd and contrived in the form of a Ram; there is no other reason I can render for it, but that Rams were of great use in the Jewish Discipline, for Batteries, as you may read in Josephus his History more at large. This work is of reasonable strength; in former times it had a watch Tower in the similitude of a Coblers shop adjoyning, from whence all the forces about are called together, upon the least approach of the Enemy. There is another, called the Maidenhead, and is impregnable, where the Enemy dares not come within shot, and in the nearest to the confines of Terra del Templo. There are other pretty contrived Platforms, as Teste Royal, the Falcon, Mitre, etc., and these in the fashion and form of Cookshops; where if a Setter or Spy chance to peep in at them (though very dark) they will make him pay for the roast before he depart. To this Ramallia, or Ramykins, belongs a very great Fleet, consisting of many Sail, well man'd, and are a great preservation to the Ramykins.

This place, according to the late Geographical Map, as well as the report of ancient Writers, cannot possibly be so besieged but that they within may go in and out at their pleasure, without impeachment; for at the Middle Temple Gate they issue in spight of the Devil; at the Inner Temple Gate they fear no colours in the Rainbow; and at the Postern of the Ramykins, in case they cannot make over to Fetter Lane, but discover Ambuscado's, they need only draw their bodies within guard of Pike, turn faces about, and retreat through the Mitre.

Now admit they stand for Rio del Plata (commonly called Fleet Street) and be so intercepted that they cannot recover the Ramykins, all that is required in that case is but to mend their March; fall downwards, as if they gave way, suddenly discharge their right-hand file, and fall easily into Sergeants Inn; where by ancient Treaty had between this famous place and Terra del Templo, it was agreed that the parties in such distress might (paying a small Fee) have convoy and conveyance without the re-hazzard of any of their persons.

If at any time they had a mind to Forrage, they are no sooner out of the Middle Temple Gate, but there is a threefold way to defend them; the Bell Inn, the Bar Gate, and Shire Lane.   The passage under the Blowers is a most excellent safe way for close contriving and retriving; neither is the Gardners Wharfage

THE WEST PROSPECT OF THE CHURCH OF S.ʳ BARTHOLOMEW THE GREAT.

ST. BARTHOLOMEW'S
From the Crace Collection in the British Museum.

(as the Tide may serve) anyways inconsiderable.   To speak the truth, the nature of Ramallia is much alter'd in few years, neither is the place so much frequented as formerly by Forreigners in Refuge, the inhabitants slighting or being careless in the preservation of their ancient privileges."

The author tells us, further, that there were formerly many other places which were considered sanctuaries for debtors, *i.e.* places where writs could not be served. These were (1) Milford Lane, at first occupied and defended by indigent officers, who held it, so to speak, by the sword :—

"And notwithstanding their title hath been much disputed heretofore, yet they have now commuted the matter, prov'd Plantation, and have withal reduced it to a most absolute Hance and free Town of itself, without dependency."

(2) Fulwoods Rents in Holborn, a place which remained to this century of bad reputation, though it contained several good houses.[1]

(3) Baldwin's Gardens was another sanctuary :—

"The Back-gate into Graies-Inn Lane, with the benefit of Bauldwins Gardens, is of excellent use ; but the passiges through certain Inns on the Field-side are not attempted without hazard, by reason of the straggling Troops of the Enemy, who lie Purdue in every ale-house thereabouts. The safest way of Sally is that through the Walks, from whence the Red Lyon in Graies-Inn Lane receives them with good quartering, and passes them through the back way into the Main Land."

(4) Another was Great St. Bartholomew's :—

"Upon whose platform a whole Army of Borrowers and Book-men might have been mustred and drawn out in length, or into what form or figure it had pleased them to cast themselves. What works, yea what variety of Art and Workmanship was within it ; What an excellent half-Moon was there cast up without it, for defence to the Eastward ; What excellent Sconces, in the fashion of Tobacco-shops and Ale houses in all parts of it.

But alas these are demolisht, for the most part, the old Soldiers discharg'd, and all delivered up into the hand of the Enemy upon composition."

The precinct of St. John of Jerusalem was also formerly held as a sanctuary, but had lost its privileges. In the precinct of Blackfriars privileges were granted to some of the oldest trades, those, probably, which were carried on in the few houses belonging to the Friars. These were feathermakers, Scotch tailors, and French shoemakers. Another is Montagu Close, on the west side of St. Mary Overies, the sanctuary of the Borough. In later years it was removed further south to the place called the Mint.

On the north side of Blackfriars is the place which the residents of all these sanctuaries are continually trying to escape. The author calls it a very strong and formidable citadel belonging to the enemy. This is Ludgate Prison.

"It is much like the apples of Sodom, better for fight without than in. Its whole prospect from within are iron grates, where, through every Transom, the forlorn Captives may take a view of the Iron Age; there is one single entrance, which, like Hell's Gate, lets many in, but few out, turn once the Ward—Et vestigia nulla retrorsum. The Cimmerians in their dwellings resemble these in their lodgings, only their lights are different ; those receive some scattered beamings by their Mountain Crannies ; these by their disconsolate loopholes.

Yet from above, the Inhabitants may take a view of all those places which club'd to their restrain ; and be reminded of the loss of time which brought them thither. The Governour hereof is careless whence they come, but infinitely cautious how they go away ; and if they go away without his favour, they are in great danger to break their necks for their labour."

The rest of the little book is made up of a Rabelaisian description of the people in sanctuary—the Ram Alley folk, with certain "special cases."

"In case of Linnen, it hath been adjudged, that if three good fellows and constant Companions have but one shirt between them, and that these three (seeing none of their other shifts will do them any good) jointly consent this shirt shall be sold, it shall be lawful for them to expose it to sale, vended and condemned for the common good of three, and that forthwith the money be spent in the cherishing that blood that retired from the extream parts, being chil'd with the fright of parting with so dear and near a friend."

---

[1] Partly obliterated in the construction of the Chancery Lane Station of the Electric Railway.

CHAPTER V

CITY GOVERNMENT AND USAGES

In this chapter I have collected certain notes which may illustrate such points in City government as differentiate the seventeenth century from that which preceded and that which followed it. For instance, the times were troubled; a man might, by bending before the successive storms, win his way through in safety; but an honest man with principles, courage, and convictions might expect fine and imprisonment if he accepted office, and might think himself lucky if he carried his ears out of office, or if he were not fined to the full extent of his worldly fortune, or if he had not to fly across the seas to Holland. In *Remembrancia*, therefore, we are not surprised to find many letters from merchants praying to be excused from office.

Among the less dangerous duties of the Mayor was the reception of the foreign Ambassadors.

On the arrival of Ambassadors the Lords of the Council sent a letter to the Lord Mayor commanding him to find a suitable residence and a proper reception. In 1580 the Spanish Ambassador was allotted a house in Fenchurch Street which he did not like, so he asked instead for Arundel House. In 1583 the Swedish Ambassador arrived; he was to have three several lodgings, with stabling for twenty horses. In 1613 the "Emperor of Muscovy" sent an Ambassador; in 1611 one came from the Duke of Savoy; in 1616 an Ambassador-Extraordinary arrived from the King of France; in 1626 two from the State of Venice; in 1628 another Spanish Ambassador; in the same year a Russian Ambassador; in 1637 an Ambassador from the "King of Morocco." All these Ambassadors were lodged and entertained in the City after a formal reception and procession through the streets to their lodging.

Mediæval London was a city of palaces and of nobles' palaces. Under the Tudors there were still some of these town houses left. Toward the end of the seventeenth century there were very few, only one or two.

A long list of noblemen and gentlemen living around London in the year 1673 may be found in the *London and Middlesex Note-book*. When one examines this list a little closely, it is remarked that the residences of far the greater number of those on the list are at St. Martin's-in-the-Fields, at Westminster, in St. James's Fields, in Leicester Fields, at Hackney, and that, though some actually belong to the outskirts of the City, none are living within the walls of the City itself except the City knights and merchants.

The houses still occupied by nobility, taking them from Ogilby's Map (see Map) were : Thanet House in Aldersgate Street, the town house of the Earl of Thanet ; the Earl of Bridgwater's house in the Barbican ; Warwick House ; Brook House and Ely House, in Holborn ; Lord Berkeley's house in St. John Street ; the Marquis of Dorchester's, Lord Grey's, and the Earl of Ailesbury's in Charter-house Lane ; in the Strand, Somerset House, belonging to, or occupied by successively, Queen Anne of Denmark, Queen Henrietta Maria, Queen Catherine of Braganza ; Arundel House, then the residence of the Duke of Norfolk, who was a great collector of statues and inscriptions ; Essex House, where Robert Devereux, Earl of Essex, the parliamentary general, was born. All these three were in the Strand. Outside Ogilby's Map, but still in the outskirts of the City, were Lord Craven's and Lord Clare's houses, in and near Drury Lane.

WARWICK HOUSE, CLOTH FAIR

If we take one parish for an example—say that of St. Benet's, Thames Street—we find that the son of the Earl of Carnarvon was christened in that church on November 26, 1633, that four children of the Earl of Pembroke were born in this parish and christened in this church, viz. Susanna, christened May 7, 1650; Mary, December 12, 1651 ; Philip, January 5, 1652 ; and Rebecca, July 18, 1655.

Before the Fire these noblemen had town houses in the parish—Lord Pembroke had Baynard's Castle ; their chaplains died in those town houses and lie buried in the church. Derby House, now the College of Heralds, was also in this parish, as was also Huntingdon House, the residence of Lord Hastings.

The departure of the nobility from their City houses was perhaps one cause of the cessation of the old connection of the country gentry with the City. This departure also contributed to a very important social change, viz. the fact that for a long time, now more than two centuries, the Mayor, the Aldermen, the City officers, and the City merchants have been socially and politically entirely out of touch with the nobility. In the next century some of the effects of this separation were greatly to be lamented. The seventeenth century, however, furnishes one very remarkable illustration of the connection between the City and the country gentry.

It is also an illustration of the way in which middle-class families went up and down. Early in the seventeenth century, one Pepys, a country gentleman of no great standing, married a girl of his own class whose sister married into the Montagu family. One of his sons, a younger son, was sent to London and entered into trade, but without conspicuous success. He became a tailor, and he was of course first cousin to Sir Edward Montagu, his mother's nephew. One of his sons succeeded him in the

Craven House Drury Lane.

From contemporary print.

business, the other became Secretary of the Admiralty, and afterwards President of the Royal Society ; he is also the writer of the finest diary ever committed to paper. Sir Edward Montagu became Lord Sandwich. In his family there were therefore, all closely connected, Lord Sandwich, the Chief Justice of Ireland, a Doctor of Divinity, a Member of Parliament, the Secretary of the Admiralty, a serjeant-at-law, a hosteller, a publican, a tobacconist, a butcher, a tailor, a weaver, a goldsmith, and a turner. As yet, however, the rest of the *Note-book* before us shows a great number of persons in the City who had the right to call themselves "Gentlemen" at a time when the title could not be assumed by any who chose, and was not conferred lightly or at haphazard. Social distinctions were much more strongly

marked then than now. Although the City contained no noble lords, it had
Baronets, Knights, Esquires, and Gentlemen. The Esquires were gentlemen of
good estate, dignified councillors at law, physicians, and holders of the King's
Commission, holders of offices of importance. The eldest son of a Knight was an

South View of Arundel Houfe in London 1646.

North View of Arundel Houfe in London 1646.

From a print published by J. Thane, London, Feb. 1, 1792.

Esquire by right; the eldest son of a Sheriff was also entitled to this distinction.
Pepys, when he received the appointment of Secretary to the Admiralty, is addressed
for the first time in his life, and greatly to his delight, as Esquire. The title of
Gentleman was more widely claimed; the son of a gentleman was also a gentleman.
A younger son, however, could not call himself, or be called Esquire unless he had
some other qualification. It is not at all uncommon to find the word "Gentleman"
on a title-page after the name of the author. There are complaints as to the illegal

use of the title. The rank of gentleman was conceded to attorneys, proctors, and notaries; but merchants, however wealthy, artists, authors, surgeons, and tradesmen could obtain no recognition of gentility on account of the nature of their work, though by descent they might be gentlemen.

The *Visitation of London* (1633-1635), published in 1880 by the Harleian Society, contains the genealogies and shields of over 900 City families. If we assume that these shields were honestly examined and allowed, we have the very remarkable fact that in the seventeenth century there were 900 City families within the walls of the City who were descended from the country gentry, and had preserved proof of their descent. The trade or calling of those whose names are given in the genealogy does not always appear; the great majority seem to be in trade of some kind. Thus we find Goldsmith, Draper, Grocer, Fishmonger, Haberdasher, Mercer, Gentleman, Skinner, "of the Temple," Doctor of Physic, Merchant Tailor, Merchant, Doctor of Divinity, Vintner, Barber, Surgeon, "of Clifford's Inn," Attorney in the office of the Pleas on the Exchequer Court, Cordwayner, "Searcher and Trier and Sealer of Madder," Dyer, Scryvener, Sadler, "Silman to Prince Charles," Merchant of the Staple, "One of His Majesty's Auditors," "One of the Commissioners for the Royal Navy," "Surveyor of Customs," Joyner, Stationer, Brewer, etc. Here are enough to show that every kind of trade was represented, but not every kind of craft. It is rare to find a craft at all, and then the person concerned was evidently an employer of working-men, a master craftsman. The names themselves have quite lost the mediæval aspect which they presented in the wills and memorials. There is hardly a name which might not belong to the London Directory of the present year. The name of Pepys is among them, but not that of Samuel, who was not yet born. "Yet I never thought we were of much account," he said thirty years afterwards. The family came from South Creake, in the county of Norfolk. The name of Milton is there, with a confusion of Mitton and Milton, but not the name of John. As for the origin of these families, it was from every part of the country. It is, however, noticeable that, whereas in the fourteenth century the names of Mayor and Sheriffs in office were frequently—nay, generally—those of men who came up from their fathers' manors young, in these lists most of them are London citizens of the second, third, and fourth generations.

Referring to the lists in the "Stow" of 1633, the following Mayors have marks of cadency on their arms. The arms, therefore, are not newly granted but hereditary :—

"Adam Bamme, 1390. Ermine, on a chief indented, sable, two trefoils, argent: an annulet for difference, being the mark of cadency for a fifth son.

John Froyshe, 1394. A fess engrailed: an annulet.

Richard Whittington, 1397. A fess checky: an annulet.

Drew Barentyn, 1397. Three eagles, displayed: an annulet.

Ralf Jocelyn, 1464. Azure, a wreath, argent and sable, with four bells, or: a mullet for difference, third son.

[Sir John] Young, 1466.   Lozengy, two unicorns' heads, erased, on a bend : an annulet.

[Sir Thomas] Mirfine, 1518.   Argent, a chevron sable : a mullet, and in dexter chief a crescent : perhaps third son of a second son.

[Sir John] Bruges, 1520.   Argent, a cross sable, a leopard's face, or : a crescent.

Dodmer, 1529.   A crescent.

Lambert, 1531.   An annulet.

Dormer, 1541.   A crescent.

Amcoates, 1548.   A crescent.

White, 1553.   An annulet.

Curteis, 1557.   A crescent.

[Sir Thomas] Rowe, 1568.   A crescent.

Ducket, 1572   A mullet.

Harvey, 1581.   A crescent.

Bond, 1587.   A crescent, thereon a mullet.

Calthrop, 1588.   A crescent.

[Sir William] Rowe, 1592.   A crescent.

Some, 1598.   A crescent."

The following have quartered coats :—

" Chalton, 1449.

Clopton, 1491.

Bradbury, 1509.

Rudstone, 1528.

Amcoates, 1548, eight coats.

Jud, 1550.

Martin, 1567.

Heyward, 1570, six coats.

Ducket, 1572.

Woodroffe, 1579.

Branche, 1580.

Osborne, 1583, three coats.

Dixie, 1585.

Barne, 1586.

Calthrop, 1588, five coats.

Heyward, 1590.

Billingsley, 1596.

Mosley, 1599.

The following is the list in full already referred to, of the nobility and gentry living in and about London in 1673.   I have omitted those names whose rank was lower than that of Baronet so as not to include the City and law knights :—

Lord Berkeley of Berkeley Castle.

Lord Berkeley of Stratton.

Sir William Boyer, Bart.

The Earl of Bridgwater, Barbican.

Baron Brooke of Beauchampe Court and Hackney.

The Earl of Buckingham and Earl of Coventry.

The Earl of Burlington, Burlington House.

Clarenceaux, Knight at Arms.

The Viscount Campden, Kensington.

Sir Robert Carr, Bart.

Sir Nicholas Crisp, Bart.

Earl of Clare, Clare House, Drury Lane.

Earl of Clarendon.

Lord Clifford.

The Viscount Courtney, Clarendon Street.

Earl of Craven.

Sir John Cutler, Bart.

Earl of Devonshire, Devonshire Square.

Marquis of Dorchester, Charter-House Yard.

Earl of Dorset.

Sir Heneage Finch, Bart.

Sir Reginald Foster, Bart.

Sir F. Everard, Bart.

Lord Grey.

Sir Harbottle Grimston, Bart., Rolls.

Viscount Halifax.

Lord Hatton.

Sir William Hicks, Bart.

Earl of Holland.

Sir Francis Holles, Bart.

Sir James Langham, Bart.

Earl of Leicester.

Earl of Lindsay.

Sir Thomas Littleton, Bart.

Sir Philip Mathews.

Viscount Mordaunt.

The Earl of Mulgrave.

Sir Herbert Price, Bart.

The Earl of Salisbury, Salisbury House.

Sir John Shaw, Bart.

Sir William Smith, Bart.

Viscount Stafford.

The Earl of Thanet at Thanet House, Aldersgate
    Street.

Sir Robert Vyner, Bart.

The Earl of Warwick, Holborn.

Sir Jervis Whitchott, Bart.

Sir William Wild, Bart.

Sir Thomas Wolstenholme, Bart.

The Earl of Worcester, Worcester House.

The freedom from taxation of certain privileged classes was a fruitful cause of quarrel and annoyance. Barristers who lived in the Four Inns of Court and in Serjeant's Inn were exempt from taxation on account of chambers. The same privilege was extended to residents in Doctors' Commons and residents in the precincts of Blackfriars and Whitefriars, who were also exempt from fifteenths and from the burdens of watch and ward, except charges for defence of the State, for pavement and clearing within the precinct, and except freemen of the City, who continued to be liable to the City charges.

A City office long discontinued was that of Chronologer. In the *Analytical Index to Remembrancia* (Guildhall) we have the following notes :—

It may not be considered uninteresting to give a list of the names of the different holders of this peculiar office, some of whom, as Thomas Middleton, Ben Johnson, and Francis Quarles, are otherwise known to fame, with some few particulars from the Civic Records concerning them.

1620, September 6, 18th James I.—Thomas Middleton, admitted City Chronologer. Item, this day was read in Court (of Aldermen) a petition of Thomas Middleton, Gent., and upon consideration thereof taken, and upon the sufficient testimony this Court hath received of his services performed to this City, this Court is well pleased to entertain and admit the said Thomas Middleton to collect and set down all memorable acts of this City and occurrences thereof, and for such other employments as this Court shall have occasion to use him in ; but the said Thomas Middleton is not to put any of the acts so by him to be collected into print without the allowance and approbation of this Court, and for the readiness of his service to the City in the same employments this Court does order that he shall receive from henceforth. out of the Chamber of London, a yearly fee of £6 : 13 : 4.

1620, November 20, 18th James I.—His salary increased to £10 per annum.

1621, April 17, 19th James I.—A freedom granted to Thomas Middleton, Chronologer and inventor of honourable entertainments for this City, towards his expenses.

1622, May 7, 20th James I.—Another freedom granted to him for his better encouragement in his labours.

1622, September 17, 20th James I.—£15 granted to him for the like.

1622 (3), February 6, 20th James I.—£20 granted to him.

1623, April 24, 21st James I.—One freedom granted to him.

1623, September 2, 21st James I.—Twenty marks given him for his services at the shooting on Bunhill and at the Conduit Head before the Lord Mayor and Aldermen.

1627, February 7, 3rd Charles I.—Twenty nobles given to his widow Magdalen.

1628, September 2, 4th Charles I.—Item, this day Benjamin Johnson, Gent., is by this Court admitted to be the City's Chronologer in place of Mr. Thomas Middleton, deceased, to have, hold, exercise, and enjoy the same place, and to have and receive for that his service, out of the Chamber of London, the sum of one hundred nobles per annum, to continue during the pleasure of this Court.

1631, November 2, 7th Charles I.—Item, it is ordered by this Court that Mr. Chamberlain shall forbear to pay any more fee or wages unto Benjamin Johnson, the City's Chronologer, until we shall have presented unto this Court some fruits of his labours in that his place.

1634, September 18, 10th Charles I.—Item, this day Mr. Recorder and Sir (Hugh) Hamersley, Knight, Alderman, declared unto this Court His Majesty's pleasure, signified unto them by the Right Hon. the Earl of Dorset, for and in the behalf of Benjamin Johnson, the City Chronologer, whereupon it is ordered by this Court that his yearly pension of 100 nobles out of the Chamber of London shall be continued, and that Mr. Chamberlain shall satisfy and pay unto him all arrearages thereof.

1639, February 1, 15th Charles I.—At the request of the Right Hon. the Earl of Dorset, signified by his letter, Francis Quarles, Gent., was admitted Chronologer. with a fee of 100 nobles per annum, during the pleasure of the Court.

1645, October 1, 20th Charles I.—Walter Frost, Esq., Sword-bearer, admitted Chronologer, so long as he shall well demean himself therein and present yearly something of his labours.

1660, February 28, 13th Charles II.—Captain John Burroughs admitted City Chronologer, the place having been void for several years, his salary to be 100 nobles per annum.

1668, November 23, 20th Charles II.—Upon the recommendation of a Committee, the yearly payment of 100 nobles to one Bradshaw, called the City Chronologer, was discontinued with the place, there appearing no occasion for such an officer.

1669, February 24, 22nd Charles II.—On the petition of Cornewall Bradshaw, Gent., late City Chronologer, for some recompense for his salary of £33 : 6 : 8, taken from him by vote of the Court (Common Council), it was ordered that, upon his resigning his said place, the Chamberlain should pay him £100 in full of all claims.

1669, March 17, 22nd Charles II.—Bradshaw (admitted in the Mayoralty of Sir T. Bludworth, 1665-6, as City Chronologer) surrendered his office, with all its rights, etc., and a freedom was given to him (*Index to Remembrancia*, pp. 305, 306).

Between 1583 and 1661 there were continual efforts made to restrain the building of new houses in the City and the erection of small tenements. The Lords of the Council pressed on the Mayor the duty of enforcing the laws. The Mayor replied that there were many places in the City that pretended to be exempt from the

Cornhill, London.
AS IT APPEARED   ABOUT THE YEAR 1630.

From an engraving published by Boydell & Co., London.

jurisdiction of the City; notably the sites of the old monasteries. One result of this activity was the driving of the poorer sort outside the City Liberties altogether, especially along the river side. Owing to this cause Southwark began to enjoy an influx of the least desirable of the population. This distinction the Borough has ever since continued to possess. The same cause built the courts and created the slums of Westminster.

The attempt to restrain the increase of London should have been accompanied by an enlargement of the City jurisdiction. Had this been done, many of the evils attendant on a rapid growth of population with no corresponding powers of justice and police might have been avoided.

The necessity of cleaning and keeping clean the streets was very much to the front after the scare of the Plague and the Fire. There were projects advanced by ingenious persons for this purpose. Thus one Daniel Nis laid a plan before the King, who sent it on to the Lord Mayor for consideration. He wanted, apparently, to raise the footpath on either side to a "convenient height, evenness, and decency,

WATCHMAN
From a print published by John Watson, *temp*. Charles II.

BELLMAN
From a rare woodcut, *temp*. James I.

leaving ample passage for coaches, carts, and horses, and reserving a competent part to be made even and easy in a far more elegant and commodious manner for the convenience of foot passengers, besides a handsome accommodation of water for the continual cleansing of the streets by lead pipes."

Daniel Nis was before his age, but one feels that when such projects are in the air, reform and improvement are at hand. Unfortunately projectors of this kind never understand the practical side of the question. Now the streets of a great city cannot be revolutionised all at once; no city is rich enough to undertake such a reform; the only thing possible is a gradual reform, taking the most important streets first. And this, in fact, was the way adopted in the City and carried on from the Great Fire to our own time.

If we go into the unreformed streets we find the kites and crows still acting as the principal scavengers, the bye-streets unpaved and unlighted—that is to say, not yet even paved with cobbles, but left quite untouched with puddles of liquid filth standing about; there were also masterless dogs by the hundred who devoured the offal.

The regulations for the standing of carts were of very early date. Standings were fixed in Tower Street and on Tower Hill in 1479. It must be remembered that most of the streets in the City were too narrow for the passage of wheeled vehicles; it was therefore necessary to regulate the traffic in the streets wide enough for carts to pass. Such Acts were passed and altered in 1586, 1605, 1654, 1658, 1661, 1665, 1667, and 1681. The last Act for licensing and regulating carts was passed in 1838. The Woodmongers' Company at one time had the management of the carts. In 1605, when Christ's Hospital had charge of the carts, a single cart was taxed 13s. 4d. a year, together with 4s. for quarterage and no more. The whole number of carts allowed was 400, viz. 100 for Southwark, 200 in the skirts of the City, and 100 in the wood wharves.

The watchmen carried bells, not rattles; they rang them as they went along to announce their coming; the thieves in this way secured timely warning and got themselves into safe hiding. But Cosmo, Duke of Tuscany, who came here in 1669, says that the streets were orderly, well lit by lanterns, and that the citizens were not afraid to go about without swords.

Such squares as then existed, as Lincoln's Inn Fields, had taken the place of Smithfield as a place of public resort. They were now laid out in three separate fields; these were surrounded by mulberry-trees. It was a common complaint that in summer evenings after work was over ballad singers stationed themselves at every street corner and bawled their songs to an admiring and a listening crowd, that their songs were coarse and lewd—perhaps it is the Puritan minister who complains,—and that young girls stood among the audience listening and laughing.

In 1618 the chimney-sweepers sent a petition to Sir Robert Naunton stating that householders generally neglected to get their chimneys swept, to the great danger of fire and the starvation of their kind, 200 in number; and they prayed that the citizens might be compelled to have their chimneys swept at proper times, and that an overseer should be appointed to look after this duty. The Lord Mayor reported that it was unnecessary to appoint another overseer, because there were already officers annually sworn to inspect chimneys. So nothing more is heard of the chimney-sweep and his grievances.

The subject of the City laystalls is unsavoury. But the removal of waste matter is always a trouble in every town. In 1670 orders were made for laystalls to be established at various points. It must be understood that all kinds of rubbish, ordure, decaying vegetables, etc., were shot out upon the laystall; when it was near the river the contents were from time to time shovelled out into the ebb tide. The following is the list of the laystalls as appointed in 1670:—

"(1) Dowgate Dock . . .   Billingsgate Ward
Bridge   ,,
Langbourn   ,,
Cornhill   ,,
Candlewick   ,,
Vintry   ,,
Walbrook   ,,
Dowgate   ,,

(2) Mile End . . . .   Portsoken Ward
Tower   ,,
Aldgate   ,,
Duke's Place Ward
Lyme Street   ,,

(3) Holloway Lane End . .   Bishopsgate Within Ward
,,   Without   ,,

(4) Bunhill Fields . . .   Cripplegate Within and Without Ward
Aldersgate Without Ward
Bassishaw   ,,
Coleman Street   ,,
Broad Street   ,,

(5) Laystall at or near 3 Cranes and in   Cheap Ward
Dunghill Lane, near Broken Wharf,   Cordwainer Ward
till Key is there laid open. After-   Queenhithe   ,,
wards a Laystall at Puddle Dock .   Bread Street   ,,

(6) Puddle Dock . . .   Farringdon Within Ward
Aldersgate Within   ,,
Castle Baynard   ,,
St. Martin's le Grand Ward

(7) Whitefriars. . . . . Farringdon Without Ward "

The Radical root-and-branch reformer is not unknown in every age. I have before me a pamphlet written by such an one in the year 1675. It will be seen that he advocates a thorough reform or rather a return to the former conditions. I quote a portion only of the pamphlet. Among other things the writer proposes—

(1) That a stop be put to any new buildings in London, or within the bills of mortality.

(2) That the nobility and gentry of the country be compelled to reside so many months in the year on their estates.

(3) That brandy, music, coffee, and tea be prohibited, and coffee-houses suppressed.

(4) That the multitude of stage coaches and caravans now on the roads be all, or most of them, suppressed.

(5) That a Court of Conscience should be established in Westminster and in every important town.

(6) That the extravagant wages of craftsmen should be reduced. The writer proceeds to advance his reasons for these proposals. For instance, the abundance of new houses tempts people to come up from the country in order to establish ale or brandy shops or to let lodgings; it also tempts the gentry to leave their estates and to live in London.

As to the prohibition of brandy, it is stated that brandy was so cheap, a quartern being sold for threepence, that the people drink spirits instead of strong beer and ale. (This is the first complaint of spirit drinking.) Whereas, if the sale of brandy were prohibited, there would be so great an increase in the consumption of barley required for beer that the farmers would rise from their impoverished condition and be once more able to pay their rents. "Brandy," he says, "burns out the hearts of his Majesty's subjects." It is not generally understood, I think, that there were complaints on the subject of brandy before the introduction of its cheaper and more destructive rival—gin.

He would suppress tea, coffee, and chocolate for the simple reason that he does not understand that they do any good to anybody, and he would shut the coffee-houses because he believes them to be mischievous places :—

"And for coffee, tea, and chocolate, I know no good they do; only the places where they are sold are convenient for persons to meet in, sit half a day, and discourse with all companies that come in, of state-matters, talking of news, and broaching of lies; arraigning the judgments and discretions of their own governors, censuring all their actions, and insinuating into the people a prejudice against them; extolling and magnifying their own parts, knowledge, and wisdom, and decrying that of their rulers, which, if suffered too long, may prove pernicious and destructive. But say there was nothing of this in the case, yet have these coffee-houses done great mischiefs to the nation, and undone many of the king's subjects; for they, being very great enemies to diligence and industry, have been the ruin of many serious and hopeful young gentlemen and tradesmen, who, before they frequented these places, were diligent students or shop-keepers, extraordinary husbands of their time as well as money " (see also p. 292).

Granted a case against tea and coffee, what can be said against the stage coach ? A great deal. Stage coaches destroy the breed of good horses, make men careless of horsemanship, and make them effeminate and afraid of cold, rain, and snow (for further on this subject see p. 338).

The crime of crimping—that is, inveigling or forcing young fellows to enter into service in the plantations—became very common in this century. It caused trouble in many ways. First, a man was encouraged to get drunk, and on recovering was told that he had enlisted, or he was knocked on the head and carried aboard, or he voluntarily enlisted and afterwards repented. In all these cases the victims complained on reaching Virginia that they had been betrayed or trapped, and they sent home sworn statements, with instructions to their friends, to indict the merchants for crimping and ensnaring them

These complaints became so numerous that rules were laid down for the enrolment of these servants, and if the rules were obeyed, the merchants were assured that there should be no prosecution :—

" I. Such servants as are to be taken by Indenture, to be executed by the servant, in the presence of the magistrate or magistrates hereafter appointed : one part thereof signed by such servant, and also underwritten or endorsed with the name and handwriting of such magistrate, which is to remain with the clerk of the Peace to be renewed to the next sessions, there to be filed upon a distinct file, and numbered and kept with the records.

II. The Clerk of the Peace is to keep a fair book, wherein the name of the person so bound, and the magistrate's name before whom the same was done, and the time and place of doing thereof, and the number of the file shall be entred ; and for the more easie finding the same, the entris are to be made alphabetically, according to the first letter of the sirname.

III. All persons above the age of one and twenty years, or who shall, upon view and examination, appear to be so in the judgment of the magistrate, may be bound in the presence of one Justice of the Peace, or of the Mayor or chief Magistrate of the place where they shall go on shipboard, who is to be fully satisfied from him of his free and voluntary agreement to enter into the said service.

IV. If any person be under the age of one and twenty years, or shall appear to be so, he shall be bound in the presence of the Lord Mayor of London, or one of the Judges, or an Alderman of London, being a Justice of the Peace, or the Recorder, or two Justices of the Peace of any other county or place, who shall carefully examine whether the person so to be bound have any parents or masters ; and if he be not free they are not to take such indenture, unless the parents or masters give their consents, and some person that knows the said servant to be of the name and addition mentioned in the indenture is to assist his said knowledge upon the said indenture.

V. If the person be under the age of fourteen years, unless his parents shall be present, and consent, he is not to be carried on shipboard till a fortnight at least after he becomes bound, to the intent that if there be any abuse, it may be discovered before he is transported. And where his parents do not appear before the magistrate, notice is to be sent to them ; or where they cannot be found, to the churchwardens, overseers of the parish where he was last settled, in such manner as the said magistrates shall think fit and direct.

And because Clerks of the Peace may conceive this not to be any part of the duty of their office, and may therefore exact unreasonable rewards for their trouble and pains therein, his Majesty doth declare that if any merchants or other persons shall be aggrieved thereby, and upon complaint to the Justices cannot obtain relief, his Majesty will take such further care for their ease herein, as in his royal wisdom he shall think meet.

And his Majestie's further pleasure is, that this order be printed and published, to the end all persons whom it may concern may take notice thereof, and govern themselves accordingly."

Here is a very curious note concerning a custom long since forgotten. Before the discovery and importation of Indian nitre, saltpetre was manufactured from animal matter. This stuff was piled in heaps, protected from rain, and watered with stable runnings. Men called saltpetre-men were employed in collecting earth thus impregnated, and were by Act of Parliament (1624) authorised to dig up the floors of stables and any other places where this saturated earth might be found. So important was the manufacture that no dove-house or stable was permitted to be paved. The appearance of the saltpetre-man and his asserted right of digging up and carrying off the earth under stables became a grievance, against which remonstrance was in vain so long as the civil wars lasted. In 1656, however, it was enacted that no saltpetre-man should dig without permission of the householder.

During the seventeenth century the 'prentices, as we have seen, became of greater importance than ever; in the eighteenth their power declined. For instance, when in 1643 it was feared that Charles would march on the City, the 'prentices turned out in great force to fortify the entrances and roads all round the City. Four years later they turned out on strike, meeting in Covent Garden, then an open space, in order to compel their masters to give them back the old holidays of which the Puritans had deprived them. These were especially Christmas, with its days of merriment and minstrelsy, Good Friday, Easter Monday, and, I think, Whit Monday. Perhaps the Puritans had also deprived them of Queen Elizabeth's Day. On Shrove Tuesday the 'prentices demolished, if they could find any, houses of ill fame. Their keepers were locked up in prison during the whole of Lent. This zeal for virtue on the part of the London 'prentice becomes a thing of suspicion when one reads *The English Rogue.* Perhaps it was a custom ordered and maintained by the masters. I conclude this chapter with the history of one of them. It will be seen that the lot of a 'prentice was not always the happiest or the most desirable. The following notes are taken from the autobiography of one of them, a scrivener's printer, named F. K. To begin with, he was very fond of reading. While he was still a boy he read *The Friar and the Boy*, *The Seven Wise men of Rome*, *Fortunatus*, *Doctor Faustus*, *Friar Bacon*, *Montelion Knight of the Oracle*, *Parismus*, *Palmerin of England*, *Amadis de Gaul.* The boy procured the latter in French, and for the sake of reading it, taught himself French, and made a French dictionary for himself. As he could not afford to buy paper, he cut pages from the middle of the other boys' copybooks, and, being found out, received a very sound and well-deserved flogging.

When he was sixteen he was apprenticed to a scrivener for eight years' servitude, his father paying £30 and giving a bond for £100 as a guarantee of the boy's honesty.

His master had already two apprentices. It was the custom that the youngest apprentice should do, so to speak, the dirty work; but in this case the master had a son who was shortly afterwards apprenticed, and should, in his turn, have taken the lowest place; but by right of his position in the family he was spared this ignominy, and so the writer continued the drudge of the whole household as long as he remained in the house. Apart from his work in the shop, where he had to write out deeds, conveyances, etc.,—the scrivener's profession exercising much the same functions as those now undertaken by the solicitor,—he says, " I was to make clean the Shooes, carry out the Ashes and Dust, sweep the Shop, cleanse the Sink, (and a long nasty one it was), draw the Beer, at washing times to fetch up Coals and Kettles; these were the within doors employs, and abroad I was to go of all errands, and carry all burthens. I dispensed with all these matters, being told thereof by my Father and Mother before I came, wherefore I was content, and did undergo all very willingly, till I had served about three years, and then being grown up to some maturity and understanding, I began to grumble. I had Money given me which I always laid out in purchasing of Books, especially such as treated of Knight Errantry, or else in buying somewhat to make me fine, and Money coming in pretty plentiful, I had bought me a very good Suit of Cloaths to wear by the by; and withal, being desirous to appear in everything like a gentleman, I had a Watch for my Pocket; being thus accoutred, I sometimes went abroad with our Neighbour Apprentices and others, and being thus fine, it troubled me that I must still carry Burthens, for whoever went empty, my Mistress would still take care that I had my Load to carry Working-day and Sunday from our London to our Countrey-house, and rather than I should want a Burthen, I was to carry earthen Pots and Pans and Ox Livers, and Bones for the Dog. This I grumbled at, and when I have bin seriously a drawing Writings in the Shop and studying and contriving how to order my Covenants the best way, a greasy Kitchin-wench would come and disturb me with one of her Errants, and tell me I must fetch a farthing worth of Mustard, or a pint of Vinegar, or some such mechanical story; nay, my Mistress hath sent me for a Pint of Purl, which when she hath warmed and tasted of, and not liked, I must carry it again to change it. And I being the youngest Apprentice was to be commanded by every one; the two eldest would appoint what I was to do in the Shop, and the Kitchin-wench would, when she pleased, command me into the Kitchin, so that I must be here and there and everywhere; and above all things, I must humor and please the Maid, or else she would pick Holes in my Coat, and tell Tales of me to my Mistress, who would not let me live a quiet hour" (*The Unlucky Citizen*, pp. 35-37).

Presently, having served for three years, and being now nineteen years of age, he complained to his father :—

"But I was little the better for it; for no sooner was I come into my Master's House, but he seeing me, enters his Closet, from whence fetches a lusty Battoon Cane (the ordinary Weapon with which I was used to be disciplined), and without by your leave, or with your Leave, he takes me by the hand, and lifting up his Sword Arm like a Fencer, he gives me a lusty Thwack over the Shoulders, and without any warning given, not so much as the least word of Defyance, that I might know his anger, or the cause of it, he follows that blow by a second and a third, and many more, so fast and so long as he could lay on, till he, being out of breath, was forced to give over, and then so soon as he had recovered the use of his Tongue, he thus breaks silence, 'Sirrah, I'le teach you to run and make complaints to your Father.' I now having heard him speak, knew whereabouts he was, but methought the News was strange and sudden, and somewhat I began to mutter, but my Tale would not be heard; he prosecuted his business with the Second Part to the same Tune, both upon my Sides and Shoulders till he was again weary, and then there being a cessation of Arms, down I sate me, not daring to speak a word; but though I said nothing, yet I paid it with thinking, but all to little purpose; he was Master, and I found so he would continue" (*The Unlucky Citizen*, pp. 43, 44).

A master at that time had a perfect right to beat his servants; nor does the writer complain, except that there was, perhaps, too much laid on. It will be remembered that the wife of Pepys caned her maids. F. K., however, does point out the vile treatment of apprentices by some of their masters, and their advantage in it :—

"And let me tell you that I have observed and known that some Citizens have much encreased their Estates by taking many Apprentices, for perhaps having fifty pounds or more with an Apprentice, and being very severe and rigid, the boy hath been so hardly used, that he hath run away within a year, and rather than return again, lose all his Money. I knew one that served eight so, one after another, and in three or four years, by this means, gained four hundred pounds for their diet, which they likewise earned, causing them to work like Porters, so that I think they paid dear enough for it; they had been better to have been boarded at the costliest Boarding-school in England; and besides the loss of the Money, there was a worse inconvenience, for the Apprentice hath been quite spoiled, so harassed and frighted, that he hath not been fit for any other service, and for the sake of his first Master, would not be perswaded to go to any other " (*The Unlucky Citizen*, pp. 144, 145).

After being taken from this master and transferred to another, who turned him out of the house for betraying confidence, F. K. was set up in business by his father, opening a small scrivener's shop on Tower Hill. If his bad luck through life was like his bad luck as an apprentice, it was due to his own folly and stupidity. For instance, he says that he was arrested a few days after he was married, for his wedding clothes. Why, then, did he not pay for them? And so on. But we need not follow the *Unlucky Citizen* any farther.

The Sumptuary Laws against Apprentices so stringently enacted in the preceding century were still in force, and a youth who dared to array himself in finery other than befitted his craft, ran the risk of being forcibly despoiled of his ribbons and adornments and being reduced to a severe simplicity of apparel.

Here is a glimpse of life furnished by Howell when he placed his two younger brothers apprentices in the City :—

"Our two younger Brothers, which you sent hither, are disposed of; my Brother Doctor hath placed the elder of the two with Mr. Hawes, a Mercer in Cheapside, and he took much Pains in it; and I had placed my Brother Ned with Mr. Barrington, a Silk-man in the same Street; but afterwards, for some inconveniences, I removed him to one Mr. Smith, at the Flower de luce in Lombard Street, a Mercer also. Their Masters both of them are very well to pass, and of good repute; I think it will prove some

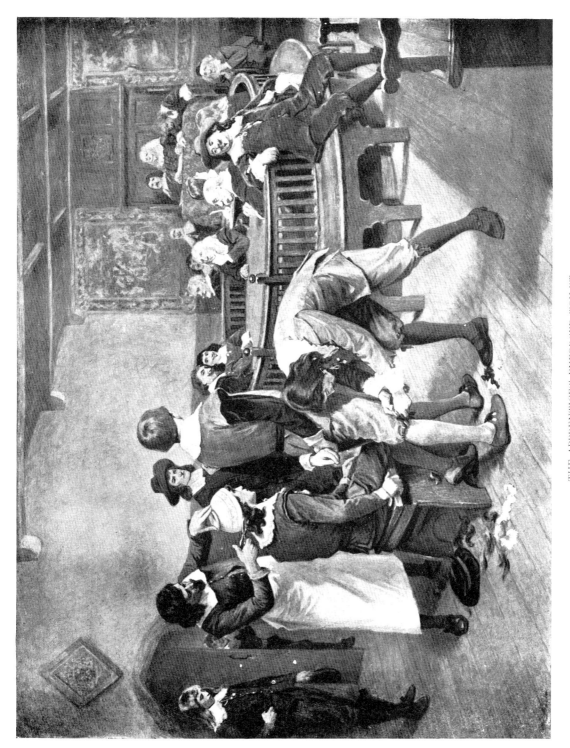

THE APPRENTICES' ENFORCED TOILET

By permission of the Artist, Ralph Hedley, R.S.A., and of the Owner, W. F. Henderson.

advantage to them hereafter to be both of one Trade; because, when they are out of their time, they may join Stocks together; so that I hope they are as well placed as any two Youths in London; but you must not use to send them such large Tokens in Money, for that may corrupt them. When I went to bind my brother Ned Apprentice in Drapers-Hall, casting my eyes upon the Chimney-piece of the great Room, I spied a Picture of an ancient Gentlemen, and underneath *Thomas* Howell; I asked the Clerk about him, and he told me that he was a Spanish Merchant in Henry VIII.'s time, and coming home rich, and dying a Batchelor, he gave that Hall to the Company of Drapers, with other things, so that he is accounted one of the chiefest Benefactors. I told the Clerk, that one of the Sons of Thomas Howell came now thither to be bound; he answered, that if he be a right Howell, he may have, when he is free, three hundred Pounds to help set up, and pay no interest for five years. It may be hereafter we will make use of this. He told me also, that any Maid that can prove her Father to be a true Howell may come and demand Fifty pounds towards her portion, of the said Hall."

CHAPTER VI

TRADE

THE chapter on trade under the Stuarts may be introduced by certain extracts from a paper written by Sir Walter Raleigh early in the seventeenth century. It was called "Observations on Trade and Commerce," in which he compares the Dutch trade and Dutch merchants with our own, very much to our disadvantage. The following, he says, are the seven points in which the Dutch surpass us :—

"1. The Merchant Staplers which maketh all Things in abundance, by reason of their Store-houses continually replenished with all kinds of Commodities.

2. The Liberty of free Traffick for Strangers to buy and sell in Holland, and other Countries and States, as if they were free-born, maketh great intercourse.

3. The small Duties levied upon Merchants, draws all Nations to trade with them.

4. Their fashioned ships continually freighted before ours, by reason of their few Mariners and great Bulk, serving the Merchant cheap.

5. Their forwardness to further all manner of Trading.

6. Their wonderful employment of their Busses for Fishing, and the great Returns they make.

7. Their giving free Custom inwards and outwards, for any new-erected Trade, by Means whereof they have gotten already almost the sole Trade into their hands."

"Thus," he goes on, "as regards the storing of merchandize, Amsterdam is never without a supply of 700,000 quarters of corn, which they keep always ready besides what they sell; and the like with other commodities, so that if a Dearth of Fish, wine, grain, or anything else begins in the country, forthwith the Dutch are ready with fifty or a hundred ships dispersing themselves at every 'Port-Town' in England, trading away their cargoes and carrying off English gold. Moreover, the Dutch have in their hands the greater part of the carrying trade of France, Portugal, Spain, Italy, Turkey, the East Indies, and the West Indies. Yet London is a much more convenient port for a store-house and for the carrying trade if our merchants would but bend their course for it."

As for small duties in foreign countries compared with the excessive customs in ours. James, it will be remembered, relied on his Customs duties, which were heavy, thereby keeping off foreign trade. In Holland the Customs duties were so much lighter that a ship which would pay £900 in the port of London could be cleared at Amsterdam for £50. Raleigh points out that what is lost by lowering the duties is more than made up by the increase of trade when the duties are low. He advocates Free Trade, observe, long before that innovation was thought of.

By the "fashion" of the ships he means the Dutch merchant vessels called "Boyers, Hoy-barks, and Hoys," constructed to contain a great bulk of merchandise and to sail with a small crew. Thus an English ship of 200 tons required a crew of thirty hands, while a ship of the same tonnage built in Holland wanted no more than nine or ten mariners.

Then, again, as to their "forwardness" in trading. In one year and a half the merchants of Holland, Hamburg, and Emden carried off from Southampton, Exeter,

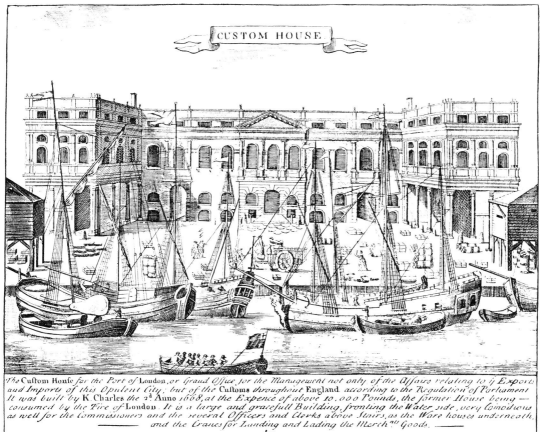

The Custom House for the Port of London, or Grand Office for the Management not only of the Affairs relating to ij Exports and Imports of this Opulent City; but of the Customs throughout England according to the Regulation of Parliament It was built by K. Charles the 2ᵈ Anno 1668, at the Expence of above 10,000 Pounds, the former House being — consumed by the Fire of London. It is a large and gracefull Building, fronting the Water side, very Comodious as well for the Commissioners and the several Officers and Clerks above Stairs, as the Ware houses underneath, and the Cranes for Landing and Lading the Merchᵗ Goods. &c.

and Bristol alone near £200,000 in gold. And perhaps £2,000,000, taking the whole of the kingdom into account. The Dutch alone sent 500 or 600 ships every year to England, while we sent but thirty to Holland.

A warning and an example is presented by the fallen and decayed condition of Genoa. Formerly this city was the most prosperous of all trading cities. All nations traded there; but in an evil moment Genoa declared a Customs duty of 10 per cent, which caused the whole of her trade to vanish. Why, again, Raleigh asks, do we not secure for ourselves the magnificent fisheries which lie off our shores? In four towns within the Sound are sold every year between 30,000 and 40,000 casts of herrings, representing £620,000. In Denmark, Norway, Sweden, etc., are sold our herrings, caught on our shores, to the amount of £170,000. This fishery represents over a million sterling in addition to all this. They are herrings caught off our shores, and yet we have no share in this great trade.

The Dutch employ a thousand ships in carrying salt to the East Kingdoms; we

Walker & Cockerell.

THE SOVERAIGNE OF THE SEAS, BUILT 1637
From a contemporary engraving by John Payne.

none. They have 600 ships in the timber trade; we none; they send into the East Kingdoms 3000 ships every year; we 100 only. They carry goods from the East Kingdoms to France, Spain, Portugal, and Italy in 2000 ships; we have none in that trade. They trade to all the ports of France; we to five or six only. They trade with every one of our ports—with 600 ships; we with three only of these ports, and but forty ships.

We neglect to take advantage of what we have. For instance, we send to Holland our cloth undressed; we let them take, for purposes of trade, our iron, our coal, our copper, lead, tin, alum, copperas, and other things on which we might employ thousands of people, and this country, which produces nothing, is enriched by carrying commodities about the world.

The arguments of Raleigh in favour of taking up the fisheries appear elementary. He thus sums up the advantages :—

" 1. For taking God's blessing out of the Sea to enrich the Realm, which otherwise we lose.

2. For setting the People on work.

3. For making Plenty of Cheapness in the Realm.

4. For increasing of Shipping, to make the Land powerful.

5. For a continual Nursery for breeding and increasing our Mariners.

6. For making employment of all Sorts of People, as blind, lame, and others, by Sea and Land, from ten or twelve years and upwards.

7. For inriching your Majesty's Coffers, by Merchandises returned from other Countries for Fish and Herrings.

8. For the increase and enabling of Merchants, which now droop and daily decay."

The trade of London during the first half of the seventeenth century decayed. The decay was due partly to the monopoly of the privileged companies, which stifled or discouraged enterprise ; partly to the civil wars ; partly to the Customs duties; and partly, it would seem, to a falling off in the vigour and enterprise which had marked the Elizabethan period. In trade, as in everything, there are times of reaction and of torpor. Meantime, in spite of everything, foreign trade increased. But Raleigh's comparison between the trade of Holland and that of London shows how small our foreign trade was, in comparison with the vast bulk carried on by the Dutch.

After Sir Walter Raleigh's " observations " let me quote Howell on the profession or calling of the merchant :—

" For my part I do not know any profession of Life (especially in an Island) more to be cherished and countenanced with honourable employments than the Merchant-Adventurer (I do not mean only the staplers of Hamburgh and Rotterdam) ; for if valiant and dangerous actions do enoble a Man, and make him merit, surely the Merchant-Adventurer deserves more Honour than any ; for he is to encounter not only with Men of all Tempers and Humours (as a French Counsellor hath it), but he contests and tugs oft-time with all the Elements ; nor do I see how some of our Country Squires, who sell Calves and Runts, and their Wives perhaps Cheese and Apples, should be held more genteel than the noble Merchant-Adventurer who sells Silks and Satins, Tissues and Cloths of Gold, Diamonds and Pearl, with Silver and Gold."

In the year 1606 James made an attempt to introduce the breeding of silk-worms. He sent mulberry-trees into the country with instructions for the feeding of the worms. There was a certain amount of English-grown silk manufactured, as is shown by an entry in Thoresby's *Diary.* " Saw at Mr. Gale's a sample of the satin lately made at Chelsea of English silkworms, for the Princess of Wales, which was very rich and beautiful." The experiment proved unsuccessful, yet it caused the immigration of a great number of silk throwsters, weavers, and dyers, who settled here and entered upon the silk trade in London. The raw silk was brought from India and China by the East India Company.

A table of imports from India in 1620 gives the most astonishing difference between the cost in India and the selling price in London (see Capper, *Port and Trade of London*, p. 82):—

Imports, 1620.	Cost on Board Ship in India.						Selling Prices in London.					
	s.	*d.*	£	*s.*	*d.*	*s.*	*d.*	£	*s.*	*d.*		
250,000 lbs. Pepper . . .	0	2½	2,604	3	4	1	8	20,833	6	8		
150,000 lbs. Cloves . . .	0	9	5,625	0	0	6	0	45,000	0	0		
150,000 lbs. Nutmegs . . .	0	4	2,500	0	0	2	6	18,750	0	0		
50,000 lbs. Mace . . .	0	8	1,666	13	4	6	0	15,000	0	0		
200,000 lbs. Indigo . . .	1	2	11,666	13	4	5	0	50,000	0	0		
107,140 lbs. China Raw Silk .	7	0	37,499	0	0	20	0	107,140	0	0		
50,000 pieces Calico . . .	7	0	17,500	0	0	20	0	50,000	0	0		
			79,061	10	0			306,723	6	8		

In 1620 the East India Company established themselves at Madras, where they had a trade in diamonds, muslin, and chintzes in return for English or European goods. They had in their service 2500 mariners, 500 ship carpenters, and 120 factors.

The story of Cockaine's patent should be (but it was not) a lesson in Free Trade. It was this man's custom to send white cloth from England to Holland to be dyed and dressed, and then sent back for sale. Alderman Cockaine proposed to the King to do the dyeing and dressing himself if he had a patent. He represented that the whole profit made by the Dutch would be saved by this arrangement. The King consented; he prohibited the exportation of white cloth to Holland, and seized the charter of the Merchant Adventurers which allowed them to export it. The Dutch naturally retaliated by prohibiting the importation of English dye cloths. It was then discovered that Cockaine could not do what he proposed to do; his cloths were worse dyed and were dearer than those dyed by the Dutch. After seven years of complaints over this business, the patent was removed and the charter restored.

The following is a statement of the trade of England at this time:—

"We trade to Naples, Genoa, Leghorn, Marseilles, Malaga, etc., with only twenty ships, chiefly herrings, and thirty sail more laden with pipes-staves from Ireland.

To Portugal and Andalusia we sent twenty ships for wines, sugar, fruit, and West Indian drugs.

To Bordeaux we send sixty ships and barks for wines.

To Hamburgh and Middleburgh, thirty-five ships are sent by our Merchant Adventurers' Company.

To Dantzic, Koningsburg, etc., we send yearly about thirty ships, viz. six from London, six from Ipswich, and the rest from Hull, Lynn, and Newcastle, but the Dutch many more.

To Norway we send not above five ships, and the Dutch above forty, and great ships too.

Our Newcastle coal trade employs 400 sail of ships; viz. 200 for supplying of London, and 200 for the rest of England.

And besides our own ships, hither, even to the mine's mouth, come all our neighbouring nations with their ships continually, employing their own shipping and mariners. I doubt not whether, if they had such a treasure, they would employ not their own shipping solely therein. The French sail thither in whole fleets of fifty sail together, serving all their ports of Picardie, Normandie, Bretagne, etc., even as far as Rochel and Bordeaux. And the ships of Bremen, Emden, Holland, and Zealand supply those of Flanders, etc., whose shipping is not great, with our coals.

Our Iceland fishery employs 120 ships and barks of our own.

And the Newfoundland fishery 150 small ships.

And our Greenland whale fishery fourteen ships.

As for the Bermudas, we know not yet what they will do; and for Virginia, we know not what to do with it; the present profit of these two colonies not employing any store of shipping" (Capper, p. 84).

The completion of the New River in 1620 was a great boon and blessing to the people, but the greatest benefit to trade in the reign of James I. was the improvement of the navigation of the upper part of the Thames by deepening the channel, so that not only was Oxford placed in communication with London, but the country all round Oxford.

The granting of monopolies was an interference with trade which would now cause a revolution. There were many complaints. Parliament declared that all monopolies were void. That was under James. Charles began, notwithstanding, to sell monopolies to whomsoever would pay him most for them. Thus the importation of alum was prohibited, for the protection of the alum works of Whitby; also brick-making, the manufacture of saltpetre, of tapestry, the coining of farthings, the making of steel, the making of stone pots and jugs, making guns, melting iron ore, and many other things. More than this, Charles made the sale of tobacco a royal monopoly; he forbade the infant colony of Virginia to sell tobacco to any foreign state; he levied a duty of four shillings a chaldron on all coal exported to foreign parts; and he actually endeavoured to establish a malting and a brewing monopoly. When we read the historian on the despotic acts of Charles and his attempts on the liberties of his people, let us bear in mind the constant exasperations of these interferences with trade—that is, with the livelihood of the people. When at last he became awakened to the danger of the position, he revoked all their "grants, licences, and privileges"; but it was then too late—revolution had already arisen.

Shops which had been open stalls confined to one or two markets in London, such as East and West Chepe, began, towards the end of the sixteenth century and early in the seventeenth, to appear along Fleet Street, the Strand, and in King Street, Westminster. Haberdashers, milliners, woollen drapers, cutlers, upholsterers, glassmen, perfumers, and others established themselves everywhere, making so brave a show every day, that, as Stow complains, "the people of London began to expend extravagantly." There were offered, among other wares, "French and Spanish gloves, and French cloth or frigarde (frieze), Flanders-dyed kersies, daggers, swords, knives, Spanish girdles, painted cruses, dials, tables, cards, balls, glasses, fine earthen pots, salt-cellars, spoons, tin dishes, puppets, pennons, ink-horns, toothpicks, silk, and silver buttons. All which 'made such a show in passengers' eyes, that they could not help gazing on and buying these knicknacks.' This great offence a contemporary writer, quoted by Stow, bitterly apostrophises. He 'marvels' that 'no man taketh heed to it what number of trifles cometh hither from beyond the seas, that we might either clean spare, or else make them within our own realm; for the which we either pay inestimable treasure every year, or else exchange substantial wares and necessaries for them, for the which we might receive great treasure."

There had then arisen outside the City a new class, and one which was becoming wealthy and important, namely, the suburban shopkeepers. They were certainly not a class that Charles could afford to exasperate. But apparently he never asked himself how far it was prudent to exasperate any class. Thus, in the blindness of his wrath against the Puritans, whose emigration was the best thing that could happen to him, he forbade them to emigrate without a certificate of having taken the oath of allegiance and supremacy, and likewise from the minister of their parish a certificate of their conversation and conformity to the orders and discipline of the Church of England. He therefore did what he could to preserve his own enemies in his kingdom, and to increase their hostility. Again, he ordered that the Weavers' Company should admit to its freedom none but members of the Church of England. He even interfered with trade to the extent of trading on his own account, on one occasion buying up all the pepper imported by the East India Company and selling it again at a profit.

The foundation of the banking business is said to date from the outbreak of the Civil War; perhaps it was partly due to that event. Banking was impossible in earlier times for several reasons: there was no system of commercial credit; there were no bank-notes; goods were bought or sold for actual coin; there was no Exchange; when men went abroad or came home, they had to take their foreign money to the Mint for re-coinage, or they had to get foreign money at the Mint; there was no recognised system of lending or borrowing; if a man borrowed money he did so as a special occasion and for a special purpose, and paid a large interest for the accommodation. The money-lenders were the Jews first, who carried on the trade as a Royal monopoly, followed by the Lombards, who came as the agents of Papal taxation; and afterwards the London merchants and goldsmiths.

When the Civil War broke out it became a serious consideration with the merchants to place their money in some place of security. The Mint, their former place of deposit, could not be trusted because Charles had already seized upon £200,000 belonging to merchants, and placed there for safety; their own strong rooms would not do, because if the City fell into the hands of the Royalists, the strong room would most certainly be plundered first.[1] They therefore began to

---

[1] The strong room was generally a recess, large or small, in the stone wall of the cellar or crypt; it was provided with a movable stone slab for a door.

THE FIRST ROYAL EXCHANGE—EXTERIOR AND INTERIOR

lodge their cash in the hands of goldsmiths, keeping what was called a "running cash" account. They probably thought that in case of need the goldsmiths could take their money and plate abroad. Country gentlemen also began to send their money up to London for greater security. This method was found so convenient that banking quickly spread and the bankers began to flourish. During the Commonwealth one Henry Robinson proposed the establishment of a "Land Bank," with branches in the country to lend money upon mortgage, the payments to be by paper.

The wars with the Dutch and the extraordinary developments of French industries caused our imports to vastly exceed our exports; every maid-servant, it was said, paid the French King half her wages; when peace came and trade was recovering, the madness of Charles II. in closing the Exchequer paralysed and ruined the City for a while. Never did monarch inflict a blow so cruel upon his people. And never did the Stuarts recover the confidence which this measure lost them.

The Plague of 1665, followed by the Fire, proved, as might be expected, a temporary check to the prosperity of the City. But the people kept up their courage.

After the Fire there was built, in place of Gresham's Exchange, which had been burned, a new Royal Exchange of which the first stone was laid by King Charles II.

The increase of trade, although petty trade, in the West was recognised in the foundation of the New Exchange, an institution which has been mostly overlooked by historians.

"This building was erected by Robert, Earl of Salisbury, somewhat after the shape of the Royal Exchange, having cellars underneath and paved walks above with rows of shops. The first stone was laid on the 10th of June 1608. It was opened by King James I., April 10th, 1609, who came attended by the Queen, the Duke of York, the Lady Elizabeth, and many great lords and ladies, but it was not successful" (*Stow*).

"In the Strand on the N. side of Durham House stood an olde long stable, the outer wall whereof on the street side was very olde and ruinate, all which was taken down and a stately building sodainely erected in the place by Robert, E. of Salisbury, Lord High Treasurer of England. The first stone of this beautiful building was laid the 10th of June last past, and was fully finished in November following. And on Tuesday, the 10th April, the year (1609), many of the upper shoppes were richly furnished with wares, and the next day after that, the King, Queen and Prince, the Lady Elizabeth and the D. of York, with many great Lordes and chief ladies, came thither, and were there entertained with pleasant speeches, gifts, and ingenious devices: there the King gave it a name and called it Britain's Burse" (Nich., *Progresses*, vol. ii. p. 248).

The exports and the imports of London during fifty years of this century are

thus tabulated.   It will be seen that they show a steady increase in the bulk of
trade :—

	Exports.	Imports.
1614	2,090,640	2,141,283
1622	2,320,436	2,619,315
1663	2,022,812	4,016,019
1669	2,063,274	4,196,139

The prosperity of the country was shown by the contemporary writers to have been
advancing steadily and rapidly, in spite of the civil wars, the Dutch wars, the
pestilence which on five separate occasions devastated the country and the City, and
the Great Fire which destroyed all the "Stock" of the merchants.   Sir William
Petty (1676) observes that the number of houses in London was double that of
1636, and that there had been a great increase of houses in many towns of the
United Kingdom, that the Royal Navy was four times as powerful as in later years,
that the coal trade of Newcastle had quadrupled, the Customs yielded three times
their former value, that more than 40,000 tons of shipping were employed in the
Guinea and American trade, that the King's revenue was trebled, and that the
postage of letters had increased from one to twenty.

The Davenant also (1698) speaks twenty years later to the same effect.   He shows
that the value of land had risen from twelve years' purchase in former times to fourteen, sixteen, and twenty years' purchase in 1666 ; and by the end of the century to
twenty-six or even more ; that great quantities of waste land had been enclosed and
cultivated ; that the merchant marine had doubled between 1666 and 1688 ; that
many noble buildings had been erected ; that the Customs duties had increased in
twenty years by a third ; that the standard of comfort among the working-classes
was greatly improved ; and that property in cattle, stock-in-trade, and personal effects
had risen from £17,000,000 in 1600 to £88,000,000 in 1688.

As already mentioned, the Revocation of the Edict of Nantes brought to this
country some 70,000 of the most highly skilled artificers.   Many thousands settled
in the suburbs of London, especially in Bethnal Green, Spitalfields, and St. Giles.
Among the things they made or prepared were "light woollens, silk, linen, writing-
paper, glass, hats, lute-string, silks, brocades, satins, velvets, watches, cutlery, clocks,
jacks, locks, surgeons' instruments, hardware, and toys" (*Capper*, p. 103).

These refugees gave the country a large and valuable industry in silk-weaving ;
it is also supposed that the manufacture of fine paper was due to the French
immigrants.   In 1670 the Duke of Buckingham brought Venetians over here who
introduced the manufacture of fine glass.

The making of linen cloth and tapestry was encouraged by an Act of 1666,
which offered special advantages to those who set up the trade of hemp dressing.
In 1669 certain French Protestants settled at Ipswich and engaged in this trade.

The old industry of woollen cloth was protected by the prohibition to export wool. In 1666 a law was passed directing that every one should be buried in wool, and the clergy were required to take an affidavit to that effect at every interment.

In 1676 the printing of calicoes was commenced in London. A writer of the day says that "instead of green say, that was wont to be used for children's frocks, is now used painted and Indian and striped calico, and instead of perpetuam or shalloon to line men's coats with is used sometimes glazed calico, which in the whole is not a shilling cheaper, and abundantly worse."

An Act passed in 1662 forbade the importation of foreign bone lace, cut work, embroidery, fringe, band-strings, buttons, and needlework on the ground that many persons in this country made their living by this work.

The art of tinning plate-iron was brought over from Germany. The first wire-mill was also put up at this period by a Dutchman.

In short, the development of the arts was largely advanced during the century, and almost entirely by foreigners—French, German, Venetian, and Dutch.

The income of the Crown does not belong to the history of London, except that the City furnished a large part of it. That of Charles II. was ordered by the Parliament, August 31, 1660, to be made up to £1,200,000 a year. To raise this sum various Acts were passed. Thus there was the subsidy called "tonnage" levied upon foreign wine, and that called "pundage" levied upon the export and import of certain commodities. These taxes were collected at the Custom House. There was also the excise upon beer, ale, and other liquors sold within the kingdom. There was the tax of hearth money, which was two shillings upon any fire, hearth, or stove in every house worth more than twenty shillings a year. There were also the Royal lands, such as the Forest of Dean, the duties on the mines in the Duchy of Cornwall, the first-fruits and tenths of church benefices, the Post Office, etc. Other duties were laid occasionally on land, on personal property, on the sale of wine, etc. It must be remembered, however, that the King maintained out of this income the Fleet and the Army.

The coinage current in London consisted of more kinds than the present simpler system. In gold there were sovereigns, half-sovereigns, crowns, and half-crowns; in silver, crowns, half-crowns, shillings, sixpences, half-groats, pennies, and halfpennies. To this there were added from time to time the Thistle crown of four shillings, the Scottish six pound gold coin valued at ten shillings, the French crown called "The Sun," valued at seven shillings. There were also farthing tokens in lead, tin, copper, and leather.

Ben Jonson shows us what kind of money was carried about. "The man had 120 Edward's shillings, one old Harry sovereign, three James shillings, an Elizabeth groat: in all twenty nobles"—a noble was worth 7s. 2d.; "also he had some Philip and Marias, a half-crown of gold about his wrist that his love gave him, and a leaden heart when she forsook him."

" Before the reign of James I. nothing beyond pennies and halfpennies in silver appear to have been attempted to supply the poor with a currency. In 1611 Sir Robert Cotton propounded a scheme for a copper coinage ; this was not, however, carried out. A scheme to enrich the king produced the farthing token, weighing six grains, and producing 24s. 3d. for the pound weight of copper ; half the profit was to be the king's and the other half the patentee's. The first patent was granted to Baron Harrington of Exton, Rutlandshire, April 10, 1613, and a Proclamation was issued May 19, 1613, forbidding the use of traders' tokens in lead, copper, or brass. The new coin was to bear, on the one side, the King's title, ' Jaco. D. G. Mag. Bri., two sceptres through a crown ; ' on the reverse, ' Fra. et. Hib. Rex., a harp crowned.' The mint mark, a rose. A Proclamation was published June 4, 1625, prohibiting any one from counterfeiting this coin. Upon the death of Lord Harrington, in 1614, the Patent was confirmed to Lady Harrington and her assigns ; subsequently it was granted to the Duke of Lennox and James, Marquis of Hamilton, and on the 11th of July 1625 to Frances, Duchess Dowager of Richmond and Lennox, and Sir Francis Crane, Knight, for seventeen years, the patentees paying to the King one hundred marks yearly. By a Proclamation issued in 1633, the counterfeiters of these tokens were, upon conviction, to be fined £100 apiece, to be set on the pillory in Cheapside, and from thence whipped through the streets to Old Bridewell, and there kept to work ; and when enlarged, to find sureties for their good behaviour. On the 3rd of August 1644 the Mayor, Aldermen, and Commons of the City of London petitioned the House of Commons against the inconvenience of this coin, and the hardship suffered by the poor in consequence. No farthing tokens being issued during the Commonwealth, private persons were under the necessity of striking their own tokens. The practice being, however, contrary to law, was subsequently prohibited by a Proclamation issued August 16, 1672. It further appears, by an advertisement in the *London Gazette*, No. 714, September 23, 1672, that an office called the ' Farthing Office ' was opened in Fenchurch Street, near Mincing Lane, for the issue of these coins on Tuesday in each week, and in 1673-4 an order was passed to open the office daily. These measures not proving effectual to prevent private coinage of tokens, another Proclamation was issued on October 17, 1673, and another on December 12, 1674. These farthing tokens encountered the contempt and scorn of all persons to whom they were tendered, as being of the smallest possible value. Sarcastic allusions were made to them by dramatists, poets, and wits. ' Meercroft,' in Ben Jonson's *Devill is an Asse*, Act ii. sc. 1, played in 1616, alludes to this coin and its patentee " (*Index to Remem.* pp. 89, 90, *note*).

In 1694 the London tradesmen began to cry out about the badness of the coinage ; vast numbers of halfpence and farthings were forged, and the chipping of the silver went on almost openly. The Government resolved on an entirely new issue, which was complete in 1699.

COINS OF THE PERIOD

1. Old Harry sovereign
2. Edward shilling.
3. James I. shilling.
4. Charles II. gold crown.
5. Elizabeth groat.
6. Charles II. half groat.
7. Charles II. sixpence.
8. Charles II. gold sovereign.
9. Charles II. half broad (gold)
10. Charles II. shilling.
11. Charles II. crown.
12. Charles II. half crown.
13. Charles II. silver Maundy penny.

It was not a time of universal prosperity; witness the following account of the Grocers' Company (Ninth Report, Historical MSS.):—

" 27th March 1673. The Grocers' proposal for payment of their debts. The Company's year rents and revenues amount to only £722:5:4, and are charged with a yearly payment of £7571:19:8 in charity. Their debts are £24,000. In 1640 they lent the king £4500, for repayment whereof some of the Peers became bound. In 1642 they advanced £9000 for suppressing the Irish Rebellion. In 1643 they lent the City of London £4500. The principal and interest of these several debts, still owing to the Company as aforesaid, amount to above £40,000. The greater part of their estate was in houses burnt down in the late Fire, and since leased out for 60, 70, and 80 years, by decrees made in the late Court of Judicature established by Act of Parliament. The several sums they owe were voluntarily lent them.

They propose that £12,000 be raised by voluntary subscriptions and equally distributed among all their creditors within six months; that, to discharge the rest of their debt, the debts owing to the Company be assigned to trustees; that a special memorandum be entered in the Company's books, that, in case the creditors be not satisfied by the means proposed, the Company shall, if ever in a capacity hereafter, pay the whole remainder to every creditor; and that, on performance of these proposals, the Company be absolutely discharged from all their debts. Meanwhile all prosecutions against the Company to be stayed, that the Company may be animated cheerfully to raise the money. The Company submit, in conclusion, that a Hall encumbered and not half finished is all the Company of Grocers have to encourage their members to a voluntary contribution to satisfy debts contracted before most of them were born, and before all the residue, save some few only, were free of the Company. (Offered this day, having been called for by the Committee on the 24th. Rejected as 'not satisfactory' on the 28th. Com. Book of date.)

28th March. Answer of the Appellants. The Company, besides their £722:5:4 for rents in England, have an estate of nearly £400 rental in Ireland, and their Hall, with appurtenances worth £200 a year more. The lands charged with charitable uses are expressly excepted by the decree. The estate is let at quit-rents, and, if rack-rented, would yield another £12,000. The yearly contributions of members amount to another £1000.

Their disbursements in 1671 were :—

	£	s.	d.
For payment for dinners and collations	172	13	10
To the Wardens	12	10	0
Corn money	25	0	0
Reparation of their Hall	281	4	6
In Gratuity given	89	0	0
Suit in Chancery and in Parliament with Appellants	89	8	11
Lord Mayor's Day	44	4	0
Interest money	46	14	0

Besides this they can at pleasure raise in a month's time, by fines for offices and calling to livery, £4000. Most of their debts are recent. Their loans to the City should be sued for by themselves. The loan of 1643 was to defend the City against the King. The Company did not suffer much by the Fire, as most of their estate was let on long leases. All the creditors have received one-sixth of their claims, except the Cholmleys, who have been promised payment since the decree, but have received nothing. The Company itself is willing to pay its debts, but is prevented by a small minority, who are the authors of the proposal, and dishonestly deny liability. Appellants cannot agree to stand equally with the rest of the creditors, who refused to join them at first before the suit commenced, and only sued the Company at its own litigation, with a view to forestall Appellants. They cannot accept the Grocers' proposals in lieu of the decree they hold. The Company have already offered more favourable terms, which have been refused. The Hall is actually sequestered, and was so before its conveyance to the Lord Mayor, etc. of London, as Governors of Christ's Hospital. The Company's estate is sufficient to cover their claim, in which Appellants are supported by several members of the Company itself. If the Company will give good personal security to discharge their debts in seven years, and to pay at once the sixth part of the principal to the Cholmleys, with interest from the time others had it, with costs, Appellants will accept these terms, assign over their sequestration, and help them to pay their other creditors ; otherwise they pray the sale may be enforced. (Put in this day, but rejected by the Grocers' Counsel. Com. Book of date.")

Another company was also struggling with difficulties, as the following extract from the same Report shows :—

" 10th March, 1675. The petition of the Master, Warden, Assistants and Commonaltie of the Corporation of Pin-makers, London, to the King ; with paper of proposals attached thereto Reminding his Majesty of a contract made between Him and their Company, for the benefit alike of His Majesty and the London Pin-makers, that came to nought in consequence of the Great Plague and the Dutch, the Pin-makers beg for an aid of £20,000—£10,000 thereof to be laid out in wire, to be bought of His Majesty at 30d. per hundred weight about the current rate of such wire ; and the other £10,000 thereof to be used as a fund by Commissioners, and the pins being distributed to buyers at a cost sufficient only to cover the charge of production. By operation of the scheme, embodied in these proposals, it is urged the trade of the pin-making will revive, the pin-makers will have full and lucrative employment, and his Majesty will by his profit on the wire receive a revenue of at least £4000 per annum."

The most important civic event in the reign of William was the foundation of the Bank of England. The bankers of the City had been, as we have seen, the goldsmiths, who not only received and kept money for their customers, but lent it out, for them and for themselves, on interest. Thus, when Charles the Second, on January 2, 1672, closed the Exchequer, his creditors could obtain neither principal nor interest. He then owed the goldsmiths of London the sum of £1,328,526.

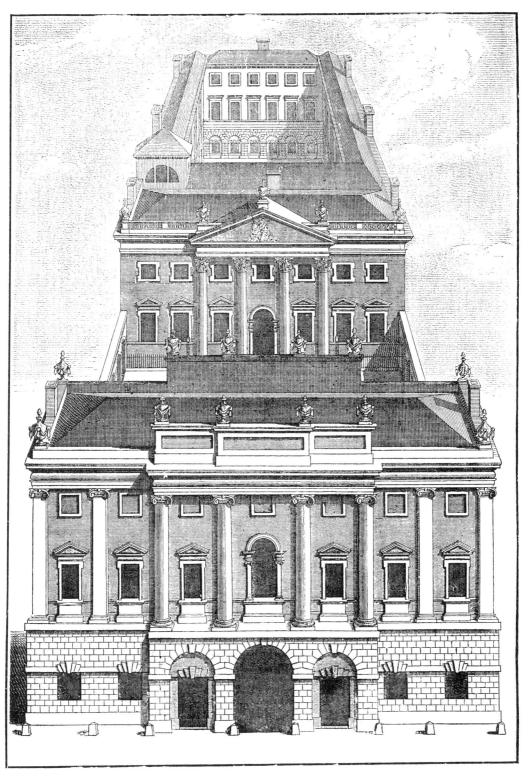

A PERSPECTIVE VIEW OF THE BANK OF ENGLAND, 1743

From Maitland's *History and Survey of London*.

Some of the older banks of London trace a descent to the goldsmiths of the seventeenth century—Child's, for instance, Hoare's, and others.

The idea of a National Bank seems to have been considered and discussed for some years before it was carried into effect. The principal advocate of the scheme was a Scotchman named William Anderson. The advantages which he put forward in defence of the Bank were the support of public credit and the relief of the Government from the ruinous terms upon which supplies were then raised. There was great difficulty in getting the scheme considered, but it was at last passed by an Act of Parliament in 1693. By the terms of this Act it was provided that the Government should take a loan of £1,200,000 from the Bank, this amount to be subscribed; additional taxes were imposed which would produce about £140,000 a year, out of which the Bank was to receive £100,000 a year, including interest at 8 per cent, and £4000 a year for management. The Company was empowered to purchase lands, and to deal in bills of exchange and gold and silver bullion, but not to buy or sell merchandise, though they might sell unredeemed goods on which they had made advances.

The subscription for the £1,200,000 was completed in ten days. The Bank began its business on July 27, 1694.

Its offices were at first the Grocers' Hall, where they continued until the year 1743. In this year the new building, part of the present edifice, was completed. Maitland describes it as

"A most magnificent structure; the front next the street is about 80 feet in length, adorned with columns, entablature, etc., of the Ionick order. There is a handsome courtyard between this and the main building, which, like the other, is of stone, and adorned with pillars, pilasters, entablature, and triangular pediment of the Corinthian Order. The hall is 79 feet in length, and 40 in breadth, is wainscotted about 8 feet high, has a fine fretwork ceiling, and a large Venetian window at the west end of it. Beyond this is another quadrangle, with an arcade on the east and west sides of it; and on the north is the Accomptant's Office, which is 60 feet long, and 28 feet broad. There are handsome apartments over this and the other sides of the quadrangle, with a fine staircase adorned with fretwork; and under it are large vaults, that have very strong walls and iron gates for the preservation of the cash."

By the charter they constituted a Governor, who must have £4000 in Bank stock; a Deputy Governor, who must have £3000; and twenty-four Directors, who must have £2000 each.

The Bank, although a year or two after its foundation its utility was fully recognised by merchants, did not command complete confidence for many years. Pamphlets were written against it. They were answered in 1707 by Nathaniel Tench, a merchant. The defence is instructive. Maitland sums it up :—

"The chief purpose of this defence was to vindicate a corporation, and the management thereof; not so much from crimes they had already been guilty of in the experiment of eleven or twelve years, as the fear of what they might do hereafter."

The charter of the Bank was renewed in 1697 to 1711; in 1708 to 1733;

in 1712 to 1743; in 1742 to 1765; in 1763 to 1786; in 1781 to 1812; and so on. There have been times of tightness. In 1697 the Bank was forced to suspend partially payment in coin, giving 10 per cent once a fortnight, and afterwards at the rate of 3 per cent once in three months. In 1720 it escaped the disaster of the South Sea Bubble. In 1745, when London was thrown into a panic by the approach of the Pretender, there was a run upon the Bank. This was staved off by paying slowly in silver. In the year 1797, by an order in Council, last payments were suspended. These events, however, belong to the after history of the Bank.

The foundation of the Bank of England brought about a complete revolution in the relations of Crown and City. We have seen that hitherto the City was called the King's Chamber; when the King wanted money he sent to the City for a loan; sometimes he asked more than the City could lend; generally the City readily conceded the loan.

In a note, Sharpe calls attention to the absurdity of representing the Chancellor of the Exchequer going about, hat in hand, borrowing £100 of this hosier and £100 from that ironmonger :—

"The mode of procedure was nearly always the same. The lords of the treasury would appear some morning before the Common Council, and after a few words of explanation as to the necessities of the time, would ask for a loan, offering in most cases undeniable security. Supposing that the Council agreed to raise the required loan, which it nearly always did, the mayor for the time being was usually instructed to issue his precept to the aldermen to collect subscriptions within their several wards, whilst other precepts were (in later times at least) sent to the master of wardens of the livery companies to do the same among the members of their companies. There were times, also, when the companies were called upon to subscribe in proportion to their assessment for supplying the City with corn in times of distress" (*London and the Kingdom*, vol. ii. pp. 586, 587).

The last loan ever asked by the King of the City was that asked by William the Third in 1697 to pay off his navy after the Peace of Utrecht. Instead of going to the City the King went to the Bank, but not then without the authority of Parliament. The City was no longer to be the Treasurer—or the Pawnbroker —of the King and the nation. This event, though the citizens did not apprehend its full meaning for many years, deprived London of that special power which had made her from the Norman Conquest alternately the object of the Sovereign's affections or of his hatred. Henceforth it mattered nothing to London whether the King loved or hated her. The power of the City was now exercised legitimately by her representatives in the House of Commons.

CHAPTER VII

THE IRISH ESTATES

THE following history of the Irish estates is taken from *London and Londonderry*, published in Belfast (1890) by Messrs. Marcus Ward and Co.

In the year 1608 the first steps were taken towards the settlement of Ulster by English and Scotch emigrants—a measure whose wisdom was shown eighty years later, when the grandson of James the First owed his expulsion largely to the descendants of the original settlers.

The greater part of six counties in the Province of Ulster, viz. Donegal, Fermanagh, Cavan, Tyrone, Armagh, and Coleraine, after the rebellions of O'Neill and O'Donnell, were declared to be escheated to the Crown. James conceived a plan for securing the peace and welfare of Ulster by replacing the Irish rebels by Protestant settlers, together with those of the Irish who were willing to conform to the English rule and religion. He therefore invited "undertakers" who would accept of lands in Ulster on his conditions.

These were, that they should not ask for large portions "in tending their private property only;" that there should be three classes of undertakers :

(1) Those who would plant with English or Scotch tenants.

(2) Servitors or military undertakers.

(3) Native Irish admitted as freeholders.

The first class were to pay to the Crown the great rent of £5 : 6 : 8 for every thousand acres. The second class, when they planted with English or Scotch tenants, were to pay the same; otherwise, the second class were to pay £8 for every thousand acres; and the third class were to pay £10 : 13 : 4 for every thousand acres.

The third condition was, that all were required to provide strongholds and arms for defence, to let their lands on easy terms, to "avoid Irish exactions," and to be resident; they were not to accept the "mere" Irish as tenants at all; they were required to create market towns, and to found at least one free school in every county for education in religion and learning. They were also privileged to import from Great Britain for three years, free of custom, everything requisite to put the plantation on a satisfactory footing.

In 1609 Commissioners were appointed to survey the escheated lands and to divide them into convenient parcels for allocation.

In the same year proposals were made in the King's name to the City that the Corporation itself should undertake the restoration of the city of Derry and the town of Coleraine, and should plant the rest of the county with undertakers. The City was offered the Customs for twenty-one years at 6s. 8d. per annum, the fisheries of the Bann and the Foyle, free license to export wares grown on their own land, and the admiralty of Tyrconnel and Coleraine.

The following were the inducements held out to the City :—

"If multitudes of men were employed proportionally to these commodities which might be there by industry attained, many thousands would be set on work to the great service of the King, strength of his realm, advancement of several trades, and benefit of particular persons, whom the infinite increasing greatness (that often doth minister occasion of ruin to itself) of this city might not only conveniently spare, but also reap a singular commodity by easing themselves of an insupportable burthen which so surcharged all the parts of the city that one tradesman can scarce live by another, which in all probability would be a means also and preserve the city from infection ; and by consequence the whole kingdom, of necessity, must have recourse thither, which persons pestered or closed up together can neither otherwise or very hardly avoid" (*London and Londonderry*, p. 7).

On July 1, 1609, the Court of Aldermen sent a precept to each of the City Companies asking them to appoint representatives to consider the propositions. The Companies refused to undertake this work. Thereupon the Mayor appointed a Committee, ignoring the refusal of the Companies, to carry out the undertaking. This Committee sent an order to the Companies to ascertain what each member would willingly undertake.

On August 1, 1609, the City sent out four "viewers" to survey the place intended for the new Plantation and "to make report to this City." The viewers returned in December, when it was resolved that £15,000 should be raised to meet preliminary expenses. The money was to be raised *in* the Companies, not by the Companies. Meantime the City asked for certain additional advantages, including forces for defence to be maintained at the King's charges. It was agreed that 200 houses should be built at Derry, leaving room for 300 more, and that 100 houses should be built at Coleraine, leaving room for 200 more, and that fortifications should be constructed. Another sum of £5000 was then ordered to be raised. In January 1610 the demands of the City were granted by the Privy Council. It is important to observe that the "undertaking" by the City was not a purchase by the Companies, but taxation of the members of the Companies by order of the City, just as any other tax was imposed and collected. Some of the poorer Companies were exempted, but not the "abler" men among them.

In July 1611 another contribution of £20,000 was raised by tax. In this case those Companies which might choose to lose the benefits resulting from their previous contributions were exempt—a privilege accepted by two of the Companies.

Power was given by the Common Council to the Committee of the Corporation, afterwards the Irish Society, to divide the land among those Companies willing to accept them, and so "to build and plant the same at their own cost and charges, accordingly as by the Printed Book of Plantation is required." Eight of the great Companies accepted at once, and the other four shortly afterwards.

Meantime the Privy Council made certain conditions, among them the following :—

"The Londoners are *first* to provide habitations for such poor and necessary men as they draw thither for their business, and afterwards to let for such rents as shall be fitting *as well for the good of the Plantation* as for some valuable rent (THE CHARGES CONSIDERED), *the Londoners always performing the Articles of Plantation*" (*London and Londonderry*, pp. 12, 13).

It would appear from this that the subscribers were intended to get rent in return for their outlay, but they never did, because the Companies added the rents of the land to their own corporate funds. As the subscribers do not appear to have objected, this was probably done openly and without any remonstrance or objection.

Complaints began to be made that the conditions were not carried out ; only twenty houses were built at Derry instead of the 200 promised ; the Londoners were converting the timber to their own profit. In December 1612 the King wrote to Sir Arthur Chichester, the Lord Deputy :—

" ' If there were no reason of State to press it forward, yet we would pursue and effect that work with the same earnestness, merely for the goodness and morality of it, esteeming the settling of religion, the introducing of civility, order, and government among a barbarous and unsubjected people to be the acts of piety and glory, and worthy also a Christian Prince to endeavour ' " (*London and Londonderry*, p. 13).

On March 29, 1613, the first charter was granted to the Irish Society as representing not the Companies, but the Corporation of the City of London for the Plantations. This charter constitutes and incorporates the Irish Society :—

" ' For the better ordering, directing, and governing all and all manner of things for and concerning the City and Citizens of Londonderry aforesaid, and the aforesaid County of Londonderry, and the Plantation to be made within the same City and County of Londonderry, and other businesses belonging to the same,' giving the Society power to purchase and hold in fee, *for these purposes*, lands, goods, etc., in England or in Ireland, to have a common seal, and to sue or be sued " (p. 14).

A grant of timber is made only for the Plantation and "not for any other causes to be merchandized or sold." In other words, the Irish Society was incorporated for the purpose of a Trust ; the members were originally Trustees.

It is charged against the Society that they began by neglecting the conditions, setting too high a rent upon their lands, and trying to make a profit for the Londoners out of the property. James himself was much dissatisfied with the conduct of the estates. He wrote to Sir Arthur again in August 1615, adding a postscript in his own hand:—"My Lord, in this service I expect that zeal and uprightness from you, that you will spare no flesh, English or Scotch, for no private man's worth is able to counterbalance the particular safety of a kingdom, which this Plantation, being well accomplished, will procure."

A year afterwards the King granted a licence to the twelve Companies to hold in mortmain whatever lands the Irish Society might grant them.

These grants contained a reservation of the right of re-entry if the conditions specified were not kept.

It is, of course, evident that if the Irish Society were Trustees they could not give away their lands, and that they could only make grants under the conditions of their Trust.

In 1620, on further complaints being made, the sequestration of the estates was granted, but not carried out. In 1624 other complaints were made that the conditions of allotting 4000 acres to Derry and 3000 to Coleraine had not been carried out. It was replied that Derry had received 1500 and Coleraine 500.

Charles I. began by making an attempt to fix a fair rent, which appears to have failed, the Society declaring that for the time it was impracticable. There were, no doubt, difficulties in the way of getting settlers, or, which seems possible, there were so many applicants that the Society was able to run up rents. In 1637 the Court of Chancery gave judgment in the case. The letters patent of March 1613 were annulled, and the premises granted to the Irish Society were seized into the hands of the King. A fine of £70,000 was also imposed upon the City.

The charges brought against the Londoners were as follows:—

" 1st, Unduly and deceitfully obtaining the letters patent, 'under pretence of a due observance of the articles'; 2nd, Obtaining more land than it was the King's intention to grant (97,000 acres of fertile land, instead of 27,000), the rents mentioned being 'one hundred and ninety-three pounds, eight shillings and fourpence, and no more;' 3rd, The neglecting to plant with English and inland Scots, and illegally many of the 'mere Irish' (names being given) in possession of the lands; 4th, Rack-renting of an atrocious type. 'Their Agents . . . do still continue the natives upon the said Plantation, and paid the Fines imposed upon them, according to the said Proclamation, for not departing from the British undertaken Lands, *because they would give greater Rents for the said Lands than the British were able to live upon*, and did prefer the Irish before the English, because they pretended they were more serviceable unto them, by which means, AND BY THEIR EXCESSIVE RAISING THE RENTS FROM FORTY SHILLINGS AND FIFTY SHILLINGS A BALLIBOE, UNTO TEN POUNDS, TWELVE POUNDS, AND TWENTY POUNDS AND THIRTY POUNDS A BALLIBOE, the English were and are much disheartened, and the natives do far exceed the British, etc.;' 5th, Spoliation of the Plantation and fraud on the Crown by cutting down the woods *for merchandise* instead of for Plantation purposes to the extent of one million oaks, two thousand elms, and two hundred thousand ash trees, of the value of £550,666 13s. 4d." (pp. 21 and 22).

The King, however, accepted a fine of £12,000 with the surrender of all the grants.

Three years later the sentence of the Court was set aside by the House of Commons with the following resolutions:—

" Resolved that it is the opinion of this House that the Citizens of London were solicited and pressed to the Undertaking of the Plantation of Londonderry.

Resolved, that the Copy attested by Mr. Goad's Hand is a true Copy of the Sentence given in the Star-Chamber against the Mayor and Commonalty of the City of London, and of the new plantation of Ulster in the Kingdom of Ireland.

Resolved, That the Order made in the Court of Star-Chamber, dated the eighth of March, in the eighth of Charles, is unlawful, both for the Matter, Persons, and Time therein prefixed.

Resolved, That this House is of Opinion that the King was not deceived in the grant which he made unto the Society of Governors and Assistants of London of the new Plantation of Ulster in the Kingdom of Ireland, in particular; nor in creating a new Corporation, called the Society of the Governors and Assistants of London of the new Plantation of Ulster in the Kingdom of Ireland.

Resolved, That this House is of Opinion that the King did not by that patent grant more Land than was by him intended to be granted, nor was he therein deceived.

That it doth not appear by sufficient Proof that the Citizens of London were tied to perform the printed Articles, and consequently not bound to plant with English and Scots, nor restrained from planting with Natives.

By the seven-and-twenty Articles, the City was to build two hundred Houses in Derry, and an hundred at Coleraine by the first Day of November 1611. Admitting that the Houses were not built, nor the Castle of Culmore repaired, by the time prefixed; yet this is no Crime, nor Cause for giving Damages, in regard the City had not that Patent until the nine-and-twentieth of March 1613.

That there is no Proof that the Governor, etc., of the new Plantation, or any of their Companies, did make any Lease unto any Popish Recusant, nor of any Decay of Religion there by default of the Planters.

There is no Proof of any Default in the Planters for not making a sufficient Number of Freeholders, nor any Articles that do tie them thereunto.

That there is no proof that the City of London, or the Governor of the new Plantations, have felled any trees in the Woods called Glancankin and Kellytrough, contrary to their covenant.

That the not conveying of Glebe Lands to the several Incumbents of the several Parish Churches, in regard their did enjoy the Lands, is no Crime punishable, nor cause of Seizure of their Lands.

That the Breach of Covenant (if any such were) is no sufficient Cause to forfeit the Lands.

That the Breach of Covenant is no Crime, but triable in ordinary Courts of Justice.

That the Court of Star-Chamber, while it stood as a Court, had no Power to examine Freehold nor Inheritance; nor had any Power to examine or determine Breach of Covenant or Trust.

That the Sentence upon these Corporations aggregate, no particular Person being guilty, it is against Law.

That in all the Proofs of this Cause there doth not appear Matter sufficient to convince the City of London of any Crime.

That, upon the whole Matter, the Sentence of the Star-Chamber was unlawful and unjust.

That this Composition and Agreement made with the City upon these Terms in the Time of Extremity ought not to bind the City.

That the Opinion of the House is, That they think fit, that both the Citizens of London, and those of the new Plantation, and all Under-Tenants, and all those put out of Possession by the Sequestration, or King's Commissioners, shall be restored to the same State they were in before the Sentence in the Star-Chamber.

That the Citizens of London, and all they against whom the Judgement is given in the Scire Facias, shall be discharged of that Judgement."

In 1650 Oliver Cromwell made a new grant of the estates to the City. In 1662 a great charter was granted by Charles II. This charter restored the Irish Society, with the same powers of management as had been granted in 1613 with all the

VIEW OF THE FRONT OF SIR PAUL PINDAR'S HOUSE ON THE WEST SIDE OF BISHOPSGATE STREET WITHOUT.

This was formerly the Residence of Sir Paul Pindar an eminent
London Merchant, Consul to Aleppo, Ambassador to Constantinople and
a public Benefactor during the reign of King James the first
The Vignette exhibits part of the First Floor Ceiling

Reٍa by Consts for the 28 Marche 1611 Paull Pyndarٍs

former conditions and reservations.   The management of these lands by a Committee in London, quite ignorant of the place and the people, and wholly dependent upon reports of their servants, presented difficulties and dangers which, to us, are obvious. But it was an age for creating companies and enterprises all governed by Committees from London, and some of them so well governed, that the plan seemed feasible and convenient for all companies.   Ireland, however, was a more difficult country than Hudson's Bay or East India.

The election of members of the Irish Society after this new charter became practically the appointment on the Board of representatives of the Companies concerned.   There were two permanent and official members, the Governor of the Society and the Recorder of London ; the other twenty-four were appointed by the Corporation.   The Society became, therefore, quite naturally, the servant of the Companies, the responsibilities of the trust were forgotten or neglected, and the custom arose of dividing among the Companies whatever surplus remained after the management expenses had been paid.

The management of the estates by the Irish Society is a chapter which belongs rather to the history of Ulster than to that of London.   The case against the Society is simply that, instead of exercising a trust for the benefit of the estates, they acted as landlords for the benefit of the Companies.

In the year 1830 the Corporation began to elect members of the Irish Society from the whole body of freemen.   The first result was that the Companies lost the division of the surplus from the undivided estate.   The Skinners' Company brought an action in the Court of Chancery intended to force the Irish Society to become Trustees for the Companies of all the rents and profits of the undivided estate.

The case was decided against the Skinners ; they appealed ; again judgment went against them ; they took the case up to the Lords.   It was a third time given against them.

The judgment of Lord Langdale, Master of the Rolls, when the case came before him, contained the following strong opinions :—

" ' It is, I think, impossible to read and consider the charter without coming to the conclusion that the powers granted to the society were more extensive than, and very different from, any which in the ordinary course of affairs are vested, or would upon this occasion have been vested, in mere private Trustees for the benefit of particular undertakers.   The powers indeed are, many of them, of a public and political nature, and . . . were given for the public purposes of the Plantation. . . . The Companies of London were, with the burthen of undertaking the plantatation of such lands as might be allotted to them, to receive such benefits as were offered to . . . ordinary undertakers. . . . The Charter of Charles appears to me to be substantially, as it is avowedly, a restoration of the Charter of James.   The property is part of that granted for the purposes of the Plantation, and the powers possessed by the Society, as well as the duties with which it is charged, *have all of them reference to the Plantation.*   I AM OF OPINION THAT THE POWERS GRANTED TO THE SOCIETY, AND THE TRUSTS REPOSED IN THEM, WERE IN PART OF A GENERAL AND PUBLIC NATURE, INDEPENDENT OF THE PRIVATE BENEFIT OF THE COMPANIES OF LONDON, AND WERE INTENDED BY THE CROWN TO BENEFIT IRELAND, AND THE CITY OF LONDON, BY CONNECTING THE CITY OF LONDONDERRY

AND THE TOWN OF COLERAINE AND A CONSIDERABLE IRISH DISTRICT WITH THE CITY OF LONDON, AND TO PROMOTE THE GENERAL PURPOSES OF THE PLANTATION, NOT ONLY BY SECURING THE PERFORMANCE OF THE CONDITIONS IMPOSED ON ORDINARY UNDERTAKERS, BUT ALSO BY THE EXERCISE OF POWERS AND THE PERFORMANCE OF TRUSTS NOT WITHIN THE SCOPE OF THOSE CONDITIONS ' " (pp. 44, 45).

Since this decision the Irish Society has remained untouched. After the Report of the Royal Commission of Inquiry into the Livery Companies of London, a Bill was prepared on lines indicated by this Report, but the Bill did not pass into law.

THE GREAT PLAGUE AND FIRE

CHAPTER I

PLAGUE

THE Plague of 1603, which is said to have swept away 30,578 persons, is one of the four great plagues of London of the seventeenth century. Historians, in their desire to account for these visitations, talk glibly about the sanitary arrangements of the City, the scant supply of good water, the crowded houses, and so forth as helping to spread the Plague. No doubt these things did help and encourage the visitation. Let us point out, however, that the City a hundred years after the plague of 1666—say, in 1766—was far more crowded than at that time, that its sanitary arrangements were no better, and that the people, though the New River water was laid on, continued to drink the water of the City wells (not, certainly, so many as before the fire), which received the filtrations and the pollutions of a hundred and fifty burial-grounds. They also continued their cess-pools, their narrow lanes, and their kennels filled with refuse of all kinds. Yet in the eighteenth century there was no plague. Let us also point out that parts of all great cities in Europe were, and are still, extremely crowded and filthy, yet no plague. In other words, it is dangerous to be unwashed, but not in itself a sufficient cause of plague. There must have been causes, of which one knows nothing, why the Plague should take hold of the City on four separate occasions in one century, and after devastating it on a grand scale, should go away for good. All the precautions observed in 1666 are recorded to have been taken in 1603. Women who had to do with the sick and the dead, if they went abroad, carried in their hands a red staff, so that people gave them a wide berth. Warnings were issued against attending funerals; dogs were killed; infected houses were marked with a red cross; streets were cleansed; bonfires were lit at street corners; the grave-diggers and the conductors of the dead carts did their work with the protection of tobacco; a thick cover of earth was laid upon the dead. The people, thrown out of work by thousands, were relieved and maintained by the Corporation and the City Companies.

There exists a strange and whimsical account of this plague entitled *The*

Wonderful Yeare 1603. The writer has no intention of setting down a plain unvarnished tale, as will be seen from the following extracts (*Phœnix Britannicus*) :—

"A stiffe and freezing horror sucks up the rivers of my blood ; my haire stands on ende with the panting of my braines : mine eye balls are ready to start out, being beaten with the billowes of my teares : out of my weeping pen does the ink mournfully and more bitterly than gall drop on the pale-faced paper, even when I do but thinke how the bowels of my sicke country have been torne. *Apollo*, therefore, and you bewitching silver-tongued *Muses*, get you gone : I invocate none of your names. Sorrow and truth, sit you on each side of me, whilst I am delivered of this deadly burden : prompt me that I may utter ruthfull and passionate condolement : arme my trembling hand, that I may boldly rip up and anatomize the ulcerous body of this *Anthropophagized Plague :* lend me art (without any counterfeit shadowing) to paint and delineate to the life the whole story of this mortall and pestiferous battaile. And you the ghosts of those more (by many) than 40,000, that with the virulent poison of infection have been driven out of your earthly dwellings : you desolate hand-wringing widowes, that beate your bosomes over your departing husbandes : you wofully distracted mothers that with dishevelled hair fall into swounds, while you lie kissing the insensible cold lips of your breathless infants : you outcast and downtrodden orphans, that shall many a yeare hence remember more freshly to mourne, when your mourning garments shall look old and be forgotten : and you the Genii of all those emptyed families, whose habitations are now among the Antipodes : joine all your hands together, and with your bodies cast a ring about me : let me behold your ghastly vizages, that my paper may receive their true pictures and eccho forth your grones through the hollow trunke of my pen, and rain down your gummy tears into mine incke, that even marble bosomes may be shaken with terrour, and hearts of adamant melt into compassion."

He goes on to describe the many who ran away :—

"It was no boot to bid them take their heels, for away they trudge thick and threefold : some riding, some on foote, some without bootes, some in their slippers, by water, by land, swom they westward : many to Gravesend none went unless they were driven : for whosoever landed there never came back again. Hacknies, water-men, and wagons were not so terribly employed many a year : so that within a short time there was not a good horse in Smithfield, nor a coach to be set eye on : for after the world had once run upon the wheeles of the pest cart, neither coach nor caroach durst appeare in his likenesse. Let us pursue these run-awayes no longer, but leave them in the unmercifull hands of the country-hard-headed Hobbinolls (who are ordained to be their tormentors), and return back to the siege of the citie.

Every house lookte like St. Bartholomew's Hospitall, and every street like Bucklersbury, for poor Methridatum and Dragonwater (being both of them in all the world, scarce worth threepence) were boxt into every corner, and yet were both drunke every hour at other men's cost. Lazarus lay groaning at every man's door : marry no Dives was within to send him a crum (for all your Gold-finches were fled to the woods) nor a dogge left to licke his sores, for they (like Curres) were knockt downe like oxen, and fell thicker than acornes. I am amazed to remember what dead marches were made of three thousand trooping together : husbands, wives, and children being led as ordinarily to one grave as if they had gone to one bed. And those that could shift for a time, and shrink their heads out of the collar (as many did) yet went they most bitterly miching and muffled up and downe with rue and worme-wood stoft into their eares and nostrils, looking like so many bores' heads stuck with branches of rosemary, to be served in for brawne at Christmas. This was a rare world for the Church, who had wont to complaine for want of living, and now had more living thrust upon her than she knew how to bestow : to have been clarke now to a parish clarke was better than to serve some foolish justice of peace, or than the yeare before to have been a benefice.

Never let any man ask me what became of our Phisitions in this massacre ; they hid their synodicall heads as well as the prowdest : and I cannot blame them : for their phlebotomes, losinges, and electuaries, with their diacatholicons, diacodions, amulets and antidotes had not so much strength to hold life and soule together ; as a pot of Pindar's Ale and a nutmeg : their drugs turned to dirt, their simples were simple things : Galen could do no more than Sir Giles Goosecap : Hipocrates, Avicen, Paracelsus, Rafis, Fernalius, with all their succeeding rabble of doctors and water-casters were at their wits end, or, I think, rather at the world's end, for not one of them durst peepe abroad, or if any did take upon him to play the ventrous knight, the plague put him to his nonplus : in such strange and such changeable shapes did this camelion-like sicknes appeare, that they could not (with all the cunning in their budgets) make pursenets to take him napping."

The Plague first made its appearance in the East End ; it raged at Gravesend. On the alarm of its spreading all those who could took flight ; those who were left behind were the working-men, craftsmen, journeymen, and servants, who lost their work and their wages. Among the fugitives were the physicians, whose place was taken by quacks ; and in the City there perished many thousands, sometimes whole families dying in a single house ; sometimes poor wretches lying down to die in the street or under a stall ; in a word, all the horrors of such a visitation with which Defoe has made the world familiar.

Twenty-one years later, on the accession of Charles, the Plague returned, and, continuing for a year, carried off 35,417 persons in London alone. I mention it in this place because the same writer, Benjamin Spencer, who gave us *The Wonderful Yeare* lived to write in 1625 *Vox Civitatis*, the Lament of London. The City complains that her children have infected the air with their sins ; we need not enumerate the sins ; in this respect every city is conservative. These and not the stinks of the City, not the reeking shambles, the noisome kennel, the malarious laystall are the cause of the Plague. Nor is her trouble only caused by sickness and death of multitudes :—

"This is not all my trouble, for my sorrows are increased like my sins : sickness hath consumed my substance : and with David, I justly say, I am weak and poor. My poverty lieth in being void of Trade, Money and victual. All which I am well nigh destitute of at this time. This I confess to be justly inflicted on me for my Pride, with which I have sought to outface Heaven. My tinckling feet, and my tip-toe Pace, my horned Tyaras, and crisp-curled locks, Shin-pride, and shoe-pride. Fulness of Bread hath made me lift my heel against my Maker, I said in my prosperity I should never be moved : but Thou, O Lord, hast turned Thy face, and I am troubled. My children have been so full-fed, that they have fallen out among themselves, the meanest thinking himself as good as the Magistrate, and the mighty refusing to look upon the cause of the mean. My Merchants have been the companions of Princes, but now are gone ; their place is scarce to be found. How hath my back groaned with heavy burdens : and now Issacher stands still for want of work. One Waine may carry all I sell in a day. I have had such trading, that I could scarce find time to serve God, but now every day is a holiday, because I have prophaned His holy day (even His blessed Sabbath) which hath been dedicated to Him, as a remembrance of His glorious resurrection. But I have laid dead in sins and trespasses. I have given liberty to my servants to execute their wills in Sabbath breaking and deceiving : now God hath proclaimed liberty for them to the pestilence, to wandering, and to idleness. My apprentices have been the children of knights, and justices of the country (which they accepted at my hands joyfully), but now my children are cast out by those Swines like dung, rated like Beggars, served like swine in Hogsties, buried in the Highway like Malefactors."

With a great deal more, from which we perceive that the same things happened in 1625 as in 1603. Aldermen, Common Councilmen, Magistrates, Physicians, Lawyers, Clergymen, all ran away, and among the dying sat the children not yet infected, crying for bread. It would seem—a fact that I have not elsewhere observed—that they turned the rooms over the City gates into hospitals or receiving houses for the children, doubtless the orphaned children.

Besides the two visitations of Plague already mentioned, there were in the seventeenth century two more, viz. in 1636 and 1665, the first of these occurring after an interval of no more than five years since the preceding one. The deaths from Plague for these four visitations were as follows; the numbers must be taken as approximate only :—

In 1603 there died of Plague 30,561 persons.
,, 1625 ,, ,, 35,417 ,,
,, 1636 ,, ,, 10,400 ,,
,, 1665 ,, ,, 68,596 ,,

That is to say, in sixty-three years there died 144,974 persons of Plague alone. There were, however, many more victims, because between 1603 and 1636 the Plague was hardly ever absent. The deaths from Plague every year ranged from 1000 to 4000, though in one or two years there were none.

For the greatest and last visitation, that of 1665, we have, besides the graphic account of Defoe, also the more sober notices of Pepys and Evelyn. There were warnings of the approach of the Plague. In the autumn of 1663 it was reported to be raging in Amsterdam; ships from Holland were placed in quarantine; in December 1664 one person died of Plague in London; in February 1665 another death was reported; in April there were two; in May the number began to increase, running up to nine, fourteen, and forty-three. The summer of 1665 was extremely hot; an unclouded sky continued for weeks; there was no rain to wash the streets; there was no wind to refresh the air; if the people made bonfires to create a draught, it was observed that the flame and smoke mounted straight up. In June all those who could escape to the country left the town in whatsoever vehicles they could get—coaches, carriages, waggons, and carts. There was a general stampede, until the villagers stopped it, driving back the people with pitch-forks, and the Lord Mayor stopped it by refusing certificates of health. Then, the mortality rising daily by leaps and bounds, the people sat down in their houses to die, or wandered disconsolately about the desolate streets, marking the crosses on the doors with sinking hearts.

It must be observed that the Lord Mayor, the Sheriffs, and the Aldermen remained at their posts, that the Archbishop of Canterbury remained at Lambeth, and that the Duke of Albemarle and Lord Craven remained in their town houses; the Court, however, went away, and the judges removed their courts to Oxford.

The physicians excused their flight by the plea that they accompanied their patients, and the City clergy—those who ran away—that they had followed their flocks.

There was no trade or craft of any kind carried on; shops, warehouses, offices, quays were closed or deserted; ships that arrived laden remained unnoticed in the

LORD CRAVEN
From a rare print.

Pool; the craftsmen and the common people had no work and drew no wages; servants and apprentices were thrust into the street; except for food there was nothing bought or sold; the quays, the port, the streets were silent; there was no grumbling of the broad wheels of waggons; there were no street cries; there were no bells; there were no children shouting and running about the streets. The churches, deserted by their incumbents, were taken over by Nonconformist ministers. It was contrary to law, but at such a time who cared for law? These preachers, braver than their persecutors, exhorted fearlessly crowded congregations, catching at every word of consolation or hope; quacks of the basest kind issued their advertisements, professing to cure the Plague. All kinds of ridiculous remedies were tried; plague water, amulets, hot spices, cupping glasses, besides old mediæval nostrums, all these were advocated and proved futile. The parishes which suffered most were St. Giles in the Fields; St. Andrew's, Holborn; St. Clement Danes; St. Martin's in the Fields, and Westminster. When the disease abated in those parts it broke out with equal force in Cripplegate, St. Sepulchre's; St. James's, Clerkenwell; St. Bride's, and St. Botolph's, Aldersgate. The City was divided into districts, each with surgeons, nurses, watchers, and grave-diggers; infected houses were closed; their doors were marked with a red cross a foot long; the grave-diggers removed the bodies of those who died in the streets; in the night the cart went round to collect the dead; the bodies were thrown into *fosses communes*, or common graves, either in the parish churchyard or some place set apart outside the town. There were hospitals erected called Pest Houses, one in Tothill Fields and one in Old Street; but those were only for people who could afford to pay. In a tract entitled "God's terrible voice to the City," by the Rev. Thomas Vincent, there is a picture, not overdrawn, of the City in August when the Plague was at its worst :—

"In August how dreadful is the increase! Now the cloud is very black, and the storm comes down upon us very sharp. Now death rides triumphantly on his pale horse through our streets, and breaks into every house where any inhabitants are to be found. Now people fall as thick as the leaves in autumn when they are shaken by a mighty wind. Now there is a dismal solitude in London streets: every day looks with the face of a Sabbath day, observed with a greater solemnity than it used to be in the City. Now shops are shut, people rare and very few that walk about, insomuch that the grass begins to spring up in some places; there is a deep silence in every street, especially within the walls. No prancing horses, no rattling coaches, no calling on customers nor offering wares, no London cries sounding in the ears. If any voice be heard it is the groans of dying persons breathing forth their last, and the funeral knells of them that are ready to be carried to their graves. Now shutting up of visited houses (there being so many) is at an end, and most of the well are mingled amongst the sick, which otherwise would have got no help. Now, in some places, where the people did generally stay, not one house in a hundred but what is affected : and in many houses half the family is swept away : in some, from the eldest to the youngest : few escape but with the death of one or two. Never did so many husbands and wives die together : never did so many parents carry their children with them to the grave, and go together into the same house under earth who had lived together in the same house upon it. Now the nights are too short to bury the dead : the whole day, though at so great a length, is hardly sufficient to light the dead that fall thereon into their graves."

During this terrible time, when all work was suspended, the people were only kept from starving by munificent gifts. The King gave £1000 a week; the City £600 a week; the Archbishop of Canterbury many hundreds every week; there was the whole industrial population of the City to be provided for. Some got employment from the Corporation as watchmen, grave-diggers, searchers, and the like; most

RESCUED FROM THE PLAGUE

From the painting by F. W. W. Topham, R.I., by permission of the Artist.

had no work and no wages; their insufficient nourishment no doubt assisted the disease, which raged with the greatest force among the poorer sort. Bartholomew Fair was forbidden. In September Pepys writes, "To Lambeth: but Lord! what a sad time it is, to see no boats upon the river, and grass grows all up and down Whitehall Court, and nobody but wretches in the street." The people began to get back and to go about their usual business in December; the Court returned in February, and it was soon observed that the streets were as full of people as ever.

SAMUEL PEPYS (1633-1703)
From the painting by John Hayles in the National Portrait Gallery, London. This picture is referred to in Pepys' *Diary*.

Yet nearly 70,000 had fallen, or perhaps one in three. If with the present population of 5,000,000 one in three were to die of Plague there would be a loss of 1,700,000. It seems as if about a third part of the population of London were cut off by this scourge. Happily it was the last of the great plagues. The history of London is no longer interrupted by the death of one-third of its people.

The following notes are a brief diary of the Plague as it was observed by Pepys—

1665
April 30th.   "Two or three houses in the City already shut up."
May 24th.   "All the news . . . is of the plague growing upon us in this town."

June 7th.   "The hottest day that ever I felt in my life.   This day I did in Drury Lane see two or three houses marked with a red cross upon the doors, and 'Lord, have mercy upon us' writ there."

June 10th.   "Hear that the Plague has come into the City."

June 15th.   "The town grows very sickly and people to be afraid of it: there dying this last week of the plague 112 from 43 the week before."

June 20th.   "There died four or five at Westminster of the plague."

June 21st.   "I find all the town almost going out of town, the coaches and waggons being full of people going into the country."

June 29th.   "The Mortality Bill is come to 267.

July 1st.   "To Westminster, where I hear the sickness increases greatly.   Sad at the news that seven or eight houses in Basinghall Street are shut up of the plague."

July 3rd.   "The season growing so sickly, that it is much to be feared how a man can escape."

July 12th.   "A solemn fast day for the plague growing upon us."

July 13th.   "Above 700 died of the plague this week."

July 20th.   "There dying 1089 of the plague this week."

July 21st.   "The plague growing very raging and my apprehensions of it great."

July 22nd.   "To Foxhall, where to the Spring Garden, but I do not see one guest there, the town being so empty of any one to come thither."

July 25th.   "Sad the story of the plague in the City, it growing mightily."

July 26th.   "Sad news of the death of so many in the parish" (his City parish) "of the plague, forty last night, the bell always going."

July 27th.   "The weekly bill . . . about 1700 of the Plague."

July 31st.   "The last week being 1700 or 1800 of the Plague."

Aug. 2nd.   "A public fast . . . for the plague."

Aug. 3rd.   "I had heard was 2020 (deaths) of the plague."

Aug. 10th.   "In great trouble to see the Bill this week rise so high, to above 4000 in all, and of them above 3000 of the plague."

Aug. 16th.   "Lord! how sad a sight it is to see the streets empty of people and very few upon the 'Change. Jealous of every door that one sees shut up, lest it should be the plague; and about us two shops in three, if not more, generally shut up."

Aug. 28th.   "To Mr. Colvill the goldsmith's, having not been for some days in the streets: but now how few people I see, and those looking like people that had taken leave of the world."

Aug. 31st.   "The plague above 6000."

Sep. 7th.   "Sent for the Weekly Bill, and find 8252 dead in all, and of them 6978 of the plague."

Sep. 14th.   "Decrease of 500 and more."

Sep. 20th.   "(Dead) . . . of the plague, 7165."

Sep. 27th.   "Blessed be God! there is above 1800 decrease."

Oct. 4th.   "The plague is decreased this week 740."

Oct. 12th.   "Above 600 less dead of the plague this week."

Oct. 16th.   "Lord! how empty the streets are, and melancholy, so many poor sick people in the streets full of sores; and so many sad stories overheard as I walk."

Oct. 31st.   "Above 400 less . . . of the plague, 1031."

Nov. 5th.   "The plague increases much at Lambeth, St. Martins, and Westminster."

Nov. 9th.   "The Bill of Mortality is increased 399 this week."

Nov. 15th.   "The plague—Blessed be God!—is decreased 400, making the whole this week but 1300 and odd."

Nov. 22nd.   "I was very glad . . . to hear that the plague is come very low; the whole under 1000, and the plague 600 and odd."

Dec. 13th.   "Our poor little parish is the greatest number in all the city, having six, from one last week."

1666

Jan. 3rd.	"Decrease of the plague this week to 70."
Jan. 8th.	"To Paternoster Row, few shops there being yet open."
Jan. 10th.	"Plague is increased this week from 70 to 89."
Jan. 16th.	"The plague 158."
Jan. 23rd.	"Plague being now but 79."
Jan. 31st.	"Plague decreased this week to 56.
Mar. 13th.	"Plague increased to 29 from 28."
April 25th.	"Plague is decreased 16 this week."
May 12th.	"The plague increases in many places and is 53 this week with us."
June 6th.	"A monthly fast day for the plague."
July 2nd.	"The plague is, as I hear, increased but two this week."
Aug. 6th.	"Greenwich worse than ever it was, and Deptford too."
Aug. 9th. Aug. 10th.	"Mrs. Rawlinson is dead of the sickness . . . the mayde also is dead."

It will be observed that the Plague lingered until the Great Fire of September 2 drove it clean away.

The best—that is, the most graphic—account of the Plague is that of Daniel Defoe. It is, perhaps, too long. The mind grows sick in the reading. He presents us, after his favourite method, with a series of pictures and portraits of individuals. When it is remembered that his book appeared in the year 1720, the year, that is, of the great Plague of Marseilles, and fifty-five years after the event, it is generally believed that his history is a work of pure fiction. I think it can be shown, however, that it was not a work of fiction at all, but simply a work of recollection. To the old man of sixty came back the memories and the tales that he had heard as a boy not yet in his teens.

Defoe was born in the year 1661. His father lived in Cripplegate, where, as we know, he had a shop. The child, therefore, was four years of age in the Plague year. A child of four observes a great deal and may remember a great deal. Children vary very much in respect to observation and memory. For instance, a child would remember, perhaps, anything out of the common in the buying and selling of goods in his father's shop, where he looked on at the customers. Defoe says: "When any one bought a joint of meat, he would not take it out of the butcher's hand, but took it off the hooks himself; on the other hand, the butcher would not touch the money, but put it into a pot full of vinegar which he kept for that purpose. The buyer carried always small money to make up any odd sum, so that he might take no change." This must surely have been seen by the child and remembered. It happened in his own father's shop before his eyes. Another thing. The Great Fire not only drove the lingering Plague out of the City, but actually drove away the memory of it. Who could talk or think about the Plague with this other awful affliction to consider? Now Cripplegate—where the child Defoe lived —was not touched by the Fire; it was very heavily afflicted by the Plague, but the

Fire spared it.   Therefore to the people of Cripplegate the Plague continued as the chief incident in their lives ; they continued to talk of their adventures, their escapes, their sufferings, and their bereavements long after the people within the walls had left off thinking of theirs.   And the boy grew up amid such talk.   Therefore he was never allowed to forget his childish impressions.   The awful silence in the streets, save for the shrieks and groans of the plague-stricken ; the rumbling of the burial carts at night ; the houses deserted, infected, no longer marked but left with open doors ready for the robber who roamed about with impunity till Death seized him

DANIEL DEFOE (1661-1731)
From a print in the British Museum.

and he fell ; the poor wretch, gone mad with terror and suffering and bereavement, moaning and crying in the street ; the closed shops ; the poor creatures sitting down in any porch or on any stall to die—all these things were told to the boy over and over again, until they were burned into his brain, to be reproduced in the most wonderful account of a plague that has ever been written.   Therefore, and for this reason, Defoe's *History* is a real history ; the incidents are not invented but remembered.   While we allow something for the embroidery of the novelist we must acknowledge that we have a contribution to the history of that terrible year larger, fuller, more human, than we can find in Pepys or in Evelyn, or in any other contemporary authority.

On the first appearance of the Plague of 1665 the Mayor and Aldermen issued orders of precaution similar to those which had been framed in the visitation of the year 1625. These orders are contained in a collection of "valuable and scarce Pieces" relating to the Plague of the latter year, published for J. Roberts at the Oxford Arms in Warwick Lane, 1721. This collection gives in full the orders of the Mayor and Council as follows :—

"Examiners to be appointed in every Parish. First, it is thought Requisite, and so ordered, that in every Parish there be one, two, or more Persons of good Sort and Credit, chosen and appointed by the Alderman, his Deputy, and Common Council of every Ward, by the Name of Examiners, to continue in that Office the space of two Months at least : And if any fit Person so appointed, shall refuse to undertake the same, the said Parties so refusing to be committed to Prison until they shall conform themselves accordingly.

The Examiner's Office

"That these Examiners be sworn by the Aldermen, to enquire and learn from time to time what Houses in every Parish be Visited, and what Persons be Sick, and of what Diseases, as near as they can inform themselves ; and upon doubt in that Case, to command Restraint of Access, until it appear what the Disease shall prove ; And if they find any Person sick of the Infection, to give order to the Constable that the House be shut up ; and if the Constable shall be found Remiss or Negligent to give present Notice thereof to the Alderman of the Ward.

Watchmen

"That to every infected House there be appointed two Watchmen, one for every Day, and the other for the Night ; and that these Watchmen have a special care that no Person go in or out of such infected Houses, whereof they have the Charge, upon pain of severe Punishment. And the said Watchman to do such further offices as the sick House shall need and require : and if the Watchman be sent upon any Business, to lock up the House, and take the Key with him ; And the Watchman by Day to attend until ten of the Clock at Night ; and the Watchman by Night until six in the Morning.

Searchers

"That there be a special care to appoint Women-Searchers in every Parish, such as are of honest Reputation, and of the best Sort as can be got in this kind : and these to be sworn to make due Search, and true Report to the utmost of their Knowledge, whether the Persons whose Bodies they are appointed to Search, do die of the Infection, or of what other Diseases, as near as they can. And that the Physicians who shall be appointed for Cure and Prevention of the Infection, do call before them the said Searchers, who are or shall be appointed for the several Parishes under their respective Cares, to the end they may consider whether they are fitly qualified for that Employment; and charge them from time to time as they shall see Cause, if they appear defective in their Duties.

"That no Searcher during this time of Visitation, be permitted to use any publick Work or Employment, or keep any Shop or Stall, or be employed as a Laundress, or in any other common Employment whatsoever.

CHIRURGEONS

"For better assistance of the Searchers, for as much as there hath been heretofore great Abuse in misreporting the Disease, to the further spreading of the Infection; it is therefore ordered, that there be chosen and appointed able and discreet Chirurgeons, besides those that do already belong to the Pest House: Amongst whom the City and Liberties to be quartered as the places lie most apt and convenient; and every of these to have one Quarter for his Limit; and the said Chirurgeons in every of their Limits to join with the Searchers for the View of the Body, to the end there may be a true Report made of the Disease.

"And further, that the said Chirurgeons shall visit and search such like Persons as shall either send for them, or be named and directed unto them, by the Examiners of every Parish, and inform themselves of the Disease of the said Parties.

"And forasmuch as the said Chirurgeons are to be sequestered from all other Cures, and kept only to this Disease of the Infection; it is ordered, That every of the said Chirurgeons shall have Twelve-pence a Body searched by them, to be paid out of the Goods of the Party searched, if he be able, or otherwise by the Parish.

NURSE-KEEPERS

"If any Nurse-keeper shall remove herself out of any infected House before twenty eight Days after the Decease of any Person dying of the Infection, the House to which the said Nurse-keeper doth so remove herself, shall be shut up until the said twenty eight Days be expired.

NOTICE TO BE GIVEN OF THE SICKNESS

"The Master of every House, as soon as any one in his House complaineth, either of Botch, or Purple, or Swelling in any part of his Body, or falleth otherwise dangerously Sick, without apparent Cause of some other Disease, shall give knowledge thereof to the Examiner of Health within two Hours after the said Sign shall appear.

Sequestration of the Sick

"As soon as any Man shall be found by this Examiner, Chirurgeon or Searcher to be sick of the Plague, he shall the same Night be sequestered in the same House. And in case he be so sequestered, then though he afterwards die not, the House wherein he sickened shall be shut up for a Month, after the use of the due Preservatives taken by the rest.

Airing the Stuff

"For Sequestration of the Goods and Stuff of the Infected, their Bedding, and Apparel, and Hangings of Chambers, must be well aired with Fire, and such Perfumes as are requisite within the infected House, before they be taken again to use: This to be done by the Appointment of the Examiner.

Shutting up of the House

"If any Person shall have visited any Man, known to be infected of the Plague, or entered willingly into any known infected House, being not allowed; the House wherein he inhabiteth, shall be shut up for certain Days by the Examiner's Direction.

"None to be removed out of infected Houses, but, etc., Item, That none be removed out of the House where he falleth sick of the Infection, into any other House in the City (except it be to the Pest-House or a Tent, or unto some such House, which the Owner of the said visited House holdeth in his own Hands, and occupieth by his own Servants), and so as Security be given to the Parish whither such Remove is made, that the Attendance and Charge about the said visited Persons shall be observed and charged in all the Particularities before expressed, without any Cost of that Parish, to which any remove shall happen to be made, and his Remove to be done by Night; and it shall be lawful to any Person that hath two Houses, to remove either his sound or his infected People to his spare House at his choice, so as if he send away first his Sound, he may not after send thither the Sick nor again unto the Sick the Sound. And that the same which he sendeth, be for one Week at the least shut up and secluded from Company for fear of some Infection, at the first not appearing.

Burial of the Dead

"That Burial of the Dead by this Visitation, be at most convenient Hours, always either before Sun-rising, or after Sun-setting, with the Privity of the Churchwardens or Constable, and not otherwise: and that no Neighbours nor Friends be suffered to accompany the Corps to Church, or to enter the House visited, upon pain of having his House shut up, or be imprisoned. And that no Corps dying of Infection shall be buried, or remain in any Church in time of Common-Prayer, Sermon, or Lecture. And that no Children be suffered at time of burial of any Corps in any Church, Church-yard, or Burying-place to come near the Corps, Coffin, or Grave. And that all the Graves shall be at least six Foot deep. And further, all publick Assemblies at other burials are to be forborn during the Continuance of this Visitation.

No Infected Stuff to be Uttered

" That no Clothes, Stuff, Bedding or Garments be suffered to be carried or conveyed out of any infected Houses, and that the Criers and Carriers abroad of Bedding or old Apparel to be sold or pawned, be utterly prohibited and restrained, and no Brokers of Bedding or old Apparel be permitted to make any outward Shew, or hang forth on their stalls, shopboards or Windows towards any Street, Lane, Common-way or Passage, any old Bedding or Apparel to be sold, upon pain of Imprisonment. And if any Broker or other Person shall buy any Bedding, Apparel, or other Stuff out of any infected House, within two Months after the Infection hath been there, his House shall be shut up as Infected, and so shall continue shut up twenty Days at the least.

No Person to be conveyed out of any Infected House

" If any Person visited do fortune by negligent looking unto, or by any other Means, to come, or be conveyed from a Place infected, to any other Place, the Parish from whence such Party hath come or been conveyed, upon notice thereof given, shall at their Charge cause the said Party so visited and escaped, to be carried and brought back again by Night, and the Parties in this case offending, to be punished at the Direction of the Alderman of the Ward: and the House of the Receiver of such visited Person to be shut up for twenty Days.

Every Visited House to be Marked

" That every House visited, be marked with a red Cross of a Foot long, in the middle of the Door, evident to be seen, and with these usual printed Words, that is to say, ' Lord have Mercy upon us,' to be set close over the same Cross, there to continue, until lawful opening of the same House.

Every Visited House to be Watched

" That the Constables see every House shut up, and to be attended with Watchmen, which may keep them in, and minister Necessaries unto them at their own Charges (if they be able) or at the common Charge if they be unable : The shutting up to be for the space of four Weeks after all be whole. That precise Order be taken that the Searchers, Chirurgeons, Keepers and Buriers are not to pass the Streets without holding a red Rod or Wand of three Foot in length in their Hands, open and evident to be seen, and are not to go into any other House than into their own, or into that whereunto they are directed or sent for; but to forbear and abstain from Company, especially when they have been lately used in any such Business or Attendance.

INMATES

" That where several Inmates are in one and the same House, and any Person in that House happen to be infected; no other Person or Family of such House shall be suffered to remove him or themselves without a Certificate from the Examiners of Health of that Parish; or in default thereof, the House whither he or they so remove, shall be shut up as in case of Visitation.

HACKNEY-COACHES

" That care be taken of Hackney-Coachmen, that they may not (as some of them have been observed to do) after carrying of infected Persons to the Pest-House, and other Places, be admitted to common use, till their Coaches be well aired, and have stood unemployed by the space of five or six Days after such Service.

ORDERS FOR CLEANSING AND KEEPING OF THE STREETS SWEET

THE STREETS TO BE KEPT CLEAN

" First, it is thought necessary, and so ordered, that every Householder do cause the Street to be daily pared before his Door, and so to keep it clean swept all the Week long.

THAT RAKERS TAKE IT FROM OUT THE HOUSES

" That the sweeping and Filth of Houses be daily carried away by the Rakers, and that the Raker shall give notice of his coming, by the blowing of a Horn, as heretofore hath been done.

LAYSTALLS TO BE MADE FAR OFF FROM THE CITY

" That the Laystalls be removed as far as may be out of the City, and common Passages, and that no Nightman or other be suffered to empty a Vault into any Garden near about the City.

CARE TO BE HAD OF UNWHOLESOME FISH OR FLESH AND OF MUSTY CORN

" That special care be taken, that no stinking Fish, or unwholesome Flesh, or musty Corn, or other corrupt Fruits, of what sort soever be suffered to be sold about the City, or any part of the same.

" That the Brewers and Tipling houses be looked unto, for musty and unwholesome Casks.   That no Hogs, Dogs, or Cats, or tame Pigeons, or Conies, be suffered to be kept within any part of the City, or any Swine to be, or stray in the Streets or Lanes, but that such Swine be impounded by the Beadle or any other Officer, and the Owner punished according to Act of Common-Council, and that the Dogs be killed by the Dog-killers appointed for that purpose."

It was further ordered, and for once the City did provide a sufficient number of constables to enforce these orders, that the multitude of rogues and wandering beggars that swarm in every place around the City shall be dispersed, and that no beggars be allowed in the City at all.   That the theatres be closed and that none of the sports be held which attract assemblies of people, such as bear-baitings, ballad-singings, buckle-play, and the like; that public feasts and dinners be discontinued, particularly those of the City companies; that tippling be discouraged, and that every tavern, ale-house, coffee-house, and cellar be closed at 9 o'clock.

And further that the Aldermen and Common Council should assemble once a week to hear reports upon the manner of carrying out these rules.

The following is a contemporary account by the Rev. John Allin; it was published in the thirty-seventh volume of *Archæologia :—*

" Loveing ffriend,—Yours of the 16th instant I have received and give you hearty thanks for that particular accompt you gave me of your affayres. If I can possibly gett time I thinke to write to you againe on Thursday : but I thought it not amiss for the inclosed's sake, to write a few lines now, and to give you my thoughts of the death of Tolhurst's sister.   According to your description of her, there hath not one of those thousands yet dyed here with all the signall characters of this present Plague more evident than she had, which this inclosed will in parte confirme to you.   Concerning the external effects of this internall infection, there are these three, with one or more or all of which this distemper is usually attended, botches, blaines, and carbuncles, to which I may add a fourth, spotts commonly called the tokens, and are very symtomatical never ariseing till the full state of the disease, even when deathe stands at the doore : for very few or none live that are so markt. For the botches or pestilential bubos, they usually aries but in 3 places, whereof the principal emunctorys of the body are :—behind or under the ears when the braine is afflicted ; under each arme when the heart or vitalls are afflicted ; in the groynes principally when the liver is afflicted.   The blaines and carbuncles may and doe aries generally in any parte of the body, necke, face, throate, backe, thighs, armes, leggs, etc., and all of them very hard: and obstinate to be dealt with withall, and must have several proceedings with them: and if any of them, after once appearing, either fall or retire backe againe, it is a very bad and dangerous symptome. The botches sometimes rise to a very great buiggnes, especially under the armes and in the groines; if so under the ears they quickly choake or kill with paine, there being no roome for them to bee extended: if they rise something in an oblongish forme, and red at the first, it is so much the better then if round, though as they grow to more maturity they will tend to a more round forme, as they come to ripen, especially on the topp; if they rise white it argues coldnes and want of heate and spot to drive them out, and must bee more carefully helpt forwards with internal drivers and externall drawers. The blaines rise first like blisters, but not puffy, as if sweld with wind or water, but hard, not yielding to the touch: but if they come forward to any maturity (which they are very difficult to bee brought to, and many dye if they have blaines) there will bee a very hard and knotty bunch of corrupt matter in them. The carbuncles, though it may be rise roundly like a pinn's head, yet presently rise up to a pointed boile, very hard: sometimes fiery red, sometimes black, and sometimes blewish in places: red the best, ye others worst. All of these risings (if they be accurately observed at the first; but especially the carbuncles and blaines) have a particular symptome annexed to them, viz. they are generally circled about with red or blew circles, sometimes with both: sometimes they are broader then a bare circle, one within another: the red colour argue the small blood affected or choler abounding: the blewish argue the arteriall blood from the hearte affected; the blacke choler adust or melancholy: white, the potre actions of cold and crude humours most. For the spotts or tokens, which most generally are forrerunns of certain death, they do more generally this year then formerly appeare in divers parts of the body, formerly usually and allmost onely to be found upon the region of the hearte and liver, or the brest, and against it on the backe; but now on the necke, face, hands, armes, amost anywhere as well as there: sometimes as broad as farthings, these are called tokens: sometimes this yeare as broad as an halfecrowne: sometimes smaller: but always of more colours than one. If they bee observed at first rising sometimes with a red circle without and blew within: sometimes with a blew circle without and red within: sometimes one more bright red, the other blewish or darker, sometimes blacker: the blew from the arteriall, the red from the venall blood affacted, the blacke from melancholy as is aforesaid. Of the swellings, or mixt as the infection is mixed more or lesse, these usually come forth about the state of the disease, when nature hath done its utmost to expell but cannot conquer: which endeavours to expel the utmost send forth these external symptomes of it: and generally when these come out the party seemes not sick as before, but dye presently within a day or 2 at the utmost after.

Many times this distemper strikes the vitalls so immediately, that nature hath not time to putt forth either spotts or blotches, and then it is the highest infection, most aptly called the Pestilence, and not the Plague: but done by a more immediate stroake of the destroying Angell.   But, if such bodyes bee kept a little length of time after death, sometimes spoots will then arise which did not before, especially whilst any warmth remayne in the body: but how many are therefore deceived, because either they view the body onely immediately when dead, or bury them whilest warme: others, wickeddly to conceal the hands of God, will drive them in agaune, and keepe them in with colde and wett cloths."

CHAPTER II

This chapter dealing with the medical literature of the Plague covers both the sixteenth and the seventeenth centuries, in which there was little change medicinally.

The sixteenth century was full of plague and pestilence. In Elizabeth's reign there was plague in 1563, in 1569, in 1574, in 1581, in 1592, and in 1603. Preventive ordinances were drawn up and issued. It is, however, evident that the people could not be possibly made to understand the necessity of caution and quarantine. The invisible enemy, to an ignorant folk, does not exist. The people of London bribed the officers, surveyors, constables, and scavengers to take down the "Bills" affixed to infected houses; they refused to carry the white rods enjoined by law upon the convalescent; they went about among their fellows while they were still dangerous; and they would not keep the streets clean. The period of seclusion was fixed at four weeks; women were appointed to carry necessaries to infected houses; every morning at six, and every evening at eight the streets were to be sluiced with buckets of water; there were to be no funeral assemblies; beggars and masterless men were to be turned out of the City. These precautions were excellent; the sanitary laws were in the right direction; but all was rendered ineffectual for want of an executive; the Plague might have been stamped out had these rules been enforced; but they were not, and so the disease continued until the Great Fire of 1666 purified the soil. New investigations rendered necessary by the outbreak of Plague in India and elsewhere will perhaps lead to an abandonment of the old theory that the Plague was caused simply by the unclean condition of the ground, saturated with the abominations of a thousand years and more. Until science, however, has spoken more definitely, I suppose that we shall continue to associate a visitation of this terrible scourge with unsanitary conditions. It is at least a useful and a wholesome belief.

I have before me certain infallible remedies prescribed in the attack of 1625. Among them are blisters, clysters, cauteries, poultices, cuppings, strong purges and emetics.   Drugs and strange compounds were also administered.   Among the former, London treacle, Venice treacle, angelica root, dragon water, and carduus play a large part.   The roots of certain wild flowers were also powdered and added to the infusion, showing that .the medicine of the time depended largely on the science of the herbwoman.   Who but she knew the properties of the roots and leaves of tormentil, sorrel, goat's rue, gentian, bay berries, scabious, bur seeds, celandine?   Who but a village herbalist could have discovered the healing powers of fresh cowdung strained with vinegar?   I transcribe one of many prescriptions to induce a strong sweat and thereby to expel the Plague.

"Take the inward Bark of the Ash Tree one Pound, of Walnuts with the Green outward Shells, to the number of Fifty, cut these small: of Scabious, of Vervin, of each a Handful, of Saffron two Drams, pour upon these the strongest Vinegar you can get, four Pints, let them a little boil together upon a very soft fire, and then stand in a very close Pot, well stopt all Night upon the Embers, after distil them with a soft Fire, and receive the Water close kept.   Give unto the Patient laid in Bed and well covered with Cloaths, two Ounces of this Water to drink, and let him be provoked to Sweat; and every eight hours (during the space of four and twenty Hours) give him the same quantity to Drink.

Care must be taken in the use of these Sweating Cordials, that the Party infected, sweat two or three Hours, or rather much longer, if he have strength, and sleep not till the Sweat be over, and that he have been well wiped with warm Linnen and when he hath been dried let him wash his Mouth with Water and Vinegar Warm, and let his face and Hands be washed with the same.   When these things are done, give him a good Draught of Broth made with Chicken or Mutton, with Rosemary, Thyme, Sorrel, succory and Marygolds; or else Water-Grewel, with Rosemary and Winter-Savory or Thyme, Panado seasoned with Verjuice, or juice of Wood-Sorrel: for their Drink, let it be small Beer warmed, with a Toast, or Water boiled with Carraway-Seed, Carduus-Seed, and a Crust of Bread, or such Posset-Drink as is mentioned before in the second Medicine; after some Nutriment, let them sleep or rest, often washing their Mouth with Water and Vinegar."

Or instead of the complicated nostrum, here are two.   By the first, it is said, "Secretary Naunton removed the Plague from his Heart."   The second, it is asserted, was prepared by Sir Francis Bacon and approved by Queen Elizabeth.

"An Ale Posset-drink with Pimpernel seethed in it, till it taste strong of it, drunk often, removed the infection, tho' it hath reached the very heart. . . .

Take a Pint of Malmsey burnt, with a spoonful of bruised Grains, i.e., Cardamom Seeds, of the best Treacle a spoonful, and give the Patient to drink of it two or three Spoonfuls pretty often, with a draught of Malmsey Wine after it, and so let him sweat; if it agrees with him, and it stays with him, he is out of Danger; if he vomits it up, repeat it again."

Let us leave the Plague for a moment and consider the general subject of medicine in the seventeenth century.

When he was ill, the Londoner had as many nostrums and infallible medicines as his successor of the present day.   We have our effervescent drinks, our pills, our ointments—so had our ancestor.   First of all, the pharmacopœia included an immense quantity of herbs, specifics for this and the other; their names still preserve some of their supposed qualities—such as fever few, eye-bright, etc.   Thus, walnut water was supposed to be good for sore eyes.   The apothecary understood how to cover a pill with sugar so as to make it tasteless ; and his pills were great boluses which we should now find it hard indeed to swallow. The physicians prescribed potions fearfully and wonderfully made, some containing thirty, forty, or even seventy ingredients. Such was "Mithidate" or "Mithridates," as a common medicine was called.

For fevers they prescribed a "cold water affusion," with drinking of asses' milk. When the Queen was ill in 1663 they shaved her head and applied pigeons to her feet. When a man fell down in a fit, they treated him vigorously. No half measures were allowed. They boxed and cuffed his ears, pulled his nose, threw a bucket of cold water into his face, and pinched and kneaded the nape of his neck. Powdered mummy for a long time was held to be a specific against I know not what diseases. It is said that the reason why it went out of use was that Jews took to embalming bodies and then sold them for genuine ancient mummies.

If a dentist was wanted he was sought in the street ; he was an itinerant tooth drawer, and he went his regular round, carrying with him his "dentist's key" and decorated with strings of teeth, while he bawled his calling and offered his services.

Ben Jonson ridicules the pretences and pretensions of the quacks of his time when he puts the following extravagance into the mouth of Bobadil :—

"Sir, believe me, upon my relation for what I tell you, the world shall not reprove. I have been in the Indies, where this herb grows, where neither myself, nor a dozen gentlemen more of my knowledge, have received the taste of any other nutriment in the world, for the space of one and twenty weeks but the fume of this simple only ; therefore, it cannot be, but 'tis most divine. Further, take it in the nature, in the true kind : so, it makes an antidote, that, had you taken the most deadly poisonous plant in all Italy, it should expel it, and clarify you, with as much ease as I speak. And for your green wound—your Balsamum and your St. John's wort, are all mere gulleries and trash to it, especially your Trinidado : your Nicotian is good too. I could say what I know of the virtue of it, for the expulsion of rheums, raw humours, crudities, obstructions, with a thousand of this kind, but I profess myself no quacksalver. Only this much : by Hercules, I do hold it, and will affirm it before any prince in Europe, to be the most sovereign and precious weed that ever the earth tendered to the use of man."

Francis Bacon—the last of his generation to be considered a quack—prescribed a regimen which would make longevity a certainty.

Every morning the patient was to inhale the fume of lignaloes, rosemary, and bay-leaves dried ; "but once a week to add a little tobacco, without otherwise taking it, in a pipe." For supper he was to drink of wine in which "gold had been quenched," and to eat bread dipped in spiced wine. In the morning he was to anoint the body with oil of almonds and salt and saffron. Once a month he was to bathe the feet in water of marjoram, fennel, and sage. . . . That diet was pronounced best "which makes lean and then renews." The great people were content with nothing less than extravagant remedies. Salt or chloride of gold was taken by noble ladies ; dissolved pearls were supposed to have mystic virtues, and even coral was a fashionable medicine.

Common folk had to submit to more desperate remedies. They were advised by Dr. Andrew Boorde to wipe their faces daily with a scarlet cloth, and wash them only once a week. Pills made of the skull of a man that had been hanged, a draught of spring water from the skull of a murdered man, the powder of antimony, the oil of scorpions, the blood of dragons, and the entrails of wild animals were all recommended for special diseases. Salves, conserves, cataplasms, ptisanes, and electuaries were made of all kinds of herbs, and freely used and believed in, though most of them must have been ridiculous. The "nonsense-confused compounds" which Burton ridiculed half a century later were in great demand, however, and the amount of general physic-taking was marvellous. Complexion-washes for ladies and fops, love-philtres for the melancholy, and anodynes for the aged, were commonly dispensed in every apothecary's establishment.

Tumours were supposed to be curable by stroking them with the hand of a dead man. Chips of a hangman's tree were a great remedy for the ague, worn as amulets. To cure a child of rickets, it was passed head downwards through a young tree split open for the purpose, and then tied up. As the tree healed, the child recovered. The king's evil, a scrofulous affection, was supposed to be cured by the royal touch, as we have already seen in considering the service for the occasion. There is a description of the process in Macbeth :—

> " *Doctor.* Ay, Sir, there are a crew of wretched souls
> That stay his cure ; their malady convinces
> The great assay of art ; but, at his touch—
> Such sanctity hath heaven given his hand—
> They presently amend.
> *Macduff.* What's the disease he means ?
> *Malcolm.* 'Tis called the evil,
> A most miraculous work in this good king ;
> Which often since my here-remain in England
> I have seen him do. How he solicits heaven,
> Himself knows best ; but strangely-visited people,
> All swollen and ulcerous, pitiful to the eye,
> The mere despair of surgery, he cures,
> Handing a golden stamp about their necks,
> Put on with holy prayers ; and 'tis spoken,
> To the succeeding royalty he leaves
> The healing benediction."

Ben Jonson contains some excellent prescriptions. Thus, for old age :—

> " Seedpearl were good new boiled with syrup of apples,
> Tincture of gold, and coral, citron-pills,
> Your elicampane root, myrobalanes— . . .
> Burnt silk and amber ; you have muscadel good in the house.—
> I doubt we shall not get
> Some English saffron, half a dram would serve ;
> Your sixteen cloves, a little musk, dried mints,
> Bugloss, and barley-meal."

On the divergence of opinions among physicians :—

> " One would have a cataplasm of spices,
> Another a flayed ape clapped to his breast,

> A third would have it a dog, a fourth an oil,
> With wild cats' skins."

Or if the patient called in the wise woman :—

> " A good old woman—
> Yes, faith, she dwells in Sea Coal Lane, did cure me
> With sodden ale and pellitory of the wall."

One learns from Ben Jonson that at St. Katherine's by the Tower there were lunatic asylums :—

> " Those are all broken loose
> Out of St. Katherine's, where they used to keep
> The better sort of mad folks."

The cunning man or woman was a kind of physician and in large practice. He undertook to cure all diseases under the sun by the " Ephemerides," the marks on almanacks of lucky or unlucky days. Besides his medical learning he knew how to advise in the matter of winning at horse races ; in card playing, how to win ; he could search for things lost, he sold charms, he told girls about their future lovers, and he erected astrological figures. Often he was a physician by profession, like that unfortunate Dr. Lambe, done to death by the crowd in the City for being an astrologer or cunning man.

The level of medical science in the seventeenth century may be judged by the prescriptions which follow :—

" (1) For Dimness of sight.
For dimness of the Eyes, eat 12 leaves of Rue in a morning with bread and butter and it will very much availe."

For the stopping of bleeding

" Take red nettles, stamp them and straine them alone, then take the juice and rubb all over the forehead and temples, so lett it dry upon the face 7 or 8 hours, after you may wash it of, but if you bleede againe, renew it."

For the plague we have

" The Medicine that the Lord Mayor of London had sent him from Q. Elisa : the ingredients are sage, rue, elder leaves, red bramble leaves, white wine and ginger. ' So drink of it till evening and morning 9 dayes together : the first spoonfull will by God's grace preserve safe for 24 dayes and after the ninth spoonfull for one whole yeare.' "

Another " safe medicine " is as follows :—

" Take a locke of your Owne hair, cutt it as small as may bee, and so take it in beere or wine. "

The next is not so appetising. For a dull hearing

" Take a grey snaile, prick him, and putt the water which comes from him into the eare and stop it with blackwool, it will cure."

" (2) To cure the biting or stinging of a Snake, as it hath often been tryed.
' Take the leaves of a Burr-dock stamp and straine them and so drinke a good quantity, halfe a pint at the least, the simple juice itselfe is best.'

(3) A most pretious Water of Wallnutts.

Cures many ailments. Among the rest : 'One drop in the eyes healeth all infirmityes, it healeth palsyes, it causeth sleep in the night. If it be used moderately with wine, it preserveth life so long as nature will permitt.'

(4) For Sciatica.

The principal ingredient is the marrow of a horse (killed by chance, not dying of any disease) mixed with some rose water. 'Chafe it in with a warme hand for a quarter of an houre, then putt on a Scarlett cloth, broad enough to cover the parte affected and go into a warme bed.'

(5) Headache.

The juice of Ground-ivy snuft up into the nose out of a spoone taketh away the greatest paine thereof. This medicine is worth gold.

(6) For consumption is recommended an infusion in which the following ingredients take part :—

"Malaga-sacke, liverwort, Dandelion-root scrapt and the pith tooke out, and a piece of Elecampane sliced.

(7) Madness in a Dog or anything :—

Pega, tega, sega, docemena, Mega. These words written and the paper rowl'd up and given to a Dog or anything that is mad, will cure him."

Floyer, for his part, placed the greatest reliance on the sovereign virtues of cold water, administered externally. He spared no pains to inculcate on sufferers from rheumatism, nervous disorders, and other maladies, the virtue of cold bathing, and maintained that the prevalence of consumption in this country dated only from the time when baptism by immersion had been discontinued.

I have mentioned the "cunning man" who was also an astrologer. But there was the astrologer in higher practice. Everybody believed in astrology, from the King downwards. The astrologer followed a profession both lucrative and honourable. Sometimes, as in the case of Dr. Nenier of Linford, he was an enthusiast who prayed continually and was in confidential communication with the archangels, being by them enabled to heal many diseases, especially ague, and the falling sickness by means of consecrated rings.

When the Civil War began there were astrologers on both sides who prophesied, each for the good of his own cause. Thus, on the Parliamentary side the astrologer prophesied disasters to the Cavaliers and victory to the Roundheads. These predictions became weapons of great weight because people believed them. Butler puts the case in his own way :—

" Do not our great reformers use
This Sidrophel to forbode news ?
To write of victories next year,
And castles taken yet i' th' air ?
Of battles fought at sea, and ships
Sunk, two years hence ? the last eclipse ?
A total o'erthrow given the king
In Cornwall, horse and foot, next spring ?
And has not he point-blank foretold
Whats'e'er the close committee would ?

> Made Mars and Saturn for the cause,
> The Moon for fundamental laws?
> The Ram, the Bull, and Goat, declare
> Against the Book of Common Prayer?
> The Scorpion take the protestation,
> And Bear engage for reformation?
> Made all the royal stars recant,
> Compound and take the covenant?"

The most important of the tribe was William Lilly, already mentioned, who wrote on the Roundhead side, publishing his predictions in an almanack called *Merlinus Anglicus*. Towards the close of the Protectorate he had the good sense to see what was coming and to predict the Restoration. When this came he made his almanack loyal to the backbone. Astrology fell somewhat into disrepute after Charles's return, or perhaps younger men got all the patronage, for Lilly abandoned astrology and took up with medicine.

The Royal Society had not yet been founded, and the only learned association was the Society of Antiquaries, formed by Archbishop Parker in 1572, meeting weekly at the College of Heralds and dissolved by James I. "from some jealousy," remarks Hallam, about the year 1604. Consequently there were no influences at work to stem the popular superstitions, and individuals who profited by them were not likely to turn reformers. The trade in charms was, however, more than half sanctioned by the learned. In his *Natural History*, Bacon lays it down as credible that precious stones "may work by consent upon the spirits of men to comfort and exhilarate them. The best for that effect are the diamond, the emerald, the hyacinth Oriental, and the gold stone, which is the yellow topaz. As for their particular properties, there is no credit to be given to them. But it is manifest that light, above all things, excelleth in comforting the spirits of men: and it is very probable that light varied doth the same effect, with more novelty, and this is one of the causes why precious stones comfort."

Bracelets of coral are recommended to cool the body, because coral loseth colour through "distemper of heat," and other varieties for similar purposes. The learned lawyer and philosopher was thus not many degrees higher than the plain and simple folk who imagined that every precious stone had some mystic virtue communicable to the wearer. The sapphire was believed to impart courage, the coral to preserve from enchantment, the topaz to cure madness, and the hyacinth to protect from lightning. As for the carbuncle, with its brilliant unborrowed light, it is referred to many times by Shakespeare, but perhaps in the happiest form in "Henry VIII.," where the Princess Elizabeth is spoken of as

> "A gem
> To lighten all this isle."

Texts of Scripture, mystic letters, cabalistic rings, and other devices were commonly worn even by the most intelligent.

CHAPTER III

The Fire

I. ASPECT OF THE CITY BEFORE THE FIRE

THERE was very little difference between the London of Elizabeth and the London of Charles II. I briefly quote a contemporary. The following humorous description was written by Sir William Davenant two or three years before the Fire :—

"Sure your ancestors contrived your narrow streets in the days of wheel-barrows, before those greater engines, carts, were invented. Is your climate so hot, that as you walk, you need umbrellas of tiles to intercept the sun? Or, are your shambles so empty, that you are afraid to take in fresh air, lest it should sharpen your stomachs? Oh, the goodly landslip of Old Fish Street, which, had it not had the ill luck to be crooked, was narrow enough to have been your founder's perspective! And where the garrets, (perhaps not for want of architecture, but through abundance of amity) are so made, that opposite neighbours may shake hands without stirring from home. Is unanimity of inhabitants in wise cities better exprest than by their coherence and uniformity of building : where streets begin, continue and end, in a like stature and shape? But yours (as if they were raised in a general insurrection, where every man hath a several design) differ in all things that can make distinction. Here stands one that aims to be a Palace, and, next it, another that professes to be a hovel; here a giant, there a dwarf : here slender, there broad : and all most admirably different in faces as well as in their height and bulk. I was about to defie any Londoner, who dares pretend there is so much ingenious correspondence in this City, as that he can shew me one house like another : yet your houses seem to be reverend and formal, being compared to the fantastical looks of the modern : which have more ovals, niches, and angles, than are in your custards, and are inclosed with pasteboard walls, like those of malicious Turks, who, because themselves are not immortal, and cannot dwell for ever where they build, therefore wish not to be at charge to provide such lastingness as may entertain their children out of the rain :

Part of CHEAPSIDE, with the CROSS, &c. as they appeared in 1660

From a contemporary print.

so slight and prettily gaudy, that if they could more, they would pass for pageants. It is your custom, where men vary often the mode of their habits, to term the nation fantastical: but where streets continually change fashion, you should make haste to chain up the city, for it is certainly mad.

"You would think me a malicious traveller if I should still gaze on your mis-shapen streets, and take no more notice of the beauty of your river: therefore, I will pass the importunate noise of your watermen (who snatch at fares as if they were to catch prisoners, plying the gentry so uncivilly, as if they had never rowed any other passengers but bearwards) and now step into one of your peascod boats, whose tilts are not so sumptuous as the roofes of gundaloes, nor when you are within are you at the ease of a chaise-à-bras. The commodity and trade of your river belong to yourselves: but give a stranger leave to share in the pleasure of it, which will hardly be in the prospect of freedom of air, unless prospect, consisting of variety, be made up with here a palace, there a wood-yard: here a garden, there a brew-house: here dwells a lord, there a dyer, and between both, *duomo commune*. If freedom of air be inferred in the liberty of the subject, where every private man hath authority, for his own profit, to smoak up a magistrate, then the air of your Thames is open enough, because it is equally free. I will forbear to visit your courtly neighbours at Wapping, not that it will make me giddy to shoot your Bridge, but that I am loth to disturb the civil silence of Billingsgate, which is so great, as if the mariners were always landing to storm the harbour: therefore, for brevity's sake, I will put to shoar again, though I should be constrained, even without my galoshoes, to land at Puddle Dock.

"I am now returned to visit your houses, where the roofs are so low, that I presume your ancestors were very mannerly and stood bare to their wives: for I cannot discern how they could wear their high-crowned hats: yet, I will enter, and therein oblige you much, when you know my aversion to a certain weed that governs amongst your coarser acquaintance as much as lavender amongst your coarser linen; to which, in my apprehension, your sea-coal smoke seems a very Portugal perfume. I should here hasten to a period, for fear of suffocation, if I thought you so ungracious as to use it in public assemblies: and yet, I see it grows so much in fashion, that methinks your children begin to play with broken pipes instead of corals, to make way for their teeth. You will find my visit short; I cannot stay to eat with you, because your bread is too heavy, and you disdain the light substance of herbs. Your drink is too thick, and yet you are seldom over-curious in washing your glasses. Nor will I lodge with you, because your beds seem no bigger than coffins: and your curtains so short, as they will hardly serve to inclose your carriers in summer, and may be held, if taffata, to have lined your grand-sires' skirts.

"I have now left your houses, and am passing that of your streets, but not in a coach, for they are uneasily hung, and so narrow, that I took them for sedans upon wheels: nor is it safe for a stranger to use them till the quarrel be decided whether six of your nobles, sitting together, shall stop and give way to as many barrels of beer. Your city is the only metropolis in Europe where there is wonderful dignity belonging to carts. I would now make a safe retreat, but that methinks I am stopt by one of our heroic games, called foot-ball: which I conceive (under your favour) not very conveniently civil in the streets, especially in such irregular and narrow roads as Crooked Lane. Yet it argues your courage much like your military pastime of throwing at cocks: but your metal would be much magnified (since you have long allowed those two valiant exercises in the streets) to draw your archers from Finsbury, and during high market let them shoot at butts in Cheapside. I have now no more to say but what refers to a few private notes, which I shall give you in a whisper when we meet in Moorfields, from whence (because the place was meant for public pleasure, and to shew the munificence of your City) I shall desire you to banish the laundresses and bleachers, whose acres of old linen make a shew like the fields of Carthagena when the five months' shifts of the whole fleet are washt and spread."

To this satirical note let us add a glance at the suburbs with the help of Hollar's map of 1665. In this map Lambeth is evidently a small village lying south of the church and Palace, with at least one street running along the road on the east leading across to St. George's Fields. On the north there are no houses; the Palace Gardens stretch out behind the Embankment, covered with trees; then comes the Lambeth Marsh, a broad field bare of trees; there is a broad mile where the river bends, and here, buried among the trees, houses begin, and continue along Bankside; on the east of Lambeth Marsh is St. George's Fields, with houses on the north side, and St. George's Church. According to Hollar, South London at this time must have been a charming and rural place divided into gardens and set with trees. Unfortunately his picture becomes unintelligible when we find St. Mary Overies on the other side of the river.

CHAPTER IV

II. THE FIRE OF LONDON

IF, as some hold, the cause of the long-continued Plague, which lasted, with intervals of rest, from the middle of the sixteenth century to 1665, was nothing but the accumulated filth of London, so that the ground on which it stood was saturated many feet in depth with poisonous filtrations, the Fire of 1666 must be regarded in the light of a surgical operation absolutely essential if life was to be preserved, and as an operation highly successful in its results. For it burned, more or less, every house and every building over an area of 436 acres out of those which made up London within the walls.

It began in the dead of night—Sunday morning, 3 A.M., September 2, 1666—at the shop of one Farryner, a baker, in Pudding Lane, one of those narrow lanes which run to north and south of Thames Street. All the houses in that lane were of wood, pitched throughout, and as the stories jutted out, the houses almost met at the top. The house itself was full of brush and faggot wood, so that the Fire quickly grew to a head, and then began to spread out in all directions at once, but especially to the west and north. Close to the house was an inn called the "Star," the court-yard of which was full of hay and straw. In a very short time Pudding Lane itself was completely destroyed; it would seem as if the people were distracted and attempted little or nothing except their own escape. When day broke the fire had caught Thames Street, which was full of warehouses containing everything combustible, as butter, cheese, brandy, wine, oil, sugar, hemp, flax, tar, pitch, rosin, brimstone, cordage, hops, wood, and coal. The only means of combating a fire fed by such materials was to blow up the houses, and this the people vehemently opposed at first. As for the supply of water, there was none at all adequate to the situation, and the water machines of London Bridge were quickly destroyed with the houses on the Bridge. In order to escape and to carry away their property, every available vehicle, cart, waggon, carriage, or boat, was in requisition. Forty pounds was offered and given by many householders for the safe removal of their property, while in some cases—those of the wealthy—£400 was paid simply to get the plate and jewels and other valuables carried out of the reach of the Fire. The things were taken out into the open fields, where they were laid on the grass, and so left in charge of the owners; open and unconcealed robberies took place, as was to be expected. Some of the people placed their things for safety in the churches, fondly thinking that the fire would spare them; the booksellers of Little Britain and Paternoster Row deposited the whole of their books in the crypt of St. Paul's; alas! they lost them all. Those who had friends in the villages near London carried away their money and their valuables and deposited them in the houses of these friends. Pepys buried his treasure in the garden of Sir W. Ryder at Bethnal Green. He afterwards describes

THE GREAT FIRE OF LONDON
From a contemporary print. E. Gardner's Collection.

how he dug it up again and how he lost some of the money by the decay of the bags.

A strong easterly wind carried the flames along from roof to roof, and from house to house, and from street to street. The fire raged almost unchecked. By Monday morning it had covered the area between Pudding Lane and Gracechurch Street and Lombard Street, and to St. Swithin's in Candlewick Street, along the river as far as the Three Cranes in the Vintry. By Tuesday night it had destroyed everything as far west as St. Dunstan's in Fleet Street. By this time the men arrived from the dockyards, and by blowing up houses the fire was stopped at a great many points at once; the Duke of York superintended the work, and gained all hearts by his powerful labours in handing the buckets and giving orders. On Wednesday the fire broke out again in the Temple, but was reduced without difficulty. The damage done by this terrible calamity was computed, to put it into figures, as follows :—of houses destroyed, 13,200; their value, £3,900,000; of streets, 400; of parish churches, 87; their value, £261,600; of consecrated chapels, 6; their value, £12,000; of wares, goods, etc., £3,800,000; of public edifices burned, £939,000; St. Paul's rebuilt at a cost of £2,000,000. The whole loss, with other and smaller items, was reckoned at £10,730,500. The public buildings destroyed included St. Paul's Cathedral, eighty-seven parish churches, six consecrated chapels, the Royal Exchange, the Custom House, Sion College, the Grey Friars Church, St. Thomas of Acon, the Justice House, the four prisons, fifty companies' halls, and four gates. By this time many of the former nobles' town houses and the great merchants' palaces had been taken down and turned into private houses, warehouses, and shops; as, for instance, the Erber, Cold Harbour, la Riole, the King's Wardrobe, and others. The mediæval buildings with the exception of the churches had all gone, but there was still left a great quantity of remains, walls, vaults, arches, and other parts of ancient buildings, the loss of which to the antiquary and the historian was irreparable.

This appalling calamity is without parallel in history except, perhaps, the earth-quake of Lisbon. Once before there had been a fire which swept London from east to west, but London was then poor; there were few merchants, and the warehouses were small and only half-filled. In 1665 the warehouses were vast and filled with valuable merchandise. There still stands south of Thames Street a warehouse[1] built immediately after the Fire, evidently in imitation of its predecessors. It consists of seven or eight stories, all low; there are still small gables, a reminiscence of the old gables; looking upon this warehouse and remembering that there was a long row of these facing the river with lanes and river stairs between, we can understand the loss to the merchants caused by the conflagration. Considering also the rows of shops along Cheapside, Eastcheap, Ludgate Hill, and Cornhill, we can understand the ruin that fell upon the retail dealers in that awful week. All they had in the world was gone save the right of rebuilding on the former site. The master crafts-men lost their tools and their workshops; the bookseller lost his books; the journey-man lost his employment as well as his sticks. I quote here certain words of my own in another book :—

" The fire is out at last; the rain has quenched the last sparks; the embers have ceased to smoke; those walls which have not fallen totter and hang trembling, ready to fall. I see men standing about singly; the tears run down their cheeks; two hundred years ago, if we had anything to cry about, we were not ashamed to cry without restraint; they are dressed in broad-cloth, the ruffles are of lace, they look like reputable citizens. Listen—one draws near another. ' Neighbour,'

---

[1] Demolished since this was written.

he says, 'a fortnight ago, before this stroke, whether of God or of Papist, I had a fair shop on this spot.' 'And I also, good friend,' said the other, 'as you know.' 'My shop,' continued the first, 'was stocked with silks and satins, kid gloves, lace ruffles and neckties, shirts, and all that a gentleman or gentlewoman can ask for. The stock was worth a thousand pounds. I turned it over six or seven times a year at least. And my profit was four hundred pounds.' 'As for me,' said the other, 'I was in a smaller way, as you know. Yet such as it was, my fortune was all in it, and out of my takings, I could call two hundred pounds a year my own.' 'Now is

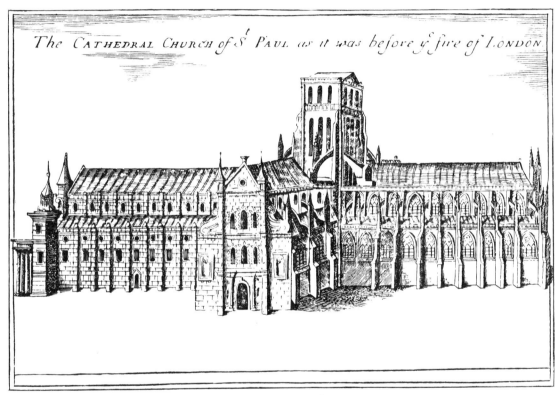

The CATHEDRAL CHURCH of St PAUL as it was before ye fire of LONDON

From a contemporary print.

it all gone,' said the first. 'All gone,' the other repeated, fetching a sigh. 'And now, neighbour, unless the Company help, I see nothing for it but we must starve.' 'Must starve,' the other repeated. And so they separated, and went divers ways, and whether they starved or whether they received help, and rose from the ashes with new house and newly stocked shop, I know not."

It is generally believed that the Fire left nothing standing where it had passed. This was not the case. Many of the church towers were left in part. Only the other day in building offices in the City on the site of a church—St. Olave's, Old Jewry—it was discovered that the lower part of the tower with the stone turret outside belonged to the old church. Many crypts escaped; the walls where they were of brick remained standing in part; in one case a whole court survived the Fire. This case is very curious. On the north-east of Apothecaries' Hall, with an entrance from Castle Street, was, until a year or two ago, a court called Fleur de Lys Court. At the time of the Fire there stood close beside the court, on the east side, the church and churchyard of St. Anne's, built after the Dissolution upon part of the old Blackfriars. Remember that the wind was easterly and strong during the Fire. When the roof of St. Anne's caught fire, therefore, the flames were driven across this court and over it. It would appear that the roof had been injured and part of the upper stories, but not the lower part. The court looked strangely out of keeping with the other buildings. I took my friend Mr. Loftie to see it. He gave it as his opinion at once that the mullions of the windows were of earlier date than the Fire. I afterwards took Mr. J. J. Stevenson, the architect, who made one or two sketches and came· to the same conclusion. A few weeks later I found that they were pulling the court down.

The causes of the Fire and the conditions which made its existence possible are thus enumerated by Strype :—

" First, They consider the time of the night when it first began, viz. between one and two of the clock after midnight, when all were in a dead sleep.

Secondly, it was Saturday night when many of the most eminent citizens, merchants, and others were retired into the country and none but servants left to look to their City Houses.

Thirdly, it was in the long vacation, being that particular time of the year when many wealthy citizens and tradesmen are wont to be in the country at Fairs, and getting in of Debts, and making up accounts with their Chapmen.

Fourthly, the closeness of the Building, and narrowness of the street in the places where it began, did much facilitate the progress of the Fire by hindering of the Engines to be brought to play upon the Houses on Fire.

Fifthly, the matter of which the Houses, all thereabouts were, viz. Timber, and those very old.

Sixthly, the dryness of the preceding season : there having been a great drought even to that very day and all the time that the fire continued, which has so dried the Timber, that it was never more pat to take Fire.

Seventhly, the Nature of the Wares and Commodities, stowed and vended in those Parts, were the most combustible of any other sold in the whole City : as Oil, Pitch, Tar, Cordage, Hemp, Flax, Rosin, Wax, Butter, Cheese, Wine, Brandy, sugar, etc.

Eighthly, an easterly wind, which is the driest of all others, had blown for several days together before, and at that time very strongly.

Ninthly, the unexpected failing of the water thereabouts at that time : for the engine at the North end of London Bridge, called the Thames Water Tower, was out of Order, and in a few hours was itself burnt down, so that the water pipes which conveyed the water from thence through the streets were soon empty.

Lastly, an unusual negligence at first, and a confidence of easily quenching it, and of its stopping at several probable places afterwards, turning at length into a confusion, consternation, and despair : people choosing rather by flight to save their goods, than by a vigorous opposition to save their own houses and the whole City."

This dry reasoning would not satisfy the people. They began to whisper among each other that this was the work of an incendiary and a stranger ; a Dutch-

A View of the Monument of London, in remembrance of the dreadful Fire in 1666. Its height is 202 Feet

man, or, more likely, a Roman Catholic. Divers strangers, Dutch and French, were arrested on suspicion of firing the City, but as there was no evidence they were released. What gave some colour to the suspicion was that, in April of that year, certain old officers and soldiers in Cromwell's army, eight in number, were tried for conspiracy and treason, their design having been to surprise the Tower, to kill the Lieutenant, and then to have declared for an equal division of lands. After taking the Tower their purpose was to set fire to the City. They were all found guilty, condemned, and executed. After the fire there was brought to the Lord Chief Justice a boy of ten, who declared that his father and uncle, Dutchmen both, were the persons who set fire to the house in Pudding Lane with fire-balls. This little villain appears to have been sent off as an impostor.

Then, however, followed Robert Hubert's confession, which was far more important. The man Hubert confessed or declared that about four months before the Fire he left his native town of Rouen with one Piedloe, and went with him to Sweden, where he stayed four months; that they came together in a Swedish ship to London, staying on board till the night when the fire began; that Piedloe then took him to Pudding Lane and gave him a fire-ball, which he lighted and put through a window by means of a long pole, waiting till the house was well alight. One Graves, a French merchant, resident in London, said that he knew both Hubert and Piedloe; that the former was a mischievous person, capable of any wickedness, while the latter was a debauched fellow, also apt to any wickedness. Next, in order to try the man's story, they took him to Pudding Lane and bade him point out Farryner's house—or the site of it. This he did very readily. Then they questioned Farryner, who declared that no fire could possibly have broken out in his house by accident. On the other hand, the Swedish captain swore that Hubert did not land until after the Fire, and his confession was full of contradictions; also he declared himself a Protestant, yet died a Catholic; in the opinion of many he was a man of disordered mind; moreover, why should Piedloe take him as companion when he might just as well have done the job himself? And how should a complete stranger taken into the dark streets of London for the first time in the dead of night be able to recognise again the street or the house?

In any case Hubert was hanged; and as he died a Catholic, it was of course abundantly clear that the whole thing was a Catholic conspiracy, a fact which was accordingly inscribed on the new monument when it was erected, so that

> " London's column pointing to the skies,
> Like a tall bully lifts its head and lies."

The inscription was removed on the accession of James the Second, but put up again on the arrival of William the Third. It remained on the monument till the year 1830, when it was taken down by order of the Common Council.

It is generally stated that the houseless people took refuge in Moorfields. This is only partly true. There were 13,200 houses destroyed and 200,000 people turned out into the streets. One remarks that if these figures are correct the crowding in the City must have been very great. For these figures give fifteen persons to every house, great and small, one with another. They did not all lie out on Moorfields simply because there was no room for them. Upper and lower Moorfields covered an area of about 840,000 square feet, or a square of 900 feet, very nearly. If we allow 15 feet × 20 feet for each hut to accommodate five people, we can find room for 2800 such houses without counting the lanes between them; so that Moorfields would contain about 14,000 people only. Evelyn says that the people were dispersed about St. George's Fields, Moorfields, and as far as Highgate. "I then went towards Islington and Highgate, where one might have seen 200,000 people of all ranks and degrees dispersed and lying along by their heaps of what they could save from the Fire."

"Pitiful huts," Maitland says, "were erected for their accommodation, and for their immediate needs the King sent a great quantity of bread from the Navy Stores to be distributed, and neighbouring Justices of the Peace were enjoined to send in all manner of victuals."

It was reputed that the loss of life was only six, but I venture to think that this loss must be greatly understated. When one considers the rapid spread of the fire, the way in which the people lingered to the last to save a little more, and when one remembers how Evelyn noticed on his first visit to the ruins the "stench from some poor creatures' bodies," we cannot but feel persuaded that the losses were more than six.

On Moorfields temporary chapels also were built. But when the fire ceased, and before the embers were cooled, the people began to creep back and the rebuilding of the City began. As there was still remaining that part of the City east of Billingsgate with the river and the shipping, business went on, though with broken wings. For the Royal Exchange they used Gresham College; the same place became their Guildhall; the Excise Office was removed to Southampton Street, near Bedford House; the General Post Office was taken to Brydges Street, Covent Garden; the Custom House to Mark Lane; Doctors' Commons to Exeter House, Strand. For temporary churches the authorities appropriated the meeting-houses which had not been destroyed. They began to rebuild their City. Within four years, ten thousand houses, twenty churches, and a great many companies' halls had been put up again. It took thirty years to complete the building of the fifty-one churches which were put up in place of the eighty-seven destroyed.

One effect of the Fire was to drive out of the City many of the shopkeepers. Thus Maitland says that before the Fire, Paternoster Row was chiefly occupied by mercers, silkmen, lacemen; "and these shops were so much resorted unto by the nobility and gentry in their carriages that ofttimes the street was so stopped up, that there was no room for foot-passengers." After the Fire, however, the tradesmen settled themselves in other parts; one supposes that they opened temporary shops, and, finding them convenient, they stayed where they were. They went to Henrietta Street, Bedford Street, and King Street, Covent Garden. Ludgate Hill, however, remained for a long time the principal street for the best shops of mercers and lacemen.

Were so great and overwhelming a calamity to befall a City in our times, we should have abundant materials for estimating not only the total value of the destruction, but also its effect upon individuals. We learn next to nothing of the Fire as it affected classes, such as merchants, shopkeepers, or craftsmen. The Plague ruined its thousands by slaying the breadwinner; the Fire ruined its tens of thousands by destroying everything that the breadwinner possessed, warehouse, goods, and all. Credit remained, one supposes; by the aid of credit many recovered. Yet, one asks, what amount of credit could possibly replace the trader's stock? What amount of credit could once more fill the great warehouse crammed to the very roof with commodities? Those who were debtors found their debts wiped off; one supposes that all prisoners for debt were enlarged; those who were creditors could not collect their amounts; rents could neither be asked nor paid; the money-lender and the borrower were destroyed together; almshouses were burnt down— what became of the poor old men and women? The City charities were suspended— what became of the poor? In such a universal dislocation, revolution, and cessation of everything, the poor man lost all that he had to lose, and the rich were sent empty away. Would that some limner of the time had portrayed for us a faithful picture of the first meeting of the Common Council after the Fire! Dryden speaks of the Fire :—

> " Those who have homes, when home they do repair
> To a last lodging call their wandering friends :
> Their short uneasy sleeps are broke with care
> To look how near their own destruction ends.
>
> Those who have none sit round where it was,
> And with full eyes each wonted stone require :
> Haunting the yet warm ashes of the place,
> As murdered men walk where they did expire.
>
> The most in fields like herded beasts lie down
> To dews obnoxious on the grassy floor,
> And while their babes in sleep their sorrow drown,
> Sad parents watch the remnant of their store."

One thing is certain: for the working man there was no lack of employment; thousands were wanted to clear away the rubbish, to get the streets in order, to take down shaky walls, to make bricks, to dig out foundations, to do carpenter's work and all those things required for the creation of a new London. And as for the artificers, they were wanted to restore the stocks of the traders as quickly as

The Names of all the Churches both in the City and Suburbs with Figures annexed refering to their situation in ye P...

1 Cathedral of S.t Paul	13 S. Mary Aldermanbury	26 French Church	42 Bow Church	56 Alhallows	73 S. Leonard	87 S. Hellens
2 Christ Church	14 S. Michael Bassian	27 S. Bennet	43 S. Matthew	57 S. Mary	74 S. Bennet	88 S. Ethelborough
3 S. Michael Paternoster row	15 S. Laurence	28 Augustin Fryers	44 S. Austins	58 S. Thomas Apostles	75 S. Margaret	89 Alhallows in ye W
4 S. Peters Wood Street	16 S. Maudlins	29 S. Martins Outwich	45 S. Gregory	59 S. John Baptist	76 S. Andrew Hubart	90 S. Botolphs Bishs.
5 S. Foster	17 Alhallows	30 S. Michael	46 S. Martins Ludgate	60 S. Michael	77 S. Georges	91 S. Botolphs Aldg.
6 S. Leonard	18 S. Martins Ironmongers Lane	31 S. Peters	47 S. Andrew	61 S. James	78 S. Botolphs	92 S. Brides
7 S. Anne Aldersga	19 S. Olaves	32 Alhallows	48 S. Bennet Thames Street	62 S. Martins	79 S. Mary Hill	93 Temple Church
8 S. Michael Wood Street	20 S. Mary Colechu.	33 S. Edmunds	49 S. Peters	63 S. Mary Botolphs L.	80 S. Dunstan	94 S. Dunstans Wes
9 S. John Zachary	21 S. Stephen	34 S. Clements	50 S. Mary	64 S. Swithins	81 Alhallows Barking	95 S. Andrew Holb
10 S. Olaves	22 S. Mildred	35 S. Nicholas	51 S. Nicholas	65 S. Mary Bush L.	82 S. Olaves	96 S. Sepulchers
11 S. Mary Staining	23 S. Margaret	36 S. Mary Woodnoth	52 S. Nicholas Olaves	66 Alhallows great,	83 Alhallows in Fen	97 S. Bartholomew
	24 S. Christopher	37 S. Mary Carwick S.	53 S. Mary Somerset	67 Alhallows ye less	84 S. Catherine Colmans	98 S. Bartholomen
	25 S. Bartholomew by the Exchange	38 S. Stephen Walbrok	54 S. John Evangelist	68 S. Laurence Pouliney	85 S. Catherine Creed C.	99 S. Botolphs Ald.
		39 S. Bennet	55 S. Mildred	69 S. Michael Crooked	church Street	100 S. Giles Crypp.
		40 S. Pancras		70 S. Magnus	86 S. Andrew Underhaft	* S. Mary Carwick
		41 S. Anthotins		71 S. Margaret		

From a ...

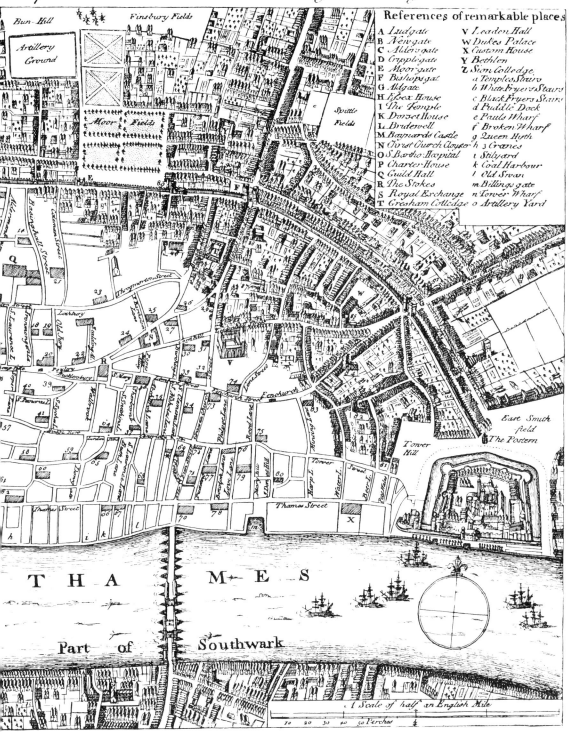

References of remarkable places

A	Ludgate	V	Leaden Hall
B	Newgate	W	Dukes Palace
C	Aldersgate	X	Custom House
D	Cripplegate	Y	Bethlen
E	Moorgate	Z	Sion Colledge
F	Bishopsgate	a	Temples Stairs
G	Aldgate	b	White Fryers Stairs
H	Essex House	c	Black Fryers Stairs
I	The Temple	d	Puddle Dock
K	Dorset House	e	Pauls Wharf
L	Bridewell	f	Broken Wharf
M	Baynards Castle	g	Queen Hyth
N	Christ Church Cloyster	h	3 Cranes
O	S. Bartho Hospital	i	Stilyard
P	Charter House	k	Coal Harbour
Q	Guild Hall	l	Old Swan
R	The Stokes	m	Billings gate
S	Royal Exchange	n	Tower Wharf
T	Gresham Colledge	o	Artillery Yard

Bun-Hill

Finsbury Fields

Artillery Ground

Moor Fields

Spittle Fields

East Smith field
The Postern

Tower Hill

Thames Street

THAMES

Part of Southwark

A Scale of half an English Mile

10 20 30 40 50 Perches

might be. Labour was never in such request before in all the history of London.

Twenty-five years later they were congratulating themselves on the changed and improved condition of the City. The writer of *Angliæ Metropolis*, or *the Present State of London*,[1] says :—

"As if the Fire had only purged the City, the buildings are infinitely more beautiful, more commodious, more solid (the three main virtues of all edifices) than before. They have made their streets much more large and straight, paved on each side with smooth free stone, and guarded the same with many massy posts for the benefit of foot passengers : and whereas before they dwelt in low dark wooden houses, they now live in lofty, lightsome, uniform, and very stately brick buildings."

Of the wooden houses commonly found in London before the Fire you will find one or two specimens still left—fifty years ago there were many. One such is in the Churchyard of St. Giles, Cripplegate. As to the total destruction of the houses I am in some doubt ; I have already mentioned one court called the Fleur de Lys, Blackfriars, which escaped the Fire. The same fact that probably saved this Court may have saved other places. Strype, for instance, mentions a house in Aldersgate Street which survived the Fire. There were, again, many houses partially destroyed, some accident arresting the Fire, and there were many walls which could be used again. These considerations are confirmed by an examination of Hollar's minute picture of London immediately after the Fire. In this picture all the churches are presented as standing with their towers ; they are roofless and their windows are destroyed, but they are standing. It would be interesting to learn how much of these old walls and towers were used in the new buildings. Half the houses on London Bridge are gone, and the Bridge is evidently cleared of rubbish. Part of the front of Fishmongers' Hall is still standing ; All Hallows the Less, which appears to have been quite a small church, has no tower, but its walls are standing. Between that church and the river is a space covered with ruins, in the midst of which stands a pillar. The Water Gate remains at Cold Harbour ; part of the front and the quay of the Steelyard, and a small part of the roof at the east end of St. Paul's still remain, melancholy to look upon ; the square port of Queenhithe is surrounded by fallen houses ; the steeple of the Royal Exchange stands over the ruins ; the river front of Baynard's Castle still stands, but the eastern side is in ruins ; the place is evidently gutted. In all directions there are walls, gables, whole houses standing among heaps and mounds of rubbish.

Two circumstances must be reckoned fortunate : the Fire, while it burned down the churches and reduced the monuments to dust, also penetrated below the surface and transformed the dreadful mass of putrefaction caused by the Plague a year before into harmless dust. It also choked most of the numerous wells, whose bright and

[1] T. Delaune, 1681.

sparkling waters charged with malarious filtrations the people had been accustomed to regard as sweet and healthy.

The King issued a Proclamation on the rebuilding of the City. No houses of wood were to be put up; cellars, if possible, were to be strongly arched; the principal streets were to be made broader and no narrow lanes to remain; the river was to have a fair quay or wharf running all along, with no houses except at a certain distance; trades carried on by means of fire and causing smoke to be placed in certain quarters where they would be neither dangerous nor noisome; a survey

SIR CHRISTOPHER WREN (1632-1723)
From the painting by Sir Godfrey Kneller in the National Portrait Gallery, London.

of the whole area covered by the Fire was to be made. There were also Acts passed by the Court of Common Council for the enlargement and the pitching and levelling of the streets. These Acts will be found in Appendix V.

Three plans were sent in to the Common Council for the laying out of the City in a more convenient manner; they were drawn up by Christopher Wren, who was appointed architect and surveyor-general, Sir John Evelyn, and Dr. Newcourt. The scheme of Wren was considered very carefully. It proved impossible, however, on account of the unwillingness of the people to give up their right of building on their old foundations. The scheme of Evelyn provided an embankment along the river,

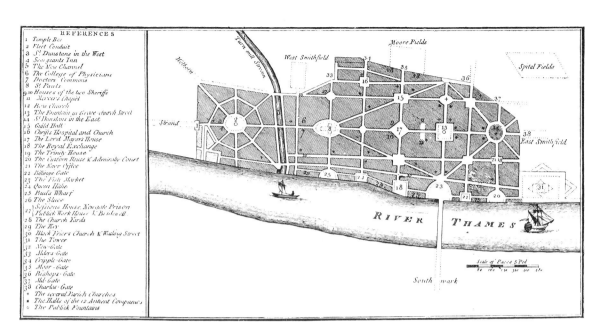

Sir John Evelyn's Plan for Rebuilding the City of London after the Great Fire in 1666.

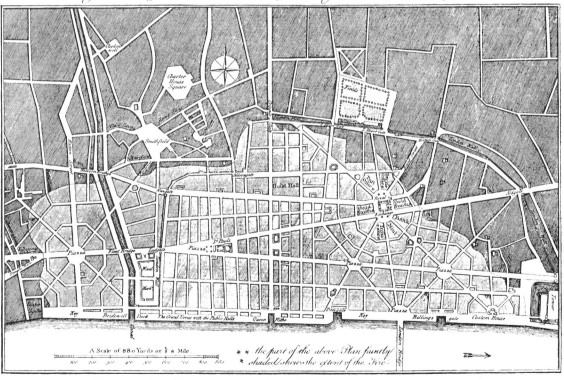

Sr Cristopher Wren's Plan for Rebuilding the City of London after the dreadfull Conflagration in 1666

From contemporary prints.

broad streets, piazzas round the churches, in which were to be shops; a Mansion House; a footway on London Bridge instead of houses; the churchyard of the whole City was to be a strip of ground under the old wall; opposite to the churchyard was to be a street set apart for inns and stations for carriers. It was, in short, a scheme quite impossible, yet remarkable for anticipating so much of what has since been carried out.

Meantime the rebuilding went on rapidly; in a few cases a street was widened; but the narrow lanes running north and south of Thames Street show that little regard was paid to the regulations. No wooden houses were built, and the old plan of high gables and projecting windows was exchanged for a flat façade and square coping. The churches were rebuilt, for the most part slowly. Some were not rebuilt at all. The last was finished thirty years after the Fire. Of the general character of Wren's churches this is not the place for an estimate. It is sufficient here to explain that Wren was guided first by the sum of money at his disposal, and next by the extent of ground; that many of the old churches were quite small buildings standing in small churchyards; but he extended the foundations and increased the area of the church; that he built in every case a preaching-house and not a mass-house, so that nearly all the churches are oblong halls instead of cruciform buildings; that he studied the interior instead of the exterior, and that some of his finest churches inside present no feature of interest on the outside.

The builders, all over the City, used as much as possible of the old foundations. Thus the Heralds' College preserves the court of Derby House; Wardrobe Square is the inner court of the King's Wardrobe Palace; while the narrow streets on either side of Cheapside preserve exactly the old lines of the streets burned down. It would be interesting to ascertain, if possible, where Wren's churches were built upon the older foundations; the north wall of the Holy Trinity Minories, for instance, belongs to the ancient convent there; the vestry of Allhallows in the Wall is on a bastion of the wall.

They altered the levels of many streets. Thames Street, "to prevent inundations," which shows that, in parts at least, it was lower than the old embankment, was raised three feet, and the streets leading out of it raised in a proper proportion; many streets were ordered to be widened, but it does not appear that the order was in every case carried into effect; several new streets were constructed; a duty on coals, one shilling at first, and afterwards two shillings on every ton, was granted to the City for the express expenses of the rebuilding; a Court of Judicature was established for the purpose of deciding quickly all disputes as to rents, boundaries, debts, etc., that might arise; the Court sat in the Hall of Clifford's Inn; rules were laid down concerning the materials, thickness of party walls, etc., rules so minute that it is perfectly certain that they could not be carried out; they divided the City into four quarters; they ordered each quarter to provide 800 buckets with brass hand squirts and ladders of various lengths; they appointed a bellman for every ward, whose duty was to walk up and down the streets all night long from Michaelmas to the Annunciation of St. Mary; that on the alarm of fire every householder was to hang up a lantern over his door and provide an armed man: that every householder should keep at his door a vessel filled with water; with a great many more regulations which may be omitted, the whole showing the terrible scare into which they had all fallen. Forty years after the Fire, Dr. Woodward of Gresham College thus wrote to Wren (*Strype*, vol. i. p. 292) in a private letter that

" The Fire of London, however disastrous it might be to the then inhabitants, had proved infinitely beneficial to their Posterity, and to the increase and vast improvement as well of the riches and opulency as of the buildings. And how by the means of the common sewers, and other like contrivances, such provision was made for sweetness, for cleanness, and for salubrity, that it is not only the finest and pleasantest, but the most healthy City in the world. Insomuch that for the Plague, and other infectious distempers, with which it was formerly so frequently annoyed, and by which so great numbers of the inhabitants were taken off, but the very year before the Fire, viz. Anno. 1665, an experience of above forty years since hath shewn it so wholly freed from, that he thought it probable it was no longer obnoxious to, or ever again likely to be infested by those so fatal and malicious maladies."

In May 1679 the people were thrown into a panic by the discovery of a so-called plot to burn down the City again. The house of one Bird in Fetter Lane having been burned, his servant, Elizabeth Oxley, was suspected of wilfully causing the fire; she was arrested and examined. What follows is a very remarkable story. The woman swore that she had actually caused the fire, and that she had been persuaded to do so by a certain Stubbs, a Papist, who promised her £5 if she would comply. Stubbs, being arrested, declared that the woman's evidence was perfectly true, and that Father Gifford, his confessor, incited him to procure the Fire, saying that it would be a godly act to burn all heretics out of their homes. The Irishmen were also implicated; the Papists, it was said, were going to rise in insurrection in London and an army was to be landed from France. Five Jesuits were executed for this business, and so great was the popular alarm, that all Catholics were banished from the City and ten miles round.

CHAPTER V

I PROCEED to quote four accounts of the Fire from eye-witnesses. Between them one arrives at a very fair understanding of the magnitude of the disaster, the horrors of the Fire, especially at night, and the wretchedness of the poor people, crouched over the wreck and remnant of their property.

"Here"—Evelyn is the first of the four—"we saw the Thames covered with floating goods, all the barges and boates laden with what some had time and courage to save, as on the other, the carts carrying out to the fields, which for many miles were strewed with movables of all sorts, and tents erecting to shelter both people and what goods they could get away. Oh the miserable and calamitous spectacle! Such as happly the world had not seene the like since the foundation of it, nor be outdone till the universal conflagration of it. All the skie was of a fiery aspect, like the top of a burning oven, and the light seene above 40 miles round for many nights. God grant mine eyes may never behold the like, who now saw above 10,000 houses all in one flame: the noise and cracking and thunder of the impetuous flames, the shrieking of women and children, the hurry of people, the fall of Towers, Houses and Churches, was like a hideous storm, and the aire all about so hot and inflamed, that at the last one was not able to approach it, so that they were forced to stand still and let the flames burn on, which they did for neere two miles in length and one in bredth. The clowds also of smoke were dismall and reached upon computation neere 56 mile in length. Thus I left it this afternoone burning, a resemblance of Sodom, or the last day. It forcibly called to my mind that passage *non enim hic habemus stabilem civitatem:* the ruines resembling the picture of Troy. London was, but is no more."

The next day he went to see the Fire again. All Fleet Street and the parts around it were in flames, the lead running down the streets in a stream, the stones of St. Paul's "flying like granados." The people, to the number of 200,000, had taken refuge in St. George's Fields and Moorfields as far as Islington and Highgate; there Evelyn visited them; they were lying beside their heaps of salvage, of all ranks and degrees, deploring their loss, and though ready to perish for hunger and destitution, yet not asking one penny for relief. It was not money they wanted, it was food and shelter. Can one conceive a picture more sorrowful than that of 200,000 people thus wholly ruined? Evelyn went home, and at once set to work on a plan for the reconstruction of the City.

Pepys has preserved fuller details :—

"So I down to the water-side, and there got a boat and through bridge, and there saw a lamentable fire. Poor Michell's house, as far as the Old Swan, already

JOHN EVELYN (1620-1706)

burned that way, and the fire running further, that in a very little time it got as far as the Steelyard while I was there. Everybody endeavouring to remove their goods, and flinging into the river or bringing them into lighters that lay off: poor people staying in their houses as long as till the very fire touched them, and then running into boats, or clambering from one pair of stairs by the water-side to another. And among other things, the poor pigeons, I perceive, were loth to leave their houses, but hovered about the windows and balconys till some of them burned their wings and fell down. Having staid, and in an hour's time seen the fire rage every way, and nobody, to my sight, endeavouring to quench it, but only to remove their goods, and leave all to the fire, and having seen it get as far as the Steelyard, and the wind mighty high and driving it into the City, and everything after so long a drought, proving combustible, even the very stones of churches, and among other things the poor steeple by which pretty Mrs. —— lives, and whereof my old schoolfellow Elborough is parson, taken fire in the very top and there burned till it fell down : I to White Hall (with a gentleman with me who desired to go off from the Tower to see the Fire, in my boat), and to White Hall, and there up to the King's closett in the Chappell, where people come about me, and I did give them an account dismayed them all, and the word was carried in to the King. So I was called for, and did tell the King and Duke of York what I saw, and that unless His Majesty did command houses to be pulled down, nothing could stop the fire." . . . "Walked along Watling Street, as well as I could, every creature coming away loaden with goods to save, and here and there sicke people carried away in beds. Extraordinary good goods carried in carts and on backs. At last met ye Lord Mayor in Canning Street, like a man spent, with a handkercher about his neck. To the King's message he cried like a fainting woman, 'Lord! what can I do? I am spent ; people will not obey me. I have been pulling down houses : but the fire overtakes us faster than we can do it.' That he needed no more soldiers : and that, for himself, he must go and refresh himself, having been up all night. So he left me, and I him, and walked home, seeing people all almost distracted, and no manner of means used to quench the fire. The houses, too, so very thick thereabouts, and full of matter for burning, as pitch and tarr, in Thames Street : and warehouses of oyle, and wines, and brandy and other things. . . . And to see the churches all filling with goods by people who themselves should have been quietly there at this time. . . . Soon as dined, I and Moone away, and walked through the City, the streets full of nothing but people and horses and carts loaden with goods, ready to run over one another, and removing goods from one burned house to another. They now removing out of Canning Street (which received goods in the morning) into Lombard Street and further : and among others I now saw my little goldsmith Stokes, receiving some friend's goods, whose house itself was burned the day after. We parted at Paul's : he home, and I to Paul's Wharf, where I had appointed a boat to attend me, and took in Mr. Carcasse and his brother, whom I met in the streets, and carried them below and above bridge to and again to see the fire, which was now got further, both below and above, and no likelihood of stopping it. Met with the King and Duke of York in their barge, and with them to Queenhithe, and there called Sir Richard Browne to them. Their order was only to pull down houses apace, and so below bridge at the water side : but little was or could be done, the fire coming upon them so fast. Good hopes there was of stopping it at the Three Cranes above, and at Buttolph's Wharf below bridge, if care be used : but the wind carries it into the City, so as we know not by the water-side what

THE GREAT FIRE OF LONDON

From the fresco painting in the Royal Exchange, London, by permission of the Artist, Stanhope A. Forbes, A.R.A., and the Donors,
The Sun Insurance Office.

it do there. River full of lighters, and boats taking in goods, and good goods swimming in the water, and only I observed that hardly one lighter or boat in three that had the goods of a house in, but there was a pair of Virginals in it. . . So near the fire as we could for smoke : and all over the Thames, with one's face in the wind, you were almost burned with a shower of fire-drops. This is very true : so as houses were burned by these drops and flakes of fire, three or four, nay, five or six houses, one from another. When we could endure no more upon the water, we to a little ale-house on the Bank-side over against the Three Cranes, and there staied till it was dark almost, and saw the fire grow : and as it grew darker, appeared more and more, and in corners and upon steeples, and between churches and houses, as far as we could see up the hill of the City, in a most horrid malicious bloody flame, not like the fine flame of an ordinary fire. Barbara and her husband away before us. We staid till, it being darkish, we saw the fire as only one entire arch of fire from this to the other side the bridge, and in a bow up the hill for an arch of above a mile long : it made me weep to see it. The churches, houses, and all on fire, and flaming at once : and a horrid noise the flames made, and the cracking of houses at their ruine. . . . I up to the top of Barking steeple, and there saw the saddest sight of desolation that I ever saw : everywhere great fires, oyle-cellars, and brimstone, and other things burning. . . . Walked into the town and find Fenchurch Streete, Gracious Streete, and Lumbard Streete all in dust. The Exchange a sad sight, nothing standing there, of all the statues or pillars, but Sir Thomas Gresham's picture in the corner. Walked into Moorfields (our feet ready to burn walking through the towne among the hot coles), and find that full of people, and poor wretches carrying their goods there, and everybody keeping his goods together by themselves (and a great blessing it is to them that it is fair weather for them to keep abroad night and day). . . . To Bishop's gate, where no fire had yet been near, and there is now one broken out : which did give great grounds to people, and to me too, to think that there is some kind of plot in this (on which many by this time have been taken, and it hath been dangerous for any stranger to walk in the streets), but I went with the men, and we did put it out in a little time : so that it was well again. It was pretty to see how hard the women did work in the cannells sweeping of water : but then they would scold for drink, and be as drunk as devils. I saw good butts of sugar broke open in the street, and people go and take handsfull out, and put into beer, and drink it. And now all being pretty well, I took boat, and over to Southwarke, and took boat to the other side the bridge, and so to Westminster, thinking to shift myself, being all in dirt from top to bottom : but could not find there any place to buy a shirt or pair of gloves, Westminster Hall being full of people's goods, those in Westminster having removed all their goods, and the Exchequer money put into vessels to carry to Nonsuch : but to the Swan and there was trimmed : and then to White Hall, but saw nobody, and so home. A sad sight to see how the River looks : no houses nor church near it, to the Temple where it stopped."

Here is a letter addressed to Lord Conway a few days after the Great Fire :—

"Alas, my lord, all London almost within the walls, and some part of it which was without the walls, lies now in ashes. A most lamentable devouring fire began upon Sunday morning last, at one of the clock, at a baker's house in Pudding Lane beyond the bridge, immediately burned down all the new houses upon the bridge, and left the old ones standing, and so came on into Thames Street, and went backwards towards the Tower, meeting with nothing by the way but old paper buildings and the most combustible matter of tar, pitch, hemp, rosin, and flax, which was all laid up thereabouts : so that in six hours it became a large stream of fire, at least a mile long, and could not possibly be approached or quenched. And that which contributed to the devastation was the extreme dryness of the season, which laid all the springs so low, that no considerable quantity of water could be had, either in pipes or conduits : and above all, a most violent and tempestuous east wind, which had sometimes one point towards the north, then again a point towards the south, as if it have been sent on purpose to help the fire to execute upon the City the commission which it had from Heaven.

From Thames Street it went up Fish Street Hill into Canning Street, Grace-church Street, Lombard Street, Cornhill, Bartholomew Lane, Lothbury, Austin Friars, and Broad Street northwards, and likewise into Fenchurch Street and Lime Street, burning down all the churches, the Royal Exchange, and all the little lanes and alleys as it went. From thence westward it swept away Friday Street, Watling Street, Cheapside, Newgate market, and the Prison, Paternoster Row, St. Sepulchre's, and so up to Smithfield Bars, and down to Holborn bridge. Also all St. Paul's Churchyard, the roof of Paul's Church, Ludgate Hill, part of Fleet Street, Blackfriars, Whitefriars, and all the Inner Temple, till it came to the Hall, a corner of which had taken fire, and was there most happily quenched, as likewise in Fleet St. over against St. Dunstan's Church : else, for aught appears, it might have swept away Whitehall and all the City of Westminster too, which is now left standing, together with all the suburbs : viz. the Strand, Covent Garden, Queen Street, Lincoln's Inn fields, Holborn as far as the Bridge, and all Hatton Garden, Clerken-well, and St. John Street.

Of the City itself, from the Tower unto Temple Bar, remains only all Smith-field and St. Bartholomew's, being stopped there before it came to Sir Elias Harvey's, wherefrom, together with Sir John Shaw's and Gresham College and so forward, are preserved : all Bishopsgate Street, Leadenhall Street, Duke's Place, and so to Aldgate.

But 'tis fit your lordship should know that all that is left, both of City and suburbs, is acknowledged, under God, to be wholly due to the King and Duke of

York, who, when the citizens had abandoned all further care of the place, were intent chiefly upon the preservation of their goods, undertook the work themselves, and with incredible magnanimity rode up and down, giving orders for blowing up of houses with gunpowder, to make void spaces for the fire to die in, and standing still to see those orders executed, exposing their persons not only to the multitude, but to the very flames themselves, and the ruins of buildings ready to fall upon them, and sometimes labouring with their own hands to give example to others: for which the people do now pay them, as they ought to do, all possible reverence

TEMPLE BARR   The West-Side

From the Crace Collection in the British Museum.

and admiration. The King proceeds daily to relieve all the poor people with infinite quantities of bread and cheese, and in this is truly God's vicegerent, that he does not only save from fire but give life too.

I believe there was never any such desolation by fire since the destruction of Jerusalem, nor will be till the last and general conflagration. Had your lordship been at Kensington you would have thought—for five days together, for so long the fire lasted—it had been Doomsday, and that the heavens themselves had been on fire; and the fearful cries and howlings of undone people did much increase the resemblance. My walks and gardens were almost covered with the ashes of papers, linen, etc., and pieces of ceiling and plaister-work blown thither by the tempest.

The loss is inestimable, and the consequence to all public and private affairs not presently imaginable, but in appearance very dreadful: yet I doubt not but the king and his people will be able to weather it out, though our enemies grow insolent upon it.

The greatest part of the wealth is saved, the loss having chiefly fallen upon heavy goods, wine, tobacco, sugars, etc.; but all the money in specie, plate, jewels, etc., were sent into the Tower, where it now lies; and the Tower itself had been fired, but that it preserved itself by beating down the houses about it, playing continually with their cannon upon all that was fired, and so stopped the progress.

So great was the general despair, that when the fire was in the Temple, houses in the Strand, adjoining to Somerset House, were blown up on purpose to save that house, and all men, both in City and suburbs, carried away their goods all day and night by carts, which were not to be had but at most inhumane prices. Your lordship's servant in Queen Street made a shift to put some of your best chairs and fine goods into your rich coach, and sent for my horses to draw them to Kensington, where they now are.

Without doubt there was nothing of plot or design in all this, though the people would fain think otherwise. Some lay it upon the French and Dutch, and are ready to knock them all on the head, wheresoever they meet them; others upon the fanatics, because it broke out so near the 3rd of September, their so celebrated day of triumph; others upon the Papists, because some of them are now said to be in arms; but 'tis no otherwise than as part of those militias which are, or ought to be, in a posture everywhere.

All the stories of making and casting of fire-balls are found to be mere fictions when they are traced home; for that which was said to be thrown upon Dorset House was a firebrand, seen by the Duke of York upon the Thames to be blown thither, and upon notice thereof given by his highness was for that time quenched. But there could be no plot without some time to form it in: and making so many parties to it, we must needs have had some kind of intelligence of it: besides, no rising follows it, nor any army appears anywhere to second such a design. Above all, there hath been no attempt upon the King or Duke's person, which might easily have been executed had this been any effect of treason.

Men begin now everywhere to recover their spirits again and think of repairing the old and rebuilding a new City. I am told this day by Mr. Chichely the City have sent to the King to desire a new model. Vaults are daily opened wherein are found immense quantities of pepper, spices, and wines, oils and sugars, etc., safe and untouched, though the houses were fired: but all the cloth laid in St. Faith's Church under St. Paul's is burnt. Gresham College is set apart for an

Exchange and Post Office. Leadenhall is to supply the uses of Guildhall; and without doubt, when the Parliament meets, as much will be done towards the restoring of the City, and in it of the kingdom, to its ancient lustre and esteem, as can be expected from the piety and policy of so dutiful an assembly."

The fourth eye-witness whom I shall quote is a certain Edward Atkyns in a letter preserved in the *London and Middlesex Note-book* (p. 171):—

"Good Brother—I received your letter and shall give you ye best account I can of our late sad fire, though it is scarcely possible for any man fully to describe it. It began at a Baker's house in Pudding Lane, near Thames Street, on Sunday morning about 2 or 3 of ye clock: and burnt doone several houses, but could not be quencht in regard it was a narrow place where engines could not play, and ye Lord Maior did not think fit to pull doone eny houses to prevent ye further spreading of ye fire: about 10 of ye clock, whilst we were at church, there was a cry in the streets yt ye Dutch and French were in armes, and had fired the Citty, and therefore ye Ministers dismist their several congregations, but wee yt were soe remote thought little of it. In the afternoon I went into the temple garden, where I saw it had made an unhappy progresse, and had consumed towards the Thames side many houses and 2 or 3 churches, as Laurence Pointney Church, which I saw strongly fired, and other churches, and at last growing violent, and meeting with many wharfes, and the wind being high, it grew very formidable, and we began to thinke of its nearer approach. By Monday morning it had burnt doone all Thames Street, New Fish Street, and some part of Cannon Street, and thereupon ye Citizens began to neglect ye fire, and in fine, and to be short, by Wednesday evening it had burnt all the City: yesterday I went from St. Dunstan's Church to Bpgates Street, and there is not one house standing betwixt those places, there one only within the wall, but a part of these 3 streets remaining, viz. part of Leadenhall Street, Basinghall and Bpgates Street, all the rest burnt to the ground, and not so much as a considerable piece of timber as I could see saved from the fire: it is impossible almost to conceive the total destruction, all the churches burnt, nay, some of ye churches, as Bow Church and . . . have not so much as the walls standing: all the Halls, as Guild-hall, Merchant Taylors, Mercers Chapel, Old Exchange, burnt downe to the ground, soe yt you can hardly tell where such a Parish or place was: I can say but this, that there is nothing but stones and rubbish, and all exposed to the open aire, soe yt you may see from one end of ye Citty almost to the other. St. Paul's Church, ye very stones, are crumbled and broken into shivers, and slatts, and you can compare London (were yt not for ye rubbish) to nothing more than an open field. The Citizens were forced to remove their goods into the open fields, and £2:10 a Cart was no deare value to carry away ye goods, the inner Temple almost all burnt, and pulled down except ye Temple Church, ye Hall much defaced, and ye Exchequer Office, Sergeants Inn in Fleet Street, and all to St. Dunstan's

Church, and soe on ye other side to Holborne Bridge: ye King and Duke of Yorke were exceedingly active, or otherwise I doubt the suburbs would have undergone ye same calamity.   Some have conceived it was a plott, but most, and ye King himself, believed yt it was only ye Hand of God.   Ye King comforts ye Citizens with ye rebuilding of ye Citty, but God knows when yt will be: ye Exchange is now kept at Gresham College, where I heard yesterday there was a full exchange of Merchants.   My father's house at St. Ellens stands well; the fire began to seize upon Chancery Lane, having burnt up Fetter Lane, and came as far as Brides Lane and Whites Alley, but, blessed be God, suppressed, and all things safe at your house and chambers: but Mr. Hainson of Cateaton Street Mr. Lowe has enquired for, and cannot hear of him, his house suffered the same calamity.   Dr. Tillotson has lost many goods and £100 worth of books: he has taken a house in Lincoln's Inn Fields, where his father-in-law purposes to remain.   40,000 quarters of Corne destroyed in Bridewell—being the City—store.   Sir William Backhouse has lost £1600 per an. in houses and in the benefit of ye New River.   Sir R. Lucy and ye Lady Allen and Lady Fairfax about 3 or 400 per an.   Sir Richard Browne's house burnt to the ground, where he has sustained great losses, and my brother Broone likewise, for my sister being then ill, all the care was to remove her.   They and all now at ye Red Lyon, Holborne, my sister at her sister Howards house at Rockhampton.   My father came up on Monday, and staid removing his goods till Wednesday morning, and I sat up all ye night, but through Mercy, Chancery Lane is yet standing, except St. John's Head next Lincolns . . . was pulled doone by way of prevention, and another house towards Holborne.   The Parliament will certainly meet at ye day: ye Duke of Albemarle is now in London.   There was a flying report of an engagement at sea, but not confirmed.   Several persons, foreigners, are in prison upon suspicion, but little will be made of it, as I am informed the Attorney-General very ill.   My father and his family are well at Albany, where my wife went on Thursday last.   I had gone my circuit and my last two counties this week, but ye fire prevented my intentions.   If we cannot find out your cousin Harrison I'le go to Totnam on Tuesday next and inquire after him, and how it stands in reference to your goods in his custody; but I believe he having notice sufficient, and being a prudent man, has secured both his owne and youre goods. Houses are now at an excessive value, and my Lord Treasurer's new buildings are now in great request.   I think it best yt you remove noe goods either in your house or chambers, for I doe believe ye danger is well over, only we have frequent alarms of fire, sometimes in one place and then in another: it only now burns in cellars and warehouses, where either coals, spirits, or other combustible matters were lodged.   I thinke it convenient yt you be here agst the sitting of Parliament, for there will be need of you: great watch is kept, for though the judgements of God have been soe remarkable, yet you would wonder at ye profaneness of people, and how little some are concerned in this sad calamity. My hearty service to my sister and nephew, Sir Robert: my father writt a letter this week to you, but no post went, and I cannot come at ye letter. My mother has had a great loss in her house by Ludgate—for what service I can perform pray command me. My paper bids me end. Our navy is come into St. Helen's Bay.—I am your ever loving brother, most ready to serve you, EDW. ATKYNS."

The following account is from Dean Milman's *Annals of St. Paul's.*

"A certain Doctor Taswell remembered well the awful event, for it happened between his election and admission as a king's scholar at Westminster. It was likely to be graven deeply on the memory of a boy. 'On Sunday between ten and eleven, just as I was standing upon the steps leading up to the pulpit in Westminster Abbey, I discovered some people below me, running to and fro in a seeming inquietude and consternation; immediately almost a report reached my ears that London was in a conflagration. Without any ceremony I took leave of the preacher, and having ascended the Parliament steps near the Thames, I soon perceived four boats crowded with objects of distress. These had escaped from the fire scarce under any covering but that of a blanket.'

The next day (Monday) Dolben, then Dean of Westminster, set gallantly forth at the head of the Westminster boys (the Dean, by Taswell's account, had frequently in the civil wars mounted guard as sentinel) to do what they could to render assistance in staying the fire. They went a long way, for they aided in saving the Church of St. Dunstan in the East by fetching water from the back sides of the building, and so extinguishing the fire. Taswell acted as a sort of aide-de-camp page to the Dean. During this expedition Taswell may have heard or seen what he relates about St. Paul's. 'The people who lived contiguous to St. Paul's Church raised their expectations greatly concerning the absolute security of that place upon account of the immense thickness of its walls and its situation, built on a large piece of ground on every side remote from houses.' Upon that account they filled it with all sorts of goods; and besides, in the Church of St. Faith, under that of St. Paul, they deposited libraries of books, because it was entirely arched over; and with great caution and prudence even the least avenue, through which the smallest spark could penetrate, was stopped up. 'But,' Taswell proceeds, 'this precaution availed them little. As I stood upon the bridge (a small one over a creek at the foot of what is now Westminster Bridge), among many others, I could not but observe the progress of the fire towards that venerable fabric. About eight o'clock it broke out on the top of St. Paul's Church, almost scorched up by the violent heat of the air and lightning too, and before nine blazed so conspicuously as to enable me to read very clearly a 16mo. edition of Terence which I carried in my pocket.' This was on Tuesday 4th; on Thursday, like a bold boy, Taswell, soon after sunrising, endeavoured to reach St. Paul's. 'The ground was so hot as almost to scorch my shoes, and the air so intensely warm, that unless I had stopped some time upon Fleet Bridge to rest myself, I must have fainted under the extreme languor of my spirits. After giving myself a little time to breathe, I made the best of my way to St. Paul's.

And now let any person judge of the extreme emotion I was in when I perceived the metal belonging to the bells melting, the ruinous condition of the walls, with heaps of stones, of a large circumference, tumbling down with a great noise just upon my feet, ready to crush me to death. I prepared myself for retiring back again, having first loaded my pockets with several pieces of bell-metal.

I forgot to mention that near the east end of St. Paul's' (he must have got quite round the church) 'a human body presented itself to me, parched up as it were with the flames, white as to skin, meagre as to flesh, yellow as to colour. This was an old decrepit woman who fled here for safety, imagining the flames would not have reached her there; her clothes were burned, and every limb reduced to a coal. In my way home I saw several engines which were bringing up to its assistance, all on fire, and those engaged with them escaping with all eagerness from the flames, which spread instantaneous almost like a wildfire, and at last, *accoutred with my sword and helmet*, which I picked up among many others in the ruins, I traversed this torrid zone back again.'

Taswell relates that the papers from the books in St. Faith's were carried with the wind as far as Eton. The Oxonians observed the rays of the sun tinged with an unusual kind of redness, a black darkness seemed to cover the whole atmosphere. To impress this more deeply on Taswell's memory, his father's house was burned and plundered by officious persons offering to aid."

A TRVE AND EXACT PROSPECT OF THE FAMOVS

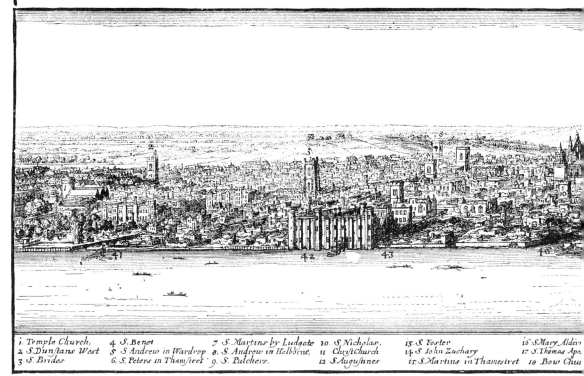

1. Temple Church,	4. S. Benet	7. S. Martins by Ludgate	10. S. Nicholas,	13. S. Foster	16. S. Mary Aldev
2. S. Dunstans West	5. S Andrew in Wardrop	8. S. Andrew in Holborne,	11. Christchurch	14. S. John Zachary	17. S. Thomas Apo.
3. S. Brides	6. S. Peters in Thamstreet	9. S. Pulchers.	12. S. Augustines	15. S. Martins in Thamestret	18. Bow Chu

APPEARETH NOW AFTER THE SAD CALAMITIE AN

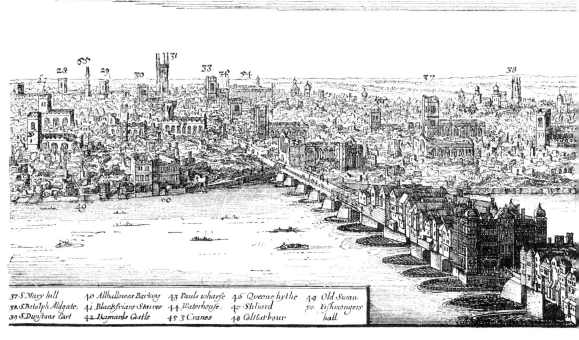

37. S. Mary hill	40. Allhallowes Barking	43. Pauls wharfe	46. Queene hythe	49. Old Swan.
38. S. Botolph Aldgate,	41. Blackfriars Staires	44. Waterhouse,	47. Stiliard	50. Fishmongers
39. S. Dunstans East	42. Baynards Castle	45. 3 Cranes	48. Colitharbour	hall.

5. Laurence	22. Allhallowes y^e great	25. S. Mary Wolnoth	28. S. Chriſtopher.	31. S. Michael, Cornhill	54. S. Denis.
S. Mary Buttolf lane	23. S. Stevens Colman ſtret	26. S. Lorence Poultney.	29. S. Bartholomew	32. Allhalloves	35. S. Magnus.
	24. S. Margaret.	27. S. Stevens in Walbroke.	30. S. Edmunds.	33. S. Peters in Cornhill	36. S. Andrew Hubart

DESTRVCTION BY FIRE, In the Yeare M. DC. LXVI.

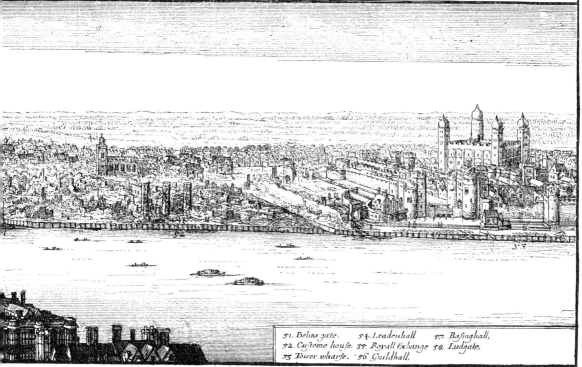

51. Belins gate.	54. Leadenhall	57. Baſinghall,
52. Cuſtome houſe.	55. Royall Exchange	58. Ludgate,
53. Tower wharfe.	56. Guildhall,	

THE FIRE
by Hollar.

Wenceſlaus Hollar delin: et ſculp: 1666.

CHAPTER VI

LET us turn to London rebuilt after the Fire. The City now began to grow outside the walls with determination; it was found impossible to stop its expansion any longer. London spread out long arms and planted colonies, so to speak; the craftsmen, driven out of their old quarters in the City by the increase of trade, and consequently of warehouses, quays, shops, and offices, settled down in the new colonies. The City joined hands with Westminster; it ran houses along Holborn to the Tyburn Road; it reared a suburb at Bloomsbury; it turned Clerkenwell into a crowded town; it made settlements at Ratcliffe, Mile End, and Stepney; it created a river-side population beyond Wapping (*see* Appendix VI.)

The map of Porter, *circa* 1660 (London Topographical Society, 1898), shows us the suburbs of that date.

Beginning with the east, we find a continuous line of houses "on the wall between St. Katherine's and Limehouse." Wapping contains two streets parallel with the river; at intervals there are stairs. What was afterwards Ratcliffe Highway is a broad road with cottages on either side, half a mile long; on the north of this road are fields intersected by country lanes. Stepney Church stands in the middle of fields. In the Whitechapel Road there are no houses beyond the church. On the north-east of the Tower is a broad open area, on the north of which stand, apparently, some of the remains of Eastminster. In the Minories, however, we look in vain for the ruins of the nunnery, though these were undoubtedly still standing at the time. Petticoat Lane, running into Wentworth Street, is the only street leading out of Whitechapel. On the north of Wentworth Street are the Spittle Fields; the Cloister and Cross of St. Mary Spital are visible. Lines of houses run north along Bishopsgate Street as far as Shoreditch Church.

North-east of Moorfields are Finsbury Fields. Cripplegate Without and Clerkenwell are thickly populated, including the Barbican, Chiswell, Red Cross, White Cross, and Grub Street. Goswell Street, as far north as the Charterhouse, Little Britain, Long Lane, and St. John Street, West Smithfield, were enclosed. There were

houses as far west as St. Giles's.   Between Holborn and the Strand, or Fleet Street,
lay Fetter Lane and Chancery Lane; between them large gardens; Lincoln's Inn
Fields was an open area of irregular shape, the gardens of Lincoln's Inn occupying the
same position as to-day.   New Inn and Clement's Inn have a garden behind them;
Drury Lane is an open road; Covent Garden is the "Piazzo."   Along the river-side
are Bridewell, Whitefriars, nearly all a garden; the Temple, Essex House, Arundel
House, Somerset House, The Savoy, Worcester House, Durham House, Buckingham
House, Northampton House, Whitehall, each in its own broad garden.   There are

SOMERSET PALACE, 1650
From a contemporary print.

no houses in Pall Mall; none in the Haymarket, except a "Gaming House"
in the north-east corner.   Piccadilly is "Pecadilly Mall" without a single house.
Westminster consists of King Street and the lanes round the Abbey.

On the south side there is a fringe of houses on the river wall, forming a street
extending for nearly a mile east of London Bridge; there are houses in "Barmisie"
Lane; a single street, ending with St. George's Church; another fringe of houses
west of the Bridge, nearly as far as the bend of the river to the south.   A theatre is
still standing—or is it a house for bear-baiting?—apparently on the site of the Globe.
There is a strange and unexpected street, with houses on either side, in the very
middle of Lambeth Marsh.   And with these exceptions, and a few cottages dotted

From a Drawing by Hollar

In the Pepysian Library at Cambridge

Durham   Salisbury   Water

DURHAM   HOUSE.   SALISBURY HOUSE.   WORCESTER HOUSE.

The three Houses   above represented, stood on the banks of the Thames, nearly adjoining each other. DURHAM HOUSE, the first in the Plate, occupied the spot called   DURHAM YARD now the ADELPHI, and was built by Ant.ᵒ Bec Bishᵖ of Durham, as a town residence for the Bishops of that See.   SALISBURY HOUSE was erected by Robert Cecil, Earl of Salisbury, in the reign of James 1 and covered the site of the present Salisbury and Cecil Streets. WORCESTER HOUSE, originally belonged to the See of Carlisle. It afterwards came into the possession of   *Salisbury*   the Earls of Worcester, Edm.ᵈ the last Earl of Worcester, died here in 1627. His son Hen.ʸ being created, Duke of Beaufort, it was called BEAUFORT HOUSE, and the Site is now called BEAUFORT BUILDINGS. The above View was taken about the year 1630

From an old print published by William Herbert, Lambeth.

271

about, there are no houses south of the river at all. The whole of the low-lying ground is covered with gardens, orchards, and meadows.

Turning now to the new London as it was after the Fire, we have Ogilby's excellent map of 1677 (*see* Map) showing the whole of London from Somerset House to St. Katherine by the Tower, and from the river to Clerkenwell, Chiswell Street, and Norton Folgate. It does not, indeed, include Westminster or Southwark. This map is an exact survey of the town as it was during the latter part of the seventeenth century, making allowance for some increase of houses in the northern suburbs. It is on the large scale of 100 feet to the inch; it presents every building, every street, and every lane, court, and alley. It consists of twenty sheets. I propose to pass this map under review, taking the streets in line from west to east.

The area of the City within the walls, according to Ogilby, was 380 acres; including the Liberties, it was 680 acres; the length from Temple Bar to White-chapel Bar is 9256 feet, or one mile, six furlongs, and a pole; the breadth from the Bars of Bishopsgate to the Bridge 4653 feet, or seven furlongs and two poles. If we include the suburbs, the distance between Blackwall inclusive and St. James's Street is nearly six miles; between St. Leonard's, Shoreditch, and the end of Blackman Street, Southwark, is two and a half miles.

In Clerkenwell, we observe, taking St. James's Church as a centre, that on the north side, apparently on the site of the Cloister, there lies a garden surrounded by buildings named " The Duke of Newcastle." On the south-east side is the church-yard; on the west and south-west are Clerkenwell Close and Clerkenwell Green. A hundred yards north-west of the church stands the " New Corporation Court Yard" with its " Bridewell Yard " and the " New Prison Walk " leading to it. Behind the Court Yard is a " Churchyard for Clerkenwell." Beyond and west of the Court are bowling fields, ponds—one of them a ducking pond—pasture lands, and private gardens; the houses are few. In the south part, however, round Hockley in the Hole, at the east end of which is a pond, the houses stand thickly with small gardens and open courts. Clerkenwell Green leads into St. John Street where the Inns begin. Here are the White Horse Yard and the Red Bull Yard; here are Aylesbury House and Gardens, 500 feet long by 200 feet broad. The east side of the street is lined with houses, apparently of the humbler kind, for they have no gardens and are divided by narrow alleys or lanes. On the north lie " Gardiners' Gardens," that is, market gardens. Between St. John's Street and Goswell Street are fields and woods, belonging to the Charter House. Old Street runs out of Goswell Street, and like the east side of that street and the east side of St. John's Street, it is lined with small houses and narrow alleys. Between Goswell Street and Bunhill Fields lies a quarter thickly inhabited and covered with houses. Golden Lane and White Cross Street run across this district in a north-west direction. Between the two streets, on the north of Playhouse Yard, is a churchyard, and on the Bunhill side are

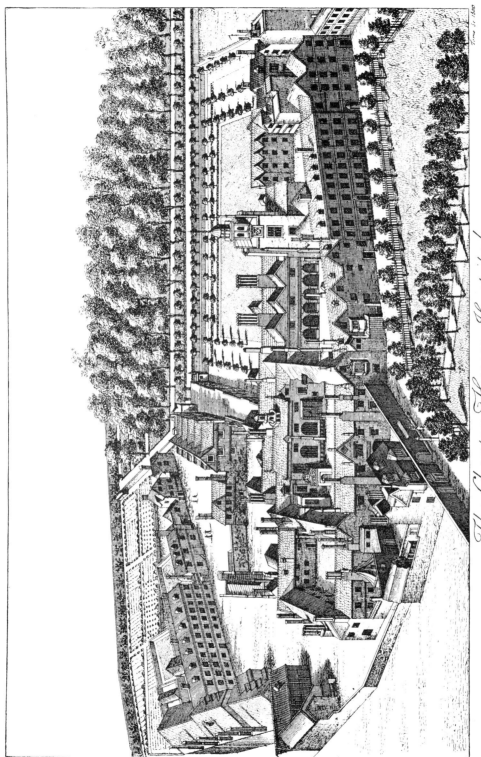

The Charter House Hospital

From a contemporary print.

18

gardens behind the houses; the largest of them is not more than 80 feet square. There is no church in this thickly populated area, more than a quarter of a mile long by nearly as much broad. It is evidently a place inhabited by the craftsmen, most of whom have ceased to live any longer in the City. The houses and gardens of Bunhill overlooking the " New Artillery Garden " remind us that many of the citizens had already begun to live out of town. Continuing east, beyond the Artillery Garden, we find Upper Moorfields, with trees planted on all four sides and paths intersecting; a large area called " Butchers' Close or Tenter Field," and a thickly built part bounded on the north by Hog Lane, and on the east by Norton Folgate. Here, again, the abundance of narrow alleys and the houses without gardens proclaim a humble population. Shoreditch is lined with houses; on its east side lies a large open space called Porter Close, with Spital Fields beyond. Two or three streets are fully built, but the vacant spaces are many and wide. No church is on this part of the map, except St. Leonard's, Shoreditch. We observe on the west of Norton Folgate two or three of the little streams which formerly ran across the moor here; they lie open for a little space and then disappear again.

The second line of maps carries us from east to west in the latitude of Gray's Inn. The only buildings of the Inn are South Square, Gray's Inn Square, and the Hall and Chapel. The rest of the Inn is planted thickly with trees, or lies open, a beautiful garden. Not far to the east of Gray's Inn are the great gardens of Furnival's Inn. Between Gray's Inn Road and the Fleet River lies a quarter thickly populated on the west and the east, but with many open spaces, especially on either side of Hatton Garden and Saffron Hill. What were these open spaces? They were not gardens, or the fact would have been indicated; they were not enclosed. Were they simply open spaces, the playground of children, the retreat of pickpockets? In this place, apparently, no gentlefolk dwelt, and there is no church.

We now cross over the Fleet and find ourselves in the classic regions of Turnmill Street, Cow Cross, and Chick Lane. Here, however, we are in a suburb which has been occupied and partly built over since the twelfth century. North of Chick Lane is the new churchyard of St. Sepulchre's, re-discovered recently when excavations took place which revealed stacks of human bones regularly laid and piled. I believe that these bones were moved from the old churchyard, which seems the only way to account for their great number, and the regular method of laying them. They have now been moved to some consecrated ground, and the place is built over. St. John's Lane leads to St. John's Gate, and Berkeley House and Gardens are on the west side; the great houses of the Elizabethan period are replaced by mean tenements. On the south side of St. John's Street is " Hix's " Hall. Further south, again, passing through the Bars, we are in Smithfield. The church of Little St. Bartholomew was not yet within the Hospital; that of St. Bartholomew the Great shows the ambulatory and the Lady Chapel, but not the transepts. Charter House shows the Courts as at present; on the east side of Charterhouse Yard are the houses and gardens of the Marquis of Dorchester and Lord Gray. St. Bartholomew's Close is a large open space; Cloth Fair and the narrow streets around it are much the same to-day as then; the whole area is covered with narrow alleys and courts with narrow openings. Between Aldersgate Street and Little Moor Fields lies a suburb thickly built over except on the northern portion south of Chiswell Street, where the houses are more scattered and there are gardens and, apparently, small fields. The same remarkable abundance of open courts approached by narrow passages that has been already mentioned may be observed here. East of Aldersgate, and just under the wall at the Cripplegate angle, are the gardens of Thanet House. North of Barbican are those of Bridgewater House. St. Giles's Church has taken over a part of the town ditch for an extension of its churchyard; the wall is encroached upon on both sides by buildings, but a strip on the south side is still left free from buildings. As regards the portion of the City included in this street, it will be noticed farther on. The upper field has trees planted along its sides and diagonally from point to point shading two intersecting fields; the lower field has also trees along its sides and two paths across at right angles, also planted with trees. On these fields the people turned out by the Fire encamped until they could rebuild their houses; it is, however, impossible to describe the great number of streets east and west of the Fields, without feeling sure that the houses afforded lodgings, better or worse, for the great majority of the homeless. On the south of Moorfields stood the New Bethlehem Hospital, a long narrow building on the outside of the wall, a piece of which has been cut down to afford an entrance from the City. The old churchyard of Bethlehem, about 200 feet by 300 feet, lay on the north-east side of Lower Moorfields; the site of St. Mary Bethlehem is preserved in the name of a street or court: "Bethlehem"—between the yard and Bishopsgate Street Without. St. Botolph's without Bishopsgate has taken a large piece of the town ditch for an extension of churchyard; the lane running along its north side leads into Petty France, now called North Broad Street. All the ground about this part is now swallowed up by the Liverpool and Broad Street Stations. Bishopsgate Street Without, with the ground east and west, is completely built up and covered with houses. The site of Old Artillery Garden is still marked by Artillery Lane, which led into it. East of Bishopsgate Street we find Petticoat Lane, Wentworth (then called Wentford) Street, Brick Lane, Carter Street, Fashion Street, Dean and Tower Streets, and other streets and lanes, lined with houses but not yet filled in with courts; the houses, in nearly all cases, have gardens behind them. One wishes for a drawing of one of these early Whitechapel streets, but in vain. Tenter fields fill up the spaces not yet built over.

We next come to the third line of maps. On the north of this line runs the noble highway of Holborn; on its north side we pass Warwick House, Gray's Inn;

and Brook House, evidently a stately building in the form of a court, with a gateway to the street and gardens behind; this is separated from Furnival's Inn by a narrow lane. The Inn, whose gardens we have already noticed, presents in plan an oblong outer court, a hall and chapel, and an unfinished inner court; Ely House has a court, gardens and buildings, and a hall. In the street itself stands the Middle Row, only taken down a few years ago; at its east end, and just west of Staple Inn, are the Holborn Bars. We next observe Chancery Lane; its west side is largely taken up with Lincoln's Inn. The Inn itself consists of the first two courts, the chapel, and the hall; the rest is all garden, open on the east to Chancery Lane, and on the west to the Fields. Lincoln's Inn Fields are not enclosed and are crossed by paths; the south side is occupied by "Portugal Row." South of the Inn, on the ground now covered by part of New Square and by part of the High Courts of Justice, is an open space called Lower Lincoln's Inn Fields, the existence of which appears to have been neglected by writers on topography. On the east side of Chancery Lane there are continuous houses, and behind them the gardens of Staple Inn, the Rolls with the Master's house, the chapel, and the gardens.

Following the south side of Holborn we find Staple Inn, much as it is at the present day, but with fine and spacious gardens; Barnard's Inn, as it was before it was turned into a school; Fetter Lane, where most of the houses still had gardens; Thavies Inn, with its two courts and its small garden; and St. Andrew's Church and Churchyard. The labyrinth of undistinguished streets called Harding Street, New Street, etc., is almost the same in 1677 as at present, save that it was not as yet the Printers' Quarter.

At the end of Holborn is Holborn Bridge, crossing the Fleet, which is here called the New Canal; barges and boats lie upon it. At the back of the street now called Farringdon Street, facing the stream, are two burial yards, one belonging to St. Andrew's, Holborn; the other, lower down, to St. Bride's, Fleet Street; on the west side a great number of narrow streets branch off to the east, ending at Snow Hill and the Old Bailey. Newgate Prison lies north and south of the Gate, quite separated from the court. The Gate and wall crossed the road 200 yards east of Giltspur Street. Passing over Holborn Bridge we can walk up Snow Hill, which leads us to St. Sepulchre's Church and Newgate, or we can keep straight on through Cock Lane to Giltspur Street, Pie Corner, and St. Bartholomew's and Smithfield. The Hospital consists apparently of one court only. Three large churchyards lie round it: that of St. Bartholomew the Less; that called "Bartholomew Church-yard," and the "Hospital Churchyard," on the site of the town ditch. In front of Newgate Prison stood a block of buildings like the Middle Row of Holborn, Butcher's Row in the Strand, or Holywell Street; on the west side the narrow street was called the Little Old Bailey. Among the courts leading out of the Little Old Bailey we observe Green Arbour Court, afterwards the residence of Oliver Cromwell.

The next sheet is altogether within the City.

We then come to Aldgate and Whitechapel. The eastern limits of the map run through Goodman's Fields, in 1677 really open fields. We observe that from Aldgate to the Tower, the site of the town ditch is still left open. A broad space not built over lies across the site of the Minories.

The last line of streets begins with Somerset House. Taking the north side

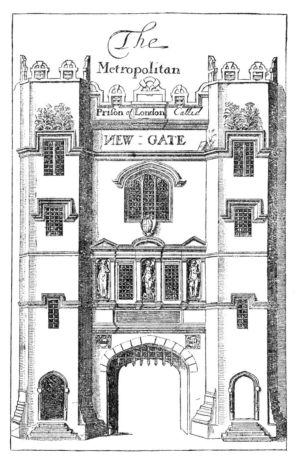

NEWGATE, 1650,
From the Crace Collection in the British Museum.

we find Lyon's Inn between Holywell Street and Wych Street; Clement's Inn and New Inn, side by side, each with its two courts and its garden; Butcher Row, built in the middle of the Strand, and a labyrinth of courts, lanes, and yards lying between Clement's Inn and Bell Yard, the whole now occupied by the High Courts of Justice; Clifford's Inn lies north of St. Dunstan's Church in Fleet Street.

On the south side we get Somerset House and Gardens, soon to be all built over; the two Temples with their gardens—a vast number of wherries are waiting at the Temple Stairs—and the Whitefriars Precinct, between Whitefriars Lane and Water Lane, where there is a dock for barges. St. Bride's is called St. Bridget's; the Palace of Bridewell, with its two courts and two gateways, is represented as still standing. The Duke's Theatre on the south-east side of Salisbury Court perhaps accounts for the number of wherries gathered at the stairs.

Passing over the City we come to the Tower, and beyond the Tower to the eastern boundary of our map. As to the crowded lanes and courts on the other side of the Tower, there is nothing to say about them; they belong to the Precinct of St. Katherine, now almost entirely converted into a dock.

We have thus gone all round the City from Somerset House west to St. Katherine's east, and from the City wall on the south to Clerkenwell on the north. These were no longer rural retreats or villages; they were, for the most part, completely built over and laid out in streets; there were among them half a dozen noblemen's houses. As there were none left in the City, it is certain that the former connection between the City and the nobility had been well-nigh destroyed; but not quite. Prince Rupert is said to have lived in the Barbican, and there are still the houses we have found in Ogilby and those along the riverside between the Temple and Westminster. In all these suburbs there are as yet no new churches, and for all these crowded suburbs, only ten old churches. There are few schools. In the seventeenth century was begun the fatal neglect of the populace, formerly living in the City under surveillance and discipline, taught, trained, and kept in their place. This was the creating cause of the terrible London mob of the next century. What could be expected, when a vast population was allowed to grow up without guidance, without instruction, without religion, and without even a police? We observe also that outside the City there was a great number of market gardens, with gardens at the back of every house until the space is wanted, when courts and alleys are run into them. The Londoner always loved a garden, and had one as long as he could (*see* Appendix VII.).

Let us next, very briefly, consider the City of 1677 as represented by this map. It is eleven years after the Fire. It is sometimes stated, loosely, that it took a great many years to rebuild London. The statement is only true as regards the churches and the companies' halls. The City itself was rebuilt with every possible despatch. As for the plans prepared by Wren and Evelyn, they came under the consideration of the Council after the people had begun with feverish haste to clear away the rubbish and to rebuild. The actual alterations made by order of the Mayor were carefully enumerated by Maitland, and will be found in their place (Appendices V. and VI.).

We must remember that the people, deprived of their shops and their warehouses, huddled together in temporary huts erected on Moorfields, with the winter before them, or lodged in the mean tenements of the suburbs, living on bounty and charity, were eager to get back to their own places. Every man claimed his own ground ; every heap of rubbish was the site of a house ; every house had its owner or its tenant ; without a workshop or his counter there was no means of making a livelihood. Therefore, even before the ashes were cooled, the people were picking their way through the encumbered lanes, crying "Mine ! Mine !" and shovelling away the rubbish in order to put up the walls anew. The improvements ordered by the Mayor were not, one fears, carried out exactly ; we know by sad experience the difficulty of getting such an order or a regulation obeyed. If we look into Ogilby's map we see plainly that as regards the streets and courts, London after the Fire was very much the same as London before the Fire ; there were the same

REMAINS OF PRINCE RUPERT'S PALACE BEECH STREET
From a print published by J. Sewell Dec. 1, 1791.

narrow streets, the same crowded alleys, the same courts and yards. Take, for instance, the small area lying between Bread Street Hill on the west and Garlick Hill on the east, between Trinity Lane on the north and Thames Street on the south : is it possible to crowd more courts and alleys into this area ? Can we believe that after the Fire London was relieved of its narrow courts with this map before us ? Look at the closely-shut-in places marked on the maps, " 1 g., m. 46, m. 47, m. 48, m. 40." These are respectively, Jack Alley, Newman's Rents, Sugar Loaf Court, Three Cranes Court, and Cowden's Rents. Some of these courts survive to this day. They were formed, as the demand for land grew, by running narrow lanes between the backs of houses and swallowing up the gardens. There were 479 such courts in Ogilby's London of 1677, 472 alleys, and 172 yards, besides 128 inns, each of which, with its open courts for the standing of vehicles, and its galleries, stood retired from the street on a spot which had once been the fair garden of a citizen's house.

The projecting upper stories had disappeared ; wooden houses and thatched roofs were no longer permitted ; moreover, the hot breath of the Fire had burned up the infected soil, the noisome laystalls, and the plague-smitten churchyards ; the wreck and rubbish of the Fire had choked the wells fed from the contaminated soil : these were not, for the most part, reopened. As for the churches, we know the date of the rebuilding of every one. In 1677 there were only about twenty rebuilt out of all the eighty-seven which were burned down ; a white square space on the map indicates the site of a church not yet rebuilt.

The picturesqueness of London had been lost ; gables, projecting stories, case-ment windows gave place to a straight façade, and flat square windows with sashes. In this map of 1677 we step from the seventeenth to the eighteenth century. And the most ardent admirer of Wren will hardly aver that his cathedral and his churches were externally more beautiful, while they were much less venerable, than those which they replaced.

The demand for land and its value was shown in the curious way in which many of the churches were built. Some had houses beside and over the porch ; some against the north or south side : as, for instance, the church of St. Ethelburga, which still has houses built before the west front ; the churches of St. Peter Cornhill, St. Mary le Bow, and St. Michael, the church of St. Alphege, all hidden by houses. The old craft quarters had by this time almost disappeared.   But there were still places which continued to keep what modern tradesmen call a "line." Linen-drapers and toymen were found in Fleet Street ; here also jewellers held raffles ; mutton was sold in Newgate Market ; beef in Leadenhall ; veal at St. James's ; the cheesemongers set up their shops in Thames Street ; second-hand booksellers round Moorfields ; second-hand clothes-men in Monmouth Street : fruit was sold in Covent Garden ; mercers were always faithful to Cheapside ; bankers and money-lenders were found in Lombard Street ; milliners had stalls in the upper rooms of the Royal and the New Exchange.

The frays and feuds between the crafts, which constantly arose during the earlier centuries, had almost become things of the past : but in 1664 the weavers and the butchers reminded the elders of the good old days by one more burst of brawling and fighting. It seems strange that so peaceful a creature as the weaver came off victorious. The weavers marched triumphantly about the streets offering a hundred pounds for the production of a butcher, and the blue smocks stayed at home in the shambles of Newgate, inglorious and defeated. And a butcher, too! a man of blood and slaughter ! The streets, with the exception of Cheapside and Ludgate Hill, were not used by ladies as a place of walking and meeting. The merchants met on 'Change; the lawyers had their Inns of Court; for social and convivial purposes there were the taverns. Nor were the streets used greatly for purposes of locomotion; if a man wished to go from the Tower stairs to Blackfriars or from the Temple to Westminster, he took a boat; the Thames was, and continued until the nineteenth century, the great highway of the City; thousands of boats and barges plied up and down the river; the old ferry—the ferry of St. Mary Overies—still crossed the

St Ethelburga within Bishopsgate

From a contemporary print.

river above the bridge; that called the Horseferry still crossed the river at Westminster. It was a great deal easier and shorter to take oars than to walk, to ride, or to take a "glass coach": one of the newly invented machines which replaced the old coach, with its perforated sides for windows. No one thought it a scandal that the watermen on the river should exchange language which in these days would drive every decent man or woman from the boats for ever. It was natural that rough and coarse men, like the watermen, should use rough and coarse language. The ladies of Charles the Second's time heard coarseness unparalleled from these fellows with much the same air with which ladies of our own time pass a group of working-men energetically strengthening every assertion with the universal adjective. They hear, but they do not hear.

As we already know, shooting London Bridge was a dangerous feat except at high and low water.   Some of the boats were tilt boats, covered, that is, with a tilt or awning of canvas to keep off the rain ; they were a kind of omnibus, and ran between Greenwich and London, with other lines.   Most of them, however, were wherries of the kind which still survive, though they are now little used.   It is melancholy to look at the river of to-day above Bridge and to compare its silence and loneliness

SPECIMEN OF ARMORIAL ARCHITECTURE FROM A HOUSE IN HART STREET, CRUCHED FRIARS, TAKEN DOWN IN 1803
From a print drawn and etched in 1792 by J. T. Smith.

with the animation and bustle of two hundred years ago, when it was covered with boats taking passengers up and down the river, barges with parties, stately barges of the Mayor and the Companies, Royal barges, cargo-freighted barges, boats with anglers moored in mid stream, tilt boats, sailing boats, and every conceivable kind of small craft.   When the Queen came down from Hampton Court ten thousand boats accompanied her.

We read a great deal about the insanitary condition of the City, the narrow lanes, the projecting storeys nearly meeting at the top, the laystalls and the stinking heaps of offal and refuse, which were not abolished by the Fire but only burnt up. No doubt these things were bad; probably they contributed to the spread of the Plague. However, the City was as healthy as any town in the world, as cities then went; it stood upon a broad tidal river which swept up a fresh wind with every tide —twice a day; the City was less than half a mile in breadth, and on all sides it was surrounded by open spaces and broad moorland. Fresh pure air on every side, without a town to speak of for twenty miles around. Moreover it stood upon a hill, or many hills; the ground sloped to the river and to the two streams; the climate had always been rainy, and the rain washed the streets and carried away the decaying matter.

There were public latrines in the streets and cesspools at the back of every house; carts went about for the collection and removal of things which require removal; they emptied their contents sometimes in the river, unless they were stopped; sometimes in "laystalls," of which there continued to be many outside the walls. One need do no more than indicate the sanitary condition of a great town without any sewers.

Pepys, in one of his observations upon the effects of the Fire, says that the Royal Exchange "is now made pretty" by having windows and doors before all the shops to keep off the cold. So that before 1666 the shops in the Royal Exchange were mere stalls open to the cold and wind. This, I take it, was the condition of nearly all the shops at that time; they had no doors, and if any glass in front, then only in the upper parts.

MANNERS AND CUSTOMS

CHAPTER I

FOOD AND DRINK

In considering the manners and customs of London during the seventeenth century we are met with the difficulty that a long civil war, followed by a visitation of Plague and a dreadful Fire, cuts the periods into two parts, and that after the war is over and the King restored we find great changes, in religious thought and ideas, in manners and customs, in society and fashions. The seventeenth corresponds in this respect with the nineteenth century; in our own time we have emerged out of eighteenth-century ideas, which prevailed until displaced by the silent though rapid revolution of the Victorian age. In the seventeenth century there is a similar revolution, but violent and created by the sword.

The City of 1670, as we have seen by our study of the map, resembled in very few details the London of 1640. We must endeavour to bear that point very carefully in mind. And if we take the latter, rather than the former half of the century for consideration, it is because the former half offers little change from the London of Queen Elizabeth.

The rents of houses varied, of course, with the site and the size. It would appear that for £30 a year one could rent a house of moderate size in any but the most expensive parts of the town. On Ludgate Hill or in Cheapside the rents were a great deal higher.

Of the furniture in such a house I have an inventory belonging to the year 1680. There were four bedrooms. One of these, the principal room, was furnished with a carved bedstead, which had a canopy and a valence; curtains, a looking-glass, and four chairs. The other three bedrooms were less splendidly furnished. There was, however, a plentiful supply of blankets, pillows, bolsters, and feather beds. There were two parlours. One of these was hung with tapestry; curtains of green cloth and a green carpet adorned it; it contained two tables, a clock case, a leather chair, a plush chair, six green cloth chairs, and two green stools. There was a cupboard and one of the tables had a drawer. The other parlour was more simply furnished, and was hung with grey linsey woolsey and gilt leather.

Carpets were advertised for sale in 1660; they were Turkey carpets and intended for the cover of tables; for the floors there was matting in those houses where rushes were not still used. Oil-cloth was introduced about the same time; made "after the German manner" either of linen, cloth, taffeta, or wool.

House in Great St Helens formerly the Residence of St Jno Lawrance Lord Mayor of London A.D. 1665

From a print published by J. Sewell, Feb. 1, 1796.

Hangings of leather and of velvet were commonly used; the furniture with tables not laid on trestles but provided with carved and decorated supports; chairs with inlaid work and carving richly upholstered; couches, sideboards, stools, all carved; paintings richly framed hanging from the walls show a great advance on the Tudor time.

The inventory of the kitchen shows that pewter was the material commonly used for plates and dishes. There is no mention of china ware. Probably it was kept for the use of the master and mistress in the parlour cupboard. There are wooden platters, pewter candlesticks and pewter pint pots. And there is no mention of forks. Yet forks by that time were well known. In 1652 Heylin speaks of "the use of silver forks which is by some of our spruce gallants taken up of late." It would seem, therefore, that twenty-five years later they had not got into general use.

The family took breakfast at eight. The meal consisted of cold meat, small beer, and oat cake. This was not an invariable rule. Pepys once breakfasts off bread and butter, sweetmeats, and strong wine; on another occasion he has oysters, anchovies, and neats' tongues. When Cosmo, Duke of Tuscany, visited England he had breakfast with a country gentleman, and it consisted almost entirely of Italian wine. Archbishop Sancroft used to take two cups of coffee and a pipe of tobacco. A learned physician recommended for breakfast two poached eggs, bread and butter, and a cup of claret.

The amount of small beer consumed in every household was enormous. It must be remembered that it was not only the national beverage, but, for a great many people, the only beverage. Children drank it as well as adults; tea was as yet only a luxury or a fashion. The household of which I am speaking drank three quarts of beer a day for every member. It seems impossible. We must remember, however, that people drank a great deal more then than now—a thing of which I have no direct proof, yet of which I am perfectly satisfied; that breakfast, dinner, and supper would easily account for two quarts, and the remaining quart was spread over the rest of the day. Benjamin Franklin's fellows in the printing office drank each his three quarts a day.

Ale, of which there were various kinds, and wine were served in the best parlour at dinner. On the variety of drinks Chamberlayne speaks :—

"Since the late Rebellion, England hath abounded in variety of Drinks (as it did lately in variety of Religions) above any nation in Europe. Besides all sorts of the best wines from Spain, France, Italy, Germany, there are sold in London above twenty sorts of other Drinks, as Brandy, Coffee, Chocolate, Tee, Aromatick, Mum, Sider, Perry, Mede, Metheglin, Beer, Ale, many sorts of Ales, very different, as Cock, Stepony, Stich-back, Hull, North-Devon, Sambidge, Betony, Scurvy-grass, Sage-Ale, Colledge-Ale, etc., a piece of wantonness whereof none of our Ancestors were ever guilty."

Howell sends a bottle of Metheglin to a friend with a recommendation to use it for a morning draught. What were the heads of our seventeenth-century ancestors made of that they could drink this heavy, powerful stuff before breakfast?

"To inaugurate a good and jovial New Year to you, I send you a morning's draught, viz. a bottle of Metheglin. Neither Sir John Barleycorn or Bacchus had anything to do with it; but it is the pure juice of the Bee, the laborious Bee, and King of Insects. The Druids and old British Bards were wont to take a Carouse hereof before they entered into their Speculations; and if you do so when your Fancy labours with any thing, it will do you no Hurt, and I know your Fancy to be very good.

But this Drink always carries a kind of State with it, for it must be attended with a brown Toast; nor will it admit but of one good Draught, and that in the morning; if more, it will keep a-humming in the head, and so speak too much of the House it comes from, I mean the Hive, as I gave a caution elsewhere."

Let us go on to repeat an observation forced upon us in every age, that London has always been a great place for good living. We learn from Pepys what a profusion of food was offered at a dinner given at his own house. The quantity of food habitually taken was much greater then than now. People got up earlier; though they took little exercise for the sake of exercise, yet they were in the open air a great deal; on the river quiescent; in the gardens sitting, strolling, or playing bowls; they all grew sleek and fat. These people had probably taken very little breakfast, a few radishes, a draught of small ale or claret, a piece of bread. The hour of dinner had advanced; it was now served at one o'clock, or sometimes at two; it was the principal event of the day. Food was simpler and less composed of made dishes than in the days of Whittington and Picard. We find served roast chicken, veal, mutton and beef, tongue, salmon, stewed carp, pies of goose, fish, turkey, eels, and everything else. The people served their dinner in courses, each course being, in fact, after the ancient custom, a complete dinner in itself. There was a great deal of dining together, as Pepys lets us see continually, and after dinner they sat and talked and drank. In the matter of drink they were catholic. It does not seem that the merchants did much business after dinner, for then began the time of rest, recreation, and drinking; then came the theatre or the tavern, later on the coffee-house, though in the evening Pepys, who was an industrious official, got through a good deal of work.

Fresh meat was scarce, and even impossible to get, in the winter. In the country, and perhaps in town as well, housewives had to lay in a great stock of beef for pickling; it was bought in pieces and in quantities of 70 lbs. at a time for the pickling tub; salt beef was the standard winter dish, garnished with a great quantity of parsnips as a corrective. Children and servants had no forks; small beer was brewed at home, and gentlemen thought no more of a pint of wine than working men think now of a pint of beer.

The fashion of putting the dinner on the table at once began to be changed soon after the Restoration, when the dishes were presented one after the other in some sort of order; but I find in boarding-houses and in private houses, long after this, the custom of putting everything on the table at the same time.

At dinner the women sat together at the upper end and helped every one, conversing freely the while.

We find some excellent specimens of dinners in the *Diary* of Pepys. Here is the menu of a grand dinner (April 4, 1665):—

"A Fricasse of rabbits and chickens, a leg of mutton boiled, three carps on a dish, a great dish of a side of a lamb, a dish of roasted pigeons, a dish of four lobsters, three tarts, a lamprey pie (a most rare pie), a dish of anchovies, good wine of several sorts, and all things mighty noble and to my great content."

About prices I find that a leg of mutton cost half-a-crown; a hand of pork eighteenpence; butter was eightpence a pound; sugar, sixpence; candles, fivepence; bacon, sevenpence; rice, sevenpence; tea was sixty shillings a pound. They seem to have had all our vegetables, all our fruit, and all our spices. But the fruit lasted only a short time; oranges appeared at Christmas, but were then unripe and sour; they lasted till April or May; strawberries lasted three or four weeks; cherries about the same time. They knew how to preserve fruit for a short time; and they pickled everything, including nasturtium buds, lime-tree buds, and elder roots. In the stillroom the housewife made wine out of cowslips, gooseberries, raspberries, and any kind of fruit; she also made certain cordials and strong waters; and she made plague water, hysterical water, fever water, and many other efficacious remedies in case of need.

The supper, of which very little is said, was served at five or six; it was, like breakfast, a mere informal stay. Cold meat with a "sallet," a tankard of strong ale, and a pipe of tobacco generally formed this meal.

As additional notes on food, one may note that asparagus was common, but as yet very dear; goose-pie was a favourite dish; buttered shrimps were also much in demand; vinegar and pepper were taken with roast beef; the potato was in use since the year 1586, but as yet by no means universally known; roast mutton was stuffed with oysters; young peacock was a stately dish, served only on great occasions; oysters were stewed with white wine; pigeons were stuffed, in the season, with green gooseberries; radishes were taken with meat as a salad; grapes were boiled in butter and served with sips of bread and sugar; turkey was stuffed with cloves; hot salmon was thought unwholesome; dates were put into broth; they used habitually mushrooms, sorrel, capers, and snails.

When a man gave a great dinner, he did not expect it to be prepared at home but ordered it at the cooks' shops, whence it was carried through the streets in a kind of triumphal procession, a server with an apron and a white cap going before. The fiddlers and the trumpeters went the round of the cooks' shops every day in order to learn where their services might be accepted.

In Howell's *Letters* we read how, on one occasion, he finds a cook for a lady, and thus describes his qualities :—

"You spoke to me for a Cook who had seen the World abroad, and I think the Bearer hereof will suit your Ladyship's Turn. He can marinate Fish, make Gellies; he is excellent for a piquant Sauce and the Haugot; besides, Madam, he is passing good for an Olla. He will tell your Ladyship that the reverend Matron the *Olla Podrida* hath Intellectuals and Senses; Mutton, Beef, and Bacon are to her as the Will, Understanding, and Memory are to the Soul; Cabbage, Turneps, Artichokes, Potatoes and Dates are her five senses, and Pepper the Common-sense; she must have Marrow to keep Life in her, and some Birds to make her light ; by all means she must go adorned with Chains of Sausages.   He is also good at larding Meat after the Mode of France."

The reign of the tavern still continued.   Most of the citizens frequented the tavern every day.   It was complained that the tradesman, who ought to have been in his shop, too often spent his mornings in the tavern, leaving his shop to the care of his 'prentices.   There were many men in London who, being visitors, strangers, unmarried, or houseless, habitually took their dinner at the tavern.

The ordinary price for dinners at a tavern was a shilling, but one might pay a great deal more ; dinners could be ordered for five shillings, or even ten shillings a head.   The most fashionable tavern was Locket's at Charing Cross, where is now

TAVERN SCENE
From a ballad in the Roxburgh Collection.

Drummond's Bank.   Adam Locket started his tavern in the reign of Charles the Second ; he died in 1688, and was succeeded by his son, Edward Locket.   It was a very famous tavern.   Cunningham quotes a column and a half of contemporary mention of Locket's house.   Here is one from Price and Montague, *The Hind and Panther, Transversed :—*

> " Come, at a crown a head ourselves we'll treat,
> Champagne our liquor and ragouts our meat ;
> Thus hand in hand we'll go to court, dear cuz,
> To visit Bishop Martin and King Buz ;
> With evening wheels we'll drive about the Park,
> Finish at Locket's and reel home i' th' dark."

It can hardly be pretended that tea was a national drink in the seventeenth century. It was not even a fashionable beverage.   It was offered as a curious foreign drink, being prepared with great care and according to rule, and taken with a certain amount of anxiety as to the possible consequences.   Precautions were taken against these consequences.   Thus in Congreve's *Way of the World*, Mrs. Millicent's lover allows her to be "Sole Empress of her tea-table," a reservation which sufficiently indicates the want of confidence in the beverage, and she must promise to banish from the table "orange brandy, aniseed, cinnamon, citron and Barbadoes water, together with ratafia and the most noble spirit of clary." The price of tea, which was then about fifty shillings a pound, though it rapidly went down, prevented any but the rich from taking it. Long after this it is noticed that the City ladies took brandy after their tea as a corrective. The earliest mention of tea in this country is an advertisement in the *Mercurius Politicus* of 1658, which is as follows :—

"That excellent, and by all physicians approved, China drink, called by the Chineans Tcha, by other nations Tay, alias Tee, is sold at the Sultaness Head Coffee-House, in Sweeting's Rents, by the Royal Exchange, London."

And Thomas Garway or Garraway at the same time issued a broadside in which he offers tea to the public at sixteen shillings to fifty shillings the pound and proclaims its virtues :—

"The Quality is moderately hot, proper for winter or summer. The drink is declared to be most wholesome, preserving in perfect health until extreme old age. The particular virtues are these. It maketh the body active and lusty. It helpeth the headache, giddiness and heaviness thereof. It removeth the obstructions of the spleen. It is very good against the stone and gravel. . . . It taketh away the difficulty of breathing, opening obstructions. It is good against lippitude distillations, and cleareth the sight. It removeth lassitude, and cleanseth and purifieth adust humours and a hot liver. It is good against crudities, strengthening the weakness of the stomach, causing good appetite and digestion, and particularly for men of a corpulent body, and such as are great eaters of flesh. It vanquisheth heavy dreams, easeth the brain, and strengtheneth the memory. It overcometh superfluous sleep, and prevents sleepiness in general, a draught of the infusion being taken, so that, without trouble, whole nights may be spent in study without hurt to the body. It prevents and cures agues, surfeits, and fevers by infusing a fit quantity of the leaf, thereby provoking a most gentle vomit and breathing of the pores, and hath been given with wonderful success. It (being prepared and drunk with milk and water) strengtheneth the inward parts and prevents consumptions. . . . It is good for colds, dropsies, and scurvies, and expelleth infection. . . . And that the virtue and excellence of the leaf and drink are many and great is evident and manifest by the high esteem and use of it (especially of late years) by the physicians and knowing men of France, Italy, Holland, and other parts of Christendom, and in England it hath been sold in the leaf for six pounds, and sometimes for ten pounds the pound-weight ; and in respect of its former scarceness and dearness, it hath been only used as a regalia in high treatments and entertainments, and presents made thereof to princes and grandees till the year 1657" (Chambers's *Book of Days*, vol. ii. p. 666).

Rugge's *Diurnal* says that tea was sold in every street in London in 1659. That statement we cannot believe, especially when we are reminded that a couple of pounds was a present fit for the King to receive. A couple of pounds of a commodity sold in every street in London? On the contrary, there is every kind of evidence that in the seventeenth century tea was perhaps the fashion, but never became a national beverage. Pepys mentions it once or twice, but tea formed no part of his ordinary diet. Evelyn, I believe, does not mention it at all. In the winter of 1683-1684 the Thames was frozen over, and in the fair that was held upon the river, tea, among other things, was sold. No one, I think, ever imagined that tea would become the national beverage, excluding beer from breakfast and from the afternoon meal. A learned physician, Dr. Lister, writing at the close of the century, says that tea and coffee "are permitted by God's Providence for lessening the number of mankind by shortening life, as a kind of silent plague." Many attacks were made upon the tea-table. It took men away from the pipe and bottle; it brought together men and women inclined for vice and gave them an opportunity; it was very costly; it offered a drink only fit for women; it destroyed the strength of man and the beauty of woman. The hostility to tea lingered during the whole of the eighteenth century.

In 1652 the first coffee-house was opened in St. Michael's Alley, Cornhill, by one Pasqua Rosee, a native of Ragusa, servant to a Turkey merchant who brought him from Smyrna. Coffee had been introduced into Oxford a little earlier. The following is a copy of Rosee's handbill (see Chambers's *Book of Days*, vol. i. p. 170):—

THE VERTUE OF THE COFFEE DRINK

First made and publickly sold in England by Pasqua Rosee.

"The grain or berry called coffee, groweth upon iittle trees only in the deserts of Arabia. It is brought from thence, and drunk generally throughout all the Grand Seignour's dominions. It is a simple, innocent thing, composed into a drink, by being dried in an oven, and ground to powder, and boiled up with spring water, and about half a pint of it to be drunk fasting an hour before, and not eating an hour after, and to be taken as hot as possibly can be endured; the which will never fetch the skin off the mouth, or raise any blisters by reason of that heat.

The Turks' drink at meals and other times is usually water, and their diet consists much of fruit; the crudities whereof are very much corrected by this drink.

The quality of this drink is cold and dry; and though it be drier, yet it neither heats, nor inflames more than hot posset. It so incloseth the orifice of the stomach, and fortifies the heat within, that it is very good to help digestion; and therefore of great use to be taken about three or four o'clock afternoon, as well as in the morning. It much quickens the spirits, and makes the heart lightsome; it is good against sore eyes, and the better if you hold your head over it and take in the steam that way. It suppresseth fumes exceedingly, and therefore is good against the head-ache, and will very much stop any defluxion of rheums, that distil from the head upon the stomach, and so prevent and help consumptions and the cough of the lungs.

It is excellent to prevent and cure the dropsy, gout, and scurvy. It is known by experience to be better than any other drying drink for people in years, or children that have any running humours upon them, as the king's evil, etc. It is a most excellent remedy against the spleen, hypochondriac winds, and the like. It will prevent drowsiness, and make one fit for business, if one have occasion to watch, and therefore you are not to drink of it after supper, unless you intend to be watchful, for it will hinder sleep for three or four hours.

It is observed that in Turkey, where this is generally drunk, that they are not troubled with the stone, gout, dropsy, or scurvy, and that their skins are exceeding clear and white. It is neither laxative nor restringent.

Made and sold in St. Michael's Alley in Cornhill, by Pasqua Rosee, at the sign of his own head."

Evelyn (writing of the year 1637) says :—

"There came in my tyme to the Coll : one Nathaniel Couopios out of Greece from Cyrill the Patriarch of Constantinople who, returning many years afterwards was made (as I understand) Bishop of Smyrna. He was the first man I ever saw drink coffee, which custom came not into England for thirty years after."

The coffee-houses, thus begun, multiplied rapidly. The new drink, which did not intoxicate, became popular ; the coffee-houses were places where men could sit and talk without getting drunk ; it was a cheap amusement, and, in a time of great political agitation and excitement, the coffee-house became a power of immense influence. For this reason the Government became alarmed, and, in 1675, endeavoured to suppress the new institution. The attempt was a failure. The coffee-houses were already the favourite meeting-places of men of all professions and of all opinions. In the graver places where physicians, divines, and responsible merchants met, the conversation was serious over coffee and tobacco. In other coffee-houses the company were diverted with songs, music, and even tumbling.

Some of the coffee-houses offered the attraction of a museum of curiosities, probably things brought from the East by sailors.

I have before me one of the earliest tracts on the subject of coffee. It is a doggerel poem dated 1665, called "The Character of a Coffee-House." How is one to know a coffee-house ? By the signs :—

> "And if you see the great Morat
> With Shash on's head instead of hat,
> Or any *Sultan* in his dress,
> Or picture of a *Sultaness*,
> Or *John's* admired curl'd pate,
> Or th' great *Mogul* in's Chair of State,
> Or *Constantine* the *Grecian*,
> Who fourteen years was th' only man
> That made *Coffee* for th' great *Bashaw*,
> Although the man he never saw :
> Or if you see a *Coffee*-cup
> Filled from a Turkish pot, hung up
> Within the clouds, and round it *Pipes*,
> *Wax candles*, *Stoppers*, these are types
> And certain signs (with many more
> Would be too long to write them 'ore),
> Which plainly do Spectators tell
> That in that house they *Coffee* sell.
> Some wiser than the rest (no doubt),
> Say they can by the smell find't out ;
> In at a door (say they), but thrust
> Your Nose, and if you scent *burnt Crust*,
> Be sure there's *Coffee* sold that's good,
> For so by most 'tis understood."

What are the benefits conferred by coffee ? The coffee-man tells you :—

> " But if you ask, what good does Coffee ?
> He'll answer, Sir, don't think I scoff yee,
> If I affirm there's no disease
> Men have that drink it but find ease.
> Look, there's a man who takes the steam
> In at his Nose, has an extreme

> Worm in his pate, and giddiness,
> Ask him and he will say no less.
> There sitteth one whose Droptick belly
> Was hard as flint, now's soft as jelly.
> There stands another holds his head
> 'Ore th' Coffee-pot, was almost dead
> Even now with Rhume ; ask him hee'll say
> That all his Rhum's now past away.
> See, there's a man sits now demure
> And sober, was within this hour
> Quite drunk, and comes here frequently,
> For 'tis his daily Mady.
> More, it has such reviving power
> 'Twill keep a man awake an houre,
> Nay, make his eyes wide open stare
> Both Sermon time and all the prayer."

The company are next treated at length. There are the usurer, the furiosol, the virtuoso, the player, the country clown, the pragmatick, the phanatick, the knight, the mechanick, the dealer in old shoes, one in an ague, the Frenchman, the Dutchman, the Spaniard :—

> " Here in a corner sits a Phrantick,
> And there stands by a frisking Antick.
> Of all sorts some, and all conditions,
> E'en Vintners, Surgeons, and Physicians.
> The blind, the deaf, the aged cripple
> Do here resort and coffee tipple."

The chocolate-house was another place of resort. It was noted for its decorations, being not only beautifully painted and gilt, but also provided with looking-glasses all round the room. But as yet the people were afraid of taking even a cup of chocolate without a dram to fortify the stomach. " Bring in," says the gallant, "two dishes of chocolate and a glass of cinnamon water." And the City ladies, if they invited friends to a tea-drinking, finished with cordials to counteract any bad effects.

The use of tobacco had by this time become universal. Sorbière says that men spent half their time over tobacco. Even women and children smoked pipes ; some men took tobacco and pipes to bed with them in case of being sleepless. I find in one of Howell's Letters a dissertation on the use of tobacco, which is more instructive than any other contemporary document :—

" To usher in again old Janus, I send you a parcel of Indian perfume, which the Spaniard calls the Holy Herb, in regard of the various Virtues it hath ; but we call it Tobacco ; I will not say it grew under the King of Spain's Window, but I am told it was gathered near his Gold-Mines of Potosi (where they report, that in some Places there is more of that Ore than Earth), therefore it must needs be precious Stuff; if moderately and seasonably taken (as I find you always do) 'tis good for many Things; it helps Digestion, taken a-while after Meat ; a leaf or two being steeped o'er Night in a little White-wine is a Vomit that never fails in its Operations; it is a good Companion to one that converseth with dead Men ; for if one hath been poring long upon a book, or is toil'd with the Pen, and stupify'd with study, it quickeneth him, and dispels those Clouds that usually o'erset the Brain. The smoke of it is one of the wholesomest scents that is, against all contagious Airs, for it o'er-masters all other smells, as King James, they say, found true, when being once a Hunting, a Shower of Rain drove him into a Pigsty for Shelter, where he caus'd a Pipeful to be taken on purpose; It cannot endure a Spider or a Flea, with such like Vermin, and if your Hawk be troubled with any such being blown into his feathers, it frees him; it is good to fortify and to preserve the sight, the smoke being let in round about the Balls of the Eyes once a week, and frees them from all rheums, driving them back by way of Repurcussion; being taken backward 'tis excellent good against the Cholic, and taken into the Stomach, it will heat and cleanse it; for I could instance in a great Lord (my Lord of Sunderland, President of York) who told me that he taking it downward into his Stomach, it made him cast up an Imposthume, Bag and all, which had been a long time engendering out of a Bruise he had received at Foot-ball, and so preserv'd his life for many years. Now to descend from the substance of the smoke to the ashes, 'tis well known that the medicinal virtues thereof are very many; but they are so common, that I will spare the inserting of them here; but if one would try a pretty conclusion, how much smoke there is in a Pound of Tobacco, the Ashes will tell him; for let a pound be exactly weighed, and the ashes kept charily, and weighed afterwards, what wants of a Pound Weight in the Ashes cannot be deny'd to have been smoke, which evaporated into Air. I have been told that Sir Walter Raleigh won a Wager of Queen Elizabeth upon this Nicety.

The Spaniards and Irish take it most in powder or smutchin, and it mightily refreshes the Brain, and I believe there's as much taken this way in Ireland, as there is in Pipes in England; one shall commonly see the serving-maid upon the washing-block, and the swain upon the plough-share, when they are tired with Labour, take out their boxes of Smutchin, and draw it into their Nostrils with a Quill, and it will beget new spirits in them, with a fresh Vigor to fall to their Work again. In Barbary, and other parts of Africk, it is wonderful what a small pill of Tobacco will do; for those who used to ride post through the sandy Deserts, where they meet not with anything that's potable or edible, sometimes three Dayes together, they use to carry small Balls or Pills of Tobacco, which being put under the Tongue, it affords them a perpetual Moisture, and takes off the Appetite for some days."

CHAPTER II

DRESS AND MANNERS

On the homely subject of washing an excellent little paper may be found in Chambers's *Book of Days.* What were the "things" put out for the lavender or laundress? The common people wore neither shirts nor socks nor any under-

From contemporary engravings by Hollar.

clothing at all. Towels, napkins, table-cloths, sheets, pillow-cases, were the things that were washed, in all houses except the very poorest; the mediæval inventories of furniture show that pillows and cushions were much used in every house. Of personal things linen shirts were not anciently worn even by great and rich nobles;

they wore their splendid velvets and silks next to the skin ; the poor man was dressed in black coarse woollen with, if he were fortunate, some kind of cloak : there were no night-shirts. When ladies began to use night-dresses they were of costly material which would not wash. Anne Boleyn slept in a night-dress of black satin, bound with black taffeta and edged with black velvet. Queen Elizabeth slept in velvet lined in fur.

A " Washing Tally " preserved at Haddon Hall, supposed to be of Charles the First's time, enumerates all the different articles then sent to the wash. They were ruffles, bandes, cuffes, " handkercher," caps, shirts, half-shirts, boot-hose, tops, socks, sheets, pillow-cases, table-cloths, napkins, and towels.

Most of these names require no explanation. The band was the white collar round the neck, which was either starched to stand up or else it lay upon the shoulders. The box that kept them was called a band-box. Boot-hose were like "tights" of the present day, drawn up the whole length of the leg. The sock, sometimes embroidered, was drawn over the hose to the calf of the leg. It was customary when the washing was done at home for the women to begin at midnight or very early in the morning. Pepys complains of being disturbed in the night by the laundresses. The basket in which the linen was thrown was called the " buck " or the " buck-basket."

The Puritanic fashions of dress, manners, and speech still continued in the City. While the Court party wore their hair long and curled, the Puritans cropped theirs close ; they drawled in their speech ; they interlarded their discourse with texts and allusions to Scripture ; they still, though the power had gone from them, denounced all sorts of merry-makings, all sports, all festivals and games as damnable ; still they continued to find their chief joy and solace at a sermon. There was reason for this ; for while their thoughts were mainly occupied with twisting texts into the support of their favourite doctrines, the preacher, who was engaged in exactly the same pursuit, gave them materials for the maintenance of their doctrines, or for discussion and controversy afterwards. The women, it is said, took down the principal points in shorthand, being as much interested and as keen in controversy as the men.

I do not know any period in which it could not be said that the dress of the gallants and courtiers, as well as that of the ladies, was not extravagant and costly. Certainly the dress of the gallants in the seventeenth century, except for the fifteen years of Puritan austerity, was costly and extravagant enough to please any one. It does not appear, however, that the extravagance in dress descended to the City or to the City madams. In the time of Elizabeth the excessive adornment of the latter was the subject of many satirical pens. Under Charles II. the sobriety of the men, still more or less under Puritan influence, was reflected in the quiet dress of the women. As for the Court ladies, Evelyn observes that they paint ; Pepys finds patches coming in with the Restoration ; he also notices, but without admiration, the hair frizzed up to the ears; in 1662 he says they began to wear perukes—by which I understand some addition to their own hair; next year he observes the introduction of the vizard. In July 1663 he witnesses the riding of the King, Queen, and Court in Hyde Park. "The King and the Queen, who looked in this dress, a white-laced waistcoat and a crimson short petticoat, with her hair dressed *à la négligence*, mighty pretty, and the King rode hand in hand with her. Here was also my Lady Castlemaine [who] rode among the rest of the ladies: but the King took, methought, no notice of her. . . . She looked mighty out of humour, and had a yellow plume in her hat, which all took notice of, and yet is very handsome. . . . I followed them up into

From contemporary engravings by Hollar.

Whitehall and into the Queen's presence, where all the ladies walked, talking and fiddling with their hats and feathers, and changing and trying one another's by one another's head and laughing. . . . But above all Mrs. Stewart in this dress, with her hat cocked and a red plume, with her sweet eye, little Roman nose and excellent taille, is now the greatest beauty I ever saw, I think, in my life."

I do not propose to dwell upon the changes of fashion, because the alterations in a sleeve, or in the length of a lady's waist, would carry us too far and would be of little profit. But there was one change in fashion which one must not pass over, because it exercised an influence upon the whole national character. This was the introduction of the peruke, perruque, or wig. Ladies began to wear wigs, presumably, as they do now, to conceal the ravages of time, and the falling off of the natural hair. Malcolm is of opinion that the wig was a natural reaction against the Roundhead rule.

For the Roundheads cropped their hair and the Cavaliers wore it long in curls. Therefore, he who had a scanty supply of curls, or was bald, to escape being taken for one of the opposite camp, put on a wig; next he excited envy by the fulness and length of his curls; finally all wore wigs, and the fashion set in which lasted a hundred years, and, as regards the clergy, for nearly two hundred years. A good deal might be said for the use of a wig. It was, to begin with, an age when the heads of all the lower classes, servants and working people, were always filled with vermin—one learns that even so late as a hundred years ago it was almost impossible

From contemporary engravings by Hollar.

to keep the children of quite respectable people clean in this respect. Next, the time and trouble of having the head dressed and the curls twisted—for not even a Cavalier could always depend upon a natural curl—were saved by sending the wig to the hairdresser. Again, when everybody wore a shaven face, the adoption of the wig went far to conceal and disguise one's age. Baldness there was none, no rany grey hairs. A man generally had two wigs; a new wig of ordinary make cost about three guineas, but one might pay a great deal more for a superior wig. "Forty guineas a year," cries an indignant writer, "for periwigs, and but ten to a poor chaplain." The wigs were at first an imitation of a man's own hair in colour, with some exaggeration in length; and although cleanliness was one reason for their introduction, they had to be sent to the barbers occasionally in order to be freed from vermin. After the Plague, for a long time, nobody would buy a wig for fear of infection. The fashion was, of course, carried to ridiculous lengths; Lord

Foppington, in the *Relapse*, is said to have a periwig down to his knees ; he also says that a periwig should be to a man like a mask to a woman ; nothing should be seen but his eyes." The various kinds of wig belong to the eighteenth century, in which they are treated more fully.

The following are a few more scattered notes on fashion :—

Both men and women carried pocket mirrors ; the women had these dangling from their girdles ; the men carried them in their hands or in their pockets, and sometimes stuck them in their hats.

It was one of the affectations of the time for the gallants to go abroad with their faces half covered by their cloaks and their hats drawn down. Hence the stage custom of throwing the cloak across from the right to the left.

The coats of inferior functionaries, such as bailiffs or catchpoles, were adorned with pewter buttons.

A country gentleman's dress consisted of Devonshire Kersey suit, coarse cloth coat, Dutch felt hat, worsted stockings, and neat leather shoes.

All craftsmen wore aprons, but these were different ; the blacksmith had a leathern apron, the grocer a white apron, the vintner a blue apron, and so on. One could formerly recognise a man's trade by his dress and appearance.

I find that this century introduced the use of the nightcap, perhaps for the sake of quiet, because, with the bawling of the watchman, the cry of the chimney-sweep, and the noise of the laundresses, who began about midnight, there was almost as much noise at night as by day.

If men disfigured themselves with wigs, the women heightened their charms, as they believed, by sticking little bits of black taffeta on their faces. The fashion began in the Commonwealth, when ladies began to cut out stars, circles, and even figures representing a coach and four, and stick them upon their cheek, forehead, or chin :—

> " Her patches are of every cut,
>   For pimples and for scars ;
> Here's all the wandering planets' signs,
>   And some of the fixed stars."

Like the fashion of the wig, the patch lasted more than a hundred years. Indeed, it lasted even into the nineteenth century. And in 1826, a lady, speaking of a toilet-table, speaks of the patch-boxes upon it. This proves, I take it, that the patch - box still retained its position on the table, though the use of it had been abandoned. I have one of these patch-boxes ; it is of silver, about the same size as a snuff-box, but a great deal deeper.

Ladies painted as well as patched. They prepared their faces for the paint with oil. The page—*The Silent Woman*—says that " my lady kisses me with her oil'd face and puts a peruke on my head." They seem all to have worn a peruke. Mrs. Otter, according to her husband, has a peruke " like a pound of hemp, made up in shoe threads." They understood the art of making up. "Her teeth were made on the Blackfriars, both her eyebrows in the Strand, and her hair in Silver Street. . . . She takes herself asunder when she goes to bed into some twenty boxes; and about noon next day is put together again like a great German clock."

In walking with a lady the custom was to take her fan and play with it for her. A fine gentleman displayed his fashion and his grace by the way he handled and waved the fan.

There was a pretty custom observed by gentlefolk on the 1st of May. The maypoles had been restored, but the old dances were well-nigh forgotten. The

From contemporary engravings by Hollar.

people on this day flocked to Hyde Park; but gentlemen escorted their mistresses into the country to bid welcome to the spring. There was always a collation in the seventeenth century to mark the day or the function, whichever it was.

Kissing was as common as shaking hands. When a man was introduced to a lady he kissed her; men kissed each other. In 1667 Pepys, having made a successful speech, was complimented by Mr. Montagu, who kissed him. It appears that husbands and lovers were not always pleased at this indiscriminate kissing, and there are instances where the ladies rebelled against the custom.

The day of St. Valentine was universally observed. Everybody chose, or received by lot, a valentine. On the eve of the 14th of February the bachelors and maidens assembled together in equal companies; each wrote his or her name on a paper. These were rolled up; the men drew the girls' names, the girls the men's.

This arrangement gave an opening for some choice, because everybody had the girl whose name he had drawn and the girl who had drawn his name. These matters settled, and every man having his Valentine chosen or assigned, it became the duty of the man to make a present to the girl and to treat her as if she was indeed his mistress. In Pepys's *Diary*, however, it is apparent that married men might have their wives for Valentines and that children might have married women. Pepys had his wife for a Valentine two years running. In the first he gave her £5, in the second a Turkey stone set with diamonds. Poets wrote Valentines. Thus in 1629 J. Howell wrote the following pretty lines to his Valentine :—

"Could I charm the Queen of Love
To lend a quill of her white Dove ;
Or one of Cupid's pointed wings
Dipt in the fair Castalian Springs ;
　　Then would I write the all-divine
　　Perfections of my Valentine.

As 'mongst all Flow'rs the Rose excels,
As amber 'mongst the fragrant'st smells,
As 'mongst all Minerals the Gold,
As marble 'mongst the finest Mould,
As Diamonds 'mongst jewels bright,
As Cynthia 'mongst the lesser Lights ;
　　So 'mongst the Northern Beauties shine,
　　So far excels my Valentine.

In Rome and Naples I did view
Faces of Celestial Hue ;
Venetian Dames I have seen many
(I only saw them, touch'd not any),
Of Spanish Beauties, Dutch and French,
I have beheld the Quintessence ;
　　Yet I saw none that could outshine
　　Or parallel my Valentine.

The Italians they are coy and quaint,
But they grosly daub and paint ;
The Spanish Kind are apt to please,
But sav'ring of the same Disease ;
Of Dutch and French some few are comely,
The French are light, the Dutch are homely.
　　Let Tagus, Po, and Loire and Rhine,
　　Then veil unto my Valentine.

Here may be seen pure white and red,
Not by feign's Art, but Nature wed,
No simp'ring Smiles, no mimic Face,
Affecture Gesture, or forc'd Grace,
A fair smooth front, free from least Wrinkle,
Her eyes (on me) like Stars do twinkle ;
　　Thus all perfections do combine
　　To beautify my Valentine."

The May Day observances, revived with the Restoration, were duly honoured. The milkmaids and the sweeps paraded the streets with music. The old custom of going out into the fields to gather May dew was kept up, though one imagines in a formal way only, and not to let good old customs decay. On New Year's Day presents were made by inferiors to their patrons, by tenants to the nobles, by the nobles to the King.

The observance of Queen Elizabeth's Day is described in the following letter from John Verney to Sir Ralph Verney, November 20, 1679 :—

"Monday being Queen Elizabeth's coronation day there were vast quantities of bonfires about town, but chief of all was at Temple Bar, over which gate Queen Elizabeth was deck't up with a Magna Charta and the Protestant religion ; there was a devil in a pageant and 4 boys in surplices under him, 6 Jesuits, 4 bishops, 4 archbishops, 2 patriarchs of Jerusalem and Constantinople, several cardinals, besides Franciscans,

MAYPOLE DANCE IN THE TIME OF CHARLES FIRST

black and grey friars ; there was also a great crucifix, wax candles, and a bell, and 200 porters hired at 2s. a man to carry lights along with the show, which came from the Green Yard in great order thro' Moor (or Cripple) Gate, and so along London Wall, then up Houndsditch, and so on again at Aldgate, from whence to Temple Bar, where they were disrobed and burnt. 'Tis believed there were above 100,000 spectators, and most say the King was at Townes' the goldsmith's ; £10 was an ordinary price for a room at Temple Bar" (Walker's MS. xi. 186).

People of position still maintained a great many servants. In 1634 Evelyn's father was appointed Sheriff of Surrey and Sussex. He had 116 servants in livery, every one in green satin doublets. Several gentlemen and persons of quality waited on him in the same habit. He says, however, that thirty or forty was the usual retinue of a Sheriff. Pepys, in his modest house in the City, apparently had a cook and housemaid, a lady's maid, and a "girl," or general assistant. The 'prentice in the tradesman's house was as we have seen a servant, and did some of the housework. A footman followed a lady who went out into the streets in the day-time; a 'prentice escorted his mistress when she went out to a card party in the evening, or when she went to an evening lecture at her parish church.

When a man was rich enough to set up his coach, part of the furniture was a

From contemporary engravings by Hollar.

pair of running footmen; these ran before the coach. The velocity of the machine did not make this exercise a great strain upon their activity; they stopped at the next stage and proclaimed the coming of the great man. Generally they were

PROCESSION IN THE CITY
From the Crace Collection in the British Museum.

dressed in white; they carried a cane with a hollow ball at the end, in which was an orange or a lemon to refresh themselves with. When the roads became smooth and the carriages began to run much faster, the running footmen were gradually abolished.

They remained, however, till late in the eighteenth century. Howell sends a running footman to a friend. He says :—

"You writ to me lately for a Footman, and I think this Bearer will fit you ; I know he can run well, for he hath run away twice from me, but he knew the way back again. Yet tho' he had a running head as well as running heels (and who will expect a footman to be a stay's man?) I would not part with him were I not to go post to the north. There be some things in him that answer for his Waggeries ; he will come when you call him, go when you bid him, and shut the door after him ; he is faithful and stout and a lover of his master ; he is a great enemy to all dogs if they bark at him in his running, for I have seen him confront a huge mastiff and knock him down ; when you go a country journey, or have him with you a hunting, you must spirit him with liquor."

The City tradesman kept one kitchenmaid. His wife and daughters made the pies and cakes, and the preserves and the pickles. We have seen the work put upon the apprentice already (p. 186).

CHAPTER III

WEDDINGS AND FUNERALS

At weddings wheat was scattered on the head of the bride; scarves, gloves, and ribbons of the bride's colours were presented to the bridesmen; at the church the company carried rosemary; after the ceremony the bride handed the cup around; it contained "sops in wine" hallowed, and was called the knitting cup; afterwards was presented the bride cake, but not in the church; there was a great feast, as sumptuous as the bride's father could afford; the bride wore her hair on this, her last appearance as a maiden, down her back. She distributed at her wedding, bride laces. At the better houses an epithalamium was pronounced; in the case of rich people there was a masque; in all houses, rich or poor, there was music, there was bride-ale, and there was feasting. There was also fooling of various kinds, with jests not the most seemly, and forms and ceremonies not the most refined, which have long since been abandoned. Even in that time voices were lifted up against the licence of the wedding sports.

Flowers, herbs, and rushes were strewed before the footsteps of the bride on her way to church. It was unlucky if the rain fell upon a wedding, and equally unlucky if the bride failed to weep during the ceremony. The lucky days for weddings were as follows :—

Jan.	2, 4, 11, 19, 21.	July	1, 3, 12, 19, 21, 31.
Feb.	1, 3, 10, 19, 21.	Aug.	2, 11, 18, 20, 30.
March	3, 5, 12, 20, 23.	Sept.	1, 9, 11, 18, 28.
April	2, 4, 12, 20, 22.	Oct.	1, 8, 15, 17, 27, 29.
May	2, 4, 12, 20, 23.	Nov.	5, 11, 13, 22, 25.
June	1, 3, 11, 19, 21.	Dec.	1, 8, 10, 19, 23, 29.

It was unlucky to have the banns called at the end of one quarter and the marriage at the beginning of the next.

The superstitions, indeed, connected with weddings were innumerable. Let it suffice to quote Herrick in the concluding ceremony :—

"And now the yellow vaile at last
Over her fragrant cheek is cast.
  *   *   *   *
You, you, that be her nearest kin,
Now o'er the threshold force her in,
But to avert the worst
Let her, her fillets first
Knit to the posts: this point
Rememb'ring, to anoint
The sides: for 'tis a charme
Strong against future harme:
And the evil deads, the which
There was hidden by the witch."

The funeral customs are described in the following (*Antiq. Rep.* iv. 585) :—

"I met nothing more pleasing to me than the funeral ceremonies at the interment of a My Lord, which mine host procured me the sight of. The relations and friends being assembled in the house of the defunct, the minister advanced into the middle of the chamber, where, before the company, he made a funeral oration, representing the great actions of the deceased, his virtues, his qualities, his titles of nobility, and those of the whole family; so that nothing more could be said towards consoling every one of the company for the great loss they had sustained in this man, and principally the relations, who were seated round the dead body, and whom he assured that he was gone to heaven, the seat of all sorts of happiness, whereas the world that he had just left was replete with misery. It is to be remarked that during this oration there stood upon the coffin a large pot of wine, out of which every one drank to the health of the deceased, hoping that he might surmount the difficulties he had to encounter in his road to Paradise, where, by the mercy of God, he was about to enter;

"Corpe Bearer."

"CORPE BEARER" IN THE TIME OF A
PLAGUE AT LONDON

From a contemporary print in the British Museum.

on which mercy they founded all their hope, without considering their evil life and that God is just. This being finished, six men took up the corpse, and carried it on their shoulders to the church: it was covered with a large cloth, which the four nearest relations held each by a corner with one hand, and in the other carried a bough. The other relations and friends had in one hand a flambeau, and in the other a bough, marching thus through the street, without singing or saying any prayer, till they came to the church, where, having placed the body on trestles and taken off the cloth from the coffin (which is ordinarily made of fine walnut-tree, handsomely worked and ornamented with iron bandages, chased in the manner of a buffet), the minister then ascended his pulpit, and, every one being seated round about the coffin, which is placed in a kind of parade in the middle of the church, he read a portion of Holy Scripture, concerning the resurrection of the dead, and afterwards sang some psalms, to which all the company answered. After this he descended, having his bough in his hand like the rest of the congregation; this he threw on the dead body when it was put into the grave, as did all the relations, extinguishing their flambeaux in the earth with which the corpse was to be covered. This finished, every one retired to his home without farther ceremony."

Poor people seem to have been lowered into the grave either quite naked or wrapped in a shroud without any coffin.

CHAPTER IV

THE places of resort in this century, and especially in the reign of Charles the Second, reveal the existence of a new class : that of the fashionable class, the people who live for amusement. They have grown up by degrees ; they inhabit a new town lying between the Inns of Court and Hyde Park, which they have built for themselves ; they have made a society composed entirely of themselves, frequenting the same coffee-houses and taverns, belonging to the same sets, and following the same kind of life. They have invented the fashionable saunter ; they have made the theatre their own ; they have introduced the *salon* and the reception. They gamble a great deal ; they lounge a great deal ; they make love a great deal ; they drink ; they dress extravagantly ; they practise affectations ; they lay bets ; they run races ; they live, in a word, exactly the same careless, useless, mischievous life which their successors have continued ever since.

Among the other things which we owe to them is the Park.

The old maps of the sixteenth and early seventeenth centuries represent the area which is now the Green Park and Hyde Park as green fields ; these fields formed part of the manors known as Neyte and Hyde, which belonged to the Abbey of Westminster until the reign of Henry the Eighth, when they fell to the Crown, being exchanged for the Priory of Hurley in Berkshire. Henry the Eighth either stocked the fields with deer, or found deer there and ran a fence round the fields so as to enclose them. During the sixteenth and part of the seventeenth centuries Hyde Park was a Royal hunting-ground. In the reign of Charles the First it was also a racecourse. In Cromwell's time it was a place for driving and for carriage races ; under Charles the Second it became a promenade and a drive, just as it is at the present day.

St. James's Park came into existence later than Hyde Park.

It began with Spring Gardens, named after a spring which here issued from the ground, but was not enough to feed the fountain which ornamented the gardens. They were not public gardens, though many people were admitted ; they contained orchards of fruit-trees, lawns and bowling greens, a bathing pond, and a butt for archery practice. James the First kept some of his menagerie in these gardens. In Charles the First's reign an ordinary was allowed to be kept here; it was six shillings a head, and all day long there was tippling under the trees with frequent quarrels. Charles was much offended by these unseemly broils and shut up the place. An enterprising barber, however, came to the rescue of the players, and set up a large establishment between St. James's Street and the Haymarket, where were two bowling greens, a tavern, an ordinary, card tables, and rooms for gaming of all kinds.

Spring Gardens were opened again during the Civil War, with the old customs of drinking; it was, however, provided that the Gardens should be closed on public fast days. In 1654 they were closed altogether; Evelyn (May 10) has an entry :—

"My Lady Gerrard treated us at Mulberry Garden, now the only place of refreshment about the towne for persons of the best quality to be exceedingly cheated at, Cromwell and his partisans having shut up and seized on Spring Gardens, which, till now, had been the usual rendezvous for the ladies and gallants at this season."

In 1658 it was open again, for Evelyn " collation'd " there on his way to see a coach race in Hyde Park.

The best account of the Garden is one quoted by Larwood from *A Character of England* [1] :—

" The inclosure is not disagreeable, for the solemness of the grove, the warbling of the birds, and as it opens into the spacious walks of St. James's. But the company walk in it at such a rate as you would think all the ladies were so many Atalantas contending with their wooers; and there was no appearance that I should prove the Hippomenes who would with very much ado keep pace with them. But, as fast as they run, they stay there so long as if they wanted not time to finish the race; for it is usual here to find some of the young company till midnight; and the thickets of the garden seem to be contrived to all advantages of gallantry, after they have been refreshed with the collation, which is here seldom omitted, at a certain *cabaret* in the middle of this paradise, where the forbidden fruits are certain trifling tarts, neats-tongues, salacious meats, and bad Rhenish (wine); for which the gallants pay sauce, as indeed they do at all such houses throughout England; for they think it a piece of frugality beneath them to bargain or account for what they eat in any place, however unreasonably imposed upon. But thus those mean fellows are enriched—beggar and insult over the gentlemen. I am assured that this particular host has purchased within few years 5000 livres of annual rent, and well he may, at the rate these prodigals pay " (J. Larwood, *The Story of the London Parks*).

A more detailed description shows us a garden laid out in square beds, each twenty or thirty paces in length and breadth, and surrounded with hedges of red currants, roses, and shrubs; in the beds were growing strawberries and vegetables, the borders were lined with flowers, and fruit-trees were growing up the walls. Pepys took his wife, his two servants, and his boy there on the King's birthday, 1662.

---

[1] *A Character of England :* As it was lately presented in a letter to a Nobleman of France, 1659. Attributed to Evelyn.

Visitors could help themselves, apparently, for the servants gathered pinks from the borders. The building of houses about Charing Cross destroyed the rural charm of these gardens; part of them were built upon; a small part still remains at the back of the street now called Spring Gardens.

Evelyn has mentioned the Mulberry Gardens. This place was on the site of Buckingham Palace. James the First in 1609, following the example of Henry

ST. JAMES'S PARK
From the Crace Collection in the British Museum.

the Fourth of France, endeavoured to establish a silk-growing industry. With this object he sent out to the various counties mulberry-trees by the hundred thousand. He enclosed four acres of St. James's Park, and planted them with mulberry-trees. In Cromwell's time the Gardens were sold; at the Restoration they returned to the King, who threw them open. They became for a time the fashionable resort; by day the non-decorous took cheese-cakes in their summer houses ; at night they were the haunt of "gentlemen and ladies that made love together, till twelve o'clock at night, the pretty leest." There were arbours for supper parties ; there were also dark paths in the "Wilderness." Dryden used to take Mrs. Reeve, an actress of Killigrew's Company, to the Mulberry Gardens. The place was closed about the year 1675.

St. James's Park began as a marshy piece of ground overflowed by the river at high tides, stretching out between St. James's Hospital and Thorney Island. The Hospital, founded by the citizens of London "before the time of any man's memory," was intended to receive fourteen poor sisters, maidens, who were leprous ; they were placed in this house to live chastely and honestly in divine service. It was endowed with land sufficient to maintain these unfortunate women in comfort ; they possessed as well a brotherhood of six chaplains and two laymen. And in 1290 Edward the First gave them a fair, to be held for seven days, beginning on St. James's Eve, July 24.

The house is said to be mentioned in an MS. in the Cottonian Library of the year 1100 ; it was, therefore, certainly the oldest hospital belonging to London.

It was rebuilt in the reign of Henry the Third. In 1450, after there had been many disputes with the Abbey of Westminster over alleged rights of visit, Henry the Sixth placed the house in the perpetual custody of Eton College. Henry the Eighth acquired it by purchase in 1537 and, according to Stow, compounded with the inmates. It has been stated that only one sister received a pension. I think the two statements may be reconciled. Thus the dread of leprosy had by this time vanished. There were very few lepers left in the country, if any. At the hospital of Sherburn, Durham, which originally contained five *convents* of lepers, of both sexes, *i.e.* sixty-five persons, in 1593 the house contained only men ; "sick, or whole, Lepers, or wayfaring." Surtees, *History of Durham*, says that it would have been difficult, long before, to find a single leper in the country.

What, then, happened at St. James's ? One of two things. Either the sisters were reduced to one, and only one, who would be considered a leper ; or that the house, like so many others, had been allowed to depart from its foundation, and had admitted as sisters, women who were not lepers at all.

However, Henry enclosed the ground belonging to the hospital, stocked it with deer, and turned it into a pleasure garden for himself.

James the First kept his menagerie here. Henry, Prince of Wales, ran at the ring and practised horsemanship here.

During the Commonwealth the Park was not sold, but preserved, though the deer seem to have run away. A certain number of people were privileged to walk in the Park.

Then Charles came back, and began at once to improve the Park. He constructed the canal, or ornamental water; he laid out the Mall; he made a rising ground beside Rosamond's pond; he erected beautiful avenues of trees. More than this, he opened the Park and gave a new place of resort, much finer than it had ever before enjoyed, to the fashionable world of London. The literature of the period is full of the Park and its frequenters.

New Spring Gardens at Vauxhall were formed in imitation of the old, and were named after them. Evelyn mentions the place in 1661, Pepys 1665; he calls it Foxhall. He went there in June and in July; on the latter day he did not find a single guest there. There were, however, plenty of guests at other times. Pepys observes how the young fellows take hold of every woman in the place. He heard the nightingale sing; he heard the fiddles, and the harp, and the Jew's trump; he heard the talk of the young men—" Lord, their mad talk did make my heart ake.' He had cheese-cakes, syllabubs, and wine in the gardens; and, as at the theatre, he and his wife were not ashamed to be seen when the company was notoriously profligate, and the women notoriously devoid of virtue.

Gray's Inn Gardens was another place of resort, probably for lawyers and their ladies. For the people of Holborn and Fleet Street there were the Lamb's Conduit Fields. These spacious fields extended from Tottenham Court Road to Gray's Inn Road, and as far to the north as what is now the Euston Road. There were no houses upon them in the seventeenth century except Lamb's Conduit, erected in 1577 For the City there were the Moor fields, then enclosed, planted with trees and surrounded by shops; there were the Hoxton Fields, the Spa Fields of Clerkenwell, and the White Conduit Fields. It was the especial happiness of London at this time that from any part of the City the open country was accessible within a quarter of an hour. All around these fields sprang up places of amusement, pleasure gardens, and taverns, which I have described fully in considering the eighteenth century.

In the City itself the favourite resorts were, for the young men, the galleries of the Royal Exchange, which were occupied by shops for the sale of gloves, ribbons, laces, fans, scent, and such things. The shops were served by girls, whose pretty faces and ready tongues were the chief attraction for the young fellows, who went there to flirt rather than to buy. Some of the younger citizens also found the Piazza of Covent Garden a convenient place to lounge and saunter. There were attractions in the Piazzas, too, of the other sex. There was also the interior of St. Paul's Cathedral.

The coffee-houses quickly became a place of resort for the graver citizen in the evening. He would not go to the theatre, where the exhibition of actresses still offended his sense of propriety; he had formerly gone to the tavern, but a dish of coffee was far more wholesome than a bowl of punch, and discourse among men who were sober was much more instructive than that of men who were drunk.

Of course, there were still left plenty of those who stuck to the tavern and

despised these new inventions of tea and coffee.   Indeed, for business purposes the
tavern continued to be used.   Transactions of all kinds were conducted in a private
room at a tavern, over a bottle.   If a customer came up to London, the shopkeeper
took him to the tavern when, in the Rose or the Sun, they performed their business.
The coffee-house never took the place of the tavern in that respect.   The most
extraordinary secrecy was expected and maintained on either side over the smallest
matter of trade.   The number of taverns was then very great.   They literally lined

INTERIOR OF ST. PAUL'S
From Pennant's *London* in the British Museum.

the two most important arteries, that from St. George's, Southwark, to Bishopsgate
Street Without, and that between the Royal Exchange and the Strand.

I have before me a pamphlet in doggerel verse of the year 1671 called *The
Search after Claret Wine: A Visitation of the Vintners.*

The following is the dedication which enumerates the favourite wines :—

> " To all Lovers, Admirers and Doters on Claret,
> (Who tho' at Deaths-Door, yet can hardly forbear it)
> Who can Miracles credit, and fancy Red-Port
> To be Sprightly Puntack, and the best of the sort ;
> To all Mornings-draught Men, who drink bitter Wine,
> To create a false Stomach against they'r to Dine ;

To all Tavern-kitchen Frequenters and Haunters,
Who go thither to hear Mistress Cooks foolish Banters
To Partake of a Dumpling, or Sop in the Pan ;
A Large Rummer Drank up, troop as fast as they can ;
To all sober Half-Pint Men, and serious Sippers ;
To all old Maudlin Drinkers, and 12 a Clock Bibbers ;
To all Drinking Committees, Knots, Clubs, Corporations
Who while others are snoaring, they'r settling the Nations ;
To all the brisk Beaus who think Life but a Play,
Who make Day like the Night, and turn Night into Day ;
To all Lovers of Red and White-Port, Syracuse,
Barcelona, Navarr, or Canary's sweet Juice ;
To all Alicant Tasters, and Malaga-Sots,
To all Friends to Straw-Bottles, and Nicking Quart-Pots,
To all Bacchus his Friends, who have Taverns frequented,
This following Poem is Humbly Presented."

The searchers after claret spend two days visiting the taverns and find none.
I suppose that the war with France had caused a stoppage of the supply.   In the
same way, during the long war with France, 1793-1815, the people forgot their old
taste for claret ; when they drank it at all, it was heavy stuff.   They visit eighty-
eight taverns between Whitechapel and Temple Bar and at Westminster, and this
without going out of the main streets.   Many of these taverns are still remembered
by the tokens which they issued for copper money.   Most of these taverns were not
hostels, and did not provide lodgings ; they were taverns and nothing more ; they
were frequented, as has been said, by tradesmen during the day ; in the evening
there were societies, clubs, and trades, which held their meetings in the taverns.
For instance, in the Mitre, Cheapside, afterwards called the Goose and Gridiron, the
Society of Musicians met and gave their concerts.   At the Cock and the Devil of
Fleet Street the lawyers thronged.

CHAPTER V

THEATRE AND ART

ON December 8, 1660, a great change was effected at the theatre. For the first time, to the exasperation of the Puritans, a woman's part was taken by a woman. The place was the theatre of Vere Street. The part first performed was that of Desdemona. The prologue written "to introduce the first woman that came to act on the stage" was as follows (Leigh Hunt, *The Town*) :—

> " I came unknown to any of the rest
> To tell the news ; I saw the lady drest :
> The woman plays to-day ; mistake me not,
> No man in gown, or page in petticoat :
> A woman to my knowledge, yet I can't,
> If I should die, make affidavit on't.
> Do you not twitter, gentlemen ?   I know
> You will be censuring : do it fairly, though ;
> 'Tis possible a virtuous woman may
> Abhor all sorts of looseness, and yet play :
> Play on the stage—where all eyes are upon her :
> Shall we count that a crime France counts as an honour ?
> In other kingdoms husbands safely trust 'em ;
> The difference lies only in the custom.
> And let it be our custom, I advise :
> I'm sure this custom's better than th' excise,
> And may procure us custom : hearts of flint
> Will melt in passion, when a woman's in't.
> But, gentlemen, you that as judges sit
> In the Star chamber of the house—the pit,
> Have modest thoughts of her : pray, do not run
> To give her visits when the play is done,
> With ' damn me, your most humble servant, lady :'
> She knows these things as well as you, it may be :
> Not a bit there, dear gallants, she doth know
> Her own deserts,—and your temptations too.
> But to the point—in this reforming age
> We have intents to civilize the stage.
> Our Women are defective, and so sized,
> You'd think they were some of the guard disguised :
> For, to speak truth, men act that are between
> Forty and fifty, wenches of fifteen,
> With bone so large and nerve so incompliant,
> When you call Desdemona, enter giant.

> We shall purge everything that is unclean,
> Lascivious, scurrilous, impious, or obscene :
> And when we've put all things in this fair way
> Barebones himself may come to see a play."

And the epilogue, much shorter, was as follows :—

> "And how do you like her?   Come, what is't ye drive at?
> She's the same thing in public as in private,
> As far from being what you call a whore
> As Desdemona injured by the Moor :
> Then he that censures her in such a case
> Hath a soul blacker than Othello's face.
> But, ladies, what think you? for it you tax
> Her freedom with dishonour to your sex,
> She means to act no more, and this shall be
> No other play, but her own tragedy.
> She will submit to none but your commands,
> And take commission only from your hands."

This change altered the whole character of the theatre.   At the beginning it lowered the tone of the stage, which was already bad enough.   When the spectators became accustomed to the appearance of women on the stage, it began perhaps to have a refining influence, but certainly not at first.

In Wycherley's *Country Wife*, Pinchwife takes his wife to the "eighteen-penny place" so that she shall not be seen.   This place was the tier called the upper boxes. Ladies sometimes went into the Pit, but not alone.   In the same play Alithea says to her lover, " I will not go if you intend to leave me alone in the Pit as you used to do."   Ladies, however, for the most part, went into the first tier or dress circle, where they received visits from their friends.   Lord Foppington says, "After dinner I go to the play, where I amuse myself till nine o'clock with looking upon the company, and usually dispose of an hour more in leading them out."

The tickets were, to the boxes, 4s.; to the Pit, half-a-crown; to the upper boxes, 1s. 6d.; and to the gallery, 1s.   There were only two theatres, the King's and the Duke of York's; the seats were simple benches without backs.

Pepys, a great lover of the stage, commends the improvement of the theatre since the Restoration :—

"The stage is now by his pains a thousand times better and more glorious than ever heretofore. Now, wax-candles, and many of them; then, not above 3 lbs. of tallow : now, all things civil, no rudeness anywhere; then, as in a bear-garden : then, two or three fiddlers; now, nine or ten of the best : then, nothing but rushes upon the ground, and everything else mean ; and now, all otherwise : then, the Queen seldom, and King never would come; now, not the King only for state, but all civil people do think they may come as well as any.   He tells me that he hath gone several times, eight or ten times, he tells me, hence to Rome, to hear good musique ; so much he loves it, though he never did sing or play a note. That he hath ever endeavoured in the late King's time, and in this, to introduce good musique, but he never could do it, there never having been any musique here better than ballads.   Nay, says, ' Hermitt poore' and 'Chevy Chese' was all the musique we had ; and yet no ordinary fiddlers get so much money as ours do here, which speaks our rudenesse still " (Pepys, vol. vi. pp. 171, 172).

Bankside had long since ceased to be the chosen seat of the drama. The Globe, after being burned down and rebuilt, was finally pulled down in 1644; the Rose, the Swan, and the Bear Garden had met the same fate; the Fortune Theatre was destroyed by soldiers in 1549; the Curtain had become, before it was pulled

INSIDE OF THE DUKE'S THEATRE, LINCOLN'S INN FIELDS
As it appeared in the reign of King Charles the Second. From a contemporary print.

down, a place for prize fights; Blackfriars Theatre, after standing empty for some years, in accordance with the law, was pulled down in 1655.

In 1642 the Parliament commanded the cessation of plays on the ground "that public sports do not well agree with public calamities, nor public stage plays with the seasons of humiliation." So the houses were closed. Then, as always happened, the law was timidly and tentatively broken; the theatres began again. In 1647, however, a second ordinance appeared calling upon the magistrates to enter houses where performances were going on and to arrest the performers. This ordinance proving of more effect, a third and more stringent law was passed denouncing stage plays, interludes, and common plays as the occasion of many and sundry great vices and disorders, tending to the high provocation of God's wrath and displeasure, ordered the destruction of all galleries, seats, and stages of the theatre. This settled the question for the time. Most of the actors went off to fight for the King; a few remained and gave private performances at the residences of noblemen. In 1658 Davenant opened the old Cockpit Theatre in Drury Lane for performances of declamation and music without being molested. Probably he ascertained beforehand what the Protector would do. On the Restoration a bookseller of dramatic propensities took possession of the Cockpit, where he played with his two apprentices, Betterton and Kynaston. Killigrew and Davenant obtained patents for opening theatres, Killigrew's company to be called the King's servants, Davenant's to be called the Duke of York's servants. Davenant associated with himself the dramatic booksellers, and after a season at the Phœnix went to the new theatre in Lincoln's Inn Fields, and from there to the larger theatre in Dorset Garden, Fleet Street, a place more commodious because it was on the river, the great highway of London. Killigrew began at the Red Bull in St. John's Street, going from that place, which seems to have been out of the way, to Gibbon's Tennis Court in Clare Market. He then proceeded to build a new theatre in Drury Lane, not far from the Phœnix. The new theatre opened with Beaumont and Fletcher's comedy of the *Humourous Lieutenant* on April 8, 1663. Ten of the company were in the Royal household, and had allowances of scarlet cloth and lace for liveries; did they wear the livery on the stage? It was here that Charles fell in love with Nell Gwynne; she was playing Valeria in Dryden's *Tyrannic Love*. She died on the stage and then jumped up and spoke the epilogue :—

> "O poet, damned dull poet ! Who could prove
> So senseless to make Nelly die for love ?
> Nay, what ! yet worse, to kill me in the prime
> Of Easter time, in tart and cheese-cake time !"

Here Pepys saw her, was presented to her, and kissed her, "and a mighty pretty soul she is." And again he mentions how he saw her in a part called Florimell, "a comical part done by Nell that I never can hope to see the like done again by man or woman."

It is sometimes stated that the theatres of the time were still without a roof. This appears to be incorrect. Pepys mentions the inconvenience of rain. "To the King's house and saw the *Silent Woman*. Before the play was done it fell such a storm of hail that we in the pit were fain to rise and all the house in disorder." A few years later, however, he notes (May 1, 1668) another visit to the same theatre, where he saw the *Surprizall*, and mentions "a disorder in the pit by its raining in from the cupola at top, it being a very foul day." There was, therefore, some kind of dome or cupola open at the side.

The time of commencing the performance was three, so that the theatre, at all

Infide of the RED BULL Playhoufe.

The Red Bull Playhouse stood on a plot of ground lately called 'Red Bull Yard' near the upper end of St Johns Street Clerkenwell, and is traditionally said to have been the Theatre at which Shakespeare first held gentlemen's horses. In the civil wars it became highly celebrated for the representation of Drolls, to a collection of which pieces published by Frauncis Kirkman in 1672, this view of it forms a frontispiece. The figures brought together on the stage, are intended as portraits of the leading actors in each Droll. The one playing Simpleton is Robert Cox then a great favorite of whom the publisher thus speaks in his preface 'I have seen the Red Bull Playhouse which was of large one so full that as many went back for want of room as had entred Robert Cox a principal actor and contriver of these pieces, how have I heard him cryed up for his John Swabber and Simpleton the Smith In which latter he being to appear with a large piece of Bread & Butter on the stage I have frequently known some of the female spectators to long for it." The above print may be regarded not only as highly curious for the place it represents but as a unique specimen of the interior economy of our antient English Theatres

From a contemporary print.

events for the first part of Charles's reign, was an afternoon amusement. The doors were thrown open soon after noon. Pepys, on one occasion, went to the theatre a little after noon ; the doors were not then open, but they were thrown open shortly afterwards. On entering the Pit he found many people there already, having got in by private ways. As he had had no dinner he found a boy to keep his seat, and went outside to get some dinner at the Rose Tavern (Wills's, Russell Street).

The play was constantly changed, and the popularity of the rival houses continually varied. On one occasion, on arriving at Drury Lane at three, the hour for beginning, Pepys found not one single person in the Pit. However, some came late, and there was a performance after all. The new fashion of having women instead of boys for the female parts was so popular, that plays acted by women alone were actually presented. One of the plays then performed, Killigrew's *Parson's Wedding*, is described as "obscene and loose," for which reason it was thought fittest for women to play.

The wearing of masks at the theatre, which was common among ladies, was due to the disgraceful licence of the dramatist. One would think, however, that if ladies disliked the grossness, they might stay away; perhaps it was rather due partly to the desire of not attracting public attention, partly to the charm of the mysterious. As for women disliking the coarseness of the play, we may simply remember that though women are in every age better than men in that respect, they are not always very much better. Like the clergy, the best we can expect of them is that they should be a little better than the men.

The seventeenth century witnessed the splendour and the death of the masque. For fifty years, if one sought for fine stage scenery, splendid dresses, curious stage effects, it was not at the theatre that it was to be found, but at the masque.

It was a very costly form of entertainment. Private persons could not attempt it. No manager of a theatre could attempt it, because the fullest house could not pay for producing it. Only great noblemen, rich bodies, and the Court could present a masque. There was orchestral music of the finest; there were songs, madrigals, choruses; there were long speeches; there was dancing, both singly and in groups; there were most costly dresses, and there were transformation scenes managed with a dexterity worthy of a modern theatre. It is remarkable that the theatre never tried to vie with the masque in scenery or dresses or music. Ben Jonson was the principal writer of the libretti; Henry Lawn was the musician; Gills the inventor of the dances; Inigo Jones the machinist and scene painter.

James the First and his Queen delighted in the masque. So did Charles and Henrietta; the Civil War put a stop to this beautiful and courtly entertainment; after the Restoration, when an attempt was made to revive it, the taste for it had gone; it had played its part and was dead.

Let me present, greatly abbreviated, one of Ben Jonson's masques :—

The masque of *Neptune's Triumph for the Return of Albion* is a favourable specimen of the scenic effects of the masque. It was played on Twelfth Night, 1624.

The scene at first showed nothing but two pillars with inscriptions; on the one NEP. RED., and on the other SEC. JOV. The masque opens with a long and tedious dialogue between a cook and a poet; in the course of it the latter explains the purpose of the masque, which is to celebrate the safe return of the Prince from Spain :—

> " The mighty Neptune, mighty in his styles,
>   And large command of waters, and of isles ;
>   Not as the ' lord and sovereign of the seas,'
>   But ' chief in the art of riding ' late did please,
>   To send his Albion forth, the most his own,
>   Upon discovery, to themselves best known,
>   Through Celtiberia ; and, to assist his course,
>   Gave him his powerful Manager of Horse,
>   With divine Proteus, father of disguise,
>   To wait upon them with his counsels wise,
>   In all extremes.   His great commands being done,
>   And he desirous to review his son,
>   He doth dispatch a floating isle, from hence,
>   Unto the Hesperian shores, to waft him thence.
>   Where, what the arts were used to make him stay
>   And how the Syrens woo'd him by the way,
>   What monsters he encountered on the coast,
>   How near our general joy was to be lost,
>   Is not our subject now ; though all these make
>   The present gladness greater, for their sake.
>   But what the triumphs are, the feast, the sport,
>   And proud solemnities of Neptune's court,
>   Now he is safe, and Fame's not heard in vain,
>   But we behold our happy pledge again."

The ground thus cleared, the cook brings in persons representing the various ingredients of an Olla Podrida. This was intended for the comic part. Then a comic anti-masque is danced by these mummers. After this the scene opens, and discloses the Island of Delos. The masquers are sitting in their "sieges." Then the heavens open and disclose Apollo, Mercury, the Muses, and the Goddess Harmony. Below, Proteus is sitting. Apollo sings :—

> " Look forth, the shepherd of the seas,
>   And of the ports that keep'st the keys,
>   And to your Neptune tell,
>   His Albion, prince of all his isles,
>   For whom the sea and land so smiles,
>   Is home returned well."

The island moves forward and joins the mainland. There is a grand chorus of Proteus and the others while the masquers land. While they prepare for their entry the chorus sings another verse :—

> " Spring all the Graces of the age,
>   And all the Loves of time ;
>   Bring all the pleasures of the stage,
>   And relishes of rhyme ;
>   And all the softnesses of courts,
>   The looks, the laughters, and the sports ;
>   And mingle all their sweets and salts,
>   That none may say, the Triumph halts."

Then the masquers "danced their entry." The dance was performed by the courtiers and the Queen's ladies. It was a dance invented for the occasion, with stately figures, arranged groups, and active "capers." Then the scene was changed and disclosed a maritime palace, the home of Oceanus, "with loud music." "And the other above is no more seen."

"Then follows the main dance, after which the second prospect of the sea is shown, to the former music."

Then Proteus and the others advance to the ladies with another song :—

> " Come noble nymphs, and do not hide
> The joys for which you so provide,
> If not to mingle with the men,
> What do you hear ? go home agen.
>   Your dressings do confess,
> By what we see so curious parts
> Of Pallas and Arachne's arts,
>   That you could mean no less.
> Why do you wear the silk-worm's toils,
> Or glory in the shell-fish spoils,
> Or strive to shew the grains of ore,
> That you have gathered on the shore,
>   Whereof to make a stock
> To graft the greener emerald on,
> Or any better-water's stone ?
>   Or ruby of the rock ?
> Why do you smell of amber-grise,
> Of which was formed Neptune's niece,
> The Queen of Love ; unless you can,
> Like Sea-born Venus, love a man?
>   Try, put yourselves unto't,
> Your looks, your smiles, and thoughts that meet,
> Ambrosian hands, and silver feet,
>   Do promise you will do't."

The revels follow, which ended, the fleet is discovered, while the three cornets play.

After a little more foolish talk between the cook and the poet, the sailors of the fleet come in and dance, and the whole is concluded with a song by ten voices accompanied by the " Whole music, five lutes, three cornets " :—

> " Although we wish the triumph still might last
> For such a prince, and his discovery past :
> Yet now, great lord of waters, and of isles,
> Give Proteus leave to turn unto his wiles.
>
> And whilst young Albion doth thy labours ease,
> Dispatch Portunus to thy ports.
>
>   And Saron to thy seas ;
> To meet old Nereus with his fifty girls,
> From aged Indus laden home with pearls,
> And Orient gums, to burn unto thy name.
>
> And may thy subjects' hearts be all on flame,
> Whilst thou dost keep the earth in firm estate,
> And 'mongst the winds, dost suffer no debate,
> But both at sea, and land, our powers increase,
> With health and all the golden gifts of peace."

It is sometimes stated that music was killed by the Puritans. If Pepys is to be considered as an average London citizen in this respect, their music was very far from being killed by the Puritans. We find him, his household and his friends, all singing, playing, taking a part; we find parties on the river singing part songs as they glided down the stream; we hear of the singing in church; at Court the evenings were always provided with singing boys; at the theatre songs were plentifully scattered about the plays. The Elizabethan custom of music at dinner had apparently vanished, yet the power of playing some instrument was far more general than it was later. As soon as possible after the Restoration the choral service was re-established in the cathedrals and the Royal chapels. Cooke, Lawn, Rogers, Wilson, and other composers were engaged in forming and teaching the choirs; new anthems were composed by Pelham Humphrey or Humfrey, Michael Wise, John Blow, and Henry Purcell. The last of these, one of the greatest of English composers, was born in 1658 and died in 1695.

It was common for people of rank to attend the service of the Chapel Royal at Whitehall or that of St. Paul's Cathedral. At Oxford an association was formed, consisting of the leading scholars and professors of the University, for the purpose of promoting the study and practice of music, vocal and instrumental. It is true that in the eighteenth century music seems to have deserted the English household; perhaps in the seventeenth it lingered only among the better sort, and had already been killed in the circles affected by the sour Puritanism of the time.

The condition and advancement of painting in the century may be briefly considered. The soil was prepared for the development of the fine arts by the learning, scholarship, and travel of the English nobles and scholars. About the year 1615 the Earl of Arundel began to collect pictures, statues, vases, and gems. Prince Henry began a collection which at his death passed to his brother Charles. On his accession Charles began to increase the Royal collections begun by Henry the Eighth, and continued slowly by his successors. Charles bought the whole of the cabinet of the Duke of Milan for £18,000. The cartoons of Raffaelle were acquired in Flanders by the agency of Rubens. Whitehall Palace contained four hundred and sixty pictures, of which twenty-eight were by Titian, eleven by Correggio, sixteen by Julio Romano, nine by Raffaelle, four by Guido, and seven by Parmigiano. Vandyke, the greatest among the pupils of Rubens, came over to this country and remained here for life. In 1630 Rubens himself came over, not as a painter but as an ambassador. However, he consented to paint the ceiling of the Banqueting Hall at Whitehall. Charles planned an Academy of Arts, but, like everything else, it had to be set aside.

Among lesser painters of the century were William Dobson, John Hoskins, Samuel Cooper, John Peiletot, and Geuteleschi, all of whom lived and painted in London.

VIOLA DA GAMBA

"For important regale of the Company the concerts were usually all viols to the organ or harpsichord. The violin came in late and imperfectly. When the hands were well supplied the whole chest went to work, that is, six viols, music being formed for it which would seem a strange sort of music now, being an interwoven hum-drum."—From *Autobiography of Roger North*, born 1653.

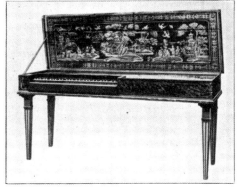

CLAVICHORD

"The Clavichord hath a tunely kynde
As the wyre is wrested high and lowe."
JOHN SKELTON, 1459-1529, Poet Laureate.

(The wrestler was the tuner, who wrested or strained the wire to the required tension.)

SPINET

This spinet was made in London about the end of the seventeenth century by Stephen Keene.
A contemporary advertisement runs thus :—" Mr. Stephen Keene, Maker of Harpsycons and virginals dwelleth now in Threadneedle St., at the sign of the virginal who maketh them excellently well both for sound and substance."

THE FLAGEOLET

Pepys, in his *Diary* (March 1, 1666), writes :—
Being returned home I find Greeting, the flageolet-master. come and teaching my wife." And (20th Jan. 1667)
"To Drumbleby's the pipe maker, there to advise about the making of a flageolet to go low and soft, and he do show me a way which he do, and also a fashion of having two pipes of the same note fastened together, so I can play on one and then echo it upon the other, which is mighty pretty."

A FINE OLD ITALIAN LUTE

A fine old Italian lute with label " 1600, in Padova Venue." A special interest attaches to it from its having been the favourite instrument of the late Carl Engel. In Evelyn's (the Diarist) time lutes by famous Bologna makers were fetching extraordinary prices.

A VIRGINAL

Pepys, in his *Diary*, Sept. 2, 1666, at the time of the great fire writes :—
" Rivers full of lighters and boats taking in goods, and I observed that hardly one lighter or boat in three, that had the goods of a house in, but there was a pair of virginals in it."

MUSICAL INSTRUMENTS OF THE PERIOD

From *Musical Instruments, Historic, Rare, and Unique* (A. & C. Black, 1888).

Lely of course belongs to the first Restoration period. So also do Hayls, Michael Wright, Henry Anderton, the two Vandeveldes, and many others. Grinling Gibbons belongs to the latter years of the seventeenth and the first quarter of the eighteenth century.

The greatest invention of the century was, without doubt, the newspaper. As far as this country is concerned, setting aside the apocryphal history of the *English Mercury*, its first newspaper was started in London by Nathaniel Butter, with whom were associated Nicholas Bonner, Thomas Archer, Nathaniel Newberry, William Sheppard, Bartholomew Dounes, and Edward Allor. The sheet was called the *Weekly News*, and it is believed to have begun on May 23, 1622. In the same year the *London Weekly Courant* also began. Twenty years later the *Mercurius Clericus* (1641) was started in the interests of the clergy; the *Mercurius Britannicus* (1642), the *Mercurius Civicus* (1643), the *Mercurius Politicus*, a Parliamentary paper, and *Mercurius Pragmaticus*, a Royalist paper.

About the year 1663 the *Kingdom's Intelligence* was started, and this was incorporated with the *London Gazette* when that was founded in 1665.

Of course it was not long before the power of the Press was discovered. The Government began to subsidise the papers; private persons began to pay for notices in them; and trade advertisements began to appear. All these papers were weekly. In 1695, however, the *Post Boy* appeared—the first daily paper.

CHAPTER VI

A LIST of sports in 1600 is quoted in Furnivall's notes to Stubbes (Part I. Series vi. No. 6, p. 316).

> " Man, I dare challenge thee to throw the sledge,
> To iumpe or leape ouer a ditch or hedge,
> To wrestle, play at stooleball, or to runne,
> To pitch the barre, or to shoote off a gunne :
> To play at loggets, nine holes, or ten pinnes,
> To trie it out at foot-ball by the shinnes ;
> At Ticktacke, Irish, Noddie, Maw, and Ruffe ;
> At hot-cockles, leape-frogge, or blindman-buffe ;
> To drinke halfe pots, or deale at the whole canne
> To play at base, or pen-and-ynk-horne sir Ihan :
> To daunce the Morris, play at Barly-breake :
> At all exploytes a man can thinke or speake :
> At shoue-groute, venter-poynt, or crosse and pile :
> At beshrow him that's last at yonder style."

The prohibition of games on Sunday by the Puritans led to the abolition of the working-class's amusements altogether, and was therefore answerable for much of that hideous brutality which possessed that class during the latter part of the eighteenth century. They were not to wrestle, shoot, play at bowls, ring bells, hold masques, wakes, play games of any kind, dance, or exercise any other pastime on Sunday. Now, as Sunday was the only day when the working people could play games or have any recreation, this prohibition destroyed the knowledge of these games, the old delight in them, the desire for them, the skill in them. After eighteen years of Puritan rule a new type of working man grew up, one who knew no games and could practise none ; a duller creature, heavy witted, slow of sight, and clumsy of hand ; one who would yield to the temptation of drink without resistance ; one who was capable of sinking lower and lower still. This is one of the many blessings which have been bestowed upon London by the Puritans.

For winter amusements the better class had a variety of games, such as " cards, tables, dice, shovelboard, chess, the philosophers game, small trunks, shuttlecock, billiards, music, masks, singing, dancing, all games, frolicks, jests, riddles, catches,

The Feasant Cook the woods doth most frequent,
Where Spanniells spring & pearch him by the sent.

And when in flight the Hawk w. quickned speed
With's beake & savage talens makes him bleede.

Angling on river banks, trowling for pike,
Ye noble Sport, when as the fish doth strike.

ANGLING.

And when your pleasure's over, then at night,
You and your freinds, doe eate them with delight.

SPORTS OF THE PERIOD

From contemporary engravings by Hollar.

purposes, questions and commands, merry tales of knights errant, queens, lovers, lords, ladies, giants, dwarfs, thieves, cheaters, witches, fairies, goblins, friars "— Malcolm [1] has picked this list out of Burton.

The shows and performances at the fairs were extremely popular. There were puppet shows, at which scriptural pieces were represented, or the Patient Grizzle, or the Lady Godiva; there were tight-rope dancers; there were performing dogs or monkeys; there were strong men and cunning men; jugglers, and conjurers.

Athletic sports were in vogue. Many of the young nobles were expert swimmers; others, among whom was the Duke of Monmouth, were fast runners, so that foot-races were a favourite amusement. Two of them once ran down a buck. Tennis was a favourite game, as was also pall-mall; skating, when there was ice, was extensively practised; bowl-racing and horse-racing were common. Bowls continued as a game which never goes wholly out of fashion. Baiting of the bull and the bear were resumed after the Restoration, but the lust for this brutal sport seems to have gone out.

The evening amusements of James the First, which seem stupid and coarse enough, may be perhaps regarded as the natural swing of the pendulum after a day spent in the maintenance of the Royal dignity by a king in whom there was naturally very little of dignity. The passage also shows the kind of amusement which rich men who could afford to keep buffoons were pleased to adopt :—

"The Monarch, it is said, would leave his dining or supping room to witness the pastimes and fooleries performed by Sir Edward Zouch, Sir George Goring, and Sir John *Finit*. The first sung indecent songs and related tales of the same description, the former of which were written by *Finit*, who procured fiddlers as an accompanyment to Zouch; and Goring was master of the game for fooleries, sometimes presenting David Droman and Archee Armstrong, the King's fool, on the back of the other fools, to tilt one at another, till they fell together by the ears; sometimes antick dances; but Sir John Millisent, who was never known before, was commended for notable fooling, and so he was the best extempore fool of them all."

Chamberlayn's *Present State of England* presents the most complete picture of the sports of this century :—

"For variety of Devertisements, Sports and Recreations, no Nation doth excel the English.

The King hath abroad his Forests, Chases, and Parks, full of variety of Game; for Hunting Red and Fallow Deer, Foxes, Otters; Hawking, his Paddock-Courses, Horse-Races, etc., and at home, Tennis, Pelmel, Billiard, Comedies, Opera, Mascarades, Balls, Ballets, etc. The Nobility and Gentry have their Parks, Warrens, Decoys, Paddock-Courses, Horse-Races, Hunting, Coursing, Fishing, Fowling, Hawking, Setting-Dogs, Tumblers, Lurchers, Duck-hunting, Cock-fighting, Guns for Birding, Low-Bells, Bat-Fowling, Angling, Nets, Tennis, Bowling, Billiards, Tables, Chess, Draughts, Cards, Dice, Catches, Questions, Purposes, Stage-Plays, Masks, Balls, Dancing, Singing, all sorts of Musical Instruments, etc. The citizen

---

[1] *Manners and Customs*, by J. P. Malcolm, 1811.

and peasants have Hand-Ball, Foot-Ball, Skittles, or Nine Pins, Shovel-Board, Stow-Ball, Goffe, Trol Madams, Cudgels, Bear-baiting, Bull-baiting, Shuttlecock, Bowling, Quoits, Leaping, Wrestling, Pitching the Bar, and Ringing of Bells, a Recreation used in no other Country of the World.

Amongst these, Cock-fighting seems to all Foreigners too childish and unsuitable for the Gentry, and for the Common People Bull-baiting and Bear-baiting seem too cruel; and for the Citizens, Foot-Ball, and Throwing at Cocks, very uncivil, rude, and barbarous within the City."

In the Directory of London, 1761, there are fifteen streets, lanes, and alleys, which are named after the game of bowls. This simple fact proves the popularity of the bowling green. These places were licensed by James the First. They were allowed to have tennis courts, rooms for cards and dice, and such diversions besides bowling greens. They were all in the suburbs; there had formerly, however, been a bowling green in Thames Street. Twenty-four were allotted to the suburbs of London and Westminster; four to Southwark; one to St. Katherine's by the Tower; two to Lambeth; one to Shoreditch; and one to every town, village, or hamlet within two miles of London or Westminster. In Charles's reign a barber set up a place provided with two bowling greens in Piccadilly, between the Haymarket and St. James Street; nothing is said about any licence being required for this venture.

Fencing schools were much frequented. The terms used in fencing, which are enumerated by Ben Jonson, were all Italian. The masters granted degrees to their disciples, *Master*, *Provost*, *Scholar*. These schools became haunts of vice, and attempts were made to suppress them, but without success.

Duke Cosmo says that the fencing masters, in order to gain reputation, give a general challenge, offering twenty or thirty jacobuses or more to any one who has a mind to fight with them.

Josevin de Rochefort, whose travels in England were published in 1672, gives a long account of a fencing match :—

"We went to see the Bergiardin, which is a great amphitheatre, where combats are fought between all sorts of animals, and sometimes men, as we once saw. Commonly, when any fencing masters are desirous of shewing their courage and their great skill, they issue mutual challenges, and before they engage, parade the town with drums and trumpets sounding, to inform the public there is a challenge between two brave masters of the science of defence, and that the battle will be fought on such a day. We went to see this combat, which was performed on a stage in the middle of this amphitheatre, where, on the flourishes of trumpets and the beat of drums, the combatants entered, stripped to their shirts. On a signal from the drum, they drew their swords, and immediately began the fight, skirmishing a long time without any wounds. They were both very skilful and courageous. The tallest had the advantage over the least: for, according to the English fashion of fencing, they endeavoured rather to cut than push in the French manner, so that by his height he had the advantage of being able to strike his antagonist on the head, against which the little one was on his guard. He had in his turn an advantage over the great one, in being able to give him the jarnac stroke, by cutting him on his right ham, which he left in a manner quite unguarded. So that, all things considered, they were equally matched. Nevertheless, the tall one struck his antagonist on the wrist, which he almost cut off: but this did not prevent him from continuing the fight, after he had been dressed, and taken a glass of wine or two to give him courage, when he took ample vengeance for his wound: for a little afterwards, making a feint at the ham, the tall man, stooping in order to parry it, laid his whole head open, when the little one gave him a stroke, which took off a slice of his head, and almost all of his ear. For my part I think there is an inhumanity, a barbarity and cruelty, in permitting men to kill each other for diversion. The surgeons immediately dressed them, and bound up their wounds: which being done, they resumed the combat, and both being sensible of their respective disadvantages, they therefore were a long time without giving or receiving a wound, which was the cause that the little one, failing to parry so exactly, being tired with this long battle, received a stroke on his wounded wrist, which dividing the sinews, he remained vanquished, and the tall conqueror received the applause of the spectators. For my part I should have had more pleasure in seeing the battle of the bears and dogs, which was fought the following day on the same theatre."

Just as, early in the eighteenth century, there was a scare about the Mohocks, so in the reign of Charles II. there was a scare about the so-called "Scowerers." There were "Roreres," in the thirteenth century; "Roaring Boys," in the sixteeenth; "Scowerers," in the seventeenth; Mohocks in the eighteenth; and Corinthian Tom in the nineteenth century. And the facts and achievements of their young bloods are always exaggerated. We are now told that the Scowerers assembled in bands, stormed taverns, broke windows, upset apple carts, and generally showed their indomitable spirit. Shadwell wrote a comedy about them. I record the common belief, but doubt the fact.

Wrestling, and the sight of wrestling, was a favourite amusement of the time :—

"In 1681," (*Manners and Customs*) "the King witnessed a wrestling match where the abettors were the Monarch and the Duke of Albemarle : a meadow below the castle was the scene of action, and the match was composed of twelve men on each side: the King's party wore red waistcoats, and the Duke's blue : a ring or inclosure was formed, and a space in it admitted the Royal coach: the Queen and her ladies viewed the contest from the terrace, but the Duke mixed with the crowd. The activity displayed on this occasion excited great applause, and only one of the number offered foul play, which the Duke punished by tripping up his heels.

The victory was gained by the blues : and they thus procured their employer 200 guineas, the wager depending : the sum of 10s. each was given to the King's men, and 20s. to the victors. After which the King's men challenged the Duke's at back-sword : in which exercise some being unskilful, others were taken in to complete the number. This was performed with great skill and courage, but not attended with those barbarous circumstances which were usual with the Roman gladiators, who, to shew the Emperor sport, sheathed their swords in one another's bowels : our most clement and gracious King abominating all acts of cruelty. The issue of this was only some broken pates, and the palm was again given to the blues. The King's men being heated, and unwilling that the Duke's should thus carry a victory, resolved to have another trial with them, and challenged them at football, which being accepted, the goals staked out, and the ball placed in the middle, the Duke held up an handkerchief over the ball, the letting fall of which was the signal to give the start, and the handkerchief a reward to him that got the first kick, which was one of the Duke's men, who (in all three exercises) behaved himself so singularly active, that his Majesty took particular notice of him, and gave him a guinea. And, notwithstanding fortune still appeared on the Duke's side, his Majesty seemed highly pleased with that day's divertisement."

"One of the most curious and ingenious amusements" ever offered to the public ear was contrived in the year 1682, when an elm plank was exhibited to the King and the credulous of London, which, being touched by a hot iron, invariably produced a sound resembling deep groans.

"This sensible and very irritable board received numbers of noble visitors : and other boards, sympathising with their afflicted brother, demonstrated how much affected they might be by similar means. The publicans in different parts of the City immediately applied ignited metal to all the woodwork of their houses, in hopes of finding sensitive timber : but I do not perceive any one so successful as the landlord of the Bowman tavern in Drury Lane, who had a mantle tree so extremely prompt and loud in its responses, that the sagacious observers were nearly unanimous in pronouncing it part of the same trunk which had afforded the original plank."

The following paragraph is from the *Loyal London Mercury*, October 4, 1682 :—

"Some persons being this week drinking at the Queen's Arms tavern in St. Martin's le Grand, in the kitchen, and having laid the fire-fork in the fire to light their pipes, accidentally fell a discoursing of the groaning board, and what might be the cause of it. One in the company having the fork in his hand to light his pipe, would needs make trial of a long dresser that stood there, which, upon the first touch, made a great noise and groaning, more than ever the board that was shewed did, and when they touched it three or four times, and found it far beyond the other. They all having seen it, the house is almost filled with spectators day and night, and any company calling for a glass of wine may see it : which, in the judgment of all, is far louder, and makes a longer groan, than the other, which to report, unless seen, would seem incredible."

The subject of fairs is treated very fully in the volume on the eighteenth century; nevertheless, they cannot be here altogether omitted, as they formed one of the chief amusements of the seventeenth century.

Fairs began by being serious markets, but later became a place of less important trade, where lace, gold and silver embroidery, jewellery, and finery of every kind were exposed for sale. A further decline took place when people of fashion ceased to attend the fair for the purchase of these things. Then the fair became frankly a

Habit of the LORD MAYOR of London in 1640. HABIT of the LADY MAYORESS of London in 1640.

From a contemporary print.

place of amusement and pleasure with booths. These are the several stages of a fair: first, the exhibition and sale of its staple as wool; next, or in addition, its ordinary trade; thirdly, a catering for children and the lower class. All this time its shows and amusements are growing of more and more importance, until at length they become the principal object of the fair. Paul Hentzner, writing in 1598, describes St. Bartholomew's Fair as follows :—

" Every year upon St. Bartholomew's Day, when the Fair is held, it is usual for the Mayor, attended by the twelve principal Aldermen, to walk into a neighbouring field dressed in his scarlet gown, and about his neck a golden chain, to which is hung a Golden Fleece, and besides, that particular ornament (the collar of SS.) which distinguishes the most noble Order of the Garter. During the year of his magistracy he is obliged to live so magnificently that foreigner or native, without any expense, is free, if he can find a chair empty, to dine at his table, where there is always the greatest plenty. When the Mayor goes out of the precincts of the City a sceptre, a sword, and a cap are borne before him, and he is followed by the principal Aldermen in scarlet gowns with gold chains, himself and they on horseback. Upon their arrival at a place appointed for that purpose, where a tent is pitched, the mob begin to wrestle before them, two at a time; the conquerors receive rewards from the Mayor. After this is over a parcel of live rabbits are turned loose among the crowd, which boys chase with great noise. While we were at this show one of our company, Tobias Salander, Doctor of Physic, had his pocket picked of his purse, with nine crowns (ecus du soleil), which, without doubt, was so cleverly taken from him by an Englishman, who always kept very close to him, that the Doctor did not in the least perceive it" (*England, as seen by Foreigners*, p. 107).

Hentzner might have observed also that by the law of England the cut-purse was liable to execution. In 1612 one John Pelman, a cut-purse, was actually hanged for stealing a purse containing forty shillings in the King's Chapel of Whitehall. It is said of him that he came in "good and seemly apparel like a Gentleman, a fair black coat laced and either lined thorow, or faced, with velvet." What says and sings Nightingale in the play?—

> " My masters and friends and good people, draw near,
> And look to your purses, for that I do say ;
> And though little money in them you do bear,
> It costs more to get than to lose in a day.
>   You oft have been told,
>   Both the young and the old,
> And bidden beware of the cut-purse so bold ;
> Then if you take heed not, free me from the curse,
> Who both give you warning, you, and the cut-purse.
> Youth, youth, thou hadst better been starved by thy nurse,
> Than live to be hanged for cutting a purse ! "

The following was the Proclamation made before the fair (Morley [1]) :—

"The Right Honourable Lord Mayor of the City of London and his right worshipful brethren the aldermen of the said city, streightly charge and command, on the behalf of our sovereign lady the Queen, that all manner of persons, of whatsoever estate, degree, or condition they be, having recourse to this Fair, keep the peace of our said sovereign lady the Queen.

That no manner of persons make any congregation, conventicles, or affrays, by which the same peace may be broken or disturbed, upon pain of imprisonment and fine, to be made after the discretion of the lord mayor and aldermen.

---

[1] *Memoirs of Bartholomew Fair*, Henry Morley, 1859.

Also, that all manner of sellers of wine, ale, or beer, sell by measures ensealed, as by gallon, pottle, quart, and pint, upon pain that will fall thereof.

And that no person sell any bread, but if it keep the assize, and that it be good and wholesome for man's body, upon pain that will fall thereof.

And that no manner of person buy or sell, but with true weights and measures, sealed according to the statute in that behalf made, upon pain that will fall thereof.

And that no manner of person, or persons, take upon him, or them, within this Fair, to make any manner of arrest, attachment, summons, or execution, but if it be done by the officer of this City thereunto assigned, upon pain that will fall thereof.

And that no person or persons whatsoever, within the limits and bounds of this Fair, presume to break the Lord's Day in selling, showing, or offering to sale, or in buying or offering to buy, any commodities whatsoever, or in sitting, tippling, or drinking in any tavern, inn, ale-house, or cook's-house, or in doing any other thing that may lead to the breach thereof, upon the pain and penalties contained in several acts of Parliament, which will be severely inflicted upon the breakers thereof.

And finally, that whatever person soever find themselves aggrieved, injured, or wronged by any manner of person in this Fair, that they come with their plaints before the stewards in this Fair, assigned to hear and determine pleas, and they will minister to all parties justice, according to the laws of this land, and the customs of this city. God save the Queen!"

The mayor, sheriffs, and aldermen sitting on horseback, robed in their violet gowns, having made this proclamation at a point between the city Fair and that owned by the Warwick or Holland family, as the rest of the official rule details, "the proclamation being made, they ride through the Cloth Fair, and so return back again, through the Churchyard of Great St. Bartholomew's to Aldersgate, and so ride home again to the Lord Mayor's house."

"It is remarkable," to quote from a scarce tract of 1641, which is given at length by Morley, "and worth your observation, to behold and hear the strange sights and confused noises in the fair. Here a Knave in a Fool's Coat, with a trumpet sounding, or on a drum beating, invites you and would fain persuade you to see his puppets; there a Rogue like a Wild Woodman, or in an antick shape like an Incubus, desires your company to view his motion; on the other side, Hocus Pocus with three yards of tape or ribbon in's hand, showing his art of Legerdemain to the admiration and astonishment of a company of cockaloaches. Amongst these you shall see a gray goose-cap (as wise as the rest), with a What do ye lack? in his mouth, stand in his booth shaking a rattle or scraping on a fiddle, with which children are so taken, that they presently cry out for these fopperies; and all these together make such a distracted noise, that you would think Babel were not comparable to it. Here there are also your gamesters in action; some turning of a whimsey, others throwing for pewter, who can quickly dissolve a round shilling into a three-halfpenny saucer.

Long Lane at this time looks very fair, and puts out her best clothes with the wrong side outward, so turned for their better turning off; and Cloth Fair is now in great request; well fare the Ale houses therein; yet better many a man fare (but at a dearer rate) in the Pig market, *alias* Pasty nook or Pie Corner, where pigs are all hours of the day on the stalls piping hot, and would cry (if they could speak), 'Come eat me'; but they are dear, and the reckonings for them are saucy."

D'Urfey's verses, written in 1655, do not present a fair quite without attractions :—

"In fifty-five may I never thrive,
    If I tell you any more than is true,
To London she came, hearing of the fame
    Of a fair they call Bartholomew.

In houses of boards, men talk upon cords,
    As easy as squirrels crack filberds ;
But the cut-purses they do bite and rob away ;
    But those we suppose to be ill-birds.

For a penny you may zee a fine puppet play,
    And for twopence a rare piece of art ;
And a penny a can, I dare swear a man
    May put zix of 'em into a quart.

Their zights are so rich, is able to bewitch
    The heart of a very fine man-a ;
Here's patient Grisel here, and Fair Rosamond there,
    And the History of Susanna.

At Pye Corner end, mark well, my good friend,
    'Tis a very fine dirty place ;
Where there's more arrows and bows, the Lord above knows,
    Than was handl'd at Chivy-Chase.

Henry III. proclaimed a fifteen days' fair to begin on the 13th of October 1248, the Day of the Translation of St. Edward (*Matthew Paris*, ii. p. 272)—

"On the 13th of October in this year, in the fortnight of Michaelmas, the king proceeded to London, to keep the feast of St. Edward, that is, of the translation of that saint, and sent word to a great number of the prelates and nobles, begging them, out of their friendship and devotion to him, to make their appearance at Westminster, to join with him in solemnly and devoutly celebrating the feast of St. Edward. At this summons, therefore, there came thither Earl Richard, Roger Bigod, earl marshal, the Earl of Hereford, some select barons, and certain knights, the bishops of Winchester, London, Ely, Worcester, and Carlisle, and a great number of abbots and priors. The king then declared it as his pleasure, and ordered it to be proclaimed by herald throughout the whole city of London and elsewhere, that he instituted a new fair to be held at Westminster, to continue for a fortnight entire. He also strictly interdicted, under penalty of heavy forfeiture and loss, all fairs which usually lasted for such a length of time in England; for instance, that of Ely and other places, and all traffic usually carried on at London, both in and out of doors, in order that by these means the Westminster fair might be more attended by people, and better supplied with merchandise. In consequence of this, innumerable people flocked thither from all quarters, as to the most famous fair, and the translation of St. Edward was celebrated, and the blood of Christ worshipped to an unexampled degree by the people there assembled. But all the merchants, in exposing their goods for sale there, were exposed to great inconveniences, as they had no shelter except canvas tents; for, owing to the changeable gusts of wind assailing them, as is usual at that time of the year, they were cold and wet, and also suffered from hunger and thirst; their feet were soiled by the mud, and their goods rotted by the showers of rain; and when they sat down to take their meals in the midst of their family by the fireside knew not how to endure this state of want and discomfort. The bishop of Ely, in consequence of the loss of his fair at Ely, which was suspended by the king's warrant, made a heavy complaint to him in the matter for introducing such novelties, but he gained nothing but words of soothing promises of future consolation."

CHAPTER VII

COACHES

THE seventeenth century witnessed the invention of the stage coach, and therefore the improvement of the roads. The horse litter was still used in the first half of the century. Marie de Medici, when she visited her daughter Henrietta in 1638, entered London in a litter. In 1640 Evelyn travelled in a litter from Bath to Wootton with his father, who was suffering from a dropsy, which killed him. The first stage coach was a waggon. A service of waggons was established between London and Liverpool; there were waggons also between London and York, and between London and other towns. M. de Sorbière, visiting London in the reign of Charles II., says that rather than use the stage coach he travelled in a waggon drawn by a team of six horses. Therefore the Dover stage coach had already begun to run, and it was not thought more convenient than the waggon. Probably it was more liable to be upset. In 1663 one Edward Parker of Preston wrote to his father saying that he had got to London in safety on the coach, riding in the boot; that the company was good, "Knightes and Ladyes," but the journey tedious.

Coaches at first had no springs, so that the occupants were tossed about. "Men and women are so tossed, tumbled, jumbled, and rumbled."

Stow attributes the introduction of coaches into England to one Guilliam Boonen, a Dutchman, who became the Queen's coachman in 1564. He is wrong about the introduction of coaches, but he is right in saying that within the next twenty years there grew up a great trade in coachbuilding, to the jealousy of the watermen.

"Coaches and sedans (quoth the waterman), they deserve both to be thrown into the Theames, and but for stopping the channell I would they were, for I am sure where I was woont to have eight or tenne fares in a morning I now scarce get two in a whole day: our wives and children at home are readie to pine, and some of us are faine for meanes to take other professions upon us."

Taylor, the water-poet, thus speaks of coaches :—

" Carroaches, coaches, jades, and Flanders mares,
Doe rob us of our shares, our wares, our fares :
Against the ground we stand and knocke our heeles,
Whilest all our profit runs away on wheeles :
And whosoever but observes and notes
The great increase of coaches and of boates,

COACHES IN ST. JAMES'S PARK

From the Crace Collection in the British Museum.

Shall finde their number more than e'r they were
By hale and more within these thirty yeares.
Then water-men at sea had service still,
And those that staid at home had worke at will :
Then upstart helcart-coaches were to seeke,
A man could scarce see twenty in a weeke.
But now I thinke a man may daily see
More than the wherries on the Thames can be."

In the year 1601 the attention of Parliament was called to the increase of coaches, and a Bill was brought in "to restrain the excessive use of coaches." This, however, was rejected on the second reading.

Attacked or defended, the stage coach, once started, could never be abolished. The first stage coach of the City was the hackney coach, which was established by one Captain Busby in 1625. He posted four coaches at the Maypole in the Strand, with instructions to his men to carry people to any part of the town. Twelve years later there were fifty; in 1652 there were two hundred; in 1694, seven hundred. The coach hire was eighteenpence the first hour, one shilling afterwards. The first coaches had no windows, but, in their place, perforated metal shutters; the glass coach was introduced about the year 1667. Lady Peterborough forgot that there was glass over the door and ran her head through it.

The sedan chair was introduced by Sir Saunders Duncombe in 1634. As for stage vehicles there were at first "long waggons," and these as early as 1564. The following extracts from Journals (*Archæologia*) show that there were many stage coaches as early as 1659 and 1660:—

"1659. May 2nd, I set forwards towards London by Coventre Coach: 4th I came to London.

1660. March 13th, my daughter Lettice went towards London in Coventre Waggon.

1662. June 28th, given 16s. in earnest, and for my passage with my man in Aylesbury Coach on Thursday next.

1663. January 27th, I went to Baginton [with his own horses, it would appear], 28th to Towcester: 29th to St. Albans, 30th by St. Albans Coach to London.

1677. April 8th, I went to Coventre: 9th thence to Woburne by Chester Coach: 10th to London.

1679. July 16th, I came out of London by the Stage Coach of Bermicham to Banbury.

1680. June 30th, I came out of London in the Bedford Stage Coach to the Earle of Aylesburie's house at Ampthill."

From the diary of a Yorkshire clergyman, lent by the Rev. Mr. Hunter, one gathers that in the winter of 1682 a journey from Nottingham to London in a stage coach occupied four whole days. One of this gentleman's fellow-travellers was Sir Ralph Knight, of Langold in Yorkshire (an officer in Monk's army), so that Mr. Parker was not singular in having as his companion in such a conveyance "persons of great quality, as Knights and Ladyes."

In 1661 there was a stage coach running between Oxford and London, taking two days, *i.e.* thirty miles a day, or about three miles an hour. The fare was two shillings. A coach with four horses carried six passengers, a long waggon with four or five horses twenty to twenty-five.

In 1663 there was a stage coach between London and Edinburgh once a month, taking twelve days for the journey, *i.e.* thirty-three miles a day. In 1697 the stage coach from York to London took six days.

Charles II. instituted tolls for the repair of the roads, but they were not extended over the whole of the country till 1767. In 1675 Lady Russell writes that it is not possible to describe the badness of the roads between Sevenoaks and Tunbridge Wells.

Post horses were threepence a mile, riding horses 2s. the first day, and 1s. a day afterwards, the hirer to pay for food and to bring back the horse.

The fare for travelling in a stage coach was a shilling for every five miles; therefore, for the journey from London to York it would be forty shillings.

There were pamphlets for and against the use of the stage coach; it caused those who travelled in it to contract "an idle habit of body; they became heavy and listless when they rode a few miles, and were not able to endure frost, snow, or rain, or to lodge in the field." This seems a very sound objection; there can be no doubt that when everybody rode or walked, people were much hardier to stand against cold or heat. On the other hand the stage coach had its defenders. One of them says that "there is of late such an admirable commodiousness, both for men and women, to travel from London to the principal towns in the country, that the like hath not been known in the world, and that is by stage coaches, wherein any one may be transported to any place sheltered from foul weather and foul ways."

The writer of a pamphlet in 1675 thus denounces them :—

" There is not the fourth part of saddle-horses either bred, or kept, now in England, that was before these coaches were set up, and would be again, if they were suppressed, nor is there any occasion for breeding, or keeping such horses, whilst the coaches are continued. For, will any man keep a horse for himself and another for his man, all the year, for to ride one or two journeys: that at pleasure, when he hath occasion, can slip to any place where his business lies, for two, three or four shillings, if within twenty miles of London : and so proportionately into any part of England: No: there is no man: unless some noble soul, that scorns and abhors being confined to so ignoble, base, and sordid a way of travelling as these coaches oblige him unto. For formerly every man that had occasion to travel many journeys yearly, or to ride up and down, kept horses for himself and servants, and seldom rid without one or two men : but now, since every man can have a passage into every place he is to travel unto, or to some place within a few miles of that part he designs to go unto, they have left keeping of horses, and travel without servants: and York, Chester, and Exeter stage-coaches, each of them, with forty horses apiece, carry eighteen passengers a week from London to either of these places : and, in like manner, as many in return from these places to London : which come, in the whole, to eighteen hundred and seventy-two in the year. Now take it for granted that all that are carried from London to those places are the same that are brought back: yet are there nine hundred and thirty-six passengers carried by forty horses: whereas, were it not for these coaches, at least five hundred horses would be required to perform this work."

We have already considered the complaint of the watermen. The stage coaches having begun to carry passengers as far as Windsor and Maidenhead up the river, and to Greenwich and Gravesend down the river, who will take a boat, which is far slower and less comfortable than the coach?

The next point of consideration is that of His Majesty's Excise. Formerly every traveller of quality rode with his servants, who consumed a great quantity of beer and wine on the journey. When coaches began, the passengers travelled without any servants at all, to the great loss of the inns on the road and the corresponding injury to the Excise. And consider the losses inflicted on trade :—

" For before these coaches were set up, travellers rode on horseback, and men had boots, spurs, saddles, bridles, saddle-cloths, and good riding-suits, coats and clokes, stockings and hats: whereby the wool and leather of the kingdom was consumed, and the poor people set at work by carding, combing, spinning, knitting, weaving, and fulling. And your cloth-workers, drapers, tailors, saddlers, tanners, curriers, shoe-makers, spurriers, lorimers, and felt-makers had a good employ: were full of work, got money, lived handsomely, and helped, with their families, to consume the provisions and manufactures of the kingdom: but by means of these coaches, these trades, besides many others depending upon them, are become almost useless: and they, with their families, reduced to great necessity: insomuch that many thousands of them are cast upon the parishes, wherein they dwell, for a maintenance. Besides, it is a great hurt to the girdlers, sword-cutlers, gunsmiths, and trunk-makers: most gentlemen, before they travelled in their coaches, used to ride with swords, belts, pistols, holsters, portmanteaus, and hat-cases: which, in these coaches, they have little or no occasion for. For, when they rode on horseback, they rode in one suit, and carried another to wear, when they came to their journey's end; or lay by the way: but in coaches, a silk suit and an Indian gown with a sash, silk stockings and beaver-hats men ride in, and carry no other with them, because they escape the wet and dirt, which on horseback they cannot avoid: whereas, in two or three journeys on horseback these clothes and hats were wont to be spoiled: which done, they were forced to have new very often, and that increased the consumption of the manufactures, and the employment of the manufacturer: which travelling in coaches doth no way do. And if they were women that travelled, they used to have safe-guards and hoods, side-saddles, and pillions, with strappings, saddle or pillion-cloths, which, for the most part, were either laced or embroidered: to the making of which there went many several trades: seeing there is not one side-saddle with the furniture made, but, before it is furnished, there are at least thirty-seven trades have a share in the making thereof: most of which are either destroyed, or greatly prejudiced, by the abatement of their trade: which being bread unto, and having served seven years' apprenticeship to learn, they know not what other course to take for a livelihood. And, besides all these inferior handy-craftsmen there are the mercers, silkmen, lacemen, milliners, linen and woollen drapers, haberdashers, and divers other eminent trades, that receive great prejudice by this way of travelling. For the mercers sold silk and stuff in great quantities for safeguards, hoods, and riding clothes for women: by which means the silk-twisters, winders, throwsters, weavers, and dyers, had a fuller employment: the silkmen sold more lace and embroidery, which kept the silver wire-drawers, lace-makers, and embroiderers: and at least ten trades more were employed. The linen-draper sold more linen, not only to saddlers to make up saddles, but to travellers for their own use: nothing wearing out linen more than riding. Woollen-drapers sold more cloth than now: saddlers used before these coaches were set up, to buy three or four hundred pounds worth of cloth a-piece in a year: nay, some five hundred and a thousand pounds worth, which they cut out into saddles and pillion-cloths: though now there is no saddler can dispose of one hundred pounds worth of cloth in a year in his trade. The milliners and haberdashers, they also sold more ribbons, and riding on horseback, spoiling and wearing them out, much more than travelling in a coach: and, on horseback these things were apter to be lost than in a coach."

And the expense :—

" Men do not travel in these coaches with less expence of money, or time, than on horseback: for, on horseback, they may travel faster: and, if they please, all things duly considered, with as little if not less charges. For instance: from London to Exeter, Chester, or York, you pay forty shillings a-piece in summer-time, forty-five shillings in winter, for your passage: and as much from those places back to London. Besides, in the journey they change coachmen four times: and there are few passengers that give twelve-pence to each coachman at the end of his stage: which comes to eight shillings in the journey backward and forward, and at least three shillings comes to each passenger's share to pay for the coachmen's drink on the road: so that in summer-time the passage backward and forward to any of these places costs four pounds eleven shillings, in the winter five pounds one shilling. And this only for eight days riding in the summer, and twelve in the winter. Then, when the passengers come to London, they must have lodgings: which, perhaps, may cost them five or six shillings a week, and that in fourteen days amounts unto ten or twelve shillings, which makes the four pounds eleven shillings either five pounds one shilling, or five pounds three shillings: or the five pounds one shilling, five pounds eleven shillings, or five pounds thirteen shillings: beside the inconvenience of having meat from the cooks, at double the price they might have it for in inns. But if stage coaches were down and men travelled as formerly, on horseback, then when they came into their inns they would pay nothing for lodgings: and as there would excellent horses be bred and kept by gentlemen for their own use, so would there be by others that would keep them on purpose to let: which would, as formerly, be let at ten or twelve shillings per week, and in many places for six, eight, or nine shillings a week.   But admitting the lowest price to be twelve shillings, if a man comes from York, Exeter, or Chester, to London: be five days coming, five days going, and say twelve days in London to dispatch his business (which is the most that country chapmen usually do stay) all this would be but three weeks: so that his horse-hire would come but to one pound sixteen shillings, his horse-meat at fourteen pence a day, one with another, which is the highest that can be reckoned upon, and will come but to one pound five shillings, in all three pounds one shilling: so that there would be, at least, forty or fifty shillings saved of what coach-hire and lodgings will cost him: which would go a great way in paying for riding-clothes, stockings, hats, boots, spurs, and other accoutrements for riding: and, in my poor opinion, would be far better spent in the buying of these things, by the making whereof the poor would be set at work, and kept from being burthensome to the parish, than to give it to those stage-coachmen, to indulge that lazy, idle habit of body, that men, by constant riding in these coaches have brought upon themselves."

CHAPTER VIII

PUNISHMENT AND CRIME

In the following chapter will be found certain notes on crime and criminals. There is little difference between the crimes of the Elizabethan and those of the Stuart period. I have added two or three stories of the period which seem to affect the manners of London. Hundreds of such stories might be found scattered up and down the annals of the seventeenth century. I have made these meagre selections with sparing hand. The crime of Lord Sanquhar; the cruelty of the Puritan in his punishments; an example of the honest citizen; the treachery of a noble lord; the origin of General Monk's wife, and one or two more persons and episodes may be taken as illustrations of the times.

The punishment of criminals under the English law remained all through the century cruel and vindictive. High treason continued to be punished with the old barbarities; we have seen what these were. The coiner, if a man, was drawn on a hurdle and hanged; if a woman, she was burned alive. For petty treason, which is the murder of a master, a husband, or a superior officer, the offender was hanged if a man; burned if a woman. For felony of all kinds, hanging. If a man refused to plead he was pressed to death. After death, the body was sometimes hung in chains. In felonies where Benefit of Clergy was still allowed, the offender was branded on the left hand. For petty larceny, the punishments were the loss of an ear, or a whipping. Perjury was punished with pillory, with branding on the forehead, while the offender's trees were pulled up in his garden and his goods confiscated. Forgery, cheating, libelling, using false weights and measures, forestalling the market, offending against the statutes in bakery and brewery, were punished with pillory, and sometimes by nailing one or both ears to the pillory, or cutting them off, or boring through the tongue with a hot iron. For striking in the King's Court the right hand was struck off. For striking in Westminster Hall while the judges were sitting, the punishment was imprisonment for life and confiscation of the offender's goods.

If a jury bought in a verdict contrary to evidence they were liable to lose the franchise; to be incapable of acting as witness or on a jury, to lose their lands and property, and to be imprisoned.

The stocks were for drunkards and vagabonds. Scolding women were to be ducked in the ducking stool.

This goodly array of punishments was in full practice during the seventeenth century.

There were other crimes not dealt with in this list, especially the crime of witchcraft. James has been held up to ridicule for believing in witchcraft. This is unjust, because there were very few in the country who had the strength of mind to disbelieve it. Fortunately the wave of superstitious terror hardly touched London.

The practice of duelling could be defended on the ground of its being a survival, in a sense, of the old ordeal by battle. James I. was the first who made an effort to restrict and abolish the practice.

Under the Commonwealth incest and adultery were made felonies. Incontinence for the first time was made a criminal offence, to be punished by three months' imprisonment.

These few notes on crime and criminal law might seem incomplete without mention of the two greatest criminals of the century, Titus Oates and Judge Jeffreys. Their crimes, however, have little or nothing to do with London save that those of the former were committed for the most part in London, and that the latter died in London.

The roguery, vice, cheateries, and thieveries practised in the City have always been on the grand scale. Perhaps there were no more of these things in King Charles's reign than in our own time. But it seems so. To begin with, there were the professed and professional sharps, men who lived by their wits. The names by which they were known under Queen Bess had been changed; these terms of endearment or of opprobrium do not last long. They were now known as Huffs, Rooks, Pads, Pompinios, Philo Puttonists, Ruffons, Shabbaroons, and Rufflers. Many of them were of good birth and of excellent manners. When one of them extorted all his money from a flat it was with an air so engaging that he could not resent it; nor could he believe that he had been cheated by loaded dice and by marked cards. Not all of them were gentlemen. Thus there was the Angler, who carried a stick with a hook at the end, which was useful in passing an open shop; there was the Ruffler, who pretended to be an old soldier of Marston Moor or Naseby; there was the Wild Rogue, a boy or girl who cut off the gold or silver buttons from people in a crowd; the Clapper Doyen, who begged about the streets with stolen children; the Abram man, a sham madman; the Whip Jack, a sham shipwrecked sailor; the Mumper, a decayed merchant; and the Dommerer, who pretended to be dumb.

If we are to believe the revelations of *Meritio Latron*, the City 'prentices contained among them a considerable number of young fellows who were common rogues and thieves; they robbed their masters as much as they dared, both of money and of goods; they met on Saturday nights when the masters were in the country, exchanged the goods, and feasted together in company with other rogues of the town. In the same edifying work we are instructed concerning the sharp practices and cheateries of the various shopkeepers. It is hardly worth while to spend any time in enumerating these. They are much the same in every age.

The case of Alexander Leighton is one of Royal cruelty. It may be placed beside that of Prynne. There are· others of Puritanic cruelty quite as bad, as will be seen presently.

Leighton, a Doctor of Divinity, in 1630, was accused of framing, publishing, and dispersing a scandalous book against King, peers, and prelate.

He was brought before the Star Chamber, where he received his sentence.

First, he was degraded. He was then whipped and put in pillory. Being taken out, his right ear was cut off and the right side of his nose slit, and he was branded on the right cheek with the letters S.S., *i.e.* Stirrer up of Sedition. He was then taken back to the Fleet for a week, after which, his wounds still fresh, he was again whipped, again set in pillory, and was then deprived of his remaining ear, had the left side of his nose slit, and the left cheek branded.

The Puritan was stern and unrelenting in his punishment. Perhaps this fact may account for something of the hatred with which he came to be regarded by the populace. Take, for instance, the case of Francis Prideaux, a poor little petty thief, who would now be let off with a month's imprisonment :—

" Francis Prideaux is now convicted of a trespas for unlawfully ripping up and taking away lead from the house of Richard Rothwell and is fined 12d., and must bee stripped naked from the middle upwards on Monday the fourteenth day of this instant January betweene the houres of 9 and 11 of the clocke in the forenoone and then openly whipped on his back untill his body be bloddy at the hinder part of a cart from the Old Gatehouse through Long Ditch, Duke Street, and Charles Street in the parish of St. Margaret's Westminster, and back againe, from the said Charles Street, through Duke Street and Long Ditch, to the said Old Gatehouse. Hee is committed to the New Prison of the Gatehouse, ther to remayne in safe custody untill he shall undergoe his said punishment, and pay his said fine, and then be delivered paying his fees iiis. viiid."

The following history of heartless duplicity in high places is told in the memoirs of De Grammont. The victim was one of the earliest actresses on the stage :—

" The Earl of Oxford fell in love with a handsome, graceful actress, belonging to the Duke's theatre, who performed to perfection, particularly the part of Roxana in a very fashionable new play : insomuch that she ever after retained that name.

This creature being both very virtuous and very modest, or, if you please, wonder-fully obstinate, proudly rejected the presents and addresses of the Earl of Oxford. The resistance inflamed his passion: he had recourse to invectives and even spells: but all in vain. This disappointment had such an effect upon him, that he could neither eat nor drink: this did not signify to him: but his passion at length became so violent that he could neither play nor smoke. In this extremity, Love had recourse to Hymen; the Earl of Oxford, one of the first peers of the realm, is, as you know, a very handsome man: he is of the Order of the Garter, which greatly adds to an air naturally noble. In short, from his outward appearance, you would suppose he was really possessed of some sense: but as soon as ever you hear him speak you are perfectly convinced to the contrary. This passionate lover presented her with a promise of marriage in due form, signed with his own hand: she would not, however, rely upon this: but the next day she thought there could be no danger, when the Earl himself came to her lodgings attended by a clergyman and another man for a witness: the marriage was accordingly solemnized with all due ceremonies, in the presence of one of her fellow-players, who attended as a witness on her part. You will suppose, perhaps, that the new countess had nothing to do but to appear at court according to her rank, and to display the earl's arms upon her carriage. This was far from being the case. When examination was made concerning the marriage, it was found to be a mere deception: it appeared that the pretended priest was one of my lord's trumpeters, and the witness his kettle-drummer. The parson and his companion never appeared after the ceremony was over, and as for the other witness, he endeavoured to persuade her that the Sultana Roxana might have supposed in some part or other of a play, that she was really married. It was all to no purpose that the poor creature claimed the protection of the laws of God and man: both which were violated and abused, as well as herself, by this infamous imposition: in vain did she throw herself at the king's feet to demand justice: she had only to rise up again without redress: and happy might she think herself to receive an annuity of one thousand crowns, and to resume the name of Roxana, instead of Countess of Oxford."

The strange story of Lord Sanquhar's revenge belongs to the reign of James the First; it is the story of a madman: a man who went mad with brooding over a sense of shame. He was a Scottish nobleman, and he came to Whitefriars to practise fencing with one or other of the fencing-masters who had lodgings in Alsatia. He was playing with a master named Turner, and in the course of their play he received the point or the button of his adversary's foil in his eye, the result of which accident was the loss of that eye altogether. The accident, it is said, was much regretted by Turner; considering how much it reflected upon his professional skill, this is not surprising. Lord Sanquhar, however, sometime visited the court of the French King Henry IV. When the King was in discourse with him he observed the loss of the eye and asked how that occurred. " By a sword," said Sanquhar. " Does the man live?" asked the King.

This question set Lord Sanquhar brooding over the thing until he persuaded himself that his honour demanded the death of Turner. It is, however, wonderful that he should have perversely believed that his honour demanded the murder of Turner by two hired assassins. It was five years after the accident of the foil. The two men went to Whitefriars about seven in the evening. They found Turner sitting before his house with a friend. Apparently Turner knew them, for he invited them to drink; whereupon one of them, Carliel, turning round to cock the pistol, presented it and fired, the bullet entering the man's heart, so that he fell back, dead. They then fled; one of them ran up a *cul de sac* and was taken on the spot; the other tried to escape into Scotland; and Lord Sanquhar tried to hide himself in the country.

They were all three caught. The two murderers were hanged opposite the great gate of Whitefriars—now the entrance to Bouverie Street; the noble lord was hanged in New Palace Yard.

We hear a great deal about debtors' prisons in the course of the eighteenth century. Some effort was made in the seventeenth century to investigate their condition.

In 1677 a committee was appointed to examine into the security, not the proper treatment, of the prisoners of the King's Bench and Fleet Street. Joseph Cooling, Marshal of the Marshalsea, deposed that he had given, for his office, security for £10,000 and paid, besides, a rent of £1400 a year. He said that he gave no liberty to the prisoners to go out; that those who would not find security were not allowed even to leave the Rules unless attended by his servants; that his servants saw that everybody was in his lodging at nightfall; that some prisoners had a whole house to themselves; that the reason of the Rules was that the prison would not hold all the prisoners; that there was a table of fees, and that he never took more than the table allowed.

Manlove, Warden of the Fleet, deposed that his office was taxed at £600 a year; that he took security from the prisoners before he suffered them to go into the Rules, and so on.

Then came the evidence of ten prisoners. They swore that when the Commissioners of Bankrupts went to the prison in order to examine one Farrington, the Marshal could only produce him twice out of eleven times that he was wanted; that when the Commissioners' messenger entered the prison, the prisoners jumped upon him. The evidence on this point is not clear. Robert Black, another prisoner, gave evidence as to the Marshal's exactions and tyranny. He himself had signed a petition against these exactions, and was in consequence forcibly removed to the poor side, where the exercise yard was encumbered with sheds and where he had to sleep in a damp cellar 4 feet underground, 18 feet square, with nineteen others: that prisoners had been locked up day and night, their friends refused admission to them. This evidence of Robert Black was confirmed by others.

Anne Moseley, another prisoner, gave evidence as to the filthy condition of the place where she had to sleep; she also accused the Marshal of taking £10 from her for permission to live at home and then putting her on the poor side. George Phillips, another prisoner, swore that he, with three others, was put into a room 16 feet by 15 feet, for which they had to pay a rent of £24 : 6 : 6 a year, though it was worth no more than £4 a year; that the Marshal let a number of such rooms, some of them worth no more than £6 a year, at rents of £24, £36, £46, and £62 a year.

Other prisoners deposed that whereas a table of fees had been laid down by a commissioner in the third year of Queen Elizabeth and exhibited in a frame hung up in the common hall of the prison; and whereas the scale of fees had been further established by the 22nd and 23rd Charles II., the warden of the Fleet, Richard Manlove, levied larger fees and threatened to put the prisoners in irons if they were not paid.

There does not appear, however, to have been any redress of these grievances. The difficulty in the minds of the judges was not as to the treatment of the prisoner by the wardens, but as to their safe custody and the keepers' court before which the wardens should be tried in case of allowing the prisoners to escape. In other words, a prisoner for debt was regarded partly as a criminal who was rightly punished by being kept in a damp dungeon, and nearly starved to death, and partly as an obstinate person who refused to pay his just debts and was therefore very properly maltreated.

In the year 1613 Mr. R. J., moved by the consideration of the wickedness to be found in this City, and of the dangers and temptations to which young men are exposed, completed a pamphlet of warning and exposure. It is entitled " Looke on me London." The title page goes on :—

> " I am an honest Englishman, ripping up the bowels
> of mischief lurking in thy Suburbs and Precincts.
> Take heed
> The hangman's halter and the Beadle's Whip,
> Will make the Fool dance and the Knave to skip."

The pamphlet shows, what one might have suspected, the protection afforded by the suburbs and parts of London outside the City and the liberties where the Lord Mayor had no jurisdiction. It was at an innocent-looking ordinary that the young man first met the companion who led him to destruction. He was a handsome, well-dressed, well-spoken gentleman; he was free with his money; his manners were easy and courteous; he laughed readily; he was known at the house, where the drawers ran to fetch him all he wanted; it was an act of courtesy when he spoke to the young gentleman come up from the country to study law, as becomes one who will be a country gentleman and will live on his estate. This brave gentleman not only condescended to speak to the stranger, but he began to talk to him of the sights and pleasures of the town. Would he see the play? The Curtain Theatre was open that afternoon. Would he cross the river to see a famous fencing match at which two would fight till one was disabled? Would he choose rather a bear-baiting? There would be one in Paris Gardens, or, if he liked it better, the gentleman knew where a gaming table could be found, or a quiet hour could be spent over the dice. Or—and here he whispered—would the young gentleman like to visit a certain *bona roba* of his acquaintance? Upon her and her friends this friendly person enlarged with so much eloquence that the young gentleman was inflamed, and, forgetting his principles and his virtue, begged his friend to take him to the house of these celestial beings.

Now this gallant of such worshipful appearance was nothing but a "shifter" who lived by picking up such simple persons, enticing them into the company of disorderly women, cheating at cards and dice.

"Yet for all this, my brave Shifter hath a more costly reckoning to give him, for being thus growne into acquaintance, hee will in a familiar kinde of courtesie accompany him up and downe the Citty, and in the end will come unto a Mercer's or Gold-smith's shoppe, of whom the young Gentleman is well knowne; there will he cheapen velvet, satten, jewels, or what him liketh, and offer his new friend's credit for the payment; he will with so bold a countenance aske this friendship, that the Gentleman shall bee to seeke of excuse to deny him: well, although the penyworths of the one bee not very good, yet the payment of the other is sure to bee currant.

Thus, by prodigall ryots, vaine company, and rash suretiship many of our English yong Gentlemen are learned to say—

> ' I wealthy was of late,
> Though needy now be :
> Three things have changed my state,
> Dice, Wine, and Venerie.' "

Presently the young gentleman falls into the hands of the money-lender :—

"After all this there seizeth upon the needy Gentleman thus consumed another Devouring Caterpillar, which is the Broker for money : one that is either an old Banker-out citizen, or some smooth-conditioned unthrifty Gentleman farre in debt, some one of these will helpe him to credit with some of their late creditors with a single protestation of meere curtesie. But by your favour, they will herein deale most cunningly. For the citizen Broker (after money taken out for his paines, considering for the time given, and losse in selling of the wares put together) will bring the yong Gentleman fifty pounds currant money for a hundred pounds good debt.

Mary, the Gentleman broker will deale more gallanter, for he will be bounde with his fellow Gentleman for a hundred pound, sharing the money equally betweene them, not without solemne promise to discharge his owne fifty, and if need be, the whole hundred pounds assurance."

The worst places are the gaming houses.

" Thus one mischiefe drawes on another, and in my opinion gaming houses are the chiefe Fountaines thereof; which wicked places first nourisheth our yong men of England in pride, then acquainteth them with sundry shifting companions, whereof one sort cozeneth them at dice, cardes, another sort consume them with riotous meetings, another sort by Brokage bringeth them in debt, and out of credite, and then awaiteth covetousnesse and usury to cease upon their livings, and the officious sergiant upon their liberties: and all this (as I said before) principally proceeds by the frequenting of gaming houses."

Where do the rogues of all kinds haunt and find refuge?

" Now remaineth the discovery of the third sort of these haunts, which are placed in the suburbs of the Citty, in Allies, Gardanes, and other obscure corners, out of the common walkes of the magistrates. The daily Guestes of these privy houses are maister-lesse men, needy Shifters, Theeves, Cut-purses, unthrifty servants, both serving-men and Prentises: Here a man may picke out mates for all purposes save such as are good: here a man may finde out fellowes, that for a bottle of wine will make no more conscience to kill a man than a butcher a beast: Here closely lie Saint Nicholas Clearkes, that with a good Northerne Gelding, will gaine more by a Halter, than an honest yeoman will with a teame of good horses: Here are they that will not let to deceive their father, to rob their brother, and fire their neighbour's house for an advantage. These brave companions will not sticke to spend frankly though they have neither lands nor goods by the dead, nor honestly by nature. But how will this hold out; Fire will consume wood without maintenance, and Ryot make a weake purse without supply.

Gentlemen (for the most part) have lands to make money, and the yong citizens way to get credite: but these idle fellowes have neither lands nor credite, nor will live by any honest meanes or occupation: yet have they hands to filch, heads to deceive, and friends to receive, and by these helpes, most commonly shift they badly well.

The other upon currant assurance, perhaps, get money for twenty pounds in the hundred, but these that worst may hold the candle: they upon their owne, or upon their maisters apparell, Brasse, Pewter, Linnin, Wollen, or such like, will find Brokers or Friperers, that for eight pence in the pound for every monthe's use, will boldly for halfe the value take these pawnes."

The writer goes on to describe some of the tricks of usurers. They are so hard-hearted—but he does not consider that the profession must begin with a flinty heart—

that they neither fear God nor reverence man ; that they will neither pardon their own father nor acknowledge their mother, nor regard their brothers, and will even make merchandise of their own children. They bear false evidence, " offend the widow and oppress the orphan. Oh, how great is this folly of theirs! to lose life, to seek death, and to banish themselves from heaven eternally." As for the various tricks that are practised :—

" I know a Broker that will take no interest for his money, but will have the lease of your house, or your land, in use, receiving rent for the same till you pay your principall againe, which will come to a greater gaine than threescore in the hundred. I knowe another that will take no interest money, but will have Pewter, Brasse, Sheetes, Plate, Table-Clothes, Napkins, and such like things, to use in his house, till his money come home, which will loose more in the wearing than the interest of the money will come to.

I know another that will take a pawne twice worth the money that hee lends, and agree with the Borrower to redeeme it at a day, or loose it, by which meanes the poore borrower is forced sometimes for want of money to loose his pawne for halfe the valew.

I know another that will not lend, but buy at small prices, and covenant with the borrower to buy the same againe, at such a price, at such a day, or loose it. This is a fellow that seekes to cozen the Law, but let him take heed lest the devill his good maister cozens not him, and at the last carry him post into hell.

I know another that will lend out his money to men of occupations, as to Butchers, Bakers, and such like, upon conditions to bee partners in their gaines but not in their losses, by which meanes hee that takes all the paines and ventures all is forced to give the Broker halfe the profit for his money.

I know another, for his money lending to a Carpenter, a Brick-layer, or a Plaisterer, will agree with them for so many daies worke, or so many weekes, for the loane of his money, which if all reckonings bee cast will come to a deere interest.

I know many about this citty that will not bee seene to be Brokers themselves, but suffer their wives to deale with their money, as to lend a shilling for a peny a weeke. To Fish-wives, Oister-women, Oringe-wenches and such like, these be they that looke about the citty like rats and weasels, so gnaw poore people alive, and yet go invisible.

This if it be well considered of, is a Jewish Brokage, for indeed the Jewes first brought usury and brokage into England, which now by long sufferance have much blemished the ancient vertues of this Kingdome: let us but remember this one example, how that in the time of King Henry the Third, the good cittizens of London, in one night slew five hundred Jewes, for that a Jew took a Christian penny in the shilling usury, and ever after got them banished the city : but surely those Brokers aforesaid deserve worse than Jewes, for they be like unto Strumpets,

23

for they receive all men's money, as well the Beggar's as the Gentleman's: nay, they will themselves take money upon Brokage, to bring their trade into a better Custome, which in my minde is a wicked custome to live only by sinne."

In the New Exchange, Strand, at the sign of the " Three Spanish Gypsies," lived from 1632 to 1649 Thomas Ratford and Ann his wife. They kept a shop for the sale of washballs, powder, gloves, and such things; the wife taught girls plain work, and about the year 1667 she became sempstress to Monk, then a Colonel, and carried linen to his place. Her father was one John Clarges, a farrier at the Savoy, and farrier to Colonel Monk in 1632. He was a man of some success in trade, because he promoted a Maypole on the site of the Strand Cross. He died in 1648. In 1649 Mrs. Ratford and her husband "fell out and parted." In 1652 she married General Monk.

Years afterwards the question arose in a court of law whether Ratford was dead at the time of the marriage. Witnesses swore they had seen him, but as he had never turned up to receive money due to him, which was inconceivable if he were living, nor had he visited any of his friends, nor was there any occasion why he should have kept out of the way, unless it could be proved that the Duchess paid him for silence, and as the question was only raised after all were dead, the verdict of the jury was in favour of the legality of the marriage. The story which represents Ann Clarges as the daughter of a washerwoman who carried the linen which her mother had washed to Monk's house is thus completely disproved. Since her father was farrier to Monk in 1632, it is possible that he noticed the girl before her marriage; it is also quite possible that some kind of *liaison* was carried on between Monk and Mrs. Ratford; this perhaps was the reason of the separation, and the marriage took place, one thinks, as soon as the death of Ratford was known.

Thomas Bancroft, grandson of Archbishop Bancroft, was for many years one of the Lord Mayor's officers of the City, who in the execution of his office, by information and summoning the citizens before the Lord Mayor upon the most trifling occasions, and for many things not belonging to his office, not only pillaged the poor, but likewise many of the rich, who, rather than lose time in appearing before the said magistrate, gave money to get rid of this common pest of citizens, which, together with his numerous quarterages from brokers, annually amassed a considerable sum of money. By these and other mercenary practices he effectually incurred the hatred and ill-will of the citizens of all denominations, that the persons who attended his funeral obsequies with great difficulty saved his corpse from being jostled off the bearers' shoulders in the church by the enraged populace, who, seizing the bells, rang them for joy at his unlamented death, a deportment heretofore unheard of among the London rabble.

CHAPTER IX

PUBLIC MORALITY

In 1679 the Lord Mayor issued a Proclamation in favour of religion, morality, and cleanliness which ought to have converted and convinced a whole City. It did not, because sinners observed with satisfaction that there was no possibility of the pains and penalties being enforced. This instructive document deserves to be set forth at length :—

"The Right Honourable the Lord Mayor, having taken into his serious consideration the many dreadful afflictions which this City hath of late years suffered, by a raging plague, a most unheard-of devouring fire, and otherwise: and justly fearing that the same have been occasioned by the many hainous crying sins and provocations to the Divine Majesty: and his Lordship also considering the present dangers of greater mischiefs and misery which seem still to threaten this City, if the execution of the righteous judgments of God Almighty be not prevented by an universal timely repentance and reformation: hath, therefore, thought it one duty of his office, being intrusted to take all possible care for the good government, peace, and welfare of this City, first, to pray and persuade all and every the inhabitants thereof to reform, themselves and families, all sins and enormities whereof they know themselves to be guilty: and if neither the fear of the Great God, nor of His impending judgments shall prevail upon them, he shall be obliged to let them know that, as he is their chief Magistrate, he ought not to bear the sword in vain: and therefore doth resolve, by God's grace, to take the assistance of his brethren the Aldermen, and to require the aid of all the Officers of this City in their several places, to punish and suppress according to the laws of the land, and the good customs of this City, those scandalous and provoking sins which have of late increased and abounded amongst us, even without shame, to the dishonour of Christianity, and the scandal of the government of this City, heretofore so famous over the world for its piety, sobriety, and good order.

To the end therefore that the laws may become a terror unto evil-doers, and that such, in whose hearts the fear of God and the love of virtue shall not prevail, being forewarned, may amend their lives for fear of punishment, his Lordship hath thought fit to remember them of several penalties provided by law against notorious offenders : as also of all Constables and Public Officers (who are to put the said laws in execution) of their duty therein.

First, every profane curser and swearer ought to be punished by the payment of twelve pence for every oath : and if the same cannot be levied upon the offender's goods, then he is to sit three hours in the stocks.

Secondly, every drunkard is to pay for the first offence five shillings : and in default thereof to sit six hours in the stocks, and for the second offence to find sureties for the good behaviour or to be committed to the common gaol : and the like punishment is to be inflicted upon all common haunters of ale-houses and taverns, and common gamesters, and persons justly suspected to live by any unlawful means, having no visible living. And no person is to sit or continue tipling or drinking more than one hour, unless upon some extraordinary occasion, in any tavern, victualling-house, ale-house, or other tipling-house, upon the penalty of ten shillings for every offence upon the master of such house : and upon the person that shall so continue drinking, three shillings four pence.

Thirdly, every person maintaining houses suspected of common bawdry, by the law, is to find sureties for their good behaviour : likewise all night-walkers, and persons using that impudent and insufferable practice of attempting others' modesty in the streets, are to be punished at the House of Correction, and find sureties for their good behaviour.

Fourthly, all persons using any unlawful exercises on the Lord's Day, or tipling in taverns, inns or ale-houses, and coffee-houses, during divine service on that day, are to forfeit three shillings four pence for every offence, to be levied by distress, and where none can be had to sit three hours in the stocks : and every vintner, inn-keeper, or ale-house keeper that shall suffer any such drinking or tipling in his house is to forfeit ten shillings for every offence : and no person may sit in the streets with herbs, fruits, or other things, to expose them to sale, nor no hackney coachman may stand or ply in the streets on that day.

And therefore all Constables and other officers, whom it doth or may concern, are required according to their oaths solemnly taken in that behalf, to take care for discovering and bringing to punishment whosoever shall offend in any of the premises : and for that end they are to enter into any suspected houses before mentioned to search for any such disorderly persons as shall be found misbehaving themselves, or doing contrary to the said laws, and to levy the penalties, and bring the offenders before some of his Majestie's Justices of the Peace of this City, to be dealt withall according to law.

And whereas there are other disorders of another nature very dishonourable, and a great scandal to the government of this City, and very prejudicial to the trade and commerce of the same : his lordship, therefore, is resolved by God's blessing, with the assistance of his brethren the Aldermen, to use his utmost endeavour to prevent the same, by putting in execution the good and wholesome laws in force for that purpose, with all strictness and severity : some of which he hath thought fit to enumerate, with the duties and penalties upon every Constable and other officers concerned therein.

At first the great resort of rogues, vagrants, idle persons, and common beggars, pestring and anoying the streets and common passages, and all places of publick meetings and resort, against whom very good provision is made by the law, viz.:—

That all such persons shall be openly whipped, and forthwith sent from parish to parish to the place where he or she was born, if known : if not, to the place where he or she last dwelt for the space of one year, to be set to work : or not being known where he or she was born or dwelt, then to be sent to the parish where he or she last passed through without punishment.

That every Constable that shall not do his best endeavour for the apprehension of such vagabond, rogue, or sturdy beggar, and cause him or her to be punished or conveyed according to law, shall forfeit ten shillings for every default.

Secondly, the not paving and cleansing of the streets : the redressing whereof being by a late act of Parliament put into Commissioners appointed by Common Council, his Lordship doth hereby recommend the same to the Deputies and Common Council of the several wards within this City, to use their utmost diligence in that affair, and especially to mind their respective Commissioners of the duty incumbent upon them, and of the daily damage which the City suffers by the neglect thereof. And his Lordship doth declare he will appear at the said Commission of Sewers as often as his more urgent occasions will give him leave, and doth expect such attendance of the other Commissioners as may render the act more effectual than hitherto it hath been.

Thirdly, the neglect of the inhabitants of this City in hanging and keeping out their lights at the accustomed hours, according to the good and ancient usage of this City, and acts of Common Council in that behalf.

Fourthly, the not setting and continuing the watches at such hours, and in such numbers, and in such sober and orderly manner in all other respects, as by the acts of Common Council in that behalf is directed and appointed.

And his Lordship doth strictly require the Fellowship of Carmen to be very careful in the due observance of the good and wholesale rules and orders which have been made for their regulation : his Lordship intending severely to inflict the penalties imposed in default thereof.

And to the end that no Constable or other Officers or Ministers of Justice may be any ways discouraged in their lawful, diligent, and vigorous prosecution of the premises, it is provided, that if they or any of them shall be resisted, in the just and lawful execution of their charge and duty, or in any wise affronted or abused, they shall be encouraged, maintained, and vindicated by the justice, order, and authority of his Lordship and the Court of Aldermen, and the offenders prosecuted and punished according to law."

CHAPTER X

GENERAL NOTES

AUBREY, writing in 1678, gives some curious notes on the changes of manners and customs. Some of his notes refer to the sixteenth century :—

"Antiently ordinary men's houses and copyholders, and the like had no chimneys, but flues like louver holes : some of 'em were in being when I was a boy.

In the halls and parlours of great houses were wrote texts of scripture on the painted cloths.

Before the last civil wars, in gentlemen's houses, at Christmas, the first dish that was brought to table was a boar's head, with a lemon in his mouth.

The first dish that was brought up to table on Easter day was a red herring riding away on horseback, *i.e.* a herring ordered by the cook something after the likeness of a man on horseback set in a corn sallad.

The custom of eating a gammon of bacon at Easter (which is still kept up in many parts of England) was founded on this, viz. to show their abhorrence of Judaism at that solemn commemoration of our Lord's resurrection.

The use of your *humble servant* came first into England on the marriage of Queen Mary, daughter of Henry IV. of France, which is derived from *votre très humble serviteur.* The usual salutation before that time was, *God keep you, God be with you*, and among the vulgar *How dost do?* with a thump on the shoulder.

Till this time the Court itself was unpolished and unmannered : King James's court was so far from being civil to women, that the ladies, nay, the Queen herself, could hardly pass by the king's apartment without receiving some affront.

Heretofore noblemen and gentlemen of fine estates had their heralds, who wore their coats of arms at Christmas and at other solemn times, and cried ' Largesse ' thrice.

A neat built chapel, and a spacious hall, were all the rooms of note : the rest were small. At Tomarton, in Gloucestershire, antiently the seat of the Rivers, is a dungeon 13 or 14 feet deep : about 4 feet high are iron rings fastened in the wall, which was probably to tye offending villains to, as all lords of manors had this power over their villains (or socage tenants), and had all of them no doubt such places for punishment.

It was well that all castles had dungeons, and so, I believe, had monasteries: for they had often within themselves power of life or death.

In days of yore lords and gentlemen lived in the country like petty kings, had jura regalia belonging to Seignories, had castles and boroughs, had gallows within their liberties where they could try, condemn and execute: never went to London but in Parliament time, or once a year, to do their homage to the king. They always eat in their Gothic Halls at the high table or orsille (which is a little room at the upper end of the hall where stands a table) with the folks at the side table. The meat was served up by watchword. Jacks are but of late invention: the poor boys did turn the spit, and licked the dripping for their pains: the beds of the men servants and retainers were in the hall, as now in the guard or privy chamber here. In the hall mumming and loaf stealing and other Christmas sports were performed.

The Hearth was commonly in the middle, whence the saying *Round about our coal fire*.

The halls of the Justice of Peace were dreadful to behold. The skreen was garnished with corslets and helmets, gaping with open mouths, with coats of mail, launces, pikes, halberts, brown bills, bucklers.

Public inns were rare: travellers were entertained at religious houses for three days together, if occasion served. The meetings of the gentry were not at taverns but in the fields or forests with their hawks and hounds, and their bugle horns in silken bawderies.

Before the Reformation there were no poor's rates: the charitable doles given at the religious houses, and the church ale in every parish, did the business.

In every parish there was a church-house, to which belonged spits, potts, etc., for dressing provision. Here the housekeepers met, and were merry and gave their charity. The young people came there too, and had dancing, bowling, shooting at butts, etc. Mr. A. Wood assures me there were few or no alms-houses before the time of Henry VIII.: that at Oxon, opposite Christ Church, was one of the most ancient in England.

In every church there was a poor's box, and the like at great inns.

Before the wake or feast of the dedication of the church, they sat there all night, fasting and praying, viz. on the eve of the wake.

The solemnity attending processions in and about churches, and the perambulations in the fields were great diversions also of those times.

Glass windows in churches and gentlemen's houses were rare before the time of Henry VIII. In my own remembrance, before the civil wars, copyholders and poor people had none. In Herefordshire, Monmouthshire, and Salop, it is so still. About 90 years ago, noblemen's and gentlemen's coats were of the fashion of the beadles and yeomen of the guard, (*i.e.*) gather'd at the middle.   The benchers in the Inns of Court yet retain that fashion in the make of their gowns.

Captain Silas Taylor says, that, in days of yore, when a church was to be built, they watched and prayed on the vigil of the dedication, and took that part of the horison when the sun arose for the East, which makes that variation, so that few stand true except those built between the two equinoxes.

From the time of Erasmus to about 20 years last past the learning was downright pedantry.   The conversation and habits of those times were as starcht as their bands and square beads, and gravity was then taken for wisdom.   The doctors in those days were but old boys, when quibbles passed for wit even in their sermons.

The gentry and citizens had little learning of any kind and their way of breeding up their children was suitable to the rest.   They were as severe to their children as their schoolmasters, and their schoolmasters as severe as masters of the house of correction.   The child perfectly loathed the sight of his parent as the slave to his torture.   Gentlemen of thirty or forty years old were to stand like mutes and fools bareheaded before their parents, and the daughters (well grown women) were to stand at the cupboard-side during the whole time of the proud mother's visits unless (as the fashion was) leave was forsooth desired that a cushion should be given them to kneel upon, brought them by the serving man, after they had done sufficient penance in standing.

The boys (I mean young fellows) had their foreheads turned up, and stiffened : they were to stand mannerly forsooth, thus—the foretop ordered as before, with one hand at the band-string, the other behind.

The gentlemen then had prodigious fans, as is to be seen in old pictures, like that instrument which is used to drive feathers : and it had a handle at least half as long with which their daughters oftentimes were corrected.

Sir Edward Coke, Lord Chief Justice, rode the circuit with such a fan : Sir William Dugdale told me he was an eye-witness of it.

The Earl of Manchester also used such a fan : but the fathers and mothers slasht their daughters, in the time of their besom discipline, when they were perfect women.

At Oxford (and I believe also at Cambridge), the rod was frequently used by the tutors and deans : and Dr. Potter of Trinity College, I knew right well, whipt his pupil with his sword by his side, when he came to take leave of him to go to the Inns of Court."

Misson, whose travels in England were published at the Hague in 1698, and a few years later were translated into English, says that he "sometimes"—as if the thing was common—met in London a procession consisting of a woman bearing the effigy of a man in straw with horns upon his head, preceded by a drum and followed by a mob making a noise with tongs, gridirons, frying-pans, and saucepans.   What should we understand if we met a procession at Charing Cross consisting of four men carrying another man, bagpipes and a shawm played before him, a drum beating, and twenty links burning around him? The significance of this ceremony would be wholly lost and thrown away upon us. It was, however, one of many processions which survived from Mediæval London, and were understood by everybody. The meaning of it was that a woman had given her husband a sound beating for accusing her of infidelity, and that upon such occasions, some kind neighbour of the poor innocent injured creature—which?—"performed this ceremony."

Again, when Prynne rode up to London to join the Long Parliament, he was accompanied by many thousands of horse and foot wearing rosemary and bay in their hats and carrying them in their hands, and this was considered the greatest affront possible to the judges who had questioned him. Why?

Of Horn Fair I have elsewhere spoken. This fair kept up to the end its semi-allegorical character. No one seems to have known why it was kept on October 18, which is St. Luke's Day, but the Evangelist is always figured with a bull's head in the corner of his portrait. The common people, however, associated horns, for some unknown reason, with the infidelity of the wife. They therefore assembled at Cuckold's Point opposite Ratcliffe, coming down the river from London, and there forming themselves into a procession, marched through Deptford and Greenwich to Charlton with horns upon their heads. At the fair horns of all kinds, and things made out of horn, were sold; the staple of the fair was work in horn, just as the staple of Bartholomew Fair was cloth. Besides the casual processions of the mob, a more formal procession was organised in London itself, especially at certain inns in Bishopsgate. This procession, which seems to have been arranged with some care and to have been interesting, consisted of a king, a queen, a miller, and other personages; they wore horns in their hats, and on arriving at Charlton, walked round the church three times. The occasion gave rise to many coarse and ribald jokes, and to much unseemliness of all kinds—hence a proverb, "All's fair at Horn Fair."

In this place the fair is mentioned as one of the last places where processions were organised, having meanings which were well understood at that time, but which would be now forgotten. The City procession, which everybody could read and understand like a printed book, lingered long, falling steadily into disuse and disrepute, until the wedding march was abandoned; the funeral, stripped of its coats of arms, the black gowns, and its torches, and even at last, the march of the milk-maids and the Mayday Jack in the Green, were seen no more.

APPENDICES

APPENDIX I

THE COURT

THE popular imagination pictures the Court of Charles the Second as a place of no ceremony or state or dignity whatever; a place where the King strolled about and where there was singing of boys, laughter of women, tinkling of guitars, playing of cards, making merriment without stint or restraint—a Bohemia of Courts. We have been taught to think thus of King Charles's Court by the historian who has seized on one or two scenes and episodes—for instance, the last Sunday evening of Charles's life; by the writer of romance, by the chronicler of scandal, by the Restoration poets, and the Restoration dramatists.

This view of Whitehall after the Restoration is, to say the least, incomplete. Charles had a Court, like every other sovereign; he had a Court with officers many and distinguished; there were Court ceremonies which he had to go through; that part of his private life which is now paraded as if it was his public life was conducted with some regard to public opinion. What his Court really was may be learned from a little book by Thomas De-Laune, Gentleman, called *The Present State of London*, published in the year 1681, for George Lurkin, Enoch Prosser, and John How, at the *Rose and Crown*. It may be useful to learn from this book the offices and management of a Stuart's Court.

I. Its Government—Ecclesiastical, Civil, and Military

i. *Ecclesiastical.*—The Dean of the King's Chapel was generally a Bishop. The Chapel itself is a Royal Peculiar, exempt from episcopal visitation. The Dean chose the Sub-Dean or *Precentor Capellæ;* thirty-six gentlemen of the Chapel, of whom twelve were priests and twenty-four singing clerks, twelve children, three organists, four vergers, a serjeant, two yeomen, and a Groom of the Chapel. The King had his private oratory where every day one of the chaplains read the service of the day. Twelve times a year the King, attended by his principal nobility, offered a sum of money in gold, called the Byzantine gift, because it was formerly coined at Byzantium, in recognition of the Grace of God which made him King. James the First used a coin with the legend—on one side—" Quid retribuam Domino pro omnibus quæ retribuit mihi?" and on the other side—" Cor contritum et humiliatum non despiciet Deus."

In addition there were forty-eight Chaplains in Ordinary, of whom four every month waited at Court.

The Lord High Almoner, usually the Bishop of London, disposed of the King's alms: he received all *deodands* and *bona felonum de se* to be applied to that purpose: Under him were a Sub-Almoner, two Yeomen and two Grooms of the Almonry. There was also a Clerk of the Closet whose duty was to resolve doubts on spiritual matters. In the reign of good King Charles the duties of this officer were probably light.

II. The Civil Government

The chief officer was the Lord Steward. He had authority over all the officers of the Court except those of the Chapel, the Chamber, and the Stable. He was Judge of all offences committed within the precincts of the Court and within the Verge. In the King's Presence the Lord Steward carried a white staff: when he went abroad the White Staff was borne before him by a footman bareheaded. His salary was £100 a year with sixteen dishes daily and allowances of wine, beer, etc. The Lord Chamberlain had the supervision of all officers belonging to the King's Chamber, such as the officers of the wardrobe, of the Revels, of the music, of the plays, of the Hunt; the messengers, Trumpeters, Heralds, Poursuivants, Apothecaries, Chyrurgeons, Barbers, Chaplains, etc.

The third great officer was the Master of the Horse. His duties are signified by his title, which was formerly *comes stabuli* or Constable.

Under these principal officers were the Treasurer of the Household, the Comptroller, the Cofferer, the Master of the Household, the two Clerks of the Green Cloth, the serjeants, messengers, etc.

In the Compting House was held the Court of Green Cloth, which sat every day with authority to maintain the Peace within a circle of twelve miles radius. It was so called from the colour of the cloth spread upon the table.

The chief clerk was an official of great power and dignity: he received the King's guests; kept the accounts; looked after the provisions and had charge of the Pantry, Buttery and Cellar. There were clerks under him. The Knight Harbinger with three Gentlemen Harbingers and seven Yeomen Harbingers provided lodgings for the King's Guests, Ambassadors, officers and servants.

The Knight Marshal was Judge in all cases in which a servant of the King was concerned: he was also one of the Judges in the Court of the Marshalsea. He had six Provost Marshals or Vergers in scarlet coats to wait upon him.

The Servants in ordinary were the Gentlemen of the Bedchamber, and the Groom of the Stole, the Vice-Chamberlain, the Keeper of the Privy Purse, the Treasurer of the Chamber, the Master of the Robes, the twelve Grooms of the Bedchamber, the six Pages of the Bedchamber, the four Gentlemen Ushers of the Privy Chamber, the forty-eight Gentlemen of the Privy Chamber, the six Grooms of the Privy Chamber, the Library Keeper, Black Rod, the eight Gentlemen Ushers of the Presence Chamber, the fourteen Grooms of the Great Chamber, six gentlemen waiters, four cupbearers, four carvers, four servers, four esquires of the Body, the eight servers of the Chamber, the Groom Porter, sixteen serjeants at arms, four other serjeants at arms who attended on the Speaker and on the Lord Lieutenant of Ireland. There were four Physicians in Ordinary, a Master and Treasurer of the Jewel House, three Yeomen of the Jewel House, a Master of the Ceremonies with an assistant and a marshal; three Kings at Arms, six Heralds, and four Poursuivants at Arms; a Geographer, a Historiographer, a Hydrographer, a Cosmographer, a Poet Laureate, and a Notary.

These were the Officers of the Wardrobe: the great Wardrobe, the standing wardrobes at Hampton, Windsor, and other places, and the Removing Wardrobe which was carried about with the King. For the wardrobes were one Yeoman, two Grooms, and three Pages.

For the Office of Tents and Pavilions were two Masters, four Yeomen, one Groom, one Clerk Comptroller and one Clerk of the Tents. The Master of the Revels ordered the plays and masques, etc. He had one Yeoman and one Groom. Attached to the Master of the Robes were workmen, each in his own craft. The Royal Falconer had thirty-three officers under him. The Master of Buckhounds had thirty-four assistants: the Master of the Otter hounds had five under him. So had the Master of the Harriers. The Master of the Ordnance had a Lieutenant, a master Armourer, and seventeen under officers. There were forty-two messengers of the Chamber. There were sixty-four Musicians in ordinary; fifteen trumpeters and kettle drummers; seven drummers and fifes; two Apothecaries; two Chyrurgeons; two Barbers; three Printers; one Printer of Oriental tongues. There were bookseller, stationer, bookbinder, silkman, woollen draper, postmaster, and a Master of Cock-fighting.

There were two Embroiderers, one Serjeant Skinner, two Keepers of the Privy Lodging, two Gentlemen, and two Yeomen of the Bows; one Cross-bow maker; one Fletcher; one Cormorant keeper; one Hand-gun maker; one master and marker of Tennis; one Mistress Semstress, and one Laundress; one Perspective-maker, one Master-Fencer, one Haberdasher of Hats, one Combmaker, one Serjeant Painter, one Painter, one Limner, one Picture-Drawer, one Silver-Smith, one Goldsmith, one Jeweller, one Peruque-maker, one Keeper of pheasants and Turkies. Joyner, Copier of Pictures, Watch-maker, Cabinet-maker,

Lock-Smith, of each one. Game of bears and Bulls, one Master, one Serjeant, one Yeoman. Two Operators for the Teeth. Two coffer-bearers for the Back-stairs, one Yeoman of the Leash, fifty-five Watermen. Upholsterer, Letter Carrier, Foreign Post, Coffee Maker, of each one.

Ten Officers belonging to Gardens, Bowling-Greens, Tennis-Court, Pall-Mall, Keeper of the Theatre at Whitehall. Cutler, Spurrier, Girdler, Corn-Cutter, Button-maker, Embosser, Enameler, of each one. Writer, Flourisher, and Embellisher, Scenographer, or Designer of Prospects, Letter-Founder, of each one. Comedians, Seventeen Men, and Eight Women, Actors.

Gunner, Gilder, Cleaner of Pictures, Scene Keeper, Coffer-maker, Wax-Chandler, of each one. Keeper of Birds and Fowl in St. James's-Park, one. Keeper of the Volery, Coffee-club-maker, Serjeant-Painter, of each one; with divers other officers and servants under the Lord Chamberlain to serve his Majesty upon occasion.

As to the Officers under the Master of the Horse, there are Twelve Querries so called of the French Escayer, derived from Escury, a Stable. Their office is to attend the King on Hunting or Progress, or on any occasion of Riding Abroad, to help His Majesty up and down from his Horse, etc. Four of these are called Querries of the Crown-Stable, and the others are called Querries of the Hunting-Stable. The Fee to each of these is only £20 yearly, according to the Ancient Custom; but they have allowance for Diet, to each £100 yearly, besides Lodgings, and two Horse-Liveries.

The next is the Chief Avener, from Avena, Oats, whose yearly fee is £40. There is, moreover, one Clerk of the Stable, four Yeomen-Riders, four Child-Riders, Yeomen of the Stirrup, Serjeant-Marshal, and Yeomen-Farriers, four Groom-Farriers, Serjeants of the Carriage, three Surveyors, a Squire and Yeomen-Sadlers, four Yeomen-Granators, four Yeomen-Purveyors, a Yeoman-Pickman, a Yeoman-Bitmaker, four Coach-men, eight Litter-men, a Yeoman of the Close Wagon, sixty-four Grooms of the Stable, whereof thirty are called Grooms of the Crown Stable, and thirty-four of the Hunting and Pad-Stable. Twenty-six Footmen in their Liveries, to run by the King's Horse. All these Places are in the Gift of the Masters of the Horse.

There is besides these an antient Officer, called Clerk of the Market, who within the Verge of the King's household, is to keep a Standard of all Weights and Measures, and to burn all that are false. From the Pattern of this Standard, all the Weights and Measures of the Kingdom are to be taken.

There are divers other considerable Officers, not Subordinate to the Three Great Officers, as the Master of the Great Wardrobe, Post-Master, Master of the Ordinance, Warden of the Mint, etc.

Upon the King are also attending in his Court the Lords of the Privy Council, Secretaries of State, the Judges, the College of Civilians, the King's Council at Law, the King's Serjeants at Law, the Masters of Requests, Clerks of the Signet, Clerks of the Council, Keeper of the Paper-Office, or Papers of State, etc.

There is always a Military Force to preserve the King's Person, which are His Guards of Horse and Foot. The Guards of Horse are in Number 600 Men, well armed and equipped; who are generally Young Gentlemen of considerable Families, who are there made fit for Military Commands. They are divided into Three Troops, viz.: the King's Troop, distinguished by their Blew Ribbons and Carbine Belts, their Red Hooses, and Houlster-Caps, Embroidered with His Majesties Cypher and Crown. The Queen's Troops by Green Ribbons, Carbine Belts, covered with Green Velvet, and Gold Lace, also Green Hooses and Houlster Caps, Embroidered with the same Cypher and Crown. And the Duke's Troop by Yellow Ribbons, and Carbine Belts, and Yellow Hooses, Embroidered as the others. In which Troops, are 200 Gentlemen, besides Officers. Each of these Three Troops is divided into Four Squadrons or Divisions, two of which consisting of one hundred Gentlemen, and Commanded by one Principal Commissioned Officer, two Brigadiers, and two Sub-Brigadiers, with two Trumpets mount the Guards one day in six, and are Relieved in their turns. Their Duty is always by Parties from the Guard, to attend the Person of the King, the Queen, the Duke, and the Duchess, wheresoever they go near home, but if out of town, they are attended by Detachments of the said Three Troops.

Besides these, there is a more strict Duty and Attendance Weekly on the King's Person on Foot, wheresoever he walks, from His Rising to His going to Bed, by one of the Three Captains, who always waits immediately next the King's own Person, before all others, carrying in his hand an Ebony-staff or

Truncheon, with a Gold head, Engraved with His Majesty's Cypher and Crown. Near him also attends a Principal Commissioned Officer, with an Ebony-staff, and Silver head, who is ready to Relieve the Captain on occasion; and at the same time also, two Brigadiers, having also Ebony-staves, headed with Ivory, and Engraven as the others.

There is added a Troop of Grenadiers to each Troop of Guards, one Division of which mounts with a Division of the Troop to which they belong; they never go out on small Parties from the Guard, only perform Centry-Duty on Foot, and attend the King also on Foot when he walks abroad, but always March with great Detachments. The King's Troop consists of a Captain, two Lieutenants, three Serjeants, three Corporals, two Drums, two Hautbois, and eighty private Souldiers mounted. The Queens Troop, of a Captain, two Lieutenants, two Serjeants, two Corporals, two Hautbois, and sixty private Souldiers mounted. The Dukes Troop consists of the like number with the Queens.

The Captains of His Majesties Guards always Command as Eldest Colonels of Horse; the Lieutenants as Eldest Lieutenant-Colonels of Horse; the Cornets and Guidons, as Eldest Majors of Horse; the Quartermasters, as Youngest Captains of Horse; the Brigadiers as Eldest Lieutenants of Horse; and amongst themselves every Officer, according to the Date of His Commission, takes precedency, when on Detachments, but not when the Three Troops march with their Colours, for then the Officer of the Eldest Troop, commands those of equal Rank with him in the others, though their Commission be of Elder Date.

Next immediately after the Three Troops of Guards, his Majestys Regiment of Horse, Commanded by the Earl of Oxford takes place, and the Colonel of it is to have precedency, after the Captains of the Guards, and before all other Colonels of Horse, whatsoever change may be of the Colonel; and all the Officers thereof, in their proper Degree, are to take place according to the Dates of their Commissions. As to the Foot, the King's Regiment, Commanded by the Honorable Colonel John Russel, takes place of all other Regiments, and the Colonel thereof is always to precede as the first Colonel. The Colestream Regiment, Commanded by the Earl of Craven, takes the next; the Duke of Yorks Regiment next, then his Majestys Holland Regiment, Commanded by the Earl of Mulgrave, and all other Colonels, according to the Dates of their Commissions. All other Regiments of Horse and Foot, not of the Guards, take place according to their Respective Seniority, from the time they were first Raised, and no Regiment loses its precedency by the Death of its Colonel.

At the Kings House, there is a guard for his Person, both above and below stairs. In the Presence Chamber, the Band of Gentlemen Pensioners wait, instituted by King Henry the VII., and chosen out of the best and antientest Families in England, to be a Guard to His Majesties Person, and also to be a Nursery to breed up hopeful Gentlemen, and fit them for Employments, Civil and Military, as well abroad as at home; as Deputies of Ireland, Embassadors in Foreign Parts, Counsellors of State, Captains of the Guard, Governors of Places, Commanders in the Wars, both by Sea and Land, of all which these have been Examples. They are to attend the King's Person to and from His Chappel, only as far as the Privy Chamber: also in all other Solemnity, as Coronations, publick Audience of Embassadors, etc. They are 40 in number, over whom there is a Captain, usually some Peer of the Realm, a Lieutenant, a Standard-Bearer, and a Clerk of the Check. They wait half at a time quarterly. Those in quarter wait daily five at a time upon the King in the House, and when he walks abroad. Upon extraordinary occasions, all of them are Summoned. Their ordinary Arms are Gilt Pole-Axes. Their Arms on Horse-back in time of War, are Cuirassiers Arms, with Sword and Pistol. These are only under their own Officers, and are always Sworn by the Clerk of the Check, who is to take notice of such as are absent when they should be upon their duty. Their Standard in time of war, is a Cross Gules in a Field Argent, also 4 bends.

In the first Room above Stairs, called the Guard-Chamber, attend the Yeomen of the Guard of His Majesties body; whereof there were wont to be 250 Men of the best quality under Gentry, and of larger Stature than ordinary (for every one was to be Six foot high) there are at present 100 Yeomen in dayly waiting, and 70 more not in waiting, and as any of the 100 die, his place is filled up out of the 70. These wear Scarlet Coats Down to the Knee and Scarlet Breeches, both richly guarded with black Velvet, and rich Badges upon their Coats both before and behind, moreover, black Velvet round broad Crown'd Caps, with Ribbons of the King's Colour; one half of them of late bear in their hands Harquebuzes, and the other half Partizans, with large Swords by their Sides; they have Wages and Diet allowed them. Their office is to wait upon the King in His standing Houses, 40 by Day, and 20 to Watch by Night; about the City to wait upon the King's Person abroad by Water or Land.

The King's Palace Royal (*ratione Regiæ dignitatis*) is exempted from all Jurisdiction of any Court, Civil or Ecclesiastick, but only to the Lord Steward, and in his absence, to the Treasurer and Comptroller of the King's Household, with the Steward of the Marshalsea, who by vertue of their Office, without Commission, may Hear and Determin all Treasons, Fellonies, Breaches of the Peace, Committed within the King's Court or Palace. The Orders and Rules for the Demeanor of all Officers and Servants are hung upon Tables in several Rooms at the Court, and Signed with the King's own hand, worthy to be read of all Strangers.

The Court or House where the King resides is accounted a Place so Sacred, that if any man presume to strike another there, and only draw blood, his Right Hand shall be cut off, and he committed to perpetual Imprisonment, and Fined. All occasions of striking are also there forbidden.

The Court of England for Magnificence, Order, Number and Quality of Officers, rich Furniture, entertainment and Civility to Strangers, and for plentiful Tables, might compare with the best in Christendom, and far excels most Courts abroad. It hath for a long time been a Pattern of Hospitality and Charity to the Nobility and Gentry of England. All Noblemen or Gentlemen, Subjects or Strangers, were freely entertained at the plentiful Tables of His Majesties Officers. Divers Dishes were provided every day extraordinary for the King's Honour. Two hundred and forty Gallons of Beer a day were allowed at the Butters-Bar for the Poor, besides all the Broken Meat, Bread, etc., gathered into Baskets, and given to the Poor, at the Court-Gates, by Two Grooms and Two Yeomen of the Almonry, who have salaries of His Majesty for that Service. The Lord Almoner hath the Privilege to give the King's Dish to whatsoever Poor Man he pleases; that is, the first Dish at Dinner which is set upon the King's Table, or in stead thereof, fourpence a day (which anciently was equivalent to four shillings now); next he distributes to 24 poor men, named by the Parishioners of the Parish adjacent to the King's Place of Residence, to each of them fourpence in money, a Twopenny Loaf, and a Gallon of Beer, or instead thereof three pence in Money, equally to be divided among them every Morning at seven of the Clock at the Court-Gate. The Sub-Almoner is to Scatter new-coined Two-pences in the Towns and Places where the King passes through in his Progresses, to a certain Sum by the Year. Besides, there are many poor Pensioners, either because so old that they are unfit for Service, or the Widows of any of the King's Servants that dyed poor, who have a Competency duly paid them: Besides, there are distributed among the poor the larger Offerings which the King gives in Collar Days.

The magnificent and abundant plenty of the King's Tables hath caused amazement in Foreigners. In the Reign of King Charles I. there were daily in his Court 86 Tables well furnished each Meal, whereof the King's Tables had 28 Dishes, the Queen's 24, 4 other Tables 16 Dishes each, 3 other 10 Dishes, 12 other 7 Dishes, 17 other 5 Dishes, 3 other 4, 32 had 3, and 13 had each 2; in all about 500 Dishes each Meal, with Bread, Beer, Wine, and all other things necessary. There was spent yearly in the King's House of gross Meat 1500 Oxen, 7000 Sheep, 1200 Veals, 300 Porkers, 400 Sturks or young Beefs, 6800 Lambs, 300 Flitches of Bacon, and 26 Boars. Also 140 dozen of Geese, 250 dozen of Capons, 470 dozen of Hens, 750 dozen of Pullets, 1470 dozen of Chickens, for Bread 36,400 Bushels of Wheat, and for Drink, 600 Tun of Wine and 1700 Tun of Beer. Moreover, of Butter 46,640, together with the Fish and Fowl, Venison, Fruit, Spice, proportionably. This prodigious plenty in the King's Court caused Foreigners to put a higher value upon the King, and was much for the Honour of the Kingdom. The King's Servants being Men of Quality, by His Majesty's special Order went to Westminster Hall in Term Time, to invite Gentlemen to eat of the King's Acates or Viands, and in Parliament-time, to invite the Parliament-men thereto.

On the Thursday before Easter, called Maundy Thursday, the King, or his Lord Almoner, was wont to wash the Feet of as many poor Men as His Majesty had reigned years, and then to wipe them with a Towel (according to the Pattern of our Saviour), and then to give every one of them two Yards and a half of Woollen Cloth, to make a Suit of cloaths; also Linnen Cloth for two Shirts, and a pair of Stockings, and a pair of Shoes, three Dishes of Fish in Wooden Platters, one of Salt Salmon, a second of Green Fish or Cod, a third of Pickle-Herrings, Red Herrings, and Red Sprats; a Gallon of Beer, a Quart Pottle of Wine, and four six-penny Loaves of Bread, also a Red-Leather-Purse with as many single Pence as the King is years old, and in face another Purse as many Shillings as the King hath reigned Years.   The Queen doth the like to divers poor Women.

The Form of Government is by the wisdom of many Ages, so contrived and regulated, that it is almost impossible to mend it.   The Account (which is of so many Natures, and is therefore very diffi- cult, must pass through many hands, and is therefore very exact) is so wisely contrived and methodized, that without the Combination of everyone of these following Officers, viz. the Cofferer, a Clerk of the Green-Cloth, a Clerk-Comptroller, a Clerk of the Kitchen, of the Spicery or Avery, or a particular Clerk, together with the conjunction of a Purveyor and Waiter in the Office, it is impossible to defraud the King of a Loaf of Bread, of a Pint of Wine, a Quart of Beer, or Joint of Meat, or Money, or anything else."

APPENDIX II

LIST OF LONDON CLERGY EJECTED

— Adams	St. Bennet, Paul's Wharf.
Dr. Samuel Baker	St. Mary at Hill.
Dr. Walter Balcanquall	Master of the Savoy.
James Batty, A.M.	St. Vedast, Foster Lane.
Matthew Bennet, A.M.	St. Nicholas Acon.
Dr. Boosie	St. Olave's, Silver Street.
— Booth	St. Botolph, Aldersgate.
Nicolas Bradshaw, A.M.	St. Mildred, Bread Street.
Dr. William Bray	St. Martin's in the Fields.
Dr. William Brough	St. Michael's, Cornhill.
— Brown	Bridewell Precinct.
Dr. Jonathan Brown	St. Faith's.
Dr. Thomas Brown	St. Mary Aldermary.
Dr. Richard Chambers	St. Andrew Hubbard.
Dr. Richard Cheshire	St. Nicolas Olave's.
Robert Chestlin, A.M.	St. Matthew's, Friday Street.
James Chibbald, A.M.	St. Nicholas Cole Abbey.
Dr. John Childerly	St. Dunstan in the East.
John Clark	St. Ethelburga.
Dr. Richard Clewet	St. Anne, Aldersgate.
Abraham Cole, A.M.	St. Leonard, Eastcheap.
John Cook, A.M.	St. Mary Somerset.
Ralph Cook, B.D.	St. Gabriel, Fenchurch
William Cooper	St. Thomas Apostle.
Thomas Crane, B.D.	St. Laurence, Jewry.
Joseph Draper	St. Thomas's Hospital.
Dr. Richard Dukeson	St. Clement Danes.
Gerard Eccop, A.M.	St. Pancras, Soper's Lane.
Phil Edlin, B.D.	St. John Zachary.
Dr. William Fairfax	St. Peter's, Cornhill.
Dr. Daniel Featley	Lambeth.
Edward Finch, A.M.	Christ Church.
— Foxley	Charter House.
Richard Freeman	St. James, Garlick Hithe.
Thomas Fuller, A.M.	Lecturer, Savoy.

Dr. William Fuller .	St. Giles, Cripplegate.
Dr. Gifford .	St. Michael Bassishaw.
(?) .	Rector of St. George's, Southwark.
Dr. John Grant	St. Bartholomew, Exchange.
Matthew Griffith, A.M.	St. Mary Magdalen, Old Fish St. and St. Bennet Sherehog.
Dr. John Hacket .	St. Andrew's, Holborn.
Abraham Haines, A.M.	St. Olive's, Hart Street.
Dr. James Halsey .	St. Alphage.
John Hanslow, A.M.	St. Christopher's.
Edward Harison	Holy Trinity the Less.
Dr. William Haywood	St. Giles in the Fields.
William Heath	Stoke Newington.
John Hill .	St. Michael, Queenhithe.
Dr. Percival Hill	St. Katherine Coleman.
Dr. Richard Holdsworth	St. Peter le Poor.
Dr. Thomas Howell	St. Stephen's, Walbrook.
— Humes .	St. Dionis, Backchurch.
Dr. Michael Jermin .	St. Martin's, Ludgate.
Dr. John Johnson .	St. Mary, Whitechapel.
— Jones .	St. Mary Magdalen, Milk Street.
Dr. William Isaacson	St. Andrew's Wardrobe.
(?) .	Rector of St. James's, Duke's Place.
Henry Kibuts, A.M.	St. Katherine's, Coleman Street.
Dr. Philip King	St. Botolph's, Billingsgate.
— Launce .	St. Michael le Queen.
Dr. Edward Layfield	Allhallows, Barking.
Jeremiah Leech	St. Mary le Bow.
Dr. John Littleton .	The Temple.
Richard Maden, B.D.	St. Mildred, Poultry.
Edward Marbury .	St. Peter's, Paul's Wharf.
Dr. James Marsh .	St. Dunstan's in the West.
Henry Mason, B.D.	St. Andrew Undershaft.
James Meggs, A.M.	St. Margaret Pattens.
— Miller .	St. Helen's.
George Moor	Hackney.
Cadwallader Morgan	St. Bennet Sherehog.
Richard Owen, B.D.	St. Swithin's.
Ephraim Paget, A.M.	St. Edmund's, Lombard Street.
Thomas Palmer, A.M.	St. Bride's.
Dr. Thomas Paske .	St. Mary Magdalen, Bermondsey.
Thomas Pierce, D.D.	St. Martin Outwich.
Robert Pory, B.D. .	St. Margaret's, New Fish Street.
John Prichard, A.M.	St. Andrew Undershaft.
— Proctor .	St. Mary Bothaw.
Luke Proctor, A.M.	St. Michael Royal.
— Quelch .	St. Bennet Gracechurch.
Nehemiah Rogers .	St. Botolph's, Billingsgate.
— Rush .	St. Katherine's Cree.
Dr. Bruno Ryves .	St. Martin's Vintry.

Josias Shute, A.M. .	St. Mary Woolnoth.
Edward Sparke, A.M.	St. Martin's, Ironmonger Lane.
— Spencer .	St. Thomas, Southwark.
John Squire, A.M. .	St. Leonard, Shoreditch.
Dr. William Stamp .	Stepney.
Dr. Matthew Stiles .	St. George, Botolph Lane.
Benjamin Stone, A.M.	St. Clement's, Eastcheap.
Dr. Thomas Swadlin	St. Botolph, Aldgate.
Humphry Tabor, A.M.	St. Margaret, Lothbury.
Thomas Thrall, A.M.	St. Mary Monthaw.
John Tireman, B.D.	St. Mary Woolchurch.
Thomas Tuke, A.M.	St. Olave's, Jewry.
Dr. Thomas Turner	St. Olave's Southwark.
Daniel Tutivall	Charter House.
Ephraim Udal	St. Augustine's.
Daniel Vochiere, A.M.	St. Peter's, Cheap.
Dr. Bryan Walton .	St. Martin's Ongars.
William Ward	St. Leonard's, Foster Lane.
— Warfield .	St. Benet Fink.
Dr. William Watts .	St. Alban's, Wood Street.
Richard Weemsley, A.M. .	St. John Baptist.
Dr. Thomas Westfield	Great St. Bartholomew.
John Weston, A.M.	Allhallows, Lombard Street.
Gilbert Wimberly .	St. Margaret, Westminster.
Thomas Woodcock, A.M. .	St. Mary At Hill.

It may be noted that of this list, 112 in number, 25 were either holders of canonries in some cathedral, or were pluralists.

APPENDIX III

ALMSHOUSES

The following is a list of almshouses belonging to and founded in the seventeenth century :—

Alleyn's . .	1614	Petty France .	10 men and women .	£2 and clothes
Alleyn's . .	1616	Old Street .	10 men, 1 woman .	26s. and clothes
Alleyn's . .	1616	Deadman's Place .	10 men, 8 women .	26s.
Amyas' . .	1655	Old Street . .	8 men or women .	£5
Aske . .	1692	Hoxton . .	8 men, 20 boys .	£3 and clothes
Badger's . .	1698	Hoxton . .	6 men and wives .	20s.
Baron's . .	1682	Shadwell .	15 women .	7s. a year
Bayning .	1631	Crutched Friars .	Parish Alms houses	
Butler's . .	1675	Wismount .	2 men and wives .	£6
Camp's . .	?	Wormwood St. .	6	34s. 8d.
Caron's . .	1623	Vauxhall .	7 women . . .	£4
Dewy's . .	1684	Soho . .	?	
Emanuel .	1601	Westminster .	20 men and women .	£10
Grey Coat Hospital	1698	Westminster .	} 80 boys. . . } 50 girls. . . }	£1457
Green Coat . .	1633	Westminster .	20 boys . . .	£300
Graham's . .	1686	Soho . .	4 women . . .	£10
Hammond .	1651	Snow Hill .	6 men . . .	£10
Haws's . .	1686	Poplar . .	6 widows. . .	30s.
Heath . .	1648	Islington . .	10 men . . .	£6
Hill's . .	1677	Westminster .	3 men and wives .	1s. 8d. a week
Jackson . .	1685	Deadman's Place .	2 women. . .	1s. 8d. a week
Lumley . .	1672	Old Street . .	6 women. . .	£4
Meggs . .	1690	Whitechapel .	12 women . .	£5 : 4s.
Melor . .	1691	Stepney . .	10 women . .	£8 : 13 : 4
Monger's . .	1669	Hackney . .	6 men . . .	£2
Newbury . .	1688	Mile End . .	12 women . .	£5 : 4s.
Owen's . .	1610	Whyton . .	10 women . .	£3 : 16s. and clothes
Palmer . .	1654	Westminster .	12 men and women .	£6
Parnell . .	1698	Mile End . .	8 women . .	1s. 8d. a week, etc.
Rogers . .	1612	Cripplegate . .	6 men and wives .	£4
St. Peter's . .	1618	Newington Butts .	Fishmongers' Company	
Sion College . .	1623	London Wall .	20 men and women .	£6
Southampton . .	1656	St. Giles .		
Spurstowe . .	1666	Hackney . .	6 women. . .	£4
Stafford . .	1633	Gray's Inn Lane .	4 men, 6 women .	£6 and clothes
Trinity Hospital .	1695	Mile End . .	28 men . . .	£10 : 12s.
Walter's . .	1651	Newington . .	16 men and women .	£3 : 10s.
Watson's . .	?	Shoreditch . .	12 women . .	20s. and coals
Whitcher . .	1683	Westminster .	6 men and women .	£5 and a gown
Wood's . .	1613	Ratcliffe . .	6 men . . .	£6 and coals
Young's . .	1694	Southwark . .	2 women. . .	1s. a week.

From the almshouses turn to the schools. Those founded in the seventeenth century were as follows :—

Allhallows, Staining . .	Will. Linton . .	1658	£26 per annum .	6 boys
Almonry	Emery Hill . .	1677	7 ,, ,, .	...
St. Saviour's Church Yard .	Applebea . .	1681	20 ,, ,, .	30 ,,
Dunhill Fields . .	Trotman . . .	1673	80 ,, ,, .	30 ,,
Castle Street . . .	Alf. Tenison .	1685	1500 ,, ,, .	30 ,,
Cherry Tree Alley . .	W. Worrall .	1689	30 ,, ,, .	40 ,,
East Smithfield . . .	Sir S. Sterling .	1673	20 ,, ,, .	16 ,,
Islington	Dame Alice Owen .	1613	20 ,, ,, .	30 children
Lambeth	R. Lawrence .	1661	35 ,, ,, .	20 ,,
Palmer's School: *see* Alms-houses				
Grey Coat ⎱ *see* Almshouses Green Coat ⎰				
Parker's Lane . . .	W. Skelton . .	1663	...	50 boys
Plow Yard	J. Hickson .	1689	£30 per annum .	20 ,,
Rotherhithe . . .	Hills and Bell .	1612	3 ,, ,, .	8 children
Tothill Fields . . .	Emery Hill . .	1677		20 boys
Whitechapel . . .	Davenant . .	1686	about £80 ,, ,, .	⎱ 60 ,, ⎰ 40 girls

APPENDIX IV

COMPOSITION OF THE LORDS AND COMMONS

In 1687 there were in the House of Lords—12 Dukes, 2 Marquesses, 66 Earls, 9 Viscounts, 64 Barons, 2 Archbishops, and 24 Bishops.   Total 181.

In the House of Commons—92 Knights of Counties, 25 cities 2 Knights each and Lords 4, 8 Cinque ports, 16 Barons, 2 Universities 2 burgesses each, and 344 burgesses for Boroughs.

APPENDIX V

ENLARGEMENT OF THE STREETS

THE following rules were laid down for the enlargement and improvement of the streets :—

"Pursuant to the said Act of Parliament, a Common Council was called for the purposes thereof; in which it was enacted, 'That the street called Fleet Street, from the place where the Greyhound Tavern stood to Ludgate, and from thence into St. Paul's Churchyard, shall be further enlarged to be of the breadth of forty-five foot.

That the street leading from the east end of St. Paul's Churchyard into Cheapside shall be further enlarged to be of the same breadth of forty-five foot.

That the street and passage at the east end of Cheapside, leading into the Poultry, shall be enlarged to be on a level line forty foot broad.

That the street and passage out of the Poultry, leading into the west end of Cornhill, shall be enlarged to be of the breadth of forty foot.

That Blowbladder Street, leading into Cheapside, shall be enlarged to be of the breadth of forty foot.

That Ave Mary Lane shall be enlarged to be of the breadth of eighteen foot.

That the street from Aldersgate, through St. Martin's le Grand, into Blowbladder Street, shall be enlarged to be of the breadth of twenty-four foot.

That the passage from St. Magnus Church to the Conduit in Gracechurch Street shall be enlarged to be of the breadth of thirty-five foot.

That the north end of Gracechurch Street from Leadenhall shall be enlarged to be of the same breadth of thirty-five foot.

That Thames Street, from the West Corner of St. Magnus Church aforesaid to Tower Dock, shall be enlarged to be of the breadth of thirty foot.

That the ground where the Middle Row in the Shambles stood, and the ground of the four late houses in Newgate Market, between Warwick Lane end and the late Bell Inn, there, and also the ground where the Middle Row in Old Fish Street stood, shall be laid into the streets.

That there shall be a new street made from the Guildhall into Cheapside, of the breadth of thirty-six foot.

That Pannier Alley, between Paternoster Row and Newgate Market, shall be enlarged to be of the breadth of nine foot, and paved with free-stone for a foot-passage.

That St. Paul's Alley, between Paternoster Row and St. Paul's Churchyard, shall be also enlarged to be of the same breadth of nine foot, and paved with free-stone for a foot-passage.

That Grocers Alley in the Poultry shall be enlarged to be of the breadth of eleven foot.

That Scalding Alley there shall be enlarged to be of the breadth of nine foot.

That Old Swan Alley in Thames Street shall be enlarged to be of the breadth of fourteen foot.

That Love Lane in Thames Street shall be enlarged to be of the breadth of ten foot.

That the cross Lane between St. Dunstan's Hill and Harp Lane shall be enlarged to be of the breadth of fourteen foot.

And be it farther enacted, ordained, and declared, That all streight and narrow passages, not fourteen foot broad, which have been or shall be staked out by the Surveyor hereunto appointed by this Court to the breadth of fourteen foot, shall be enlarged accordingly, and in such manner, as they now are, or shall be staked and set out.

And this court was farther consenting and desirous, that all other streight and narrow passages, not before particularly mentioned (which should be found convenient to be enlarged for the common benefit and accommodation, and should receive his Majesty's Order and approbation), should and might be enlarged and made wider, and otherwise altered, before the twenty-ninth day of May now next ensuing, as should be fitting for the beauty, ornament, and conveniency thereof, and staked and set out accordingly'" (*Maitland*, vol. i. p. 443).

Rules for the Pitching and Levelling the Streets

" 1. Tower Dock in Thames Street is to be raised 3 foot: At 147 foot upwards from Thames Street to be raised 2 foot 10 inches: At the highest part in Tower Street, against the middle of St. Allhallows Barking churchyard, to be sunk 6 in.

2. Beer Lane is to be raised at Thames Street 8 ft., at 90 ft. upwards 4 ft., and to be abated at 192 ft. upwards 3 inch., and at Tower Street 6 inch.

3. Water Lane is to be raised at Thames Street 6 ft., at 83 ft. upwards nothing, and to be abated at 128 ft. upwards 1 ft. 11 inch., at Tower Street 3 ft. 10 inch.

4. Harp Lane is to be raised in Thames Street 7 ft., at 100 ft. upwards 4 ft. 7 inch., and to be abated at 180 ft. 1 ft. 6 inch., at 270 ft. 6 ft. 4 inch., at Tower Street 6 ft. 4 inch.

5. Idle Lane is to be raised in Thames Street 7 ft., at 90 ft. upwards 4 ft. 2 inch., and to be abated at 165 ft. upwards 2 ft. 3 inch., at 262 ft. 5 ft. 10 inch., in Tower Street 3 ft. 6 inch.

6. St. Dunstan's Hill, beginning at Idle Lane, is to be raised 4 ft. 2 inch., at 76 ft. upwards 3 ft. 3 inch., at 126 ft. 1 ft., and to be abated at 226 ft. 2 ft. 1 inch., at Tower Street 2 ft. 10 inch.

7. St. Mary Hill is to be raised in Thames Street 5 ft., at 87 ft. upwards 2 ft. 6 inch., and to be abated at 187 ft. 1 ft. 8 inch., at 287 ft. 5 ft. 8 inch., at 387 ft. 6 ft. 4 inch., at little East Cheap 3 ft. 8.

8. Love Lane is to be raised in Thames Street 4 ft., at 100 ft. upwards 6 ft., at 200 ft. 2 ft. 3 inch., and to be abated at 270 ft. 3 ft. 10 inch., at 370 ft. 8 ft., at 470 ft. 6 ft. 5 inch, at East Cheap 3 ft. 10 inch.

9. Botolph Lane is to be raised at Thames Street 4 ft., at 133 ft. upwards 4 ft. 5 inch., at 233 ft. 10 inch., and to be abated at 333 ft. 2 ft., at 433 ft. 2 ft., at East Cheap 3 inch.

10. Pudding Lane is to be raised in Thames Street 7 ft., at 115 ft. 5 ft. 5 inch., at 212 ft. 1 ft. 8 inch., and to be abated at 300 ft. 3 ft. 7 inch., at 400 ft. 6 ft., at East Cheap 5 ft. 9 inch.

11. New Fish Street Hill is to be raised at Thames Street 2 ft., at 80 ft. upwards 2 ft., and to be abated at 280 ft. nothing; at 380 ft. 2 ft. 9 inch., at East Cheap 4 ft.

12. St. Michael's Lane is to be raised in Thames Street 7 ft., at 80 ft. upwards 6 ft. 9 inch., at 280 ft. 6 ft. 6 inch., at 380 ft. 2 ft. 10 inch., and to be abated at 380 ft. 8 inch., at East Cheap 5 inch.; the current of it is 13 inch. upon 20 ft.

13. St. Martin's Lane is to be raised in Thames Street 6 ft., at 103 ft. 6 ft., at 203 ft. 4 ft. 3 inch., at 303 ft. 2 inch., and to be abated at 403 ft. 1 inch, at Cannon Street 2 ft. 8 inch.

14. Green Lettice and Duck's Field Lanes are to be raised at Thames Street 3 ft., at 135 ft. 1 ft. 10 inch., and abated at 235 ft. 2 ft. 11 inch., at 297 ft. 4 ft. 5 inch., at 397 ft. 5 ft. 5 inch., at Cannon Street 10 inch.

15. St. Lawrence Pountney Lane is to be raised in Thames Street 4 ft., at 157 ft. 3 ft. 7 inch., and abated at 261 ft. 11 inch., at 361 ft. 4 ft., at Cannon Street 2 ft. 8 inch.

16. Suffolk Lane is to be raised in Thames Street 3 ft., at 110 ft. upwards 2 inch., and to be abated at 190 ft. 3 ft. 6 inch., at 290 ft. 7 ft. 9 inch., at the entrance into Duck's Field Lane 4 ft. 4 inch.

17. Bush Lane is to be raised in Thames Street 3 ft., at 103 ft. 2 ft., and to be abated at 203 ft. 8 inch., at 303 ft. 4 ft. 4 inch., in Cannon Street nothing.

18. Dowgate is to be raised in Thames Street 3 ft., at 134 ft. 1 ft. 4 inch., and to be abated at 288 ft. 1 ft. 8 inch., the current 1 upon 34.

19. College Hill is to be raised at Thames Street 3 ft., at 216 ft. 3 inch., the current 1 upon 35.

20. Garlick Hill is to be raised at Thames Street 3 ft., at 216 ft. 11 inch., the current 1 upon 26.

21. Little Trinity Lane is to be raised in Thames Street 4 ft., at 75 ft. 2 ft. 11 inch., and to be abated at 150 ft. 1 ft. 4 inch., at 250 ft. 3 ft., at Great Trinity Lane 5 ft. Current 1 upon 18.

22. Huggen Lane is to be raised in Thames Street 4 ft., at 63 ft. 3 ft. 1 inch., and abated at 153 ft. 1 ft. 10 inch., at 253 ft. 5 ft. 7 inch., at Trinity Lane 7 ft. Current 1 upon 18½.

23. Bread Street Hill is to be raised in Thames Street 4 ft., at 53 ft. 3 ft., at 153 ft. 3 inch., and abated at 253 ft. 2 ft. 11 inch., at Trinity Lane end 3 ft. 6 inch. Current 1 upon 20.

24. Old Fish Street Hill is to be raised at Thames Street 4 ft. and abated at 100 ft. 1 ft. 7 inch., at 200 ft. 4 ft. 9 inch., at 300 ft. 3 ft. Current 1 upon 16.

25. Lambeth Hill is to be raised in Thames Street 4 ft., at 73 ft. 11 inch., and to be abated at 173 ft. 3 ft. 6 inch., at Old Fish Street 3 ft. Current 1 upon 17½.

26. The Old 'Change is to be abated at Fish Street 3 ft. 6 inch., at St. Austin's Gate 1 ft. 9 inch., the current 1 upon 68.

27. St. Paul's Chain, or St. Bennet's Hill, is to be raised in Thames Street 8 ft., at 100 ft. 3 ft. 11 inch., and to be abated at 190 ft. 2 ft. 5 inch., at 340 ft. 4 ft. 3 inch., at 490 ft. 1 ft., in St. Paul's Churchyard as it was.

28. Puddle Dock is to be raised at Thames Street end 8 ft., at 56 ft. 6 ft. 2 inch., at 196 ft. 3 ft. 3 inch., at 286 ft. 3 ft. 3 inch., at 386 ft. 9 inch., and to be abated at Carter Lane 1 ft. 7 inch.

29. Creed Lane at Carter Lane end is to be abated 3 ft., and so gradually to Ludgate Hill.

30. Ludgate Hill is to be raised at Fleet Bridge 6 ft., at 200 ft. upwards 8 ft. 7 inch., at 300 ft. 5 ft. 2½, at 400 ft. 11 inch., and to be abated at Ludgate 10 inch., at Ave Mary Lane end 1 ft. 8 inch., at St. Paul's Churchyard nothing.

31. Mark Lane is to be abated at the ending in Tower Street 3 ft., and so gradually to about 150 ft. up the lane.

32. Rood Lane is to be abated all the length of it. In Eastcheap 3 ft. 8 inch. In Fenchurch Street 1 ft ; the descent for the current is 1 upon 41.

33. Grace Church Street is to be sunk at Eastcheap 4 ft., at the conduit 4 ft., at Lombard Street end 2 ft. 10 inches, the descent for the current 1 upon 68.

34. Cannon Street is to be abated in Eastcheap, at Grace Church Street 4 ft., the highest ground at 200 ft. within the street, near St. Michael's Lane end ; the other parts of it are to be sunk according to the endings of the streets before-mentioned.

35. Lombard Street is to be abated at Grace Church Street 2 ft. 10 inch , and so gradually to about 250 ft. within the street, where is to be the highest ground of it.

36. Bread Street is to be abated at Trinity Lane end 3 ft. 6 inch., at Watling Street 3 ft. 2 inch., and so gradually to Cheapside ; the descent for its current 1 upon 60.

37. Friday Street is to be abated at Old Fish Street 3 ft., at Watling Street 2 ft., the Current 1 upon 70.

38. Watling Street is to be abated at the places mentioned.

39. Cheapside, about Wood Street end, is to be raised 2 ft., and so gradually eastward and westward, and that raising to end at the Old 'Change westward, and Soper Lane eastward.

40. The Stocks to be abated 2 ft., and that abatement to be gradually extended into Cornhill, Lombard Street, Threadneedle Street, and the Poultry, and a little way into Wallbrook, which about the South end of the churchyard of St. Mary Woolchurch is to be raised about 2 ft., that the current of the water that way may be stopt, and turned back toward the Stocks, whence it is to be conveyed by a grated Sewer into the main Sewer not far distant " (*Maitland*, vol. i. pp. 444, 445).

APPENDIX VI

THE NEW BUILDINGS OF LONDON

THE following is taken from a contemporary pamphlet :—

"A Particular of the new buildings within the Bills of Mortality, and without the City of London, from the year 1656 to 1677, according to the account now taken by the churchwardens of the several Parishes and the old account of New Houses from 1620 to 1656, and what they did amount to at one whole year's value, as appears by the Duplicate in the Exchequer :

	1677.	1656.	Value.		
			£.	s.	d.
Westminster	490				
Martins in the Fields	1780				
St. Giles in the Fields	889	141	4855	8	6
Convent Garden	59	342	10,859	4	0
Savoy	37				
St. Clement Danes	253	183	3794	0	0
S. Dustan in the West	72				
St. Bridget	126	146	1475	15	0
St. Andrews, Holbourn	550				
St. Bridewell Precinct					
St. Sepulchre	35	127	725	11	2
Clerkenwell	199				
Bartholomew Great	11	47	205	15	0
Bartholomew Less					
Aldersgate	102	30	390	0	0
Criplegate		517	3362	1	0
Bishopsgate	208	265	1925	7	0
Algate	50	520	2855	7	8
Minories	16	6	45	0	0
St. Katherines	24	51	370	7	0
White Chappel	423	291	2620	4	4
Shoreditch	144	348	1170	7	0
Stepney	2137	1625	11,719	6	10
Shadwell	289				
Hackney	51				
Islington	25				
S. Saviours, Southwark		339	2137	11	4
S. Olave, Southwark	385	147	963	12	4
S. George, Southwark	231	144	595	18	0
S. Thomas, Southwark		160	788	19	10
Redriff	219	59	397	7	0
Bermondsey	349	428	3669	9	10
Christ-Church	100				
Newington	107	247	995	2	8
Lambeth	185	383	1684	6	4
		6646	57,606	1	10

The total of the New Buildings from 1656 to 1677 is about Ten Thousand.

The Total from 1620 to 1656 was about Seven Thousand Five Hundred.

Their value at one year's rent about Seventy Thousand Pound if it had been collected.

Though the particular makes the number but 6646, and the sum but 57,606 Pounds, some Parishes being wanting.

As there have been great mistakes about the Damage and Nuisance by the increase of New Buildings in the Suburbs: so by this we may see the mistake to be as great about their number and value; some reporting their number to be Twenty Thousand; others Thirty Thousand: though it is very plain to any man that considers that their number cannot be much above Ten Thousand, for that the Total of all the Houses, both New and Old, both in the City and in the Bills of Mortality, are not Threescore Thousand.

That this is true, and that the number from 1656 to 1677 cannot much exceed Ten Thousand, will appear by comparing the Increase of the Burials from 1620 to 1656 with the particular of the New Houses built within that time. . . .

The Medium is the Increase of two Burials for every five houses that were built, so that the Increase of Two Thousand Five Hundred Houses raises the Burials One Thousand.

And If we examine the Increase of the Burials from 1656 to 1677 we shall find them to be about Four Thousand, which being but a fourth more than were from 1620 to 1656. The new houses since that time cannot be reckoned above a Fourth, which makes the Total about Ten Thousand.

And this way of calculation, though it may not exactly discover the particular number of Houses, yet it is sufficient to prove there can be no mistake of Thousands in the Account: for that the Inhabitants of two or three Thousand Houses would have added a visible Increase to the Burials.

And to fully justify this computation, it agrees very well with the calculation made by the Ingenious Mr. Grant both of the Total number of the Inhabitants within the Bills of Mortality, and his probable guess that about three in one hundred die, allowing twelve Inhabitants to every House, one with another, which no man I suppose will dispute.

This will apparently confute that wild conjecture of some, who report that there is Three Thousand Five Hundred New Houses in St. Martin's Parish, when the Burials of that Parish are not above Eighteen Hundred in a year: so that the Total of New and Old in that Parish cannot be above Four Thousand Five Hundred, and therefore it is probable that the Account of 1780 now given in is very true.

The conjectures of many concerning the value of these Houses, that they will make twenty pounds a year one with another, and raise two or three Thousand pounds, are as false as about the number of them.

For Ten Thousand Houses will not raise about fifty Thousand pounds, it being the half years value at ten pounds a year one with another, which is the most they can be reckoned at.

As will plainly appear from the account of the value of those seven thousand five hundred Houses, which did not amount to Seventy Thousand pound at a whole year's value, as appears by the Duplicate in the Exchequer, they are making one with another ten pound a year.

Now the great houses in the Piazza, Lincolns-Inn-Fields, and Queen-street, were equal in value to these twenty-two Houses in St. James Square, or Bloomsbury Square, or other places: and are more in number of that sort of Houses than have been built since.

Besides the middle sort of Houses in the streets of Covent-Garden, Long-Acre, Clare-Market, Old-Southampton Buildings, and other places have equall'd both the number and value of Leicester-Fields, Bloomesbury, York-Buildings, Essex-Buildings and the rest. And the number of the small houses at four and five pounds per Annum since 1656 are much greater.

So that upon enquiry it is plain that the Houses that were built before 1656 were equal in value to what have been built since. And therefore it is not probable that a Tax upon the New foundation can raise above Fifty Thousand Pound, which considered with the charge of collecting it, and the loss of His Majesties customes upon Timber, Boards, Wainscot and Iron, being not less than Ten Thousand pound per annum, which will be occasioned by the discouraging of Building will not bring in Thirty Thousand pounds clear into the Exchequer, if it were possible to make the Law so that all might be collected.

But not to mention how hard the purchasers of New Houses will believe such a Law to be, having paid a valuable consideration for them and offended no Law.

Nor how severe the Workmen Builders will think they are dealt with, to be punished for exercising their lawful Trades.

Nor how partial it will be to those that build since 1656, that have already paid a year's value. Not to mention what the owners of the great houses that have been altered think, not being allowed the £500 a year which their Houses yielded before: since they pay for improvement by the building of their Gardens.

Nor what is general all those sufferers will think, who believe they have done good service to the nation by Building. The Law will have this peculiar disadvantage, it will be impossible so to word it, or to comprize all men's interests, so as to raise that money as shall be designed by it. For after the Commissioners of Oliver's Act had set four years, they did pay in Twenty Thousand pounds into the Exchequer of the £70,000 that was returned upon the Duplicates."

APPENDIX VII

GARDENS

"THE garden played a large part in the recreation of the citizens. A contemporary account of the principal London gardens is here subjoined :—

Chelsea Physick Garden has a great variety of plants both in and out of greenhouses. Their perennial green hedges and rows of different coloured herbs are very pretty, and so are their banks set with shades of herbs in the Irish stitchway, but many plants of the garden were not in so good order as might be expected, and as would have been answerable to other things in it. After I had been there, I heard that Mr. Watts, the keeper of it, was blamed for his neglect and that he would be removed.

My Lord Ranelagh's Garden being but lately made, the plants are but small, but the plants, borders, and walks are curiously kept, and elegantly designed, having the advantage of opening into Chelsea college walks. The kitchen garden there lies very fine, with walks and seats, one of which, being large and covered, was then under the hands of a curious painter. The house there is very fine within, all the rooms being wainscoted with Norway oak, and all the chimneys adorned with carving, as in the council-chamber in Chelsea College.

Arlington Garden, being now in the hands of my lord of Devonshire, is a fair place, with good walks, both airy and shady. There are six of the greatest earthern pots that are anywhere else, being at least two feet over within the edge : but they stand abroad, and have nothing in them but the tree holy-oke, an indifferent plant, which grows well enough in the ground. Their greenhouse is very well, and their green-yard excels : but their greens are not so bright and clean as farther off in the country, as if they suffered something from the smutty air of the town.

Kensington Gardens are not great nor abounding with fine plants. The orange, lemon, myrtles, and what other trees they had there in summer, were all removed to Mr. London's and Mr. Wise's greenhouse at Brompton Park, a little mile from them. But the walks and grass laid very fine, and they were digging up a flat of four or five acres to enlarge their garden.

The Queen Dowager's Garden, at Hammersmith, has a good greenhouse, with a high erected front to the South, whence the roof falls backward. The house is well stored with greens of common kinds : but the Queen not being for curious plants or flowers, they want of the most curious sorts of greens, and in the garden there is little of value but wall trees : though the gardener there, Monsieur Hermon Van Guine, is a man of great skill and industry, having raised great numbers of orange and lemon trees by inoculation, with myrtles, Roman bayes, and other greens of pretty shapes which he has to dispose of.

Sir Thomas Cooke's Garden at Hackney is very large, and not so fine at present, because of his intending to be at three thousand pounds charge with it this next summer, as his gardener said. There are two greenhouses in it, but the greens are not extraordinary, for one of the roofs, being made a receptacle for water, overcharged with weight, fell down last year upon the greens, and made a great destruction among the trees and pots. In one part of it is a warren, containing about two acres, very full of coneys, though there was but a couple put in a few years since. There is a pond or a mote round about them, and on the outside of that a brick wall four feet high, both which I think will not keep them within their compass. There is a large fish-pond lying on the South to a brick wall, which is finely clad with philaria. Water brought from far in pipes furnishes his several ponds as they want it.

The Archbishop of Canterbury's Garden at Lambeth has little in it but walks, the late archbishop not delighting in one, but they are now making them better: and they have already made a greenhouse, one of the finest and costliest about the town. It is of three rooms, the middle having a stove under it: the forsides of the room are almost all glass, the roof covered with lead, the whole part (to adorn the building) rising gavel wise higher than the rest: but it is placed so near Lambeth church that the sun shines most on it in winter after eleven o'clock: a fault owned by the gardener, but not thought on by the contrivers. Most of the greens are oranges and lemons, which have very large ripe fruit on them.

Mr. Evelyn had a pleasant villa at Deptford, a fine garden for walks and hedges (especially his holly on which he writes of in his *Sylva*) and a pretty little greenhouse with an indifferent stock in it. In this garden he has four large round philarias, smooth clipped, raised on a single stalk from the ground, a fashion now much used. Part of his garden is very woody and shady for walking: but his garden not being walled, has little of the best fruits."

INDEX

INDEX